THE KAʿBA ORIENTATIONS

THE KAʿBA ORIENTATIONS

Readings in Islam's *Ancient House*

Simon O'Meara

EDINBURGH
University Press

Edinburgh University Press is one of the leading university presses in the UK. We publish academic books and journals in our selected subject areas across the humanities and social sciences, combining cutting-edge scholarship with high editorial and production values to produce academic works of lasting importance. For more information visit our website: edinburghuniversitypress.com

Edinburgh University Press Ltd
The Tun – Holyrood Road
12 (2f) Jackson's Entry
Edinburgh EH8 8PJ

Typeset in 11/13 Adobe Garamond by
IDSUK (DataConnection) Ltd, and
printed and bound in Malta at Melita Press

A CIP record for this book is available from the British Library

ISBN 978 0 7486 9930 8 (hardback)
ISBN 978 0 7486 9931 5 (webready PDF)
ISBN 978 1 4744 6650 9 (epub)

Contents

Figures

Acknowledgements

It is my honour to acknowledge the many people who enabled or informed the research that underpins this book, the first full years of which were supported by a postdoctoral fellowship on the European Research Council Starting Grant, 'The Here and the Hereafter in Islamic Traditions' (no. 263308, 2011–15), but which began with a postdoctoral fellowship at the Kunsthistorisches Institut in Florenz in early 2010. In alphabetical order, those people are: Hamra Abbas; Anahita Alavi; Hannah Baader; Joachim Backes; Christoph Baumgartner; Carel Bertram; Sheila Blair; Jan Böttger; Crispin Branfoot; Barbara Brend; Adam Bursi; Moya Carey; Walter Sasson Chahanovich; Chris Chaplin; Mounia Chekhab-Abudaya; Anna Contadini; Pieter Coppens; Yorgos Dedes; Yavuz Demir; Abdelghani El Khairat; Raymond Farrin; Narguess Farzad; Barbara Finster; Walid Ghali; John Gibson; María Gomez; Valerie Gonzalez; Caroline Goodson; Charlie Gore; Corné Hanssen; Mónica Herrera Casais; Ruba Kana'an; Anna Marazuela Kim; Naomi Koltun-Fromm; Saeid Kordmafi; Scott Kugle; Nico Landman; Nicholas Lua; Christian Luczanits; Norbert Ludwig; Shane McCausland; Charles Melville; Birgit Meyer; Meraj Nawab Mirza; Esra Müyesseroglu; Stefan Neuner; Güngör Öğüt; Glenn Peers; Karen Pinto; Marcel Poorthuis; Arjan Post; Hind Qirwan; Jessica Rahardjo; Scott Redford; Kevin Reinhart; Aila Santi; Jochen Sokoly; Rana Sowwan; Maria Subtelny; Jörn Thielmann; Marina Tolmacheva; Lale Uluç; Cornelis van Lit; Jamel Velji; Muhammad Isa Waley; Jan Just Witkam; Yunus Yaldiz; Malikabonui Zekhni; Holger Zellentin. I thank you all. Where you have shared translations, personal images and unpublished work and insights, I thank you again and again.

I am especially indebted to the following individuals and groups, who in different ways gave considerably of themselves to the book: Dale Eickelman; Péter Nagy; Robert Nelson; and the Arabic reading group at Utrecht University, led by Christian Lange.

To the last-named individual I am irrevocably beholden, as I am also to Jonathan Bloom: titans both. This book could not have happened without your better wisdom and greater knowledge, not to mention your belief in it and me. A satyr to two suns I am.

The book would not be in print without the editorial rigour and expertise of Edinburgh University Press. I thank everyone involved, most especially Nicola Ramsey. Robert Hillenbrand's reading of the penultimate draft prompted robuster argumentation and an improved structure; Kirsty Woods and in particular Eddie Clark patiently saw the book through to completion. Externally, Lel Gillingwater improved the final copy and narrative flow; Ælfwine Mischler provided the index.

The book began in Florence and ended in London, via Kuwait and Utrecht. Its anchorage has been Rena. Its dedicatee is Adam: 'Auf einen Stern zugehen, nur dieses.'

Introduction

Charles Long's definition of religion as orientation makes Islam an unusually religious religion.[1] Not only are Muslims required to orient themselves to the *qibla*, or the direction of the Kaʿba, for ritual prayer, but being oriented to the *qibla* is compulsory for bodies placed in the grave and the performance of certain rituals of the pilgrimage to Mecca, and it is recommended for ritual ablution and petitionary prayer (*duʿāʾ*). Depending on the jurist and law school, turning the heads of animals about to be ritually slaughtered towards the *qibla* is also either compulsory or recommended.[2] Conversely, it is forbidden to orient oneself to the *qibla* when defecating or urinating;[3] and transgressing the requirement to have a *qibla* orientation for the other actions is sometimes regarded as an ingredient of sorcery (*siḥr*).[4] For good reason, then, Muslims are known as 'the people of the *qibla*' (*ahl al-qibla*), an appellation that allegedly dates to the time of the Prophet.[5]

Arguably, these acts of orientation about the Kaʿba have their apotheosis in the annual pilgrimage, or Hajj, to Mecca, the site of the Kaʿba. This event has proven sufficiently fascinating to outside observers to make Mecca enter the English language as the very definition of a desirable, popular destination. This interest notwithstanding, for a building that does more than just fascinate but in Islamic culture functions variously and profoundly, the Kaʿba has received little attention in architectural scholarship and barely figures in the many survey texts of Islamic art.[6] The aim of this book is to correct that neglect, by studying how the Kaʿba works or is alleged to work in the Islamic world, and what that work enables for Islam and generates for the Islamic world. In brief, the book studies the work of a building the Qurʾan calls the Ancient House (*al-Bayt al-ʿAtīq*).[7]

The Work of Art

The idea that a building, painting or sculpture works in this or that culture should need no special pleading. From Hegel's talk of art *liberating* 'the real import of appearances' and *presenting* 'the Absolute itself', to Heidegger's notion of the artwork *setting up* and *opening* a world, one speaks about the *work* of art with good reason.[8] And one does so without contrivance. Because an artwork is by definition the result of action, or work in the cultural sphere called art, it follows that in the expression 'the work of art' the word 'work' refers to something in addition to the artwork itself. One does not say, for example, 'the artwork of art'. Does not the word refer to the action, or verb of the artwork? In the case of Hegel and Heidegger, the verbs include 'liberating', 'presenting', 'setting up' and 'opening'. In the case of Jacques Rancière, they include 'transforming', 'recomposing', and, again, 'opening.' Rancière writes: 'Art anticipates work because it carries out its principle: the transformation of sensible matter into the community's self-presentation . . . [Art] opens up a form of visibility [that recomposes] the landscape of the visible.'[9]

These and other verbs are the work of art. As the philosopher and cognitive linguist Mark Johnson notes: 'The work of art is a *working of art*.'[10] Nelson Goodman speaks similarly when he says: '[A] work of architecture, or any other art, works as such to the extent that it enters into the way we see, feel, perceive, conceive, comprehend in general, [participating] in our continual remaking of a world.'[11]

Should this talk be considered too Eurocentric for non-Western art, the anthropologist of Melanesia and India, Alfred Gell, talks of the artwork there and elsewhere as 'a system of action, intended to change the world'.[12] Robert Layton, another anthropologist, says this of the work of art in West African societies: '[A]rt objects [help] bring the political systems to life.'[13] A third anthropologist, Arjun Appadurai, writes of how the prevalent contemporary Western notion of the non-working artwork is at odds with the notion of art held in many non-Western societies, where 'things have not been so divorced from the capacity of persons to act'.[14] Lastly, in Jean-Pierre Warnier's ethnological account of the material culture of calabashes, baskets and other containers in the western Cameroons, the author shows why this art of containment should not just be understood 'for what it might "signify" in a system of communication, [but also] for what it enables in terms of the perception, action, achievement, and performance on the part of the subject'.[15] As we shall see in Chapters Five and Six, the Kaʿba is a container, albeit of a very particular sort. What might *it* enable on the part of the subject?

In sum, whether Western or non-Western, the artwork ought to be studied for the work it does, a methodological directive that is not new in Islamic art history.[16] To ignore this work is effectively to imperil the artwork to aesthetic appreciation only. Thus has Islamic architectural scholarship largely imperilled the Kaʿba, which partly explains but does not justify why the Kaʿba features so poorly in this scholarship. As an object of disinterested aesthetic appreciation only, it has proven troublingly easy to dismiss. In the words of Richard Ettinghausen and Oleg Grabar, the founding figures of Islamic art history: '[The Kaʿba is] not too impressive as an architectural creation.'[17]

Other reasons for the relative obscurity of the Kaʿba in architectural scholarship are discussed below and in Chapter Four. One reason not discussed there, which needs stating here, is that not every Islamic architectural historian is allowed to go the Kaʿba; only those professing the faith of Islam. It is questionable, however, whether seeing the Kaʿba with one's own eyes really is required to write about it, because what is there to see that a photograph cannot record, especially when one's chances of being able to enter it are staggeringly slight? The present book, for example, has been written without the author visiting the Kaʿba. This objection notwithstanding, the restricted access to the building yet remains a valid explanation for the Kaʿba's poor coverage in Islamic architectural scholarship.

The Structure and Content of the Book

As noted, this book studies the work of the Kaʿba in the Islamic world. For the most part, the modern Islamic world is excluded from this study, as the book is restricted to the work of the Kaʿba in the early, medieval, and pre- and early modern Islamic periods only. Tackling modernity would almost demand a book of its own.

To each aspect of the Kaʿba's work a chapter is dedicated, commencing with the work occurring furthest from Mecca and then drawing closer in. Together the chapters comprise the orientations in the book's title: readings in the work of the Kaʿba. Pertaining predominantly to the spatial aspects of this work, these readings cover: the urban and world orientations that the Kaʿba as both *qibla* and navel effects (Chapters One and Two); the continuity of the Islamic world that the Kaʿba's substructure ensures even when its superstructure lies in ruin (Chapter Three); the unions that the Kaʿba as beloved enables and shares in when circled and cleaved to (Chapter Four); and the animating force that the Kaʿba as container is imagined to shelter temporarily, the void that it otherwise holds, and the role that its covering robe, or *Kiswa*, plays in this housing and holding work (Chapters Five and Six).

Topics covered in the first chapter include: the history of the *qibla* and its literal, customary and symbolic meanings; Kaʿba-related decoration of mosques' *mihrab*s; and the early and medieval history of Islamic urbanism as it pertains to the *qibla*. Topics covered in the second chapter include: the orientation of the Kaʿba itself and the question of orientation per se; the different methods for determining the *qibla*; the creation of the world according to Islamic tradition and as reflected in *mappae mundi*; and the bilateral bodily structure of the Kaʿba, again according to Islamic tradition. Topics covered in the third chapter include: the destructions the Kaʿba has endured in its history and is predicted to endure at the apocalypse; the relationship between the Kaʿba and its alleged celestial archetype, the Frequented House (*al-Bayt al-Maʿmūr*); and the relationship Sufis allege to exist between the Kaʿba and the human heart. In the fourth chapter the topics include: the ritual circumambulation of the Kaʿba, or the *ṭawāf*; the experience of pilgrims, especially Sufis and mystics and above all Ibn ʿArabī (d. 638/1240), as they perform the *ṭawāf*; the Kaʿba as a site of momentary divine union; and the representation of the Kaʿba in Islamic tradition as a building inaugurating the Islamic epoch and in architectural inscriptions as a building without equal. In the fifth chapter the topics include: the contents of the Kaʿba before and after the Prophet's conquest of Mecca in 8/630, again as represented in Islamic tradition; the nature of the Kaʿba after it was emptied as part of this conquest, including the representation of this emptiness in diagrams of the Two Sanctuaries (*al-Ḥaramayn*) of Mecca and Medina; and the relationship between its emptied state and the dot, or 'primordial point' (*nuqṭa*) of the Arabic alphabet as interpreted in Islamic letter symbolism. In the sixth and final chapter, the topics include a history and description of the Kaʿba's robe, the *Kiswa*; the different ways it is hung in the course of the Islamic year; and the representation of these different ways in popular sayings, travel narratives and Persian miniatures.

Although space and politics are inseparable, these six readings of the Kaʿba do not explicitly pertain to the political domain. In part this is because there exists a growing body of Kaʿba- and especially Hajj-related publications pertaining to this domain.[18] In other part it is because I hold the view that the study of Islamic art insufficiently engages with the insights and methods of a relatively new subject of study, material religion. Contrary to the tired and anxious caricature that derides as essentialist the study of Islamic art in terms of Islam, studying Islamic art this way, via a material religion lens, is to ask what Islamic art has made possible for Islam: how Islamic art has materialised Islam.[19] These materialisations of Islam are spatial before they are political, no matter how momentarily.

On account of the fact that the book commences with the work of the Kaʿba occurring furthest from Mecca (Chapters One and Two) and then draws closer in (Chapters Three to Six), so the reader comes to understand the Kaʿba in the conventional manner: from the outside in. He or she does so exclusively on the basis of primary sources: pictorial and textual, Arabic and Persian, Sunni and Shiʿite, scriptural and theological, historical and geographical, legal and mystical, cartographic and cosmological, archaeological, poetic and biographical. These sources are wide ranging and inevitably call into question my disciplinary competences to use them. The validity of this question notwithstanding, when architecture is understood as the work it does in a culture, then its study must be multidisciplinary, for better or worse. One either accepts limitations in competency and proceeds in spite of them or one continues to approach architecture as if it were a text to be described and categorised, historicised and decoded.[20] This enduring approach to architecture, however, has long been questionable. Decades ago, the architect and theorist Christian Norberg-Schulz said this of it, for example:

> So far, [architectural meaning] has mostly been approached in semiological terms, whereby architecture is understood as a system of conventional 'signs'. Considering architectural forms as representations of 'something else', semiological analysis has, however, proved incapable of explaining works of architecture as such.[21]

Arguably, approaching architecture as just so many conventional signs is how Islamic architectural scholarship tends to operate; proof is the relative obscurity of the Kaʿba in this scholarship. The approach cannot make much of the Kaʿba, because it is all but blind to it. Describing the Kaʿba takes little more than two paragraphs: one each for the exterior and interior. Categorising the Kaʿba's architectural type takes even fewer words: an Arabian sanctuary. Historicising the Kaʿba, as in seeking its origins and builder's intentions, seems inappropriate, given its traditionally alleged builder, either Abraham or Adam. Decoding it takes no words at all, because not only is it composed of blank walls, its exterior is covered in a cloth. From this dead end, Ettinghausen and Gabar's negative aesthetic judgement follows almost logically.

Even though the Kaʿba has reasonable claim to be the Islamic world's most important building, when it is all but invisible in a subject that proclaims Islamic architecture as its object, alarm bells must sound. One must either acknowledge and try to circumvent this methodological blind spot or ask what type of knowledge the subject produces and for whom it speaks.

With time, more orientations in the work of the Kaʿba could have been added to the book; which is to say, the book does not pretend to be the last word on the Kaʿba. Nor does the book purpose to be a guide to the Kaʿba, a kind of coffee-table companion for those curious as to its history and lore. Much of this history and lore is traversed in the course of the book, but the book is not a report of them. The book, rather, is a series of arguments built upon primary sources, not an extended encyclopedia entry.

Lastly, although the book might seem to some to be but an idiosyncratic meditation on the Kaʿba by one who, additionally, has never set foot in Mecca, Shahab Ahmed's book *What is Islam?* allows me to explain why that is not so. In one section of this posthumously published, paradigm-shifting publication, Ahmed discusses Islamic art and shows how the hermeneutic developed in the course of his book can advance its study. With a few caveats he approvingly references Ernst Grube's understanding of what Islamic art historians should be doing with their objects of study. This understanding, he rightly notes, is derived from the iconological method developed by Erwin Panofksy.[22] As Panofsky himself explains the iconological method, by way of it art historians check what they think is an artwork's intrinsic meaning against the intrinsic meaning of as many 'other documents of civilization historically related to that work' as possible.[23] Such is all I am doing with my object of study. This book on the Kaʿba is thus no meditation, but a kind of iconology that moves to and fro between the Ancient House of Islam and its representation in the myriad documents pertaining to Islam.

Importantly, and quite contrary to what might popularly be believed, Sufism is part and parcel of Islam. Sufism is neither necessarily esoteric in practice and noticeably mystical in content nor marginal to Islamic thought and a negation of Islamic worship (*ʿibāda*). The scholarship on the matter is unambiguous.[24] Therefore, to refer to Sufi documents as being representative of Islam, as this book will frequently do, is neither to speak exceptionally nor fancifully. The commonplace distinctions bandied about in the media and elsewhere today that make of Islam so many categories – for example, good Islam, orthodox Islam, Sufi Islam and so forth – cannot be allowed to substitute for knowledge of Islam. This is true even of one of the most prolific but divisive figures of Sufism: the Andalusian mystic Ibn ʿArabī (d. 638/1240).[25] Although his influence within Sufism is well known because well studied, less well known is his influence outside Sufism. Recently, however, three university press monographs have been published that spell out just how extensive this influence was, informing tenth/sixteenth-century political conceptions of the Ottoman caliphate and thirteenth/nineteenth- and twentieth-century Salafism.[26] In view of these and related publications, the lingering academic prejudice that the writings of Ibn ʿArabī can be referenced only with regard to Sufism must be rejected as baseless.[27]

Kaʿba Nomenclature

With the rationale, methodology and content of the book explained, what remains for this Introduction is to provide a description of the Kaʿba, intended to give a basic context for the chapters that follow. Before proceeding to that description, however, some terminological distinctions need to be made.

There is a case to be made for referring to the Kaʿba as a temple. Usage of that term would not only follow the nomenclature established by Francis Peters, who has written widely on the Kaʿba,[28] but it would also be validated by applying to the Kaʿba John Lundquist's fifteen-point typology of the ancient Near East temple.[29] In that application, all the criteria would obtain, with the clear exception of two: points 8b and 9.[30] The first exception concerns the calamity that befalls a community on its temple's destruction, something that can hardly be said to pertain to the Kaʿba, as will be demonstrated in Chapter Three. The second exception concerns the oblation rituals held inside a community's temple. As will be shown in Chapter Five, such rituals have no bearing on the Islamic Kaʿba.

Referring to the Kaʿba as a temple would also fit Ernst Cassirer's definition of the word: '*Templum* (Greek τέμενος) goes back to the root τεμ, "to cut", and thus signifies that which is cut out, delimited. It first designates the sacred precinct belonging to the god and consecrated to the god.'[31] This definition is especially suitable for the Kaʿba, for it speaks to traditional Islamic accounts of the building's origins. As we shall see in Chapter One, Islam's most sacred precinct, the Sanctuary, or *Ḥaram* of Mecca, is coterminous with the Kaʿba, because it is alleged to have come into existence at the moment the Kaʿba came into existence. To enter the precinct, approximately 127km in circumference, is thus in some way to enter the Kaʿba: its projected boundaries.[32] (By 'projected boundaries' I mean the inner perimeter of the Sanctuary, as demarcated by the numerous boundary markers, the furthest of which is approximately 20km from the Kaʿba and the nearest approximately 7km.[33] I do not mean the much more remote, outer perimeter of the Sanctuary, as demarcated by the five Stations, or *Mawāqīt*. At these *Mawāqīt*, male pilgrims to Mecca who do not reside within either perimeter must don the pilgrimage garb, the *iḥrām*, to be discussed below.[34])

The foregoing justifications for the use of the term 'temple' notwithstanding, referring to the Kaʿba this way is not without its critics, most notably Jacqueline Chabbi, who explains that calling it such effaces the Kaʿba's origins as a betyl. These betylic origins, Chabbi asserts, have no bearing on the ancient Near East temple and its origins.[35] Compounding matters, the use of the term also risks connoting activities and features unrelated to the Islamic history of the Kaʿba – for example, sacrificial slaughter, offerings and altars. Those erroneous connotations could conceivably prove offensive, and so another term must be found. For the most part, that term will be 'the House', in ostensible adherence to Qurʾanic usage, where the word *al-Bayt* (the House) is traditionally taken to mean the Kaʿba.[36] For reasons that will be discussed in Chapter Three, the Qurʾan qualifies this usage by twice calling the Kaʿba 'the Ancient House'. The title of this book reflects that usage.

Referring to the Kaʿba as 'the House' also makes good sense for a Western audience, for whom a church, say, is commonly called a house of God. However, even here, there is a risk of effacing the putative betylic origins of the Kaʿba, for the Arabic word *bayt* (house) is etymologically relatable to the very word betyl.[37]

I shall also occasionally refer to the Kaʿba as a palladium, following the usage of the celebrated Islamicist, Arent Jan Wensinck.[38] As will become apparent over the course of the book, it is particularly meaningful to refer to the Kaʿba as a palladium, as a source of protection for the Islamic world.

The Nature of the Early Islamic Sources

Any attempt to describe the Kaʿba as it stands today and present that description as beneficial for understanding the Kaʿba of the medieval, pre-modern and early modern Islamic periods, and above all the early Islamic period, must address the following fact. Until approximately the early fifth/eleventh century, the only information we have regarding the House comes from the Qurʾan and early Islamic sources. Nothing that is related about the Kaʿba in either can be independently verified and thus considered factual by a scholar endeavouring to reconstruct the history and appearance of the pre-Islamic, Qurʾanic and early Islamic period Kaʿba. What is related in them could be historically true, but it could also be only a pious truth, a form of theology masquerading as history.[39]

Suspicious that what these sources relate is indeed theology not history, a number of Western historians, often labelled revisionists, have tried to prise apart the historical lacuna concerning the origins of the Kaʿba, as well as other lacunae concerning the origins of Islam as a whole. In the process, they have thrown into doubt the value of the traditional, early Islamic accounts of both.[40] The history of the Kaʿba only escapes this epistemological predicament in approximately the fifth/eleventh century, for that period sees the advent of a number of Muslim travellers' independent, eyewitness accounts of the building. That period sees, in other words, the Kaʿba entering verifiable historical time. To describe the Kaʿba of today, as will shortly be done below, is thus to give the reader simultaneous access to near certainties concerning the form and dimensions of the Kaʿba of the medieval, pre- and early modern past only. The matter is less clear concerning the early Islamic Kaʿba, and decidedly unclear for the Qurʾanic and pre-Islamic period Kaʿba. In those earlier periods, most especially the two earliest, we cannot be sure of the Kaʿba's form and dimensions. The diagrams reproduced below, created for the Islamic archaeologist Barbara Finster, are probably the closest we can get to knowing them (Figure I.1).[41] The details of these diagrams will be expanded on in the course of the book.

Throughout this book, the foregoing distinction between unverifiable historical time, circa the fourth/tenth century and before, and verifiable historical time, circa the fifth/eleventh century and after, will be maintained. Neither time will be valorised over the other, however.

Throughout this book, too, the term 'early Islamic sources' will refer to the aggregate of texts originating in the centuries before the fifth/eleventh century, with the exception of the Qurʾan, which will be referred to by name. Be they biographies and sayings of the Prophet, his companions and successors, accounts of Arab military conquests, reports of pre-Islamic religions, Qurʾanic exegeses, sacred histories or world geographies, the majority of these early Islamic sources date from the third/ninth and fourth/tenth centuries.

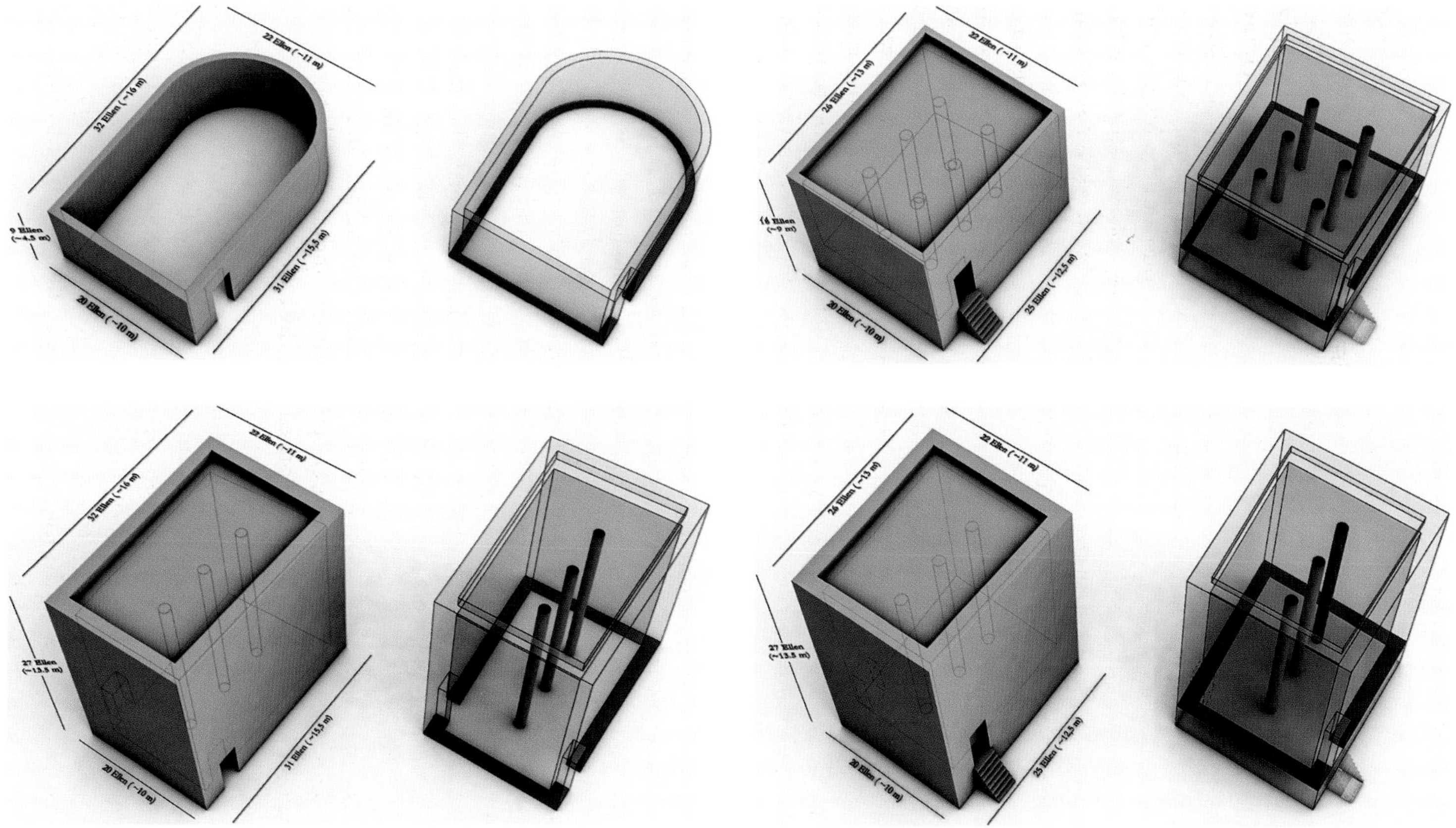

Figure I.1 *Reconstructions of the earliest forms of the Kaʿba by Joachim Backes, TU Darmstadt. Top, left to right: (a) the pre-Islamic period Kaʿba, c.400 CE, with averaged dimensions of 15.75 × 10.5 × 4.5m (L × W × H); (b) the pre-Islamic-cum-Qurʾanic period Kaʿba, c.605 CE, as allegedly reconstructed with the help of Muḥammad, but without showing the excluded Ḥijr outside it (see page 12 below for details), 12.75 × 10.5 × 9m. Bottom, left to right: (c) the early Islamic period Kaʿba, c.64/684, as allegedly reconstructed by Ibn al-Zubayr (d. 73/692), with the Ḥijr reincorporated inside it, 15.75 × 10.5 × 13.5m; (d) the early Islamic period Kaʿba, c.74/693, as allegedly reconstructed by al-Ḥajjāj b. Yūsuf (d. 95/714), but without showing the excluded Ḥijr outside it, 12.75 × 10.5 × 13.5m. Courtesy: Joachim Backes and Barbara Finster.*

The First Eyewitness Account of the Kaʿba?

The last mentioned of these early Islamic sources, world geographies, merits additional discussion. That is because this corpus is related to the corpus of the aforementioned Muslim travellers of approximately the fifth/eleventh century, with their eyewitness accounts of the Kaʿba.[42] Conceivably, therefore, the world geographies might contain personal accounts of the Kaʿba that pre-date the first incontestably eyewitness account, that of the Persian traveller, Nāṣir-i Khusraw (d. *c.*481/1088), in the mid-fifth/eleventh century.[43]

One world geography in particular suggests itself as a likely candidate for this status of earliest. It is *Kitāb al-Aʿlāq al-nafīsa* ('The book of precious things') by Ibn Rusta (*fl.* 290–300/903–13). Two reasons exist as to why one should be cautious about accepting this suggestion, however. First, what remains of this text is written according to a particular school of geography current then, thus indicating that the account might be more formulaic than personal.[44] (This is not simultaneously to say that he never visited the places described in his book.[45]) Second, corroborating this indication, the author's exceptionally extensive and minutely precise information concerning the Kaʿba and its surroundings seems to outstrip the capability of ordinary memory.[46] Ibn Rusta's account, therefore, might just repeat the information contained in the early sources.[47] Again, this is not simultaneously to say he never undertook the Hajj and thus never saw the Kaʿba with his own eyes. Scholars think that he did, in 290/903.[48] It is to say only that his account might not be based on his personal, eyewitness experience of the Kaʿba.

The same possibility must also be entertained for another fourth/tenth-century text that similarly has some claim to containing the earliest eyewitness account of the Kaʿba: *al-ʿIqd al-farīd* ('The unique necklace') by Ibn ʿAbd Rabbih (d. 328/940).[49] The doubt about the reliability of this text takes the form of an anecdote, written in the first person, regarding the pigeons of Mecca and how they never overfly the Kaʿba but descend to a height below the building, where they split to the left and right and regroup once they have passed it.[50] According to Muḥammad Shafīʿ, the twentieth-century translator of the account, this anecdote is proof that Ibn ʿAbd Rabbih's entire account is eyewitness.[51] There is, however, every reason to think that it is simply a reworking of a literary trope, for the same anecdote is found in an earlier work, namely, *Kitāb al-Ḥayawān* ('The book of animals') by al-Jāḥiẓ (d. 255/869).[52] Additionally, a related anecdote is presented by Ibn Rusta, although not in the form of a personal observation;[53] and subsequent to both Ibn Rusta and Ibn ʿAbd Rabbih, a number of later accounts contain the anecdote, although again not in the form of a personal observation.[54]

These admittedly inconclusive doubts concerning the two foregoing fourth/tenth-century accounts explain why in the present work the moment when the Kaʿba enters verifiable historical time is set at the fifth/

eleventh century. Only then can we be reasonably sure that the dimensions and form of today's Kaʿba are the same or at least very similar to those Nāṣir-i Khusraw observed, experienced and spoke of in his expressly eyewitness account from that century.[55]

To say that, however, is not simultaneously to say that today's Kaʿba is the one Nāṣir-i Khusraw observed and experienced. As will be detailed in Chapter Three, throughout its history the Kaʿba has been rebuilt a number of times. On the conservative reckoning of Muḥammad al-Mūjān, what stands today is the eleventh reconstruction.[56]

A Description of the Kaʿba Today

Centrally located in the courtyard of Mecca's Sacred Mosque (*al-Masjid al-Ḥarām*), the Kaʿba comprises two structures, not one. Each structure is adjacent to, but does not touch, the other. The larger structure is an irregular oblong. It has a height of 14m and a sloping base that measures at its widest 11.53m × 13.16m × 11.28m × 12.84m (Figure I.2).[57] This sloping, marble-clad base is called the *Shādharwān*.

Over this larger structure, anchored to a cable that passes through brass rings in the *Shādharwān*, is draped a covering robe, the *Kiswa*. As will be discussed in Chapter Six, since the seventh/thirteenth century, this robe has almost always been black, a colour that has proved instrumental in creating for the Kaʿba its instantly recognisable, iconic quality.

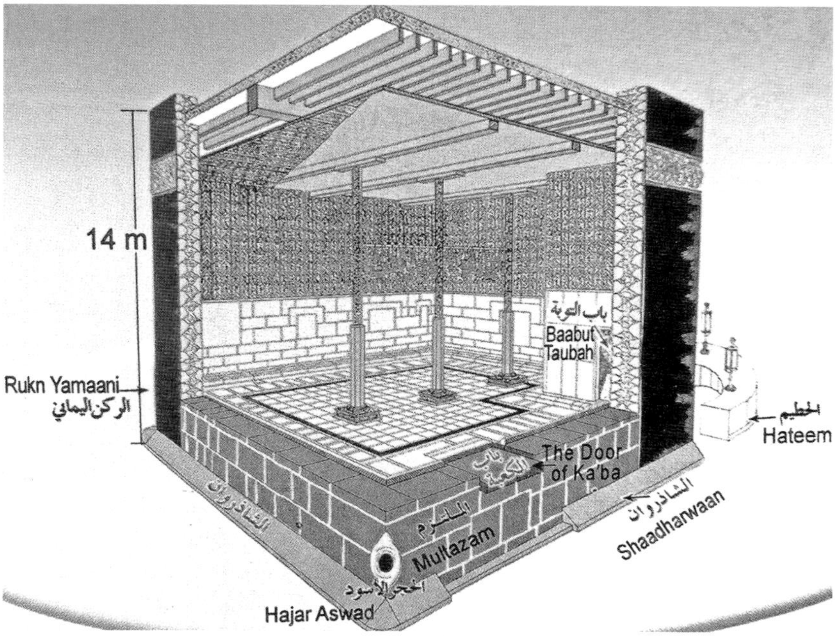

Figure I.2 *Cut-away isometric diagram of the Kaʿba. (Source: Abdul Ghani 2004, p. 73.)*

Iconic though this larger structure undoubtedly is, as its dimensions indicate, in form it is not cubic but cuboid: approximately cubic. Related to this observation, contrary to what is commonly said, the name Kaʿba should not automatically be presumed to mean 'cube', because other explanations are possible.[58] These other possible meanings notwithstanding, it is hard to gainsay Finster when she asserts: 'The word *kaʿba* refers to a cubic architectural body.'[59]

Explanations have also been given for the name of the Kaʿba's base, the *Shādharwān*; for contrary to what might be expected, the term is not Arabic but Persian in origin, where it once signified a precious curtain suspended on tents and palaces of sovereigns and leaders.[60] This linguistic origin of the *Shādharwān* supports Travis Zadeh's tentative explanation that its usage at the Kaʿba is evidence of an early historical attempt to graft Persians into the sacred history of the Sanctuary and thus make Islam accommodating of more than just Arabs.[61]

Recently linked by swing gates to the northern face of the cuboid structure is the smaller of the Kaʿba's two structures: a low, semicircular, marble-clad wall, 1.32m high and varying in thickness from 1.55m to 1.62m. This wall, sometimes called the *Ḥaṭīm* (from the verb 'to smash'), encloses the area of the Kaʿba known variously as: *pars pro toto*, the *Ḥaṭīm*; the *Ḥijr*; and the *Ḥijr* of Ishmael, the last name being a reference to the widespread belief that the biblical personage of that name lies buried there.[62] In this book, *Ḥijr* only will be used. Its literal meaning is 'the interdicted'. The early Islamic sources allege that part of it, some 3m, was once incorporated within the larger structure, which accordingly was longer then than now (Figure I.1, a and c).[63] Although both structures are shown in the diagram above (Figure I.2), they are more clearly shown in the plan below (Figure I.3).

Set 2.25m off the ground in the eastern face of the larger structure is the door to the Kaʿba. Made today of solid gold, it comprises two leaves, both of which are extensively worked with Qurʾanic verses and other inscriptions. It is 3.1m high and 1.9m wide.[64] Using stairs wheeled up to it, one passes through this door into the structure's interior, to find there a mostly empty space (Figure I.4).

Visible in this photograph of the Kaʿba's interior (Figure I.4) is one of the three wooden columns that support the building's false ceiling and roof. Visible, too, are a number of lamp-shaped decorations hanging between these columns. Possibly, glass lamps once hung there instead, but even they would have been largely ornamental, because at least until 1996 when especially far-reaching repairs of the House began, there was a glass-covered opening in the roof, measuring 1.27m x 1.4m.[65] This aperture allowed for a degree of illumination to filter into the interior through the four or five translucent skylights (*rawāzin*, *maḍāw*ⁱⁿ) set within the ceiling.[66] Nowadays, the use of crystal, not wood, for the internal staircase leading to the roof provides a source of illumination.[67] This staircase is accessible via a narrow door, the Door of Repentance (*Bāb al-Tawba*), located next to the building's internal north-eastern corner. At 2.3m high

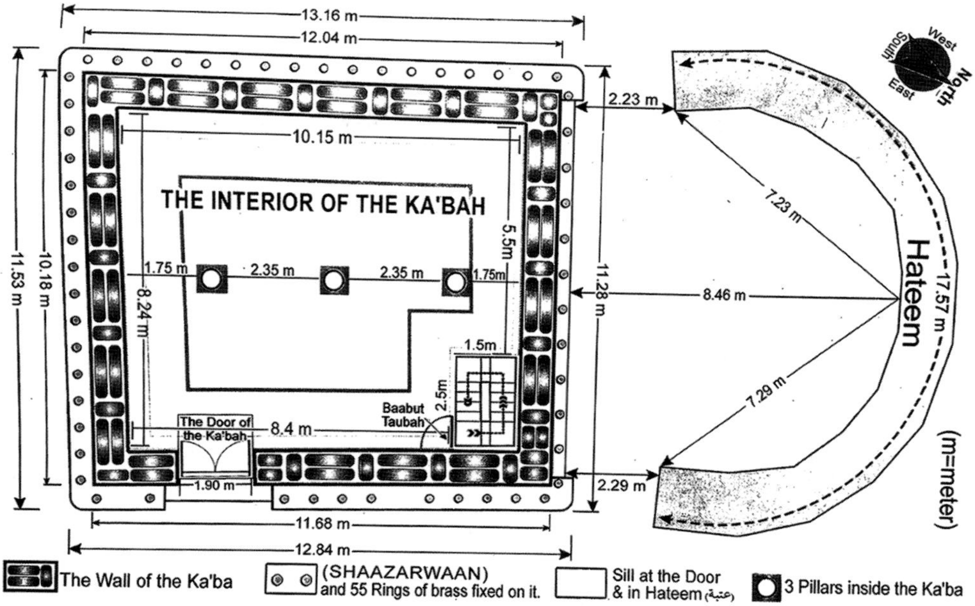

Figure I.3 *Plan of the Kaʿba. (Source: Abdul Ghani 2004, p. 75.)*

Figure I.4 *King Salmān b. ʿAbd al-ʿAzīz al-Saʿūd (r. 1436–/2015–) of Saudi Arabia, third from right, praying inside the Kaʿba on the occasion of its washing on 31 May 2015. The king is royally stockinged, not profanely shod. The chair behind him does not belong to the Kaʿba but is there to facilitate his prayer movements. (Source: online edition of the Kuwaiti newspaper* al-Anbāʾ. *Available at: <http://tinyurl.com/zsddo56> [last accessed 15.06.19].)*

and 0.7m wide, it is not visible in the photograph, but is marked in both the diagram and plan as 'Baabut Taubah'.[68]

As for the roof of the Kaʿba itself, it is slightly sloped to allow for the egress of water, which falls onto the pavement below via a rainspout that projects 1.54m over the *Ḥijr* from its location high on the building's northern face. This golden conduit, 2.585m long, is called the *Mīzāb al-Raḥma* (Spout of Mercy). It is highly worked with pious and historical inscriptions, and since at least 1273/1857 it has been made of teak and coated externally with plates of gold.[69]

Concerning the exterior of the Kaʿba, the main structure's four corners (sing. *rukn*) all have individual names, two or perhaps three of them deriving from the regions that the corners abut, a subject discussed in Chapter Two. These names are: the *Yamānī* corner, for the south-western corner; the *Shāmī*, or Syrian corner, for the north-western corner; and the *ʿIrāqī*, or Iraqi corner, for the north-eastern corner. The south-eastern corner has no such regional name, being commonly known as just *al-Rukn*, the Corner. This singular appellation is related to the fact that set in this corner is the Black Stone (*al-Ḥajar al-Aswad*, but also *al-Rukn*). This revered stone, traditionally said to be from Paradise, comprises a number of small pieces, having first been damaged in an early siege, the details of which will be related in Chapter Three. A thick bezel, presently of silver, holds these pieces together; its base is 1.1m from the ground.

In Western scholarship, the *Yamānī* corner is sometimes said to hold a stone, too: the Fortune Stone (*al-Ḥajar al-Asʿad*).[70] Having found no primary-source mention of this stone before the thirteenth/nineteenth century, I am excluding it from this description of the Kaʿba.[71] As the corner takes its name from the Arabic root *yamana*, 'to be fortunate', I am tempted to suppose that the scholars asserting the historical existence of the Fortune Stone are mistaken. In support of this supposition, I note that the traveller Ibn Jubayr (d. 614/1217) reports seeing silver nails in the *Yamānī* corner; he explains that they once held a split-off piece of the granite stone used for constructing the Kaʿba.[72] Muḥammad al-Kurdī al-Makkī, a modern-day historian, corroborates this explanation with reference to damage done to the *Yamānī* corner in 559/1163, twenty years before Ibn Jubayr's visit.[73] He adds that in the Ottoman period a broken stone in the same corner was repaired by filling it with molten lead.[74] Quite possibly the Fortune Stone is Ibn Jubayr's fissured fragment: a segment of sheared-off builder's stone, not a betyl.

In Western scholarship, too, the Black Stone is sometimes taken as the kernel of the Kaʿba, the original betyl for which the two architectural structures that comprise the Kaʿba are said to be only a supplementary support and stage.[75] In Islamic law, meanwhile, the Black Stone is always taken as the point where each circuit (*shawṭ*) of a pilgrim's ritual sevenfold circumambulation (*ṭawāf*) of the Kaʿba begins and ends. The Stone should be gestured to at each circuit's start and, pressing crowds permitting, touched or kissed, as will be described in more detail in Chapter Four.

The pavement on which the Ka'ba stands takes its name from these ritual circuits: the *Maṭāf*, or 'place of the *ṭawāf*'. In miniature paintings and other historical images of the Sacred Mosque, if the *Maṭāf* is represented it appears as a granite-clad circle in the middle of the courtyard: a Ka'ba island, commonly shown connected it to the Mosque's peristyle (*riwāq*) by narrow, pavemented walkways (Figure I.5). Today the *Maṭāf* has lost this circular, insular aspect and instead has the oblong aspect of the courtyard, because now all of the courtyard is paved. Today, too, the crowds circling on it and pressing towards the Black Stone are monitored by a guard who stands next to the Stone on a modern dais, 'the supervision platform' (*maṣṭabat al-ḥirāsa*), where he is cooled by air from an underground vent.[76]

Although not bonded to the Ka'ba's exterior, another stone allegedly from Paradise stands in proximity to the Black Stone.[77] This is the *Maqām Ibrāhīm*, or Station of Abraham, so called because it is said to bear the imprint of the prophet Abraham's feet when he was building the Ka'ba.[78] Visible today through a crystal case that is protected by a gold-plated copper dome 3m high, the stone is located almost opposite the door of the Ka'ba, at a distance of approximately 14m.[79] The area between it and the Black Stone is considered to be especially auspicious.[80] Since it is portable, it has sometimes been relocated during the pilgrimage season.[81]

In the early twelfth/eighteenth-century view of Mecca reproduced below (Figure I.5), the Sacred Mosque takes centre stage, with most of the foregoing elements of or related to the Ka'ba shown. Also shown are additional elements of the Mosque, not all of which still stand today. They include: the pitched-roof pavilions (sing. *maqām*) of three of the four Sunni law schools, placed at intervals just outside the *Maṭāf*;[82] the free-standing arch on the *Maṭāf*'s boundary, called the Banū Shayba Gate, after the Kaaba's custodians, the Banū Shayba; the ornate posts ringing the *Maṭāf*, between which lanterns hang for night time circumambulation;[83] the stepped *minbar* just within the *Maṭāf* (not for entering the Ka'ba, of course, but for sermons);[84] and again within the *Matāf*, directly opposite the Ka'ba's door, the pavilion housing the well of Zamzam, the Mosque's sacred spring, which today is accessed below ground. To the left of the Zamzam pavilion are two additional structures: the *Qubbatān* ('the two domes'). Before they were demolished in the late thirteenth/nineteenth century, they served variously as stores and depositories, especially for the Mosque's treasury.[85]

There is considerably more that could be said about Mecca's Sacred Mosque on the basis of this painting, not least its construction history from the second/eighth century onwards, including its multiplying number of minarets.[86] By 170/786, for example, there were four such minarets, and by 974/1566 there were seven.[87] Seven is the number shown in the painting and what can still be counted today.

Were one then to compare and contrast the view of the Mosque as represented in the painting with the view confronting today's pilgrims, there would be even more to say, so unsparing has the Saudi government's

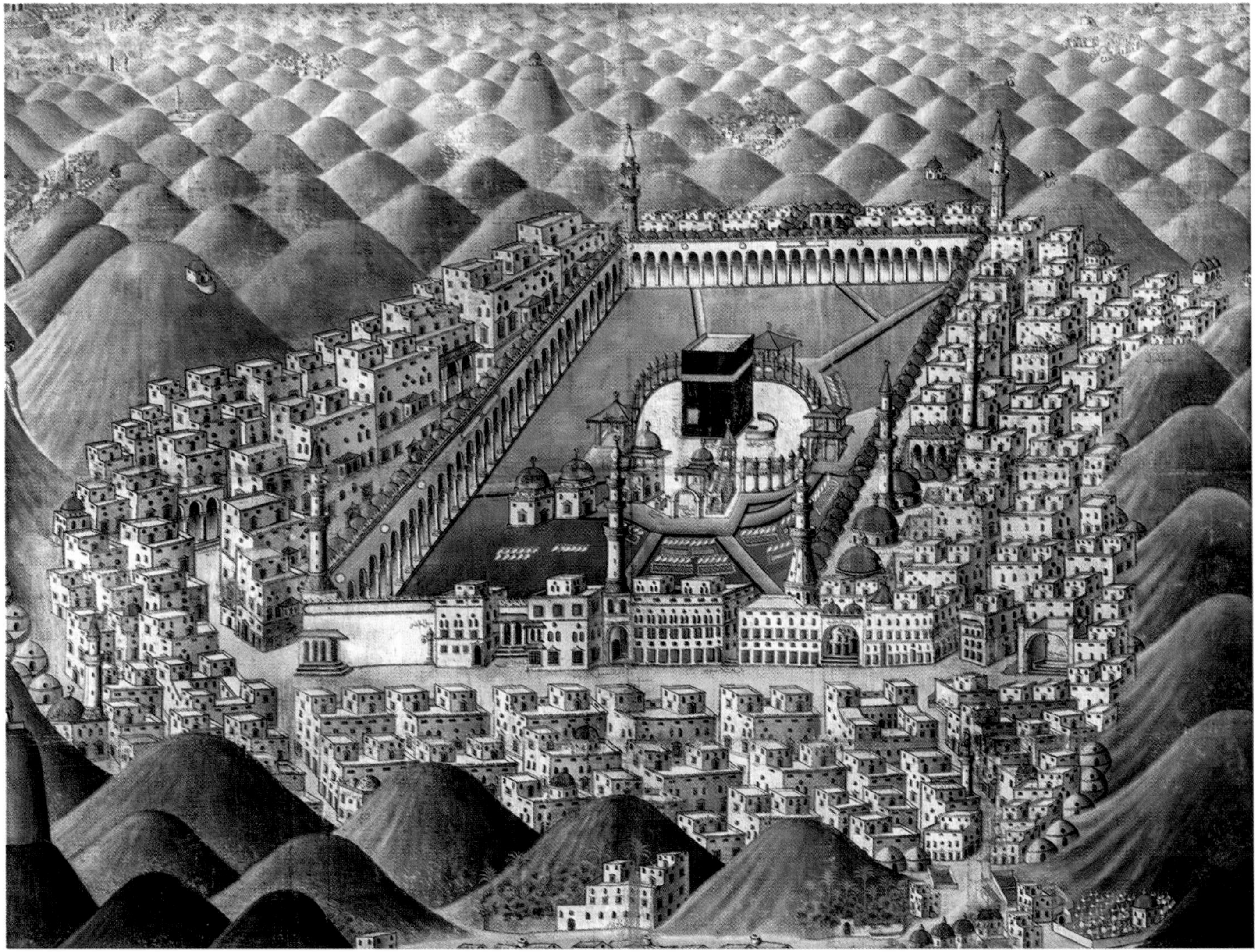

Figure I.5 *Topographical view of Mecca and its environs by an anonymous artist, dated to c.1122/1710. Oil on canvas; 112.2 × 84.5cm. Courtesy: Uppsala University Library.*

redevelopment of the Mosque and its environs been during the past sixty years.[88] Nevertheless, despite the importance of these topics, to treat them in detail would be to distract from the overarching topic of the book, namely, the work of the Kaʿba.[89]

One topic related to the painting must, however, be treated, because as with the description of the Kaʿba it helps provide context for the chapters that follow. That topic is the pilgrimage itself, the ritual sites of which are shown in the painting, both within the Sacred Mosque and, especially, outside it, in the Mosque's near and distant environs.[90]

Hajj and Umrah: the Major and Minor Pilgrimages

The Hajj pilgrimage occurs once a year over a five-day period, during which time the pilgrim must execute a precise and physically demanding roster of rituals, having first attained the requisite state of ritual purity and assumed the ritual dress, both called *iḥrām* (literally, declaring taboo, or consecrated).[91] This dress is gender specific, for only men don it. It comprises two pieces of seamless white cloth: one tied about the waist, the other covering the upper body. Women must attain the same state of ritual purity, but their clothing remains quotidian, although no face coverings are allowed.

Other than the same requirement for *iḥrām*, the Umrah pilgrimage is not restricted in its time of occurrence, being accomplishable throughout the year. Nor is it so restrictive in its roster of rituals, because it necessitates hours, not days, for its completion.[92] The rules for these rituals and those of the Hajj, and possibly even the rituals themselves, almost certainly have an early Islamic development history, a subject outside the scope of this book.[93]

In both pilgrimages, the only ritual that involves the Kaʿba is the aforementioned *ṭawāf*, or sevenfold counterclockwise circumambulation of the House's exterior. This ritual is performed once for the Umrah and either twice or thrice for the Hajj, depending on whether or not the pilgrim has already performed the *ṭawāf al-qudūm*, or circumambulation of arrival.[94] As the *ṭawāf* ritual will be discussed in detail in Chapter Four, all that needs emphasising about it here are two things. First, the ritual can be undertaken at any time of the year, such that the circling pilgrim need not be in the *iḥrām* state to perform it.[95] Second, the ritual excludes entry inside the Kaʿba, whether the cuboid building or the semicircular *Ḥijr*.

Kaʿba Copies

To bring this Introduction to a close, I would like to dispel a popular misconception concerning the Kaʿba's form.[96] Although scholars have asserted that the Kaʿba may not be copied or has only rarely been copied, neither statement is true.[97] It is especially untrue when one remembers that to copy the dimensions of the Kaʿba, specifically its iconic, larger structure, is simultaneously to copy its form. For example, during the lifetime of the Prophet a number of publicly sited cultic buildings in Arabia are said to have existed that either somehow resembled or precisely imitated the Kaʿba. These buildings were likely intended as rivals to the Kaʿba, which was conceivably the most visited of the cultic sites in central Arabia and thus the richest and most enviable.[98] At least four such buildings are known from the early Islamic sources, each one referred to as a 'kaʿba'.[99] One of these four rivals was ordered by the Prophet to be destroyed, but the others were left to stand.[100]

Long after the Prophet's lifetime, the early and later Islamic sources continue to report the erection of publicly sited copies of the Kaʿba in the Islamic world. For example, in the third/ninth century, the ʿAbbasid caliph al-Muʿtaṣim (r. 218–27/833–42) allegedly built a replica of the Kaʿba in the palatine city of Samarra, Iraq, adding to it a pavement for its ritual circumambulation, similar to the pavement around the Kaʿba.[101] In the fourth/tenth century, a mosque with the same dimensions as the Kaʿba is said to have been built in Fusṭāṭ, Egypt.[102] In the same century and city, a pavilion (*jawsāq*) in the form of the Kaʿba was built in the Qarāfa cemetery by the ʿAbbasid director of finances in Egypt, Abū Bakr al-Mādharāʾī (d. 345/957), for the celebration of religious festivals.[103] In the seventh/thirteenth century, the Iraqi-born luminary, ʿAlī b. Abī Bakr al-Harawī (d. 611/1215), is said to have been buried in a mausoleum that was shaped like the Kaʿba.[104] Later, in the eighth/fourteenth century, another mosque with the dimensions of the Kaʿba is recorded as standing opposite the church of Erzurum, in present-day Turkey; it was allegedly called the 'Kaʿba model'.[105] Later still, in tenth/sixteenth-century Timbuktu, Mali, the interior walls of the courtyard of Sankoré Mosque were allegedly modelled on the dimensions of the Kaʿba.[106]

These examples represent just an overview of the phenomenon of Kaʿba copies in the early, medieval and pre-modern periods. Other examples exist.[107] Clearly, whatever it is that makes the Kaʿba unique in the Islamic world has nothing to do with the incorrect claim that its form is sanctified and may not be copied.

CHAPTER ONE

The Kaʿba as *Qibla*

This chapter concerns the Islamic prayer direction, or *qibla*. Facing the House by adopting the *qibla* is the most ubiquitous use of the Kaʿba, undertaken at every ritual prayer and every other ritual listed in the Introduction. In a book on the work of the Kaʿba, a chapter on the Kaʿba as the *qibla* is thus an appropriate place to start. As I shall show, throughout Islamic history not only have mosques been constructed in alignment with the *qibla*, something one has learnt always to expect, but much less consistently, urban settlements, too. Can it really be the case that the exorbitant, painstaking labour required to align these latter, ostensibly secular constructions results from 'trivia', as two celebrated academics have separately asserted?[1] One aim of the chapter is to address this question, by bringing to the fore the extent to which rulers and patrons have lavished wealth to achieve this urban-wide alignment.

Another aim of the chapter is to ensure that the term *qibla* really does denote the direction of the Kaʿba. This aim is necessary, because from the very beginnings of Islam such an exclusive denotation was not always the case. Rather, as I shall show, the term was sometimes anchored not to the palladium of the Islamic world but to an absolute, mostly divinely sanctioned authority in this world: a ruler, principally. Because the chapter is premised on the judgement that one of the works of the Kaʿba is its role as the *qibla*, it is necessary to verify at the outset that the *qibla* is indeed the direction of the Kaʿba and denotes the Kaʿba by implication. The chapter starts, hence, with a review of the history and meaning of the term, looking at its literal and symbolic meanings, not just its Islamic customary meaning as the direction of the Kaʿba.

Part One: The History and Meaning of the *Qibla*

When a *qibla* was first adopted for ritual purposes in Islam, and to where and what it first pointed, are questions without uniformly accepted answers.[2] Because, as I shall show, the *qibla* was probably tied to the Kaʿba as the sole sacred direction of Islam no later than the end of the rule of the Umayyad caliph ʿAbd al-Malik (r. 65–86/685–705), answers to the questions have to be sought in the unverifiable and often contradictory history presented in the early Islamic sources. Nevertheless, some attempt to answer the questions is necessary, especially as doing so illuminates the usage and thus significance of the term *qibla*.

Taking the Qurʾan as her primary evidence, not Islamic tradition, Angelika Neuwirth has repeatedly argued that Jerusalem's Temple Mount was the first *qibla* of Islam, inaugurated at some unspecified time during the latter years of the Prophet's Meccan period (*c.*610–22).[3] According to Neuwirth, prior to that moment there had been no ritually prescribed *qibla* for the proto-Muslims, the Believers (*muʾminūn*), even though the increasingly harsh reality of their life in a hostile Mecca had generated a desire for an inner exile, a psychological escape from the hardships they were experiencing on the ground. With the establishment of Jerusalem as the Believers' first prescribed *qibla*, Neuwirth argues, this desire was answered and 'understood as an emulation of the practice of Moses, who in Egypt, equally in a situation of external pressure, ordered the Children of Israel to adopt a *qibla* for their prayer [as recounted in Q 10:87]'.[4] As Neuwirth interprets this inaugural moment in Mecca, in initiating an imaginary exodus to the sanctuary of Jerusalem via oriented prayer, the community of Believers created for themselves 'a self-consciousness . . . no longer based solely on the rites inherited from the Kaʿba worship, but much more on the awareness of being among the receivers and bearers of a scripture and of having a share in the memory of salvation history'.[5]

Neuwirth's argument is important, not because it is conclusive, which it is not, but because it is based on a sophisticated, holistic engagement with the Qurʾan and a measured acceptance of Islamic tradition. Other scholars' arguments have sometimes been based on neither.[6] This does not necessarily invalidate their arguments, but it does make them mostly immaterial to a book that explores the work of the Kaʿba within Islamic culture.

A strand of Islamic tradition concurs with Neuwirth on the target of the first *qibla*. There exists, for example, the honorific term 'First of the Two Qiblas' (*ūlā al-qiblatayn*), which was applied to Jerusalem no later than the Ayyubid period (564–658/1169–1260), when it is first found recorded.[7] The exact moment when this *qibla* was inaugurated does, however, differ in Islamic tradition from Neuwirth's account, being mostly dated to an unspecified time soon after the Prophet's Hegira, or flight from Mecca and arrival in Medina in 1/622.[8]

Contradicting Neuwirth and this strand of Islamic tradition, another strand of Islamic tradition supposes the Kaʿba to have been the first *qibla*, either alone or in conjunction with the Temple Mount, a conjunction the Prophet was allegedly able to achieve by standing before the Kaʿba in the direction of the Temple.[9] This strand does not, however, disagree regarding the Prophet's use of the Temple Mount as the sole *qibla* following his arrival in Medina, as just mentioned.

Although there is uncertainty in Islamic tradition regarding the precise duration of the Temple Mount *qibla*,[10] there is agreement that the Kaʿba became the Believers' sole official *qibla* at some point during the first seventeen or eighteen months of the Prophet's stay in Medina.[11] This agreement is based upon the evidence of the Qurʾanic verse:

> We have seen you looking up into heaven, turning this way and that, so We will turn you towards a *qibla* which will please you. Turn your face, therefore, towards the Sacred Mosque (*al-Masjid al-Ḥarām*) [in Mecca].[12] Wherever you are, turn your faces towards it.[13]

With regard to this verse, it should be noted that, outside Islamic tradition, its meaning is anything but agreed. That is because the absence of a precise geographical location for the 'Sacred Mosque' mentioned in the verse has prompted some revisionists to wonder if the Kaʿba was ever a Qurʾanic *qibla* and if Mecca was ever the Qurʾanic Sanctuary (*al-Ḥaram*).[14] This absence of a precise geographical location explains my parenthetical interpolation of 'in Mecca' in the verse's translation.

Without wading too far into an issue that is beyond the purview of this book, the revisionists' conjecture is countered by certain early Islamic traditions. These allege two important matters. First, that the Sanctuary either came into existence or took definition only because of the presence of the Kaʿba, specifically the prototypical, celestial Kaʿba, the Frequented House (*al-Bayt al-Maʿmūr*), which temporarily descended to earth in the form of a paradisiacal tent of red hyacinth at the time of Adam.[15] Second, that light emanating from the Black Stone at the time of Abraham's sojourn in Mecca reaffirmed the Sanctuary's inner perimeter.[16] On the basis of these traditions, effectively Mecca, the Sanctuary, is the Kaʿba. It exists because the Kaʿba exists.

The revisionists' conjecture aside, there would be little reason to doubt the immediate implementation of the *qibla* change announced in the above Qurʾanic verse, were it not for some archaeological evidence and some suggestive but inconclusive details contained in a number of early Islamic traditions.[17] Regarding the archaeological evidence, it primarily concerns a site in the southern Negev that is rectangular in shape and marked out not just with a southern, or Kaʿba-oriented apse but an eastern one, too. Moshe Sharon, the site's archaeologist, has interpreted the site as an early Umayyad mosque and seen in the existence of the two apses, or *mihrab*s, evidence that an East-oriented *qibla* continued to be used by the community of Believers long after the Qurʾan had announced that the *qibla* was the Kaʿba.[18] Although Sharon's interpretation of the site as a mosque has since been disputed,[19] there exists additional archaeological evidence in support of his conclusion that the Kaʿba did not become the Believers's sole *qibla* for quite some time. That evidence comes from the medieval Palestinian cemetery of Tell el-Hesi, where several bodies have been found with their faces oriented towards Jerusalem.[20]

Regarding the details contained in a number of early Islamic traditions, they equally indicate that long after the change of *qibla* was announced in the Qurʾan the Believers continued to pray in other directions.[21] In combination with the archaeological evidence, these details have promoted the idea, again outside traditional Islamic scholarship, that the Kaʿba did not automatically become the sole official *qibla* but that others persisted. Primary among these other *qibla*s are the Temple Mount and, under Christian influence, the non-site specific, cardinal direction of East.[22]

The duration of these alternative *qibla*s is not always specified by their proponents. Regarding the East-oriented *qibla*, however, Sharon has argued on the basis of the aforementioned archaeological evidence that it came to an end in or just after 76/695, via a decree from the Umayyad caliph ʿAbd al-Malik.[23] Given this caliph's activity in developing and systematising elements of the Qurʾan as part of his efforts to create the first Islamic state, not to mention his likely role in standardising the Qurʾan itself, such a date is plausible.[24] Related to these activities, Michelina Di Cesare has shown that ʿAbd al-Malik's son, al-Walīd (r. 86–96/705–15), was as interested as his father in unifying the *qibla*, and perhaps much more so.[25] Possibly the end of the East-oriented *qibla* should be credited to him.

Sacred direction and the play of analogies between kingship and divinity

On the basis of the foregoing history, it is possible to assert that although the literal meaning of the term *qibla* is 'what faces the front of something' (*mā qābala wajh [al-shayʾ]*),[26] and thence direction or goal, the customary meaning of the term is a direction or goal deemed sacred.[27] The cardinal direction of East, the Temple Mount, and the Kaʿba are three such sacred goals. The literal meaning is useful to bear in mind, however, as it conveys something essential about the etymology of the term. That is because another word from the same root as *qibla*, *qubul* (also *qubl*), means a body's front part, and thus, sometimes, face (*wajh*).[28] This physiognomic aspect is at play, for example, in the gloss by Fakhr al-Dīn al-Rāzī (d. 606/1210) of the Qurʾanic phrase 'the face (*wajh*) of God' (Q 2:115) as 'His *qibla*'.[29] It is similarly at play in the assertion by ʿAyn al-Quḍāt Hamadānī (d. 526/1131) that the Prophet's 'face (*rū*) is the religion (*dīn*) and *qibla*';[30] and also in the assertion by Rūzbihān Baqlī (d. 605/1209) that 'the face (*rū*) of Adam is the *qibla* of the passionate lovers'.[31] In view of this play,

Frederick Denny's literal definition of *qibla* as 'facing point' is helpful, for it captures the term's physiognomic resonance.[32]

Early Arabic sources confirm the customary meaning of the term. For example, in the allegedly pre-Islamic poetry of the legendary sixth-century poet ʿAntara, there is a reference to the Sasanian emperor Khusraw I (Anūshirwān, r. 531–79 CE) as 'the *qibla* of the ambassadors (*qiblat al-quṣṣād*)'.[33] In the early Islamic period poetry of al-Farazdaq (d. *c.*112/730), there is a similar reference to the Umayyad caliph Sulaymān b. ʿAbd al-Malik (r. 96–9/715–17): 'You are to this religion like the *qibla* by which people are guided from going astray.'[34] As the heads of theocracies, Khusraw and Sulaymān were in certain verbal, ceremonial and discursive contexts perceived as sacral beings.[35] It is therefore unsurprising to find them likened to the *qibla*.

Explaining this perceived sacrality of the ruler, at least with regard to the early Islamic caliphate, Aziz Al-Azmeh writes: '[T]he person and rule of individual kings [had] a correlative cosmic signature. They were not simply the lynchpins of the mundane social order, but were appointed as part of the divine order.'[36] The Muslim philosopher Abū Sulaymān al-Sijistānī (d. *c.*375/985) even contended that a king was a human god.[37]

This likening of the ruler to the *qibla* is neither a literal nor an obviously customary usage of the term. It needs investigating in case it conflicts with the almost universal assumption today that the *qibla* is the Kaʿba.

The usage continued during the rule of the ʿAbbasids (132–656/750–1258), the dynasty which succeeded the Umayyads (41–132/661–750). For them, it would seem the term was deployed not just honorifically, but also architecturally.[38] According to Samer Ali, in at least three of the third/ninth-century palaces at Samarra, the caliph's audience hall was oriented against the *qibla*; only the caliph faced Mecca.[39] This orientation, Ali contends, forced visiting dignitaries to choose between giving the caliph or the Kaʿba their backs when retreating, thereby 'creating a hierarchical conflict between God and his first executive'.[40]

The impropriety of walking with one's back turned to the Kaʿba is well attested in early Islamic sources.[41] Although it would be absurd to interpret this evidence as meaning that no matter where a Muslim went in the world never could they turn their back to the Kaʿba, something of the great piety the evidence expresses can still be found today, as Annemarie Schimmel explains: 'As Mecca and the Kaʿba are, for the pious, certainly the most sacred place on Earth to which the living and the dead turn, one should not spit or stretch out one's legs in the direction of the Kaʿba, nor perform bodily needs in its direction.'[42]

The impropriety of walking with one's back turned to the ruler is equally well attested in Islamic sources. A good example concerns the visit of the deposed Christian ruler Ordoño IV (r. 958–60) to the Umayyad caliph in al-Andalus, al-Ḥakam II (r. 350–66/961–76), as described by the chronicler Ibn Ḥayyān (d. 469/1076). Having prostrated himself before al-Ḥakam and submitted his petition for military assistance, Ordoño 'rose to retire, walking backwards so as not to turn his face from the caliph'.[43]

At Samarra, the two conflicting improprieties were put to good use, at least according to Samer Ali. Although Ali cites no archaeological sources in support of his interpretation, the orientation of the sites of at least one, and possibly two, of the Samarra palaces in question would seem to bear it out, as does the late Umayyad or possibly early ʿAbbasid palace at Mshatta in Jordan, with its processional axis oriented against the *qibla*.[44] Much later, during the Mughal period of India, the contemporary planning principle of *qarīna*, or counter-image, was deployed by Shah Jahan (r. 1037–68/1628–57) for the counter-*qibla* axis of his audience hall at Agra.[45] Similar to the aforementioned Umayyad caliph Sulaymān; the Ghaznavid ruler Maḥmūd (r. 388–421/998–1030); the Fatimid imam–caliph al-Mustanṣir (r. 427–87/1036–94); the ʿAbbasid caliph al-Nāṣir li-Dīn Allāh (r. 575–622/1180–1226); the Marinid ruler Abū al-Ḥasan ʿAlī (r. 732–49/1331–48); the eponym of the Timurid dynasty (771–912/1370–1506), Tīmūr (r. 771–807/1370–1405); the Safavid ruler Muḥammad Khudābanda (r. 985–996/1578–88); the Mughal rulers Akbar (r. 963–1014/1556–1605), Jahangir (r. 1014–37/1605–27) and Aurangzeb (r. 1068–1118/1658–1707); the de facto Mughal regent Qudsiyya Begum (Udham Bai) (*fl.* 1161–7/1748–54); and various rulers of the Qajar dynasty (1193–1342/1779–1924), Shah Jahan was honorifically referred to as the *qibla*.[46] As seems also to be true of Akbar at Fatehpur-Sikri, at Agra he rendered this honorific architectural.[47]

What we are witnessing here, in both the architectural and honorific realms, is the deliberate play of analogies between kingship and divinity. According to Al-Azmeh, the purpose of this play was to construct a 'self-conscious rhetoric of kingship which [was] impervious to all but the most officious of doctrinal or legalistic questioning'.[48] Precisely because the honorific use of the term *qibla* for the ruler could be passed off as mere metaphor, and the architectural use of the counter-*qibla* for the throne-room could be dismissed as the inevitable consequence of orienting a palace to the Kaʿba, the analogies were efficacious. Their elusiveness, their non-literalness, was their strength. As this efficaciousness is explained by Al-Azmeh:

> Although [the rhetoric of sovereignty] is not a theoretical enunciation or regulation of sovereignty methodically systematised in a comprehensive and coherent statement, [it] is a locus of significant conceptions that, in addition to their discursive consequence, have social and political effect.[49]

The cumulative social and political effect of analogies like the ruler as the *qibla* is described by the same scholar as 'creative of a sublime and holy authoritarianism, one which flows in the social and imaginary-conceptual capillaries of Muslim political traditions'.[50]

As noted, Samer Ali explains the architectural deployment of the counter-*qibla* axis for certain ʿAbbasid throne-rooms as a strategy of power; one might consider it a type of psychological domination. The same explanation likely holds true for Shah Jahan's audience hall, too. In these architectural usages, the *qibla*'s sole denotation as the Kaʿba is not challenged, and even reinforced. What, though, of the honorific deployment of the term: if a ruler is referred to as the *qibla*, does that not mean the term no longer exclusively denotes the Kaʿba? With reference to what Al-Azmeh considers the clearest source of the play of analogies between kingship and divinity, namely, manuals of dream interpretation, the answer is no.[51] For in these manuals, to dream of the Kaʿba is to dream of the ruler.[52] During the Fatimid period (297–567/909–1171), this interpretation seems to have been developed and simultaneously removed from the realm of dreams, because the Fatimid missionary al-Qāḍī al-Nuʿmān (d. 363/974) devotes a number of pages to the relationship between the imam-caliph and the architecture of the Kaʿba.[53]

On the basis of this dream interpretation, the steps leading to the negative answer to the foregoing question are as follows: the ruler is the embodiment of the Kaʿba; the ruler-as-*qibla* honorific denotes this embodiment; thus there remains just one exclusive referent for the term *qibla*, namely, the Kaʿba.[54] Apart from dream manuals and the subtleties of Fatimid theosophy, however, the possibility still exists that in the royal courts where the honorific was deployed, the ruler and the Kaʿba were in competition with each other, playfully or otherwise.[55] If one is to believe the story related by the early Islamic historian al-Ṭabarī (d. 310/923), the Umayyad caliph al-Walid II (r. 125–6/743–4) was perhaps invoking this competition and cheerfully submitting to it when in 125/743 he took a royally domed canopy (*qubba*) of the same proportions as the Kaʿba to the Kaʿba. He allegedly planned to erect it over the Kaʿba and sit beneath it, inside the building, drinking wine: a king, the King, the divine King (*al-Mālik*) enthroned. Only his companions' fear of what the people would do if they saw him acting thus stopped him from executing his plan![56]

Is the qibla *the Sanctuary?*

As noted at the outset of this chapter, before proceeding to the chapter's second aim, namely, a history of the extent to which rulers and patrons have endeavoured to have even their secular constructions oriented towards the Kaʿba, the following is required. It must be proved that in post-second/eighth-century usage, if not a century earlier, the term *qibla* always refers to the Kaʿba. In the foregoing pages, we have achieved this with regard to the potential *qibla* rivals of the Temple Mount, the cardinal direction of East, and for the most part the ruler. One last potential *qibla* rival is the Meccan Sanctuary itself; for the possibility exists that the term's referent is not the Ka'ba in specific but the Meccan Sanctuary in general. This possibility arises from an Imāmī (Shi'ite) and Sunni tradition, both of which speak of a nested *qibla*: the Sanctuary nesting the Sacred Mosque nesting the Ka'ba.[57] One version of the Imāmī tradition reads as follows:

> God made the Ka'ba the *qibla* for the people of the [Sacred] Mosque. He made the [Sacred] Mosque the *qibla* for the people of the Sanctuary; and He made the Sanctuary the *qibla* for the people of this world (*ahl al-dunyā*).[58]

The Sunni tradition is almost identical in its wording, the difference being that in one version of it 'the people of this world' are specified as coming from the Prophet's community (*umma*). That version is found, for example, in the hadith collection compiled by Abū Bakr al-Bayhaqī (d. 458/1066), who considers it unreliable.[59]

Is the purport of this tradition that the *qibla* varies according to one's distance from the Ka'ba, such that for Muslims in Morocco, say, the *qibla* is Mecca in general, not the Ka'ba in specific? At least until the modern period, the answer to this question was yes, scientifically speaking, but no, popularly speaking.[60] The issue at stake was how to determine the *qibla* when at a far remove from the Ka'ba. Science and popular tradition diverged on how to solve the problem.

The mathematical, scientific solution was to make the calculations with reference to Mecca and its terrestrial coordinates, the *qibla* at any given locality being 'a trigonometric function of the local latitude, the latitude of Mecca, and the longitude difference from Mecca'.[61] As the Muslim polymath al-Bīrūnī (d. *c*.442/1050) explains in his scientific work *The Determination of the Coordinates of Localities*:

> For the pillar and also pole of Islam [viz., ritual prayer] to be performed, we note that ascertaining and verifying the azimuth of the *qibla* is an urgent need. God says: 'Turn your face, therefore, towards the Sacred Mosque. Wherever you all are, turn your faces towards it' [Q 2:144]. It is already axiomatic that this direction varies in accordance with one's location relative to (*bi-ḥasabi jihāt al-tanaḥḥī*) the Ka'ba. As this is witnessed in the Sacred Mosque itself, how much more so elsewhere! . . . There are men for every job: [some] have determined the longitudes of cities, which are the measures of their eastern or western displacements, and their latitudes, which are the measures of their northern or southern displacements . . . But [even these men] are confused about [ascertaining and verifying the azimuth of the *qibla*]. You see them trying to equate the qibla with the directions of the wind, with the risings of the lunar mansions, and so forth, all to no advantage . . . [And so] even if the need to determine the distances between cities and compute the habitable

> world (*ḥaṣr al-maʿmūra*) in order to know the azimuths of cities relative to each other were a need that achieved the correction of the *qibla* only, it would be incumbent on us to devote our care and attention to it.[62]

Using Mecca for its terrestrial coordinates in the way outlined by al-Bīrūnī does not, however, mean that the scientists were confused regarding the precise identity and ultimate direction of the *qibla*. The opening page of a treatise for scientifically determining the *qibla*, written not by an astronomer but the mathematically inclined al-Bazdawī (d. 493/1100), shows this well: 'One of the conditions required in every prayer is that one should face the Kaʿba, wherefore one has to know in which direction is the Kaʿba.'[63]

Folk astronomy: the qibla *is the Kaʿba*

In the above long quote from al-Bīrūnī, his disparaging remarks about people trying to determine the *qibla* by the directions of the winds, the risings of the lunar mansions, and so forth, all refer to the second means for solving the *qibla* problem: the non-mathematical ways advanced by popular tradition. David King, a historian of Islamic science, has extensively researched these trenchantly upheld and widely pursued ways. He refers to them collectively as the folk astronomical tradition of Islamic geography, as opposed to the scientific astronomical tradition.[64]

The practitioners of this folk tradition formed a disparate group that included judges and other members of the *ulema*, such that the appellation 'folk' is perhaps not one which we might automatically associate with them.[65] Even so, as King explains regarding them and their craft:

> The scholars of the sacred law of Islam created a sacred geography based on the notion that in order to face the Kaʿba in any region of the world one should face the same direction in which one would be standing if one were directly in front of the appropriate segment of the perimeter of the Kaʿba . . . From the 9th to the 16th century [they] developed a tradition of sacred geography in which the *qibla*s of different regions of the world around the Kaʿba were associated with particular astronomical horizon phenomena. Some 20 different schemes of this kind of sacred geography – sometimes illustrated in manuscripts, sometimes described in word – are known from some 30 different medieval sources, and there are surely more yet to be rediscovered. These directions adopted for the *qibla* obviously corresponded only roughly to the *qibla*s that were calculated by the Muslim astronomers.[66]

As a number of the schemes of this folk astronomical tradition are discussed at greater length in Chapter Two, they will not be treated further here. Instead, the following assertion alone must suffice: in historical

Figure 1.1 *ʿAbd al-Qādir al-Jīlānī has a vision of the Kaʿba when performing his ablutions. From a copy of* İbretnümā *('The exemplar') by the Ottoman author Lamiʿī Çelebi (d. 938/1532), dated 995/1587. Gouache, gold and ink on paper; 15.5 × 24.75cm (folio). Courtesy: The Keir Collection. PT2–26, fol. 37r. © The Keir Collection of Islamic Art on loan to the Dallas Museum of Art, K.1.2014.38.A-Z.*

diagrams of these popular schemes, the Kaʿba is always shown at their epicentre (Figures 2.2 and 2.3). The *qibla*, in other words, is the Kaʿba.

This conclusion is replicated in popular Sufi traditions, where claiming to see the Kaʿba with one's inner vision when commencing the ritual prayer is a marker of one's elevated spiritual station.[67] A visual representation approximating such a claim is reproduced above (Figure 1.1). It shows a vision of the Kaʿba as experienced by ʿAbd al-Qādir al-Jīlānī (d. 561/1166), the eponym of the Qadiriyya Sufi order, when performing his ablutions in preparation for the ritual prayer.[68]

Coda

With reference to this tradition of seeing the Kaʿba prior to or at the moment of ritual prayer, it might be conjectured that its logical upshot would be the placement of a representation of the Kaʿba within the *mihrab* of a mosque, as occurs in the early modern *mihrab* of the Mosque of the

Figure 1.2 *Diagrammatic representation of the Kaʿba and the Sacred Mosque in the tiled* mihrab *of the Mosque of the Black Eunuchs at Topkapı Palace, Istanbul, dated to c.1077/1666. © Peter Eastland / Alamy Stock Photo.*

Black Eunuchs at Topkapı Palace (Figure 1.2). This Ottoman *mihrab* is, however, almost unique in that regard, at least for the medieval and pre-modern periods.[69]

Somewhat more common for the pre-modern period is the placement next to the *mihrab* of a wall tile consisting of a reserve-painted outline suggestive of a *mihrab*, at the centre of which is a representation of the Kaʿba.[70] A medieval record of a related practice is contained in a text by Muḥammad b. Shākir (d. 764/1362), who alleges that in the decorative programme of the second/eighth-century Umayyad Mosque of Damascus, a representation of the Kaʿba was placed above the *mihrab*.[71] Another related practice is the placement in or above the *mihrab* of a piece of the Black Stone, or what is alleged to be such a piece.[72] At least three Ottoman mosques evidence this practice.[73]

One last related practice of visually tying the *mihrab* to the Kaʿba is exhibited at the Marinid necropolis and pilgrimage site of Shāla, just outside Rabat, Morocco. There, in the early twentieth century, on what would have been the second day of the Hajj, two French academics witnessed rituals being performed at one of the ruined site's medieval *mihrabs*.[74] They saw people making sevenfold circumambulations of this *mihrab*, in apparent anticipatory imitation of the pilgrims in Mecca who, on the third day of the Hajj, perform a sevenfold circumambulation of the Kaʿba, the *ṭawāf al-ifāḍa*, or circumambulation of 'overflowing'.[75] The academics add that while these people circled the *mihrab* they were chanting the *talbiyya*, the ritual phrase used by pilgrims to Mecca to announce their intention to begin the pilgrimage. They further note that the people moved with the distinctive gait, *ramal*, recommended for the initial three circuits of the *ṭawāf* ritual.[76]

In this particular prayer hall at Shāla, for these particular visitors, the *mihrab* was more than just an architectural element aligned to the Kaʿba. In some vital sense, it *was* the Kaʿba. Conceivably, this usage dates to the eighth/fourteenth century.[77]

Part Two: A History of the Materialised *Qibla*

Mosques are aligned with the *qibla*, because of the requirement to pray in the prophetically sanctioned direction, and disputes regarding the *qibla*'s correct angle, commonly politically or ideologically motivated, have frequently led to mosques being reoriented, either by force or miracle.[78] Why, though, should urban settlements have been oriented to the Kaʿba?[79] Given their essentially religious purpose, madrasas and mausolea are sometimes aligned with the *qibla*.[80] Why, though, should domestic housing, especially vernacular domestic housing of recent centuries, sometimes have this alignment?[81] (That ceremonial housing, above all palaces, should sometimes have this alignment is less perplexing, given the transference potential of *qibla*-based symbolism onto the ruler, a phenomenon treated in part one.)

The focus of this part of this chapter is on these more surprising, less immediately explicable findings, especially the *qibla*-aligned urban settlements. As stated at the outset of the chapter, the aim is to bring to the fore the extent to which rulers and patrons have found it expedient to lavish wealth to achieve this alignment. An additional aim is to try to account for their doing so; for as also briefly noted at the chapter's outset, the explanation that the alignment results from 'trivial facts', as independently propounded by Keppel A. C. Creswell and Paul Wheatley, is perhaps premature.[82] Could matters be that simple? Can their explanation even begin to account for all the subsequent endeavours in the history of Islamic urbanism to repeat this 'trivially realised' *qibla* alignment?

The early Islamic city: Kufa, Basra and the other amṣār

With regard to the protracted debate about whether the academic concept of the Islamic city has any basis in historical reality, the above sub-heading indicates that yes, it does, at least for the very earliest period of Islamic urbanism.[83] This period is the first 100 years or so, and is predominantly the period of the *amṣār* (sing. *miṣr*), or garrison towns, and the so-called Umayyad desert palaces.[84] After this period, things become more complex. However, as will appear in the following review, some of the apparently original, or proper-to-Islam, seemingly ritualistic urban planning elements of several of the *amṣār* live on in cities that belong to a later period of Islamic urbanism. The *qibla* orientation of a city's central or earliest quarter is one such element.

Kufa

Although contemporary with Basra, Kufa's foundation and early development are more fully treated in the early Islamic sources. So Kufa is where this *qibla*-focused review of early and medieval Islamic urbanism begins.

The two earliest reports in the Islamic sources concur that Kufa was founded in 17/638. Exactly how it was founded, they slightly disagree. One report states:

> When Saʿd [b. Abī Waqqāṣ (d. *c*.55/675)] reached the place [destined to be] the mosque, on his orders an archer shot one arrow towards the *qibla* (*mahabb al-qibla*), another towards the north, another to the south, and a fourth to the east, marking the spots where the arrows fell. [Saʿd] then established the mosque and the governor's residence on and about the spot where the archer had stood.[85]

In this report, the mosque is laid out only after the archer has demarcated the limits of a wide, open square. In the second report, the reverse is true: the open square is demarcated only after the mosque has been laid, or traced out (*ikhtaṭṭa)*:

> The first thing to be marked out in Kufa, and that was subsequently erected when they had finally decided to make a beginning with building, was the mosque . . . Its ground plan was traced out. Then a man stationed himself in the center of this ground plan. He was an archer of prodigious strength. He shot (one arrow) to his right and ordered that anyone who wanted could start building for his own beyond where the arrow had landed. (Then he did the same with an arrow that he shot to the left.) Next he shot an arrow straight ahead of him and one in the opposite direction and ordered that anyone who wanted could start building for himself beyond where these two arrows had landed. Thus they left a square (*murabbaʿ*) for the mosque, that the people could enter from all sides.[86]

Whether the tracing out of the mosque occurred before or after the demarcation of the square is, for present purposes, insignificant.[87] What matters, rather, is that the square was oriented towards the *qibla*, as the first report clearly states. This *qibla* direction was not determined mathematically, but by astronomical horizon phenomena, exactly as also achieved by the folk astronomical tradition of Islamic geography discussed in part one.[88] The ritualistic nature of the square's orientation process is apparent in both reports, in the form of the actions of the archer, because the use of arrows for ritual, often divinatory purposes was a part of pre-Islamic Central Arabian culture.[89]

As just noted, the *qibla* orientation of the square is stated in the first report only. In the second report, it is suggested by the fact that the square echoes the plan of the mosque, the latter presumably having a *qibla* orientation. About this oriented square the rest of the town unfolded: the surrounding land was marked out into plots (sing. *khiṭṭa*), each assigned to the different tribes, with the direction of the principal thoroughfares (*manāhij*) being dictated by the square's orientation. As a later section of the second report describes this process:

> North of the congregation area (*ṣaḥn*) five main thoroughfares branched out, from the south side four such thoroughfares branched out, while from the east and the west (sides) three such roads were planned. All these roads were marked out (by Saʿd). North of the congregation area, adjacent to it, he settled [the following tribes . . .]. South of the congregation area he settled [the following tribes . . .]. East of the congregation area he settled [the following tribes . . .]. Finally, west of the congregation area he settled [the following tribes . . .]. Thus, all those who lived right next to the congregation area, as well as all the other people, were housed between (the main thoroughfares) and beyond them, the entire territory having been divided up into plots.[90]

Modern archaeological excavations at Kufa appear to confirm the concerted efforts at town planning that are recounted in this report.[91] Indeed, scholars have since used the excavations to see in the foundation of Kufa the application of precise planning principles, with one scholar even supposing that the town was intended to be orthogonal in design.[92] Although Hichem Djaït, the historian most associated with the study of early and medieval Kufa, has not gone that far in interpreting the textual and archaeological evidence, his reference to the town plan's 'grande perfection géométrique', and his comparison of this plan to the square plan of ancient Babylon, are acknowledgements of at least some degree of orthogonal principles at work.[93] Certainly, in his analysis of the town's earliest orientation, Djaït confirms what is most important to the present review, namely, the role of the *qibla*. He writes: 'It is the *qibla* that must have been the point of reference.'[94] Against such a conclusion, how perplexingly aberrant appears Creswell's and Wheatley's rejection as 'trivial' the reports concerning the demarcation of the town's central square by means of an archer with his four arrows.

Where the charge of triviality has some justification is in the two scholars' dismissal of the traditional reason given for the relocation of Kufa's mosque to the side of the governor's residence, the *dār al-imāra*. The sources explain that this relocation occurred after a theft allegedly from the town's treasury, which was housed at the residence. The theft prompted the then caliph, ʿUmar (r. 13–23/634–44), to issue the following order: 'Relocate the mosque in order to place it to the side of the residence, and make the residence its *qibla*. For in the mosque there are always people present, day and night; they will act as guards of what is also their treasure.'[95] In this relocation, the residence ended up immediately behind the mosque's *qibla* wall, a spatial arrangement of mosque and gubernatorial or royal residence that would be repeated in other towns and cities for approximately the next 200 years.[96]

As others, including Wheatley, have observed, there was clearly more to the relocation than just a theft, because the mosque could have been placed on any side of the residence for the treasury to be protected. Why was the chosen side the one that put the residence in the path of the congregation's ritual prayers? Addressing just this question, Jere Bacharach wonders if the intention was to enable these prayers 'to "travel" through the official residence of the Muslim ruler'.[97] For his part, Jeremy Johns argues that the same configuration at Basra was an expressive political gesture, because as the earliest report from the Islamic sources explains, '[it was] unseemly that the *imām* should have to pick his way through the congregation on his way to the *miḥrāb*'.[98] Whatever the exact motivations were for this oriented pairing, they were surely not trivial. As Wheatley himself memorably conceives of the pairing: it formed one of the 'signatures of power in the urban landscape'.[99]

Basra and the other amṣār

As just mentioned, Basra also had its mosque and gubernatorial residence configured as a paired, oriented unit, if not at the moment of its foundation, then three decades later during the governorship of Ziyād b. Abīhi (d. 53/673) from 45/665.[100] Whether the city as a whole was also oriented towards the *qibla*, as at Kufa, is not stated in the earliest sources. Only in the seventh/thirteenth century, in the history of Ibn al-Athīr (d. 630/1233), do we find it implied that it was, with both Basra and Kufa being spoken of by Ibn al-Athīr as founded in the manner that the earlier sources reserve for Kufa alone.[101]

Of the conventionally defined *amṣār*, and excluding al-Jābiya in Syria, the next major garrison town to be founded after Kufa and Basra was Fusṭāṭ in Egypt in 21/642. Wladyslaw Kubiak, the scholar most associated with the early history of this town, flatly denies, however, that planning principles were applied at its foundation, especially orthogonal ones.[102] Compounding matters, he adds that there was no gubernatorial residence, no *dār al-imāra*, until the 'Abbasid period, more than 100 years later.[103] Thus appears to grind to a halt any attempt to assert meaningfully the concept of the early Islamic city and to see in this concept a *qibla*-based organisation of space.

More recently, however, Donald Whitcomb has argued that Kubiak's excavations at Fusṭāṭ excluded a key area, the *Ahl al-Rāya* (People of the Banner), the town's central land plot, or *khiṭṭa*. Whitcomb supposes that had Kubiak excavated there, the principles of geometrically ordered town planning would have been apparent, similar to Kufa's central *khiṭṭa* discussed above.[104] He considers it likely that the core of Fusṭāṭ's central *khiṭṭa*, what he calls this and every other garrison town's 'institutional centre', was oriented towards the *qibla*, exactly like Kufa's institutional centre.[105] Additionally, he argues that the pre-existence of a Roman and Byzantine legionary fort in the southern part of the *Ahl al-Rāya* plot, Babylon, obviated at the outset the need for a purpose-built *dār al-imāra*.[106]

Whitcomb's arguments have subsequently been buttressed by the work of another archaeologist, Peter Sheehan, who argues that the orthogonally planned Babylon significantly determined the alignment and layout of Fusṭāṭ.[107] Referring to the same work and findings of Kubiak as Whitcomb, Sheehan concludes: '[T]he evidence suggests a much more formal layout of the central quarter of al-Fustat than has previously been proposed.'[108]

According to Whitcomb, 'early Islamic urban foundations were planned orthogonal structures'.[109] If the garrison town of Kufa and probably also Basra and Fusṭāṭ, and the so-called Umayyad desert palaces of 'Anjar in Lebanon and Qaṣr al-Ḥayr al-Sharqī in Syria, not to mention Mshatta and Qaṣr al-Ṭūba in Jordan, are taken as proof, then early Islamic urban foundations were additionally *oriented*, planned orthogonal structures. For all of these settlements are *qibla* aligned, either at their institutional centres or in their entirety.[110]

I leave it to others to draw the conclusions, but if early Islamic urban settlements were indeed oriented to the Ka'ba, then contrary to revisionist claims, already in the first half of the first Islamic century the cultic importance of Mecca would seem to be beyond reasonable doubt.[111] Even if this conclusion is considered too bold, the same evidence regarding the orientation of these early settlements should certainly encourage scholars of Islamic urbanism to heed Wheatley's penetrating definition of a city. '[T]he city,' he writes, 'is not merely an aggregation of population of critical size and density but also an organizing principle . . . a creator of effective space.'[112] At least for the study of early Islamic urbanism, the orientation of space is perhaps as important to consider as data concerning size, infrastructure, and so forth.

Lastly in this review of early Islamic urban settlements, another town, Ayla (present-day ʿAqaba in Jordan), founded in *c.*29/650 and counted by Whitcomb as one of the *amṣār*, is notably not *qibla* aligned.[113] However, the corners of its perimeter walls are cardinally oriented.[114] More importantly, the so-called large enclosure, which is thought to have been the town's mosque, has the same orientation as these walls.[115] Given what we have already shown regarding the other *amṣār*, that is exactly what one would have predicted, the mosque's orientation dictating the settlement's orientation. As just mentioned, however, the orientation in question does not adhere to any traditional *qibla* angle that can be derived from the town's geographical location.[116]

Later Islamic urban foundations

In the literature on Islamic architecture and urbanism, it is common to find only sporadic mention of site orientation, and often none at all.[117] As has been noted by others, a case in point is Creswell's monumental survey of Egyptian architecture.[118] A comprehensive survey of the orientation of urban settlements for the period 132–905/750–1500 is therefore out of the question. Instead, one must make do with informed speculation regarding Baghdad, occasional observations, and two titles that explicitly pursue the theme by way of *in situ* measurements.

The Round City of Baghdad was quite likely *qibla* oriented. Founded in 145/762 by the ʿAbbasid caliph al-Manṣūr (r. 136–58/754–75), it became known as *al-Zawrāʾ*, the Askew, most probably because of the caliph's imposition of a *qibla* orientation upon what the formerly Sasanian inhabitants of the region expected to be a cardinally bisected circle.[119] Robert Hillenbrand speaks evocatively of this probable orientation:

> The available data do not permit any further refinement of this line of argument, but its implications are nonetheless striking. They suggest that the entire city – and perhaps, by extension, the whole world of which it was the centre and the image – was in fact orientated to Mecca. Thus [Baghdad's] entire political ideology should be seen *sub specie aeternitatis*. It is in this light, too, that the name of the city assumes its full significance; for Baghdad means 'god-given' in Persian, while its other name, Madinat al-Salam, or 'City of Peace', has been interpreted as a deliberate echo of a term used in the Qurʾan (Sura VI, 127) to refer to Paradise.[120]

With reference to Hillenbrand's final sentence, it is appropriate to note that another early medieval palatine city with a plausible claim to be paradisiacal in the Qurʾanic manner is definitely not *qibla* oriented. The city in question is Madīnat al-Zahrāʾ, founded outside Cordoba in 327/939, or shortly thereafter.[121]

Moving now to occasional observations in scholarship on site orientation, two come from the Islamic archaeologist Alastair Northedge. In the first he says that the late-second/eighth-century ʿAbbasid foundation al-Rāfiqa, Syria, has 'lines of streets parallel to the *qibla* wall of the mosque', and that 'the *qibla* wall of the mosque and the south wall of the city are aligned'.[122] Al-Rāfiqa would thus seem to have continued the early Islamic city foundation principles discussed above. This interpretation is buttressed by another Islamic archaeologist, Michael Meinecke, who notes in an article unusually focused on orientation that the road network at the core (*Kernbereich*) of this ʿAbbasid city was *qibla* oriented.[123]

Northedge's second observation concerns the vast, mid-third/ninth-century ʿAbbasid palace-cum-garrison foundation, al-Iṣṭablāt, 13km south of Samarra. It is, says Northedge, 'roughly' oriented towards the *qibla*.[124] Essentially a city within a city, al-Iṣṭablāt thus also seems to have continued the earlier foundation principles. Interestingly, a number of ʿAbbasid palaces at al-Rāfiqa were also *qibla* oriented.[125]

A third observation comes from David King. Concerning medieval Cairo, specifically the Fatimid urban settlement al-Qāhira, he writes: 'When in the tenth century the Fatimids built the new city of al-Qāhira alongside the pharaonic Red Sea Canal, it turned out that the canal was exactly perpendicular to the *qibla*.'[126] King does not assert that the choice of site was made because of the canal's direction at this point of its course, saying only that the canal's direction was 'fortuitous'. However, it could be said that he implies as much when he adds that, as a result of this choice of site, 'the largely orthogonal street plan of Fatimid Cairo was aligned [to] the *qibla*.'[127]

Lastly, a fourth observation, also from King, states that the medieval cities of Taza in Morocco and Khiva in Uzbekistan are both *qibla* oriented. Unfortunately, no evidence is adduced to support this statement.[128] It is likely, however, that the reference to Taza is based upon the data marshalled by the geographer Michael Bonine in his *in situ* measurements of the *qibla* orientations of medieval cities of Morocco.[129] In the publication presenting this scientific data, as well as in a later publication presenting the *in situ* measurements for Tunisian cities, Bonine shows that a number of cities in these two countries are *qibla* oriented. 'Similar to the *qibla*'s influence in Moroccan cities,' he writes in the second publication, 'the sacred direction to Mecca appears to be significant for the orientation of many of the traditional Tunisian cities.'[130] In both publications, however, Bonine adds the caveat that other factors, including especially the prevailing slope conditions in Morocco and the pre-existence of a Roman centuriation system in Tunisia, might have been the real reason behind the orientation of the cities, such that their *qibla* alignments were only a fortuitous bonus.[131] Unsurprisingly, perhaps, King is of the opinion that deliberate choice, not serendipity, was at play in these alignments.[132] The following conclusion by Bonine regarding the Moroccan cities would seem to substantiate his opinion:

> [T]he number of instances in which the *qibla* directions of major buildings, principal streets, and the axis of the city and the main slope orientation are aligned leads to the conclusion that the site of a building or a city was selected because it had a slope which was in the correct direction, that is, a slope that corresponded to the *qibla*.[133]

Nevertheless, until further research is undertaken, Bonine's more cautious attitude, as evidenced by his aforementioned caveat, remains sensible to heed.[134]

Bonine's caution might, however, be considered as excessive when his data, all of which concerns the medieval and pre-modern periods, is placed within the context of the data for the early Islamic city. In that context, the medieval and pre-modern data seems less open to the charge of happenstance and serendipity. Rather, on the basis of the admittedly limited information we have for the *amṣār*, one might have expected these later cities also to be *qibla* oriented, at least in part. The part in question is the area corresponding to the political and institutional heart of the *amṣār*, the central *khiṭṭa*. In other words, one might have expected a *qibla* orientation to have been a desideratum for at least this part of a medieval city's foundation, even if it was also not always a practical, attainable one.

In the foundation narrative of Fez, Morocco, as recorded some 600 years later in the earliest extant history dedicated to the city, it is possible to see this desideratum being either enacted and attained or retroactively superimposed, written into the facts. (The latter interpretation seems more likely, given the challenging topography and varying slope conditions of the site, as also noted by Bonine.[135]) The narrative identifies Idrīs b. Idrīs (r. 187–213/803–28) as the founder of Fez. It alleges that Idrīs first asked for God's benedictions on the incipient city, and then proceeded to erect the city's first structure, the perimeter walls, beginning 'from the *qibla* side' (*min jihat al-qibla*), where he also then built the city's first gate, *Bāb al-Qibla*, Qibla Gate.[136]

Whether superimposed onto an otherwise purportedly accurate history or not, these actions by Idrīs suggest the existence of a desire to orient urban settlements to the *qibla*.[137] Bonine's raw data substantiates this suggestion for Tunisia, if not for Morocco.[138] Of the seven cities he surveyed in Tunisia, where there is a detectable *qibla* orientation to a settlement's principal axis, by happenstance or otherwise, it is commonly most apparent in relation to that settlement's earliest core.[139] Kairouan is, however, a notable exception to this possible pattern, most especially because it was a new foundation. The exception of Sousse is scarcely less notable.[140]

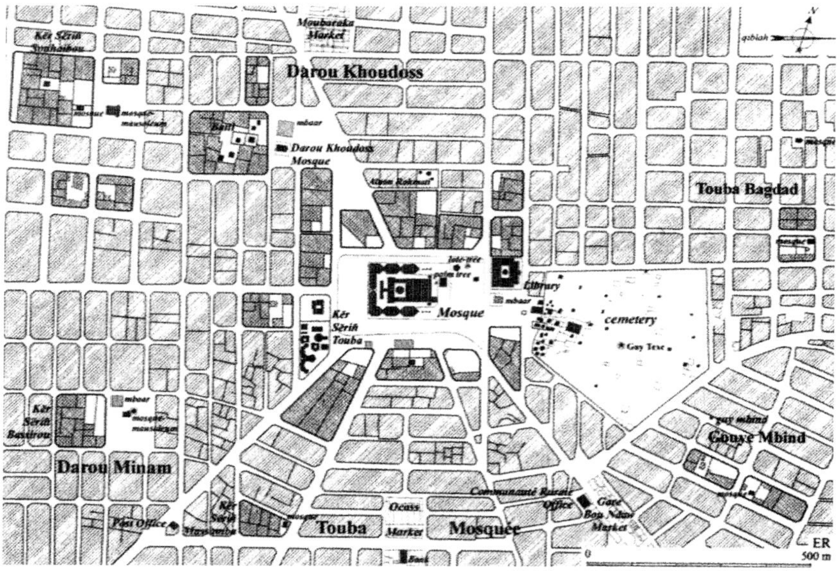

Figure 1.3 *Touba, Senegal: map of the central wards. (Source: Ross 2006, p. 80. Courtesy: University of Rochester Press.)*

Against these two Tunisian exceptions, modern-day Touba in Senegal might be adduced in support of the atavistic desire for a *qibla* orientation; for as the map of its central, earliest wards shows, it is oriented to the Ka'ba (Figure 1.3).[141] Although Touba falls outside the timespan of the present review, having been founded in the late thirteenth/nineteenth century, it may represent the continuation of a foundation practice, the archaeological traces of which have over time been transformed beyond recognition by land movement and the deformations caused by repeated rebuilding. Interpretations more positive than that must evade us for now.

Conclusion

In this chapter we have first investigated the history and meaning of the Islamic *qibla*, and second reviewed the extent to which Islamic urban settlements have been oriented to the *qibla*. Concerning the investigation, we saw how after the second/eighth century, if not much earlier, there was little or no reason to suppose that the Islamic *qibla* meant anything other than the direction of the Ka'ba. This was an important finding for a chapter premised on the judgement that one of the principal works of the Ka'ba was its role as the *qibla*. In the investigation, too, we saw how rulers could be compared to the *qibla* and thus benefit from, or perhaps vie with, its symbolic register.

Concerning the review, its focus was not on the elements that extensively comprise a settlement, the buildings, many of which we already knew had a *qibla* orientation. The focus, rather, was on the urban site as a whole and the extent to which one could talk of a practice, a tradition, of orienting it to the *qibla*. Although the evidence for the very earliest period was necessarily limited and often textual, sufficient data existed to argue for a tradition of orienting at least the central core of urban settlements. For the later periods, although the evidence was again limited, this time because of the paucity of *in situ* measurements, the possibility of this early orientation tradition having continued into the medieval centuries was apparent from some, but not all of the data. The *qibla* orientation of modern-day Touba could thus plausibly be interpreted as a very late survival of this tradition. Such a tradition would not be unprecedented, because orienting cities in auspicious, symbolic and/or sacred directions is well attested for other cultures.[142] That there was an equivalent tradition of orienting Islamic cities, too, albeit one observed as much in principle as in practice, would therefore be unsurprising.

Even if one dismisses these partly conjectural conclusions concerning the *qibla* orientation of Islamic urban settlements, as also referenced in the course of the chapter definitive evidence exists in plenty regarding the *qibla* orientation of Islamic architecture other than religious architecture; domestic housing, for example. This evidence alone prompts one to ask: (1) why the effort to orient architecture was made, and (2) if only politics explains why the conquering leader of the Almohad dynasty (524–668/1130–1269) allegedly refused to enter Marrakesh because of what he deemed to be an incorrect *qibla* angle used in that city by its founders, the vanquished Almoravids (454–541/1062–1147).[143] When this evidence is combined with the conjectural tradition of settlement orientation, the requirement for answers becomes insistent. Because the next chapter investigates the issue of orientation as a whole, not just site orientation, the matter is better left until then. For now, though, with reference to site orientation only, two related answers suggest themselves. First, if as discussed in part one, Neuwirth is correct and the Prophet's initial adoption of a *qibla* created for the Believers a share in biblical salvation history, then imposing a *qibla* orientation on later settlements was a way for the Believers to remain participants in that history, though in its superseding, Qur'anic version. Second, echoing the thought of Akel Kahera, I would argue that Islamic settlement orientation was very plausibly about the establishment of a 'transcendent and eschatological vision'.[144] This vision, I would add, comprised two vectors: a horizontal vector towards the Ka'ba, facilitated by the *qibla*, and a vertical vector towards God, facilitated by the Ka'ba.

CHAPTER TWO

The Kaʿba as Navel

This chapter concerns the work of the Kaʿba as the Islamic world's navel: its axis and generative matrix. The aim is not to rehearse Mircea Eliade's ideas of the sacred centre as they apply and can be applied to Mecca. Those ideas have been covered by others.[1] Rather, the aim is to understand how the Kaʿba is said to orient the world, and then to explain what it is about the Kaʿba that makes this orientation conceivable. To achieve these aims, the chapter is in two parts.

Part one discusses the Kaʿba's orientation of the world, as represented in the early Islamic sources. This part would seem to be an extension of the previous chapter's discussion of the Kaʿba's orientation of urban space; and indeed it is, except that in discussing world orientation we shall simultaneously see what it is about the navel of Mecca that distinguishes it from other alleged omphaloi in the Islamic oikumene. On the basis of the early Islamic sources, we shall see that the world is said to be oriented to the Kaʿba because it is generated from the Kaʿba.

Part two argues that the Kaʿba has a world-orienting capacity because, as evidenced in the early Islamic sources, the Kaʿba is construed as having the attributes of a bifurcated, bilateral body – a human body. As I shall show, only this type of body can orient space. The crux of the matter of orientation per se will be addressed at this point, namely, why a human being is fundamentally an orienting being.

Part One: The Orientation of the Kaʿba

David King is widely regarded as the academic who brought to scholarly light what had been unknown, ignored or forgotten regarding the Kaʿba's astronomical function and its celestial-cum-meteorological orientation.[2] In his account of those findings in the *The Encyclopaedia of Islam*, he succinctly – perhaps, too succinctly – explains the complexities of this celestially motivated function and orientation, whilst simultaneously correcting the widespread view that the Kaʿba is cardinally oriented. He writes:

> [It is] asserted that the corners of the Kaʿba face the cardinal directions. In fact, the Kaʿba has a rectangular base with sides in the ratio *c*.8:7 with its main axis at about 30° counter-clockwise from the meridian. When one is standing in front of any of the four walls of the Kaʿba, one is facing a significant astronomical direction; this fact was known to the first generations who had lived in or visited Mecca.[3]

In an earlier, less compressed account, King explains his findings less technically, judiciously referring to a simple diagram that is reproduced below (Figure 2.1). He writes:

> The earliest recorded statements about the astronomical alignment of the Kaaba date from the 7th century, being attributed to Companions of the Prophet. From these it is clear that the first generations of Muslims knew that the Kaaba was astronomically aligned, and this was why they used astronomical alignments in order to face the Kaaba when they were far away from it. In fact, they often used the same astronomical alignments to face the appropriate section of the Kaaba they would have faced had they been standing directly in front of that particular section of the edifice. Furthermore, the same texts provide a clue to why the Kaaba is astronomically aligned: in the most popular of the pre-Islamic wind schemes, the four winds are considered to blow in such a way that they strike the four sides of the Kaaba head-on (see [Figure 2.1]). Modern plans of the Kaaba and the surrounding mountains based on aerial photography essentially confirm the information provided by the medieval texts, but reveal yet more. The alignment to Canopus is close, but the alignment to midsummer sunrise is off by several degrees. On the other hand, the minor axis is in fact accurately aligned to the southernmost limit of the setting Moon at midwinter. Roughly every 19 years, the Moon would be seen along the northwest or southeast walls of the Kaaba setting over the local horizon. This fact raises interesting questions about the regulation of the calendar in pre-Islamic times, not least because the intercalators used to make their pronouncements in front of the Kaaba.[4]

On the basis of these and other findings, King interprets the pre-Islamic orientation of the Kaʿba to mean that the building was 'laid out as an architectural representation of a microcosm of the pre-Islamic Arab universe'.[5] For the reasons stated in the Introduction concerning the absence of historically verifiable sources for this period, there is no means of confirming King's argument. It certainly seems plausible, and if correct it would contradict the academic commonplace that the concept of a celestial protype for the Kaʿba, the Frequented House (*al-Bayt al-Maʿmūr*), is a borrowing of Jewish Temple lore.[6] For if King is correct in interpreting the Kaʿba as a pre-Islamic microcosm, then we have, as he says, an indigenous explanation for the concept.[7]

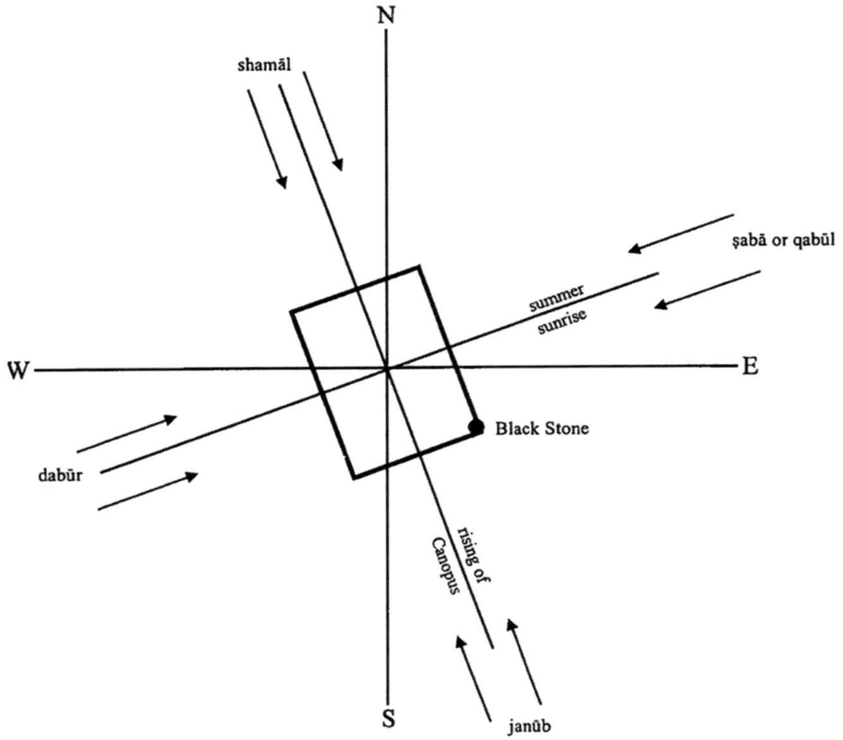

Figure 2.1 The alignments of the axes of the Kaʿba and the directions of the four cardinal winds as described in medieval Arabic sources. (After King 1985, p. 327.)

Folk astronomy

Indisputable in King's findings is the fact that the Kaʿba's astronomically motivated orientation allowed for the development of what he calls the folk astronomical tradition of Islamic geography for determining the *qibla* direction. This tradition was discussed in Chapter One. As he notes in both of his statements quoted above, there is evidence that the Kaʿba's astronomical-cum-meteorological orientation was known to the Believers and earliest Muslims. For example, a tradition reports al-Ḥasan al-Baṣrī (d. 110/728) allegedly saying:

> The winds are determined in relation to the Kaʿba. So when you want to ascertain this, lean your back against the door of the Kaʿba, then [the North wind] *al-Shamāl* will blow from your left side, namely, the side on which the *Ḥijr* is. [The South wind] *al-Janūb* will blow from your right side, where the Black Stone is. [The East wind] *al-Ṣabā* will be opposite you, in front of the door of the Kaʿba. And [the West wind] *al-Dabūr* will blow from behind the Kaʿba.[8]

In another purportedly early tradition, this time attributed to the Prophet's cousin and son-in-law ʿAlī (d. 40/661), the four-wind compass-rose schema referenced by al-Ḥasan al-Baṣrī recurs.[9] Although other wind schemas existed in the Islamic world, this particular Arabian schema was a prevalent, popular one, presumably in part because it enabled one to determine the *qibla* direction so simply.[10]

Determining the *qibla* direction this way was not the only method in the folk astronomical arsenal. This was fortunate, as the method was considered most unreliable (*aḍʿaf*) by some practitioners of the folk tradition.[11] More reliable methods of determining the *qibla* direction included mentally partitioning the Kaʿba's exterior and then associating the different sectors with particular astronomical horizon phenomena and/or regions of the Islamic world.[12] In the first of the two diagrams reproduced below, the Kaʿba has been divided this way into eight sectors and associated with eight regions of the Islamic world (Figure 2.2). In the second diagram, the Kaʿba

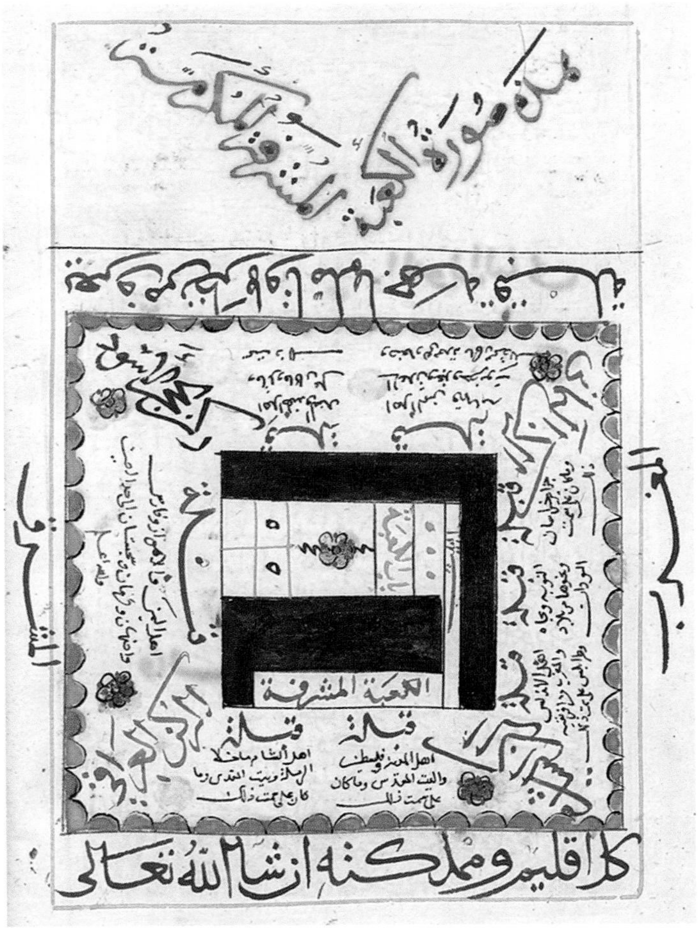

Figure 2.2 *Eight-sector division of the Kaʿba for determining the* qibla *direction. From a copy of* Kharīdat al-ʿajāʾib wa farīdat al-gharāʾib *('The pearl of wonders and the uniqueness of strange things') by the Arab cosmographer Sirāj al-Dīn b. al-Wardī (d. after 822/1419), dated 908/1503. The captions in the diagram's upper two and lowest margins read: 'This is an image of the noble, venerable Kaʿba. He who views and studies it knows the* qibla *direction of every region plus its realm, God willing.' Gouache, gold and ink on paper. Courtesy: Topkapı Palace Library. TSMK A.3025, fol. 30b.*

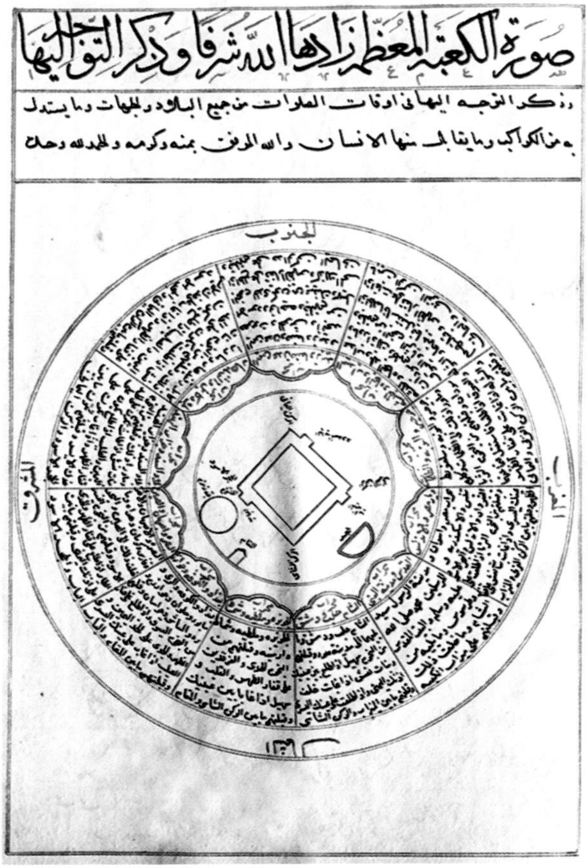

Figure 2.3 *Eleven-sector division of the Kaʿba for determining the* qibla *direction. From an unattributed manuscript dated* 960/1553. *The three-line caption at the top of the diagram reads: 'Image of the exalted Kaʿba, may God increase its honour, and aide-memoire [for] facing it. An aide-memoire [for] facing it at ritual-prayer times from all cities and districts, and what is to be gleaned from the stars [for achieving this] and which of them a person [should] turn towards.' Ink on paper. Courtesy: Leiden University Library. MS Leiden, Or. 5, fol. 37a. Photo by J. J. Witkam.*

has been divided into eleven sectors and associated with eleven regions of the Islamic world and eleven celestial phenomena (Figure 2.3).

With specific regard to Figure 2.3, although an eleven-sector division was proposed by the Yemeni jurist Muḥammad b. Surāqa al-ʿĀmirī (d. 410/1019), it is likely that the division in the diagram is erroneous and should instead comprise twelve sectors. As King notes with reference to an almost identical diagram, such copyists' errors are not uncommon in *qibla* diagrams.[13] Equally common in diagrams and descriptions of the Kaʿba is a discrepancy regarding the names of the two northern corners, the north-eastern *ʿIrāqī* corner and the north-western *Shāmī* corner. Sometimes the two names are switched, as in Figure 2.3, which reverses the order of Figure 2.2.[14]

Orienting the world

Reproduced below is a third diagram of a multi-sector division of the Kaʿba for determining the *qibla* direction (Figure 2.4). It comprises a

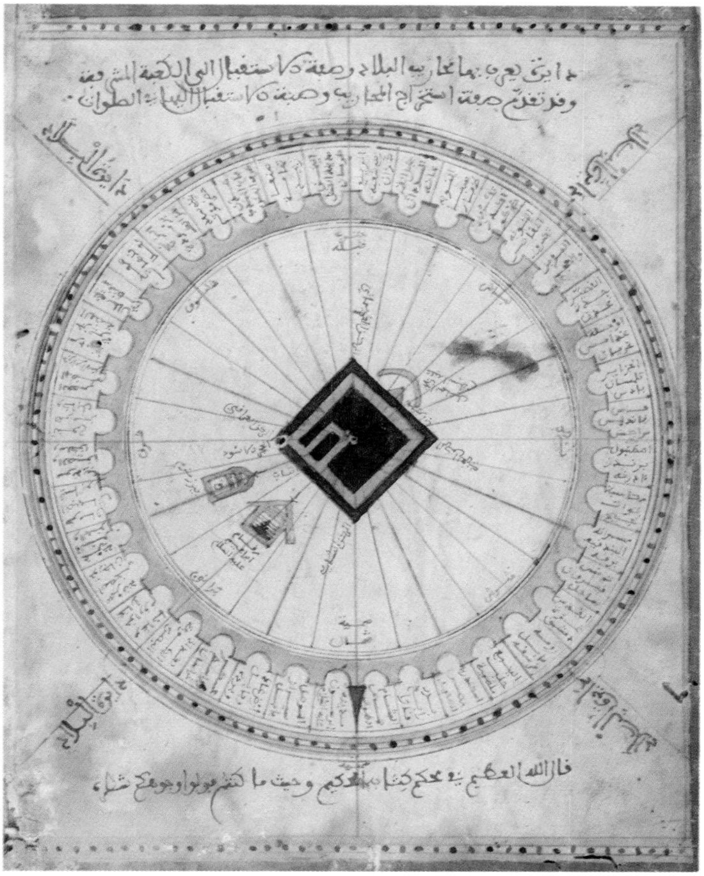

Figure 2.4 *Forty-sector division of the Kaʿba for determining the* qibla *direction, superimposed upon a thirty-two-division wind rose. From a nautical atlas by the chart maker ʿAlī al-Sharfī of Sfax (*fl. *mid-to-late tenth/sixteenth century), dated* 979/1571. *The caption at the top of the image reads: 'A compass by which is known the* mihrab *[angle] for each country, and a depiction for facing the noble Kaʿba.' The caption at the bottom reads: 'God the exalted says in His perfectly planned Book, "Wherever you are, turn your faces towards [the Sacred Mosque]" [Q 2:144].' Gouache and ink on paper;* 20.7 × 26.8*cm. Courtesy: The Bodleian Libraries, University of Oxford. MS. Marsh* 294, *fol.* 4*v.*

forty-sector division superimposed upon a thirty-two-division wind rose. It was made in 979/1571 by the chart maker ʿAlī al-Sharfī of Sfax, Tunisia (*fl.* mid-to-late tenth/sixteenth century).[15]

At first glance, the diagram looks like a more elaborate version of the two preceding diagrams, because it has more detailed partitioning. There are, however, two important differences. First, this diagram has no practical utility. As King cautions: '[W]oe betide anyone who would *measure* the *qibla* of any specific locality from [it]!'[16] Second, in the event of King's warning going unheeded, the *qibla* directions that would then be measured would in fact be the counter-*qibla* directions. That is to say, the *qibla* directions of the cities and localities listed on the chart do not show the angles from the perspective of the people living in these locations. Rather, the chart shows the diametrically opposite angles: the angles from the perspective of the Kaʿba, as if the Kaʿba were 'looking' towards the people. For someone to use them, they must first be converted to the *qibla* angle.[17]

In this diagram, the cities and localities are not merely tied to the Kaʿba, similar to the two other diagrams; they appear to have been set there by the Kaʿba. That is to say, the Kaʿba of this diagram is not just organising these cities and localities, in the sense that by facing the Kaʿba and being tethered to it, they seem to rotate around the Kaʿba. This sense I shall refer to as sense 1. Rather, the Kaʿba seems to be assigning their locations, too, in the sense that the Kaʿba seems to be placing them, as if its outlook were organisational of the world. This sense I shall refer to as sense 2.

In sense 1, as exemplified by Figures 2.2 and 2.3, the vector of the diagrams is centripetal: *from* the locations *to* the Kaʿba. The diagrams, in other words, portray a world turned towards the Kaʿba and then fastened to it. In sense 2, as exemplified by Figure 2.4, the diagram's vector is centrifugal: a world ordered from the Kaʿba and umbilically tied to it. Visually speaking, the outcome in both cases is identical: a Kaʿba-centred world in which the Kaʿba occupies the centre and the cities and localities occupy everywhere else. The centrifugal representation of this world, however, belongs to a geographic practice that is centuries older.[18]

In their discussion of the use of the counter-*qibla* in Islamic geography, Petra Schmidl and Mónica Herrera Casais note that its first extant deployment is the division of the Islamic oikumene in the third/ninth-century *Kitāb al-Masālik wa al-mamālik* ('Book of routes and realms') by Ibn Khurradādhbih (d. *c.*299/912). They suggest that its usage possibly preceded this text. They write:

> The scheme of Ibn Khurradādhbih is based on counter-*qibla* directions from the perspective of the Kaʿba looking out to other regions. The concept surely derives from the earliest geographical divisions of the world around the Kaʿba that were implied in the naming of the corners of the building . . . Similar schemes constructed with counter-*qibla*s might have been in circulation even before Ibn Khurradādhbih's time, but none of them have apparently survived.[19]

They add that ʿAlī al-Sharfī's use of the counter-*qibla* directions in the tenth/sixteenth century is an unexpected anachronism, because by the end of the fourth/tenth century those directions no longer seem to be used. They explain that this was 'most probably for practical reasons, to avoid the conversion of counter-*qibla* into *qibla* directions'.[20]

In the context of the present chapter, the existence of an early geographic practice, short-lived or otherwise, of mapping the inhabited Islamic world from the perspective of the Kaʿba is significant for two reasons. First, the practice echoes equally early Islamic traditions that represent the Kaʿba as the site of the world's generation. Second, the practice additionally echoes other related early traditions alleging that the corners of the Kaʿba gave their names to regions of the world and that the Kaʿba's sides named the four winds. To these Creation and naming traditions the chapter now turns.

The origin of the world

In the early Islamic sources, a number of traditions are recorded concerning God's creation of the world. In them, the Kaʿba is portrayed as the Creation's hub. Examples include: 'He created the House two thousand years before the earth (*al-arḍ*), and from it the earth was spread out (*duḥiyat minhu*)';[21] 'Two thousand years before He created the world (*al-dunyā*), the House was placed upon the water on four pillars. The earth was then spread out from under it (*min taḥtihi*)';[22] and 'Forty years before God created the heavens and the earth, the Kaʿba was spume (*ghuthāʾ*) upon the water. From it, the earth was spread out.'[23] A longer example reads as follows:

> Before the creation of the heavens and the earth, when the Throne (*al-ʿArsh*) was on the water, God sent a beating wind which drove the water back and exposed on the [future] site of the House a stony mound in the form of a dome (*qubba*). From under it, God spread out the lands (*al-araḍīn*). They stretched and they strained, so God staked them with mountains.[24] . . . The first mountain He placed on them was Abū Qubays [that overlooks the Sacred Mosque]. For that reason Mecca is called Metropolis (*Umm al-qurā*).[25]

With reference to the 'stony mound' mentioned in this last example – the domical outcrop whence the earth allegedly spread and where the Kaʿba would eventually stand – an undated and unsourced late medieval or pre-modern Persianate *mappa mundi* is reproduced below (Figure 2.5).[26] Represented at its epicentre is this outcrop, labelled 'Dome of the earth' (*qubbat al-arḍ*): the zero degree of longitude and latitude. The Kaʿba is shown next to it.[27]

As regards the Qurʾanic epithet for Mecca, *Umm al-qurā*, that is also referenced in the last tradition (where I translated it as 'Metropolis', but whose literal translation is 'Mother of the towns'), it makes sense to consider the Creation this and the other traditions narrate as unfolding less from the Kaʿba qua the Creation's hub and more from the Kaʿba qua the Creation's matrix.[28] That is because a hub denotes an impersonal object, whereas a matrix denotes a living organ, a womb. As the exegete Muqātil b. Sulaymān (d. 150/767) explains the Qurʾanic epithet: 'Mecca is called *Umm al-qurā* because from under the Kaʿba the entire earth was spread out.'[29] On this view, the world was born of the Kaʿba: a vertical – traditional – accouchement.[30]

Navel gazing

At this juncture of the discussion of the Kaʿba as the world's navel, the objection will likely be made that because the early Islamic sources mention a number of sites claiming this status, one cannot restrict it to the Kaʿba.[31] In response to this potential objection, although it is true that (1) other *umm al-qurā*s and navels (sing. *surra*) are presented in the sources, for example, Merv and Jerusalem,[32] and (2) Mecca seems not to be referred

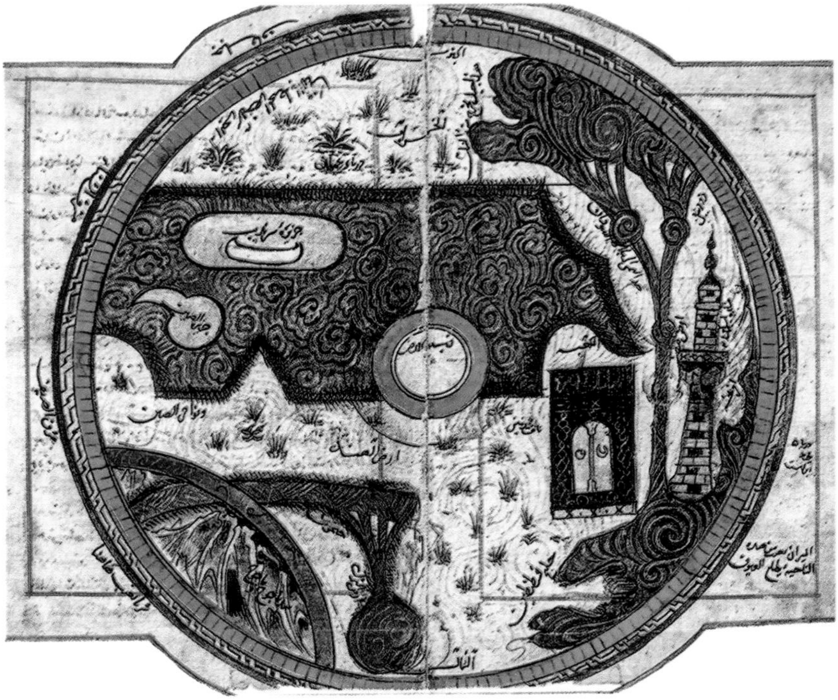

Figure 2.5 Mappa mundi *with the 'Dome of the earth' (*qubbat al-arḍ*) at the centre, the Ka*ʿ*ba next to it, and the Lighthouse of Alexandria at the perimeter. From an unidentified late medieval or pre-modern Persianate manuscript. Gouache and ink on paper. (Source: al-Mūjān* 2010, *p.* 31.*)*

to as a navel at all in these sources,[33] what distinguishes the Kaʿba from these other sites is the fact that the world is imagined as actually coming out from under it, generated from it.

The one exception to this distinction is Jerusalem, specifically the Rock of the Temple Mount (*al-Ṣakhra*).[34] Here one does find the graphic birthing image, with God saying to the Rock: 'From under you I spread the earth.'[35] However, not only do the traditions that represent Jerusalem this way appear to be considerably fewer than those for the Kaʿba,[36] more importantly, precarious though it is to argue *ex silentio*, to the best of my knowledge none is found in the early sources.[37] Rather, the two earliest recorded instances both date from the fourth/tenth century.[38] The first comes from *Mukhtaṣar Kitāb al-Buldān* ('The abridged book of countries') by Ibn al-Faqīh Hamadhānī (d. after 290/903).[39] The second comes from *Faḍāʾil al-Bayt al-Muqaddas* ('The merits of Jerusalem'), a work written in 410/1020 by the preacher of the Temple Mount's al-Aqsa Mosque, Abū Bakr al-Wāṣiṭī (*fl.* 410/1020), but which is largely based on a lost work by al-Walīd b. Ḥammād al-Ramlī al-Zayyāt (d. 299/912).[40] The dates of these two recorded instances mean that the Rock's graphic representation as *matrix mundi* comes approximately 150 years after the Kaʿba was represented thus by the aforementioned Muqātil b. Sulaymān and effectively represented thus (missing is the preposition 'under') by Ibn Isḥāq (d. *c.*150/767) and allegedly Abū Ḥanīfa (d. 150/767).[41]

In view of this *ex silentio* argument, it is germane to note Ofer Livne-Kafri's observation that the epithet *Umm al-qurā*, Metropolis, is attributed to Jerusalem only rarely in the Arabic sources. 'It seems,' he writes, 'to be connected to the Qurʾānic expression related to Mecca.'[42]

Naming the world

In the earlier cited quote from Schmidl and Herrera Casais regarding the wind scheme used by Ibn Khurradādhbih, the authors make reference to the view, advanced by David King, that the Kaʿba's corners took their names from the divisions of the world. On this plausible but historically undocumented view, the south-western, or *Yamānī* corner is called thus because it abuts Yemen; the north-western, or *Shāmī* corner is called thus because it abuts Syria (al-Shām); and the north-eastern, or *ʿIrāqī* corner is called thus because it abuts Iraq.[43] The south-eastern corner, in which is set the Black Stone, is the exception to this view, because as noted in the Introduction this corner seems to have no geographically derived nomenclature and is instead commonly called just *al-Rukn*, the Corner.[44]

Undermining this view is a tradition that dates to at least the time of the renowned hadith collector al-Bukhārī (d. 256/870). In it, two regions of the world are said to take their names from the Kaʿba. 'Yemen,' al-Bukhārī reports, 'was called so because it is situated at the right hand (*yamīn*) of the Kaʿba, and Syria was called so because it is situated at the left hand (*yasār*) of the Kaʿba.'[45] In this tradition, the outlook from the Kaʿba is once again generative: once again organisational of the world.

The Kaʿba's naming capacity is also alleged to be behind the earlier cited wind schema referenced in the tradition attributed to al-Ḥasan al-Baṣrī: the four-wind compass-rose schema with the Kaʿba at the centre, which King considers to be the most popular of the early Islamic wind schemas.[46] In the seventh/thirteenth century, the jurist and philologist Abū Isḥāq al-Aṣbaḥī (d. *c.*660/1262) explained the nomenclature of this schema, commencing his explanation with this pivotal sentence: 'The *ulema* say the winds are named thus on account of God's Sacred House (*sumiyat al-riyāḥ bi-hādhihi al-asmāʾ bi-Bayt Allāh al-ḥarām*), because it is the *qibla* of the world.'[47] He continues as follows:

> When the Arabs observed the wind that came and struck the wall of the Kaʿba's left hand (*shimāl*), they named it *Shamāl* (the North wind). When they observed the wind that came from the other side (*al-jānib*), they named it *Janūb* (the South wind). When they observed the [East] wind that struck

> the Kaʿba's face (*wajh*), they named it either *Ṣabā*, because it struck (*aṣābat*) the Kaʿba's face or *Qabūl*, because it came from in front of (*min qubuli*) the Kaʿba. When they observed the [West] wind that came from the Kaʿba's back (*ẓahr*), they called it *Dabūr* (literally, the rear-comer).[48]

Al-Aṣbaḥī's explanation will be referenced again in part two below. Here all I note is that in his mystical cosmology, Ibn ʿArabī (d. 638/1240) says something similar about the naming capacity of the House when he talks of the cardinal directions being 'apportioned from' (*taqsīm min*) the Kaʿba.[49] Preserving these directions, he continues, are the four divinely appointed saints (*awliyāʾ*) known as the Pillars, or *Awtād*.[50] These cosmic figures commonly comprise the second highest degree in the Sufi hierarchy of saints, just below the Pole, or *Quṭb*.[51] No matter who or where they are in the cosmos at any one time, the Pillars carry out their universe-preserving duties at the centre of the world, Mecca.[52] There, says Ibn ʿArabī, each Pillar corresponds to one of the four corners of the Kaʿba.[53] By extension, therefore, each also corresponds to one of the four corners of the celestial Kaʿba, the Frequented House.[54] If not umbilically tied to the Kaʿba, in this cosmology the entire universe is at least anchored to it.

Although it is beyond the scope of the present book to discuss the overlap of Ibn ʿArabī's Kaʿba-centric cosmology with mystical currents in Shiʿism or to chart its continuity in Sufism and Islamic culture more broadly, such overlaps and continuities exist.[55] In Shiʿism, it is also worth noting, mystical cosmological conceptions of the Kaʿba long pre-date Ibn ʿArabī.[56]

'Very like a whale'

The foregoing discussion of the origin and naming of the world shows that the Kaʿba is distinguished in the early Islamic sources as being not only the world's navel and axis, but also its matrix and partial nomenclator. To assert this distinction is not to take anything away from the importance of the other alleged navels, most notably Jerusalem; nor is it to refute the widely held academic view that Jewish Temple lore was translated into Islamic Kaʿba lore at an early period of Islamic history.[57] Rather, to assert that the Kaʿba is the world's matrix is to distinguish the Kaʿba from the other navels mentioned in the Islamic sources.

In some late medieval and pre-modern Islamic *mappae mundi*, often of the form associated with the cosmographer Sirāj al-Dīn b. al-Wardī (d. after 822/1419), this distinction can almost be said to be visible, with the world represented as if uncoiling from the Kaʿba.[58] The circa eleventh/seventeenth-century *mappa mundi* reproduced below (Figure 2.6) is perhaps the clearest expression of this reading.[59]

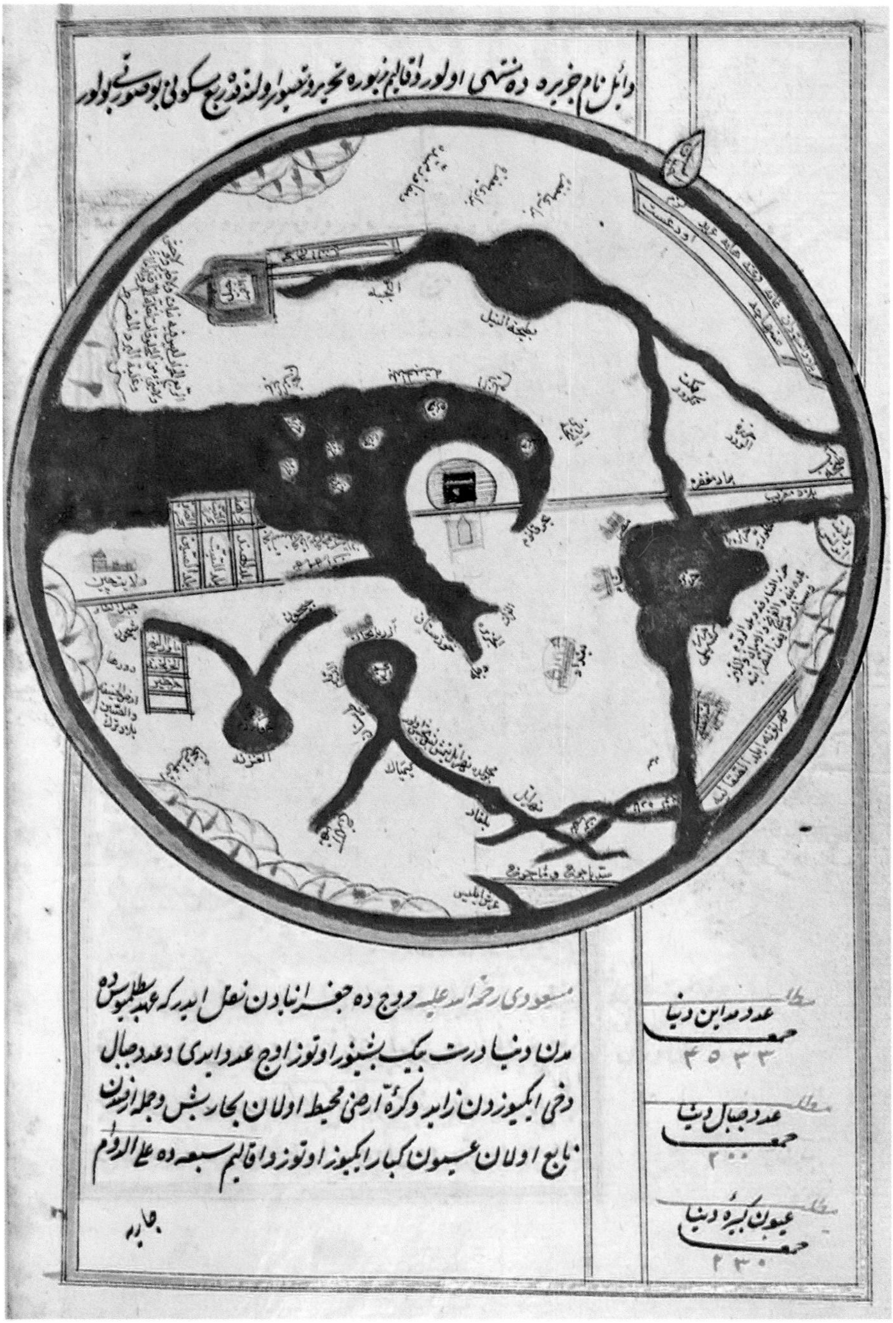

Figure 2.6 Mappa mundi *with the Kaʿba at the centre, dated* 1060/1650 *and pasted into a copy of an anonymous tenth/sixteenth-century Ottoman work,* Tarih-i Hind-i garbi *('History of the West Indies'). Gouache, gold and ink on paper;* 13.6 × 23.2*cm. Courtesy: Leiden University Library. MS Leiden, Or.* 12.365, *fol.* 90*b.*

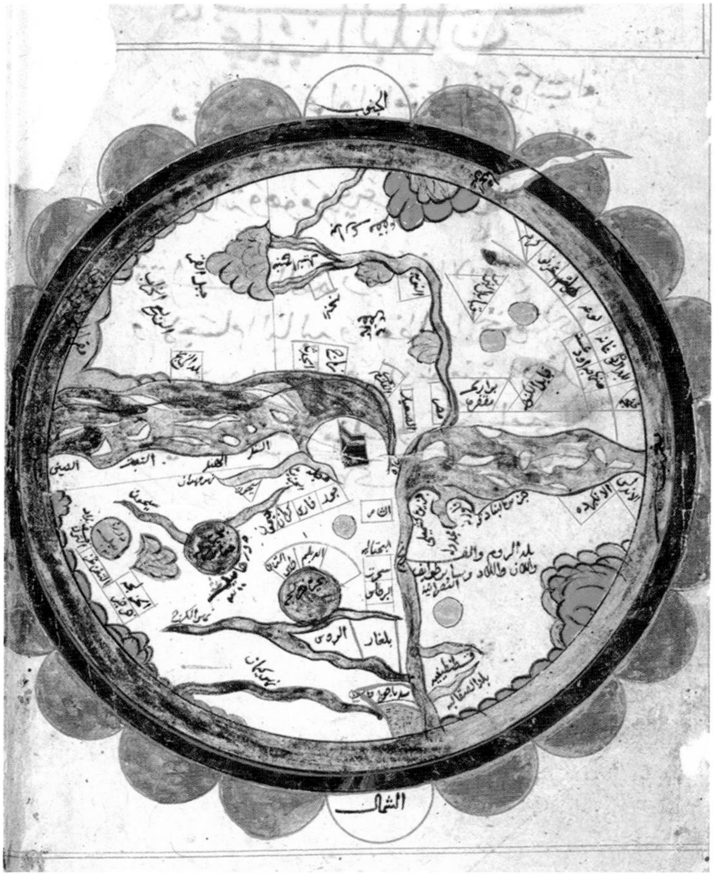

Figure 2.7 Mappa mundi *with the Kaʿba at the centre. From a copy of* ʿAjāʾib al-makhlūqāt *('The wonders of creation') by the Arab cosmographer and geographer Zakarriyāʾ al-Qazwīnī (d. 682/1283), dated* 990/1582. *Gouache, gold and ink on paper. Courtesy: The University of Manchester Library. Arabic MS* 313 *[668].*

In another *mappa mundi* of the same period, the sea encircling the Kaʿba has a zoomorphic quality to it, as if it were swallowing the Kaʿba (Figure 2.7). This reading, though, is unquestionably fanciful. With regard to another map from the same century, however, it is less fanciful to side with its publishers when they say it shows the Kaʿba being swallowed, this time by a whale (Figures 2.8 and 2.9).[60]

Pace the authors of this interpretation, the map in question is not strictly speaking a *mappa mundi*, but a map of the Arabian Peninsula (*diyār al-ʿarab*) according to the so-called Balkhī tradition of cartography.[61] Its scalloped outer frame is, however, reminiscent of many *mappae mundi*, where it commonly signifies Mount Qāf, the cosmological mountain range that is said to surround the terrestrial world.[62] Figure 2.7, for example, represents Mount Qāf in just that way. As such, the map does seem to share in the cosmographic, non-empirical nature of *mappae mundi*.[63] More importantly, the authors' identification of the whale at the heart of the map is plausible.

Figure 2.8 *Map of the Arabian Peninsula with the Kaʿba at the centre. From a copy of* Kharīdat al-ʿajāʾib wa farīdat al-gharāʾib *('The pearl of wonders and the uniqueness of strange things'), attributed in the copy not to Ibn al-Wardī but one al-Marrākshī (lifetime unknown), dated* 983/1575. *Gouache and ink on paper;* 19 × 28.5*cm. Courtesy: The Museum of Islamic Art, Doha. MS.*523.1999. *© The Museum of Islamic Art, Doha.*

The authors make this identification on the basis of two elements: first, on Islamic traditions which say that God created the earth upon a giant fish or whale (*ḥūt*),[64] a cosmic creature akin to the biblical Leviathan, but sometimes confusingly named Bahamūt, the biblical Behemoth;[65] and second, on the apparent likeness of the map's seemingly zoomorphic component to a whale. This step of their argument is problematic, because it assumes that a modern-day viewer's expectations of a representation of a whale are more or less the same as those of a medieval viewer. Fortunately, there exist representations of whales conforming to just this modern-day expectation in copies of *Kitāb Ṣuwar al-kawākib al-thābita* ('The book of fixed constellations') by ʿAbd al-Raḥmān al-Ṣūfī (d. 376/986). The representations pertain to the constellation of Piscis Austrinus, or the Southern Fish (*al-Ḥūt al-Janūbī*). An example is reproduced below (Figure 2.10).[66] The similarity is clear.

With the identification of the whale corroborated, it remains to be asked (1) why this particular map and not the others has this zoomorphic

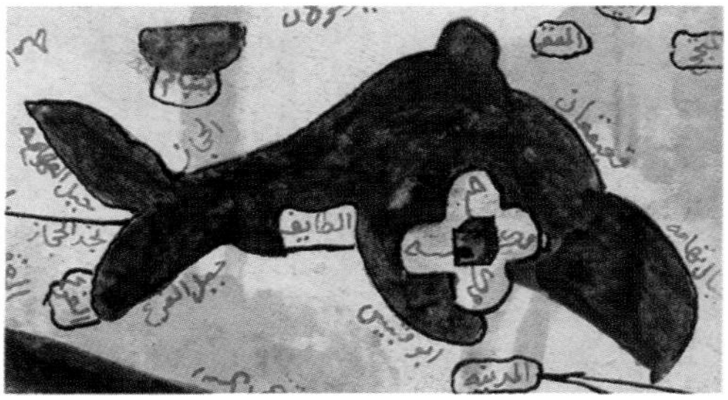

Figure 2.9 *(L): Detail of Figure 2.8, showing the Kaʿba inside the cosmic whale. The legend, Makka (Mecca), is twice written across this Kaʿba.*

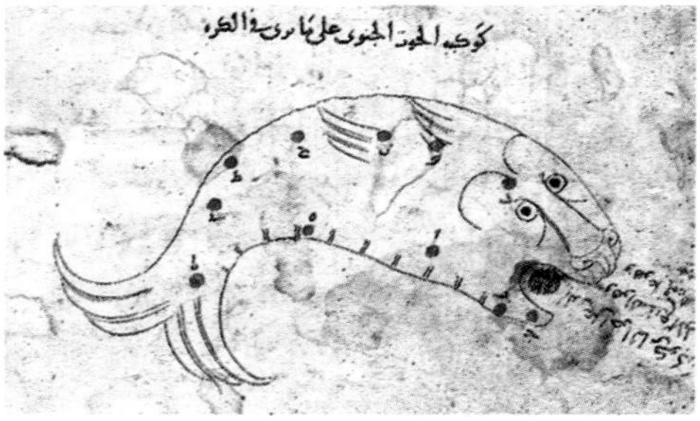

Figure 2.10 *(R): The constellation of Piscis Austrinus, or the Southern Fish (*al-Ḥūt al-Janūbī*). From a copy of* Kitāb Ṣuwar al-kawākib al-thābita *('The book of fixed constellations') by ʿAbd al-Raḥmān al-Ṣūfī (d. 376/986), recently re-dated to the late sixth/twelfth century. Ink on paper; 15 × 11cm. Courtesy: The Bodleian Library, University of Oxford. MS. Marsh 144, f. 417.*

element, and (2) what this element underscores concerning the foregoing discussion of the Kaʿba qua matrix.

Concerning the first of these two questions, although no definitive answer can be given, one likelihood is that the artist was attempting a visual pun, something not unknown in medieval Islamic art.[67] On this view, the artist would have known of the traditions regarding the world's creation upon a giant fish or whale, a number of them being deeply rooted because they are pre-Islamic.[68] Likewise, he would have known of traditions of the Kaʿba being the world's matrix. He thus transformed the mountainous areas in the near and distant vicinities of Mecca into this whale, colouring the creature as he had also coloured the map's seas, in brown. From the perspective of the map's aerial viewpoint, the Kaʿba rests on the whale – a representation which accords with the traditions. From the perspective of the approximately isometric projection used for the whale and the Kaʿba, the Kaʿba is wholly swallowed by the whale – a representation which delights the viewer.

That this map is an idiosyncratic visual pun would seem to be corroborated by two images produced in the same period, both belonging to copies of a Turkish translation of *ʿAjāʾib al-makhlūqāt* ('The wonders of creation') by Zakarriyāʾ al-Qazwīnī (d. 682/1283). Like the map, both images show a Kaʿba-centred world supported on the giant fish or whale. Unlike the map, however, the Kaʿba is not shown inside the fish or whale. One of these two images is reproduced below (Figure 2.11).[69] In it, the Kaʿba is the small rectangle at the centre of the Mount Qāf-ringed world. Other elements

Figure 2.11 *The Ka'ba-centred world hierarchically supported on the cosmic bull, the giant fish or whale, and an angel. From a Turkish translation of al-Qazwīnī's* ʿAjāʾib al-makhlūqāt, *dated to c.960/1553. Gold, gouache and ink on paper. Courtesy: Library of Congress, Washington, DC. MS Turkish 185.*

include the cosmic bull (*thawr*), which stands between the Kaʿba-centred world and the fish or whale; and an angel, who supports all.

Concerning now the second of the two questions about the whale map, what the cosmic behemoth underscores regarding the discussion of the Kaʿba qua matrix is the scarcely imaginable force that the Kaʿba once channelled for the world's creation. In a related image, an early thirteenth/nineteenth-century diagram of the Islamic cosmos in its entirety, the Kaʿba appears to have channelled the force for all of the Creation, both its sub- and super-lunar aspects (Figure 2.12).[70]

Given the Kaʿba's appearance of sub- and super-lunary generative potency in this diagram, one should possibly understand that what is labelled in it as the Kaʿba represents more than just the earthly Kaʿba; this would explain why it is represented in such a distorted manner. In this conjectural explanation, the Kaʿba's odd shape in the diagram would be accounted for by the following early cosmological tradition:

> The Apostle of God said: 'This House is one of fifteen, seven in the heavens up to the Throne and seven up to the limits of the lowest earth. The highest situated one, which is near the Throne, is the Frequented House. Every one of these Houses has a sacred precinct (*ḥaram*), like the sacred precinct of this House. If anyone of them fell down, the rest would fall down, one upon the other, to the limits of the lowest earth.'[71]

As the diagram maker's visual response to this cosmological tradition, the Kaʿba in the diagram would represent all fifteen of the Houses. However, because of (1) the artist's decision to show cosmological elements of the uppermost terrestrial world, for example, Mount Qāf, and (2) the two-dimensional limitations of his medium, he was unable to show the other fourteen Houses directly above and below the Kaʿba of Mecca. He thus represented, distortedly, just the eighth of these Houses, the middle one, the Kaʿba of Mecca, and thereby he effectively represented them all.

This conjectural explanation is corroborated by another early cosmological tradition in which the Kaʿba is said to be the terrestrial version of the uppermost celestial Kaʿba, the Frequented House, sharing 'its form and dimensions' (*mithālihi wa qadrihi*).[72] Quite possibly all the Houses have this form and dimensions, so that to see the outward aspect of one of them, in a diagram, say, is to see the outward aspect of all of them.

Samer Akkach comes to a similar understanding of the multiple, fifteen-in-one quality of the terrestrial Kaʿba when, with reference to the two cosmological traditions only, he writes: 'At the center of the earth the Kaʿba reveals a vertical relationship with the center of heaven . . . The cosmic axis that passes through the Kaʿba connects it to its infraterrestrial, celestial, and supracelestial counterparts.'[73]

What Akkach calls the 'cosmic axis' quickening the terrestrial Kaʿba seems to be alluded to in a third tradition: 'When rain strikes one of the

Figure 2.12 *Diagram of the Islamic cosmos with the Kaʿba at the centre. From a copy of* Maʿrifetnāme *('The book of gnosis') by the Ottoman Sufi and scholar İbrahim Hakkı (d. 1194/1780), dated 1235/1820. Gold, gouache and ink on paper; 8.5 × 18.5cm. Courtesy: The British Library. MS Or. 12964, fol. 23v. © The British Library Board.*

sides of [the Ka'ba], in that year fertility will be on that side. When rain strikes all of its sides, fertility will extend everywhere.'[74] This tradition implies that the Ka'ba is a microcosm of the world: to affect one side of it is to affect one side of the world. The Ka'ba has this meteorologic effect, I would argue, because it forms the Islamic universe's core.[75]

Part Two: The Ka'ba's Body and the Question of Orientation

The purpose of this second, shorter part of the chapter is to examine what rationally comprehensible attributes the Ka'ba is said to have which explain how it could conceivably orient the world. These attributes, it will be argued, are human ones. They become apparent by way of a discussion of Kant and the orientation of space.

Attempting to derive dimensionality from the nature of physical space, Kant introduces the body, specifically the bilateral, bifurcated human body. In a key essay from 1768, 'Concerning the Ultimate Ground of the Differentiation of Directions in Space', he explains that our concept of directions in space is derived from the sides of our bodies. This concept, he says, gives us knowledge of three-dimensionality and location. With this concept, he adds, we can orient things.[76] As Edward Casey glosses Kant's thought: 'Things are not oriented in and by themselves; they require our intervention to *become* oriented. Nor are they oriented by a purely mental operation: the a priori of orientation belongs to the body, not to the mind.'[77] Things in the world occupy positions relative to each other; only the bilateral body gives them directionality, orientation.

As we have seen in this and the previous chapter, not only is the Ka'ba said to orient the Islamic world as a whole, but empirically it orients a significant proportion of the architectural space of this world. In view of Kant's argument, it can come as no surprise, therefore, to find that in the early Islamic sources the Ka'ba is conceptualised as a bifurcated, bilateral body. To that evidence we now turn. Before doing so, however, it is important to emphasise that Kant's argument is not one whose applicability is restricted to just modern, Western bodies. Not only has his argument proven to be both widely accepted in academia and not culture specific,[78] but an account of a mystical illumination (*ru'ya*) that Ibn 'Arabī experienced in 593/1197 highlights the validity of the argument for non-Western, medieval, Muslim bodies, too. In this account, the mystic recalls the perceived loss of his own bodily bifurcation at the time of the illumination. Momentarily, he says, he became spherical, not bilateral, losing all orientation: 'I could not distinguish between my sides. Rather, I was like a ball, with no sense of direction.'[79]

The Ka'ba's bilateral body

Earlier in this chapter we encountered an anonymous geographical tradition, adduced by al-Bukhārī, which purported to explain the origin of the regional names Yemen and Syria. Analysing this tradition in his study of the word 'Yemen' (*Yaman*), Suliman Bashear shows that although by the third/ninth century this Ka'ba-centred explanation for the regional name Yemen predominated, others still existed, and not everyone was confident about accepting it.[80] A late example of such a reluctant scholar is the geographer Yāqūt (d. 626/1229), for whom it was nonsensical to assign the origins of the name to the Ka'ba, because 'the Ka'ba is a square and so has no right hand or left hand'.[81] For Yāqūt, the tradition could only make sense if it was referring to the south-western, or *Yamānī* corner of the Ka'ba. '[Only when] someone faces the *Yamānī* corner,' he says, 'is it correct.'[82] For Yāqūt, in other words, when facing that particular corner one may indeed speak of the Ka'ba as having a right hand and a left hand.

Of the three corners of the Ka'ba not holding the Black Stone, the *Yamānī* corner is the most venerated. In addition to its alleged status as one of the gates of Paradise, it is the corner at which the angel Gabriel is said to stand forgiving the sins of those who greet it, and where the mother of 'Alī, the Prophet's cousin, is said to have miraculously emerged from inside the Ka'ba holding her newborn child.[83] In the words of Yāqūt once more, it is the most august (*ajall*) of the corners.[84] It is also the corner that is shown on the cover of this book.

In the early Islamic sources, it and the corner holding the Black Stone are frequently referred to simply as the 'two Yamānī Corners' (*al-Ruknān al-Yamāniyān*).[85] In the early sources, too, the Black Stone that is attached to one of these two corners is alleged to be God's right hand. As reported by the hadith scholar Ibn Qutayba (d. 276/889): 'Ibn 'Abbās said: "The Black Stone is God's right hand (*yamīn Allāh*) on earth. With it He greets those whom He wants from His creation."'[86] Such a claim did not go unnoticed by Muslims, and elaborations of the tradition developed.[87]

With this anthropomorphic, left- and right-hand quality of the Ka'ba established so early in the Islamic sources, it can come as little surprise to find the Ka'ba also being early spoken of as having a front, or face (*wajh*), a rear (*dubur*) and a back (*ẓahr*).[88] The early Islamic wind schema discussed in part one, for example, the four-wind compass rose with the Ka'ba at the centre, avails itself of this 'anatomy'. As we saw in al-Aṣbaḥī's explanation of that schema, in addition to the 'left-hand' (*al-Shamāl*) wind, there is the 'front-comer' (*al-Qabūl*) wind, and the 'rear-comer' (*al-Dabūr*) wind.[89] Less consequentially, perhaps, at some point in the medieval history of the Ka'ba, the discrete section of the Ka'ba's robe (*Kiswa*) used for covering the front of the building, specifically the door, became known as the *Burqu'*: literally, the face veil.[90]

In conclusion, although it might seem to some that in detailing these anthropomorphic conceptualisations of the Ka'ba one is discussing mere metaphor and the blindingly obvious, the rebuttal is as follows. While it is indeed true that none of these conceptualisations is specific to the Ka'ba, but all are common to how one talks about buildings in general, the aim of this book is to find out what the Ka'ba does. As shown in this and the previous chapter, a principal work of the Ka'ba is the orientation of space. To do this work means it must share the characteristics of the bilateral, bifurcated human body. It does. As Avinoam Shalem has argued on the basis of different evidence: the 'cubic building in Mecca should . . . be regarded as a body with lower and upper parts.'[91]

Disorientation

This book began with Charles Long's definition of religion as orientation. Lindsay Jones, another religious studies scholar, concedes that although this definition is problematic, because it privileges thought over practice, it is also productive.[92] Jones borrows it, for example, to develop the first of the three heuristic propositions used in his magnum opus, *The Hermeneutics of Sacred Architecture*. '[O]rientation, or the human quest for a "place" in the world,' he writes, 'is *the* fundamental religious question in traditional (and perhaps all) cultures.'[93]

In this proposition, Jones might well have considered dispensing with the idea of orientation as a religious question, for in addition to Charles Long, the insights of a number of disciplinarily diverse scholars are invoked in the proposition's development. For example, Jones invokes Norberg-Schulz, who writes: 'Human life cannot take place anywhere; it presupposes a space that is really a cosmos.'[94] Similarly, he invokes the philosopher of aesthetics, Suzanne Langer, who writes: '[A] human being can adapt himself somehow to anything his imagination can cope with: but he cannot deal with Chaos . . . Therefore our most important assets are always the symbols of our general orientation in nature.'[95] Lastly, he invokes the philosopher of science, Elisabeth Ströker, for whom an individual's pre-reflexive 'attunement in space' – their having a world to know, negotiate and experience – presupposes orientation.[96]

These voices from outside religious studies suggest that orientation is fundamental not just to religious being, but to human being in general: to all of us, whether we are religious or not. This suggestion can be corroborated by approaching the question of orientation from the opposite direction: from the perspective of *dis*orientation. To approach it this way, one need not resort to anecdotal evidence, such as that given by the urban planner Kevin Lynch, who speaks of disoriented Africans 'stricken with panic, and plung[ing] wildly into the brush'.[97] Rather, one can proceed philosophically.

In his book *Phenomenology and Mysticism*, Anthony Steinbock speaks of disorientation, referring to it as the destruction of what he calls the vertical dimension of life, the dimension 'of mystery and reverence'.[98] He terms it 'idolatry'.[99] He specifically intends the term 'idolatry', because, he says, 'it cannot accommodate itself to a postmodern worldview'.[100] He contends that in our postmodern age, idolatry, or disorientation 'becomes actualized in many ways: injustice, hatred, racism, institutionalized poverty, militarism, misogyny, ecological terrorism, and general earth-alienation'.[101] On Steinbock's view, therefore, orientation is not restricted to religious being, because all human beings are creatures of orientation and, especially, disorientation.

As is well known, *shirk* is a common term in the Qurʾan and early Islamic sources, where it denotes any action or belief that compromises the absolute monotheism Islam proclaims and demands. It is routinely translated as idolatry.[102] In the light of the previous chapter that detailed the degree to which orientation to the Kaʿba has historically been pursued at the urban level, and in view of the degree to which practising Muslims daily orient themselves to the Kaʿba, disorientation would thus seem to be an appropriate way of conceiving of *shirk*. It is the antithesis of the absolute monotheism Islam proclaims and demands, and this helps explain why identifying Muslims go to such lengths, often exorbitant, to avoid it.

Conclusion

This chapter has pursued further the space-orienting function of the Kaʿba discussed in Chapter One. In that chapter, the space in question was architectural and primarily urban; in this chapter, it was global and sometimes cosmic. In this chapter, we have not only seen how the Kaʿba is said to have acted as the matrix of the Creation, but also how it is said to orient the world by assigning the coordinates of localities within the world and by naming the four winds and two regions of the world. Searching for attributes of the Kaʿba that might rationally explain how it could effectuate such a global orientation, we saw in the early Islamic sources how the Kaʿba had been conceptualised as a bifurcated, bilateral body. As this body, orientation was an effect open to it, because as we saw in the thought of Kant, only bifurcated, bilateral bodies can orient space.

The question of orientation per se has also been addressed in this chapter. With so many pages devoted in Chapter One to the subject of the Kaʿba's spatial orientations, including the exorbitant lengths to which Muslims have sometimes gone to try to facilitate an enduring state of orientation, it was appropriate to at least raise the question of why attaining that state was so important in Islam. In an attempt to answer the question by looking at it in reverse, via the question of disorientation, we saw how the philosopher Anthony Steinbock had spoken of disorientation as idolatry. We argued that referring to disorientation as idolatry was a good way of understanding why orientation was so important in Islam, for it spoke of the absolute antithesis of Islam's absolute monotheism, *shirk*.

CHAPTER THREE

The Kaʿba as Substructure

This chapter concerns the Kaʿba when its superstructure lies in ruins and only its substucture remains. Beginning with an account of destructions the Kaʿba has suffered throughout its history, the chapter explores what those ruinations tell us about the Kaʿba. Motivated by the knowledge that they have not occasioned the kind of apocalyptic anxiety that might be expected after the collapse of the world's alleged axis, the chapter asks how that could be. Four reasons are adduced in answer, two for each of the chapter's two parts. One reason speaks of the role of the Kaʿba at the apocalypse; another speaks of the fact that what ultimately matters about the Kaʿba are its allegedly unnatural, awesome foundations; a third speaks of the Kaʿba's incorporation in Sufism as the human heart; and the fourth speaks of the role of the Kaʿba in structuring foundational concepts of Islamic thought.

Part One: Destructions of the Kaʿba

> The Lord gave full vent to his wrath;
> he poured out his hot anger,
> and kindled a fire in Zion
> that consumed its foundations.
> (Lamentations 4:11)

For the Kaʿba, there is no equivalent of the Old Testament's Book of Lamentations, even though the Kaʿba, like the Temple, has seen wrath and fury rain down upon it at the hands of warring forces.[1] That it has done so on a number of occasions, detailed below, makes the absence of poetically charged commentary even more remarkable, especially as lamentation (*rithāʾ*) over fallen towns and cities occupies an important position in Islamic literature.[2] Lamentation is, for example, movingly employed to recount the destruction of al-Andalus at the hands of the Christians during the *reconquista*.[3] Regarding the Kaʿba, however, following its first alleged martial destruction in 64/684 during the siege led by al-Ḥusayn b. Numayr (d. 67/686), and its second alleged martial destruction in 72/692 during the siege led by al-Ḥajjāj b. Yūsuf (d. 95/714), at the most its ruins are compared to 'the bosoms of [mourning] women' (*juyūb al-nisāʾ*).[4]

It is not that these two sieges have no significance in the early Islamic sources; to the contrary, many pages and verses are dedicated to what occasioned them and arose from them.[5] Rather, what is noteworthy is the fact that in these pages and verses the actual destruction of the Kaʿba, including the splitting of the Black Stone during the first siege, does not provoke the kind of grief, anxiety and trauma among the chroniclers that one might have expected, given the House's function as *axis mundi*.[6] Even an eyewitness account of the ruined Kaʿba after its destruction in the first siege is presented in rather neutral imagery:

> I came to Mecca with my mother on the day the Kaʿba was burned. The fire had reached it, and I saw that it was without its silk veil. I saw that the [*Yamānī*] corner of the Kaʿba was black and had been cracked in three places. I asked, 'What has happened to the Kaʿba?' They pointed to one of the followers of [Mecca's de facto ruler] Ibn al-Zubayr [d. 73/692] and said, 'It has been burned because of this man. He put a firebrand on the tip of his spear; the wind made it fly off. It struck the veils of the Kaʿba between the [*Yamānī*] corner and the Black Stone.'[7]

Here and elsewhere in the sources, including, notably, the treatment of the two sieges by al-Jāḥiẓ (d. 255/869), factional politics are the focus of interest, not the world's potential collapse.[8] As such, the contrast with the biblical laments for the destruction of the Temple remains instructive.[9] Instructive, too, is the observation that in the Islamic calendar there is no day of collective mourning similar to the Jewish Tisha B'Av, the day on which the destruction of both the First and Second Temple is commemorated.[10] Scarcely less instructive is the fact that there exists no Islamic equivalent to the other mourning practices regarding the Temple.[11]

In part, this absence of apocalyptic language regarding destructions of the Kaʿba is because there are hadiths which prophesise that it will be a bow-legged Abyssinian called Dhū al-Suwayqatayn (literally, the short-legged one), not an Arab, who attacks and destroys the Kaʿba and thus heralds the apocalypse.[12] In other words, the Dhū al-Suwayqatayn prophecy prevents this or that destruction of the Kaʿba from being interpreted as a sign of the apocalypse, because the prophecy's details present a reassuring contrast to what is actually being witnessed during these destructions. To that prophecy we now turn.

Apocalyptic destructions of the Kaʿba

A sound (*ṣaḥīḥ*) version of the Dhū al-Suwayqatayn prophecy reads as follows:

ʿAbd Allāh b. ʿAmr said: 'I heard the Prophet say, "Dhū al-Suwayqatayn from Abyssinia will destroy the Kaʿba, plunder its ornaments, and strip it of its *Kiswa*. It is as if I could see him: he is slightly bald and slightly misshapen, and he strikes at [the Kaʿba] with his shovel and pick."'[13]

A version of it is recalled in relief by the inhabitants of Mecca at the time of the second alleged siege and destruction of the Kaʿba in 72/692: 'When the army of al-Ḥajjāj came, [because of this prophecy] we did not doubt it was them, the army of al-Ḥajjāj [and not the army of the Abyssinian].'[14] Another version of it is illustrated below (Figure 3.1).[15]

Figure 3.1 *An apocalyptic attack on the Kaʿba by Abyssinians wielding picks. From a late ninth/sixteenth-century copy of* Tercüme-i Miftāḥ-ı cifru el-cāmi, *a Turkish translation of a book of apocalyptic prophecy called* The Key of Comprehensive Divination. *This book was begun by Kamal al-Dīn b. Ṭalḥa (d. 652/1254) as* al-Durr al-munaẓẓam fī al-sirr al-aʿẓam *('The strung pearls concerning the greatest secret') and then both preserved and expanded as* Miftāḥ al-jafr al-jāmiʿ *('The key of comprehensive divination') by ʿAbd al-Raḥmān al-Bisṭāmī (d. 858/1454). Gold, gouache and ink on paper. Courtesy: Topkapı Palace Library. TSMK B373 fol. 256r.*

Elsewhere in the Islamic sources, however, a less-reported hadith predicts the apocalypse being heralded by the divine removal of the Kaʿba, following two unspecified occasions of its destruction and, presumably, reconstruction. In this hadith, no mention is made of Dhū al-Suwayqatayn. 'Make the most of this House,' the hadith reads, 'because it has been destroyed on two occasions, and on the third occasion it will be removed.'[16] A commentary on it specifies that the meaning of 'on the third occasion' is not the third occasion of the Kaʿba's destruction but its third reconstruction, because, the commentary explains, one would not use the word 'House' to refer to ruins.[17]

Another less reported hadith, a 'divine hadith' (*ḥadīth qudsī*) – so-called because God is the speaker – predicts the apocalypse commencing with the Kaʿba's destruction. Again, no mention is made of the Abyssinian or indeed any intermediary acting as God's hammer. The hadith reads: 'When I want to destroy the world, I will begin with My House.'[18]

These two less reported hadiths do not, however, contradict the Dhū al-Suwayqatayn prophecy, because neither excludes the possibility that Dhū al-Suwayqatayn is the agent of the Kaʿba's destruction. More importantly, neither hadith undermines the potential imminence of the prophecy. The details of the Dhū al-Suwayqatayn prophecy are imaginable as pertaining to the present, the here and now; in contrast, the two hadiths refer to a less imaginable, more obviously remote time, when seven consecutive years have already elapsed with no one making the Hajj, and Gog and Magog have been unleashed to roam the earth.[19]

In summary of the foregoing discussion, the Dhū al-Suwayqatayn prophecy might have acted as a brake against viewing historical or allegedly historical destructions of the Kaʿba in apocalyptic terms. This argument might even have a bearing on the partial destruction of the Kaʿba and brutal sacking of Mecca in 317/930 by the adherents of a dissident branch of Ismaʿili Shiʿa, the Qarmatians (*Qarāmiṭa*) of Bahrain.[20] For although this group's profanation of the town and desecration of the Kaʿba are represented in the sources as a profoundly traumatic moment in the history of Islam, to the best of my knowledge the group's actions are not viewed apocalyptically.[21] The late medieval chronicler of Mecca, Quṭb al-Dīn al-Nahrawalī (d. 990/1582), for example, says only this of the event: 'What those brazen, evil people did was one of the greatest catastrophes (*maṣāʾib*) to strike Islam. For the religion, it was the harshest of all of them. It dissolved the hearts of the faithful.'[22] These words are, to be sure, expressive of searing pain, but the representation remains free of apocalyptical overtones. Could that be because of the existence of the prophecy? The only people who viewed the Kaʿba's desecration apocalyptically were the Qarmatians themselves, especially their leader Abū Ṭāhir (d. 332/944). For him, the barbaric attack was intended as the harbinger of a new era: the end of the Islamic cycle of time and the dawn of the seventh, final cycle.[23]

In view of Abū Ṭāhir's motivation, it is both tempting and problematic to see what he did to the Kaʿba as a conscious reference to the Dhū al-Suwayqatayn prophecy. It is problematic, because the prophecy is a Sunni one and may well not have been known to the Qarmatians or accepted by them. A Shiʿite tradition concerning the apocalypse, for example, prophesises only that the Mahdi (*al-Qāʾim*) will 'destroy the Sacred Mosque to its foundations'. Does the Mahdi's destruction include the Kaʿba? It would seem not, for the prophecy continues by saying that the Mahdi will 'restore the House to its site and erect it upon its foundations', hanging from it the amputated hands of its erstwhile custodians, the 'thieving Banū Shayba'.[24] Another version of the prophecy, however, says that it is the Station of Abraham that is restored to its site, not the Kaʿba.[25]

Notwithstanding what is problematic about interpreting Abū Ṭāhir's actions as a conscious reference to the prophecy, it yet remains tempting to interpret his actions thus. That is because although Abū Ṭāhir did not totally destroy the Kaʿba, he did remove its door and tear out its Black Stone, and he tried to have its rainspout, the golden *Mīzāb,* wrenched off. Additionally, he plundered the Kaʿba's treasury and stripped it of its *Kiswa*.[26]

Were Abū Ṭāhir imitating the details of the prophecy so as to fulfil it, it would not be the first time the prophecy had been imitated. Mecca's de facto ruler, Ibn al-Zubayr, had allegedly light-heartedly done the same when, at the start of his rebuilding of the Kaʿba following the first siege, he ordered some Abyssinian slaves to the top of the Kaʿba in order to raze what remained of the walls. He hoped, it is reported, that in the slaves 'was the attribute (*ṣifa*) of . . . Dhū al-Suwayqatayn.'[27]

Later destructions of the Kaʿba

The foregoing argument that the Dhū al-Suwayqatayn prophecy might have acted as a brake against people interpreting destructions of the Kaʿba in apocalyptic terms, does not, however, hold entirely true for later periods of the building. That is so for two reasons. First, in 1019/1610, so precariously leaning were the Kaʿba's walls that, as described by a contemporary source: '[I]t almost fell to pieces. (And) the world, which was embellished and decorated with its illustrious form . . . [was] almost torn asunder.'[28] Second, in 1039/1630, the Kaʿba was destroyed by torrential floods, and the people of Mecca took that as a sign of the world's end.

Before the expansion and redevelopment of the town in the twentieth century, the inhabitants of Mecca had been used to the flooding of the Kaʿba and Sacred Mosque.[29] That is because the town lies in a hollow in a steep wadi known as Baṭn Makka (literally, the Belly of Mecca), with the Kaʿba located at the hollow's lowest point.[30] This location is called al-Baṭḥāʾ: a toponym directly derived from the geography of the site, because the term *baṭḥāʾ* means the bottom of a watercourse.

Notwithstanding this familiarity with flooding, for the inhabitants of Mecca the flood of 1039/1630 was especially violent, doing more than just damaging the Kaʿba but ruining it.[31] According to Eyüp Sabri Paşa (d. 1308/1890), an Ottoman naval officer writing in the thirteenth/nineteenth century but drawing from earlier and contemporary sources to describe this calamitous event:

> The roar that the walls made as they collapsed, combined with the sound of the thunder and lightning, provoked such fear in the inhabitants of Mecca, that some of them died from fright . . . The inhabitants believed that what happened that day was one of the signs of the apocalypse.[32]

Helpfully for his readers, Sabri Paşa visualises this apocalyptic scene with an illustration (Figure 3.2).

Interestingly, although Sabri Paşa does not mention it, the inhabitants might have referred to a prophetic hadith in confirmation of their dreadful conclusion. It speaks of the Kaʿba's destruction by flooding, though metaphorically: 'The sea will boil with people from the Sudan, who will then flood towards the Kaʿba as a torrent of ants (*sayl al-naml*) and destroy it.'[33]

In view of Sabri Paşa's historical account, an additional explanation must be found to account for why in the Islamic sources the world does not seem to collapse with the various destructions of the Kaʿba. The existence of the Dhū al-Suwayqatayn prophecy is an insufficient explanation, because in Sabri Paşa's account the inhabitants of Mecca do think

Figure 3.2 *Flooded pavilions of the Sacred Mosque and the last remaining corner of the ruined Kaʿba following the inundation of* 1039/1630, *as visualised in* Mirat ül-Harameyn *('Mirror of the two sanctuaries') by Eyüp Sabri Paşa (d.* 1308/1890*), dated* 1301/1883. *(Source: Sabri Paşa* 1884, *pp.* 328–9.*)*

the apocalypse is at hand, even if they soon realise they are mistaken, so promptly do they start working towards the Kaʿba's reconstruction.[34] The sought-for explanation, I shall argue, lies in the fact that all these destructions are superficial, related only to what stands ephemerally above the ground, not to what lies preternaturally beneath: the Kaʿba's foundations. As I shall show, these foundations often seem to matter more in the Islamic sources than what stands upon them, a paradox which a historian working in an idiom similar to the revisionists might simply explain with reference to a theory of Gerald Hawting. This theory states that the way the Islamic-period Kaʿba is represented in the early Islamic sources results from an amalgamation of two different religious traditions, a Judaic, *axis mundi*-based Temple tradition (viz., a foundations-based tradition) having been grafted imperfectly onto an important but local, pre-Islamic shrine tradition.[35]

The Kaʿba's foundations

That the foundations of the Kaʿba seem to matter more in the Islamic sources than what stands upon them is sufficiently easy to demonstrate, even if the reasons why are harder to ascertain. On the two occasions that the Kaʿba is allegedly destroyed or severely damaged by implacable forces, either warring or natural ones, and the sources expatiate on the ensuing reconstruction process, what causes the inhabitants of Mecca the greatest anxiety is not the fact that the Kaʿba has been destroyed. What terrifies them, rather, is the fact that the remains of the House must first be demolished in order for it to be rebuilt. In that activity of demolition, the Kaʿba's foundations must necessarily be struck.

The later of these two occasions is the alleged siege and destruction of the Kaʿba of 64/684, mentioned at the beginning of the chapter. According to Mecca's pre-eminent local historian, al-Azraqī (d. *c.*250/864), as soon as Ibn Numayr's army had withdrawn from the town, the de facto ruler Ibn al-Zubayr turned his attention to rebuilding the ruined Kaʿba. He asked the town's notables whether he should first tear down what remained standing of the building. On the basis of a prophetic hadith that warned against the repeated dismantling and rebuilding of the Kaʿba because of the risk of belittling thereby its sacrality (*ḥurma*), most of the notables advised him against razing the remains, but to 'renovate it' (*irfaʿhā*).[36] Dissatisfied with this advice, Ibn al-Zubayr resolved to raze the remains and rebuild from the foundations (*qawāʿid*) up:

> [When he was ready for the demolition to commence], the people of Mecca left the town and went to Mina, where they stayed for three days, fearing a punishment would befall them if they razed the ruins. Ibn al-Zubayr then

gave the order for the demolition, but no one dared to do it. When he saw this, he climbed the ruins himself and, taking a pick, he started demolishing the ruins and throwing down the stones. When the people saw that nothing had happened to him, they were emboldened and got up to demolish [the ruins], too . . . When Ibn al-Zubayr had demolished the Kaʿba and levelled it to the ground, he discovered the foundations (*asās*) of Abraham.[37] These extended into the [semicircular] *Ḥijr* about six-and-a-bit cubits, and were like intertwined fingers or the necks of camels joined one to another. Disturbing (*tuḥarraku*) the *Ḥijr* at the foundations (*qawāʿid*), disturbed all the cornerstones (*arkān*) [of the Kaʿba's foundations].[38] Ibn al-Zubayr then called fifty of Mecca's notables and made them witness these foundations. A strong man from among them, ʿAbd Allāh b. Muṭīʿa al-ʿĀdawī, inserted a crowbar into one of the House's cornerstones, and all the cornerstones shook together. It is said that Mecca convulsed violently at the moment the foundations (*asās*) shook, and the people were extremely frightened, to the point that those who had advised Ibn al-Zubayr to raze the ruins regretted doing so, and all were aghast and extremely distressed.[39]

The earlier of the two occasions happened during the lifetime of the Prophet. According to some reports, this was when he was thirty-five, making the year 605, according to the standard chronology.[40] At that time, the inhabitants of Mecca set about rebuilding the Kaʿba, either because it had been ruined by a flood or fire, or because its walls needed heightening and roofing and its door raising off the ground to prevent the ingress of thieves (see Figure I.1, b).[41] In the earliest biography of the Prophet, as composed by Ibn Isḥāq (d. 150/767) and redacted and transmitted by Ibn Hishām (d. 213/828 or 218/833), this act of rebuilding is recounted as follows:

When they had decided to demolish and rebuild [the Kaʿba], Abū Wahb b. Makhzūm stood up and took a stone from the Kaʿba, but it leapt out of his hand and returned to its place.[42] . . . The people were afraid . . . and withdrew in awe. Al-Walīd b. al-Mughīra said, 'I will begin the demolition.' So he took a pick and went up to [the House], saying all the while, 'O God, do not [mind], O God, we intend only what is best.' Then he demolished the part at the *Yamānī* and Black Stone corners. That night the people watched, saying, 'We will look out. If he is smitten, we won't destroy any more of it and will restore it as it was; but if nothing happens to him, then God is pleased with what we are doing and we will demolish it.' In the morning al-Walīd returned to the work of demolition and the people worked with him, until they got down to the foundations (*asās*) of Abraham. They came upon green stones likes camels' humps joined one to another. A certain traditionist told me that a man of [the Prophet's tribe] the Quraysh inserted a crowbar between two stones in order to get one of them out, and when he moved the stone the whole of Mecca shuddered, so they left the foundations alone.[43]

The frequently identical narratives of these two purportedly historical occasions might suggest that the information recounted therein is more literary fantasy than fact. It might, however, also point to the spread, hold and nature of the belief that the Kaʿba's foundations are unearthly, unnatural and extraordinary. Pursuing the latter surmise only, what more do we know about the Kaʿba's foundations?

The Kaʿba's foundations in the Qurʾan

In the Qurʾan, the foundations of the Kaʿba are referred to once, at the moment that Abraham either builds or rebuilds the Kaʿba. The verse reads: 'And when Abraham, and Ishmael with him, raised the foundations (*yarfaʿu al-qawāʿid*) of the House, [they said]: "Our Lord, accept [this] from us! You are the All-Hearing, the All-Knowing."'[44]

It is unclear what 'raising the foundations' means in this verse, especially as the word used for foundations, *qawāʿid*, has been interpreted by some exegetes to mean columns, walls or even rows of bricks. These exegetes have done so in part because of the word's other occurrence in the Qurʾan, where 'columns' more obviously makes for a plausible translation of *qawāʿid*. That occurrence reads: 'Those that were before them plotted, so God came upon their building from the *qawāʿid*, and the roof collapsed on top of them.'[45]

Notwithstanding this uncertainty over the word's precise meaning, whether it denotes walls, columns or rows of bricks, *qawāʿid* is clearly some kind of load-bearing structure: a seat, as its etymology indicates.[46] In that sense, 'foundations' makes for a satisfactory translation. What, though, does it mean for Abraham 'to raise them'?

The Qurʾanic exegetical tradition is too voluminous and varied to be characterised as having a univocal view on much of the Qurʾan, and the interpretation of this Qurʾanic verse is no exception. Nevertheless, one dominant narrative thread is that Abraham does not build the Kaʿba from scratch, but rebuilds what Adam had either first built or received complete from heaven, namely, the prototypical Kaʿba.[47] This Kaʿba either eventually collapsed of its own accord or was elevated to heaven at the time of the Flood, only its foundations remaining. Those foundations Abraham raises.[48]

As might be expected, not only does Mecca's historian al-Azraqī confirm this narrative, he also elaborates on it.[49] He claims, for example, that the foundations of Adam's Kaʿba reached right down to the seventh earth. He additionally claims that the prototypical Kaʿba is in fact the celestial Kaʿba, the Frequented House (*al-Bayt al-Maʿmūr*).

Regarding the first claim, al-Azraqī reports a tradition alleging that Gabriel's wing struck the ground at the point where the Kaʿba was to be built, and a 'firm foundation' (*uss thābit*) became exposed on the lowest earth (*al-arḍ al-suflā*). Angels then filled the chasm between this firm foundation and the earth's surface with huge rocks, and upon those rocks Adam built.[50] Regarding the second claim, the celestial Kaʿba, al-Azraqī devotes a short chapter to the subject. He explains (1) how the first thing that God placed on earth was the Kaʿba (*al-Bayt al-Ḥarām*), which God also designated as the future celestial Kaʿba (*al-Bayt al-Maʿmūr*), and (2) how at the time of the Flood this Kaʿba was elevated to heaven in silken brocades, destined to remain there until the Day of Resurrection.[51] More simply, he also says that the celestial Kaʿba was sent down to earth for Adam's benefit, returning to heaven at the time of the Flood.[52] Al-Ṭabarī says something similar, with the additional clarification that when God removed the celestial Kaʿba from the earth and returned it to heaven, 'its foundations remained' (*wa baqiya asāsuhu*).[53]

The 'foundations that remained' are those, then, of an archetype: the prototypical Kaʿba. What stands today in Mecca, and what has been destroyed from time to time in the past, is only a copy of that archetype. As a copy whose original was safe elsewhere, its destruction was never likely to spell calamity.

Part Two: The Kaʿba of the Heart and Mind

Still pursuing reasons why the various Kaʿba destructions have not proven cataclysmic to the Islamic world, I shall now argue that the Kaʿba was bodily incorporated as part of Islamic thought, where it contributed to structuring this thought. I shall conclude by saying that, with the Kaʿba bodily incorporated and functioning in this specific structural way, whether or not a tectonic Kaʿba stands or falls at Mecca is almost immaterial.

Journeying to the Kaʿba of the heart

In the Qurʾan, the human heart (*qalb*) is conceptualised as the locus of piety and understanding, and appraised both positively and negatively. It is associated with disease and hardness (*maraḍ*, *qaswa*), resulting in irreligious behaviour; but also with the notion that God acts directly upon it.[54] In post-Qurʾanic thought, most especially in Sufism, this latter association is formalised and expanded, the heart becoming viewed in at least two ways. First, as the seat of religious knowledge and sensitivity, or conscience; for example, the statement of al-Ghazālī (d. 505/1111) that 'the heart is the part of man that perceives and knows and experiences. It is addressed, punished, rebuked and held responsible'.[55] Second, as a locus of theophanies (*tajalliyāt*); for example, the statement of Sahl al-Tustarī

(d. 283/896) that 'the heart has a thousand lives, the last of them is the encounter with the Transcendent (*liqā' al-Ḥaqq*)';[56] and the statement of Ibn 'Arabī (d. 638/1240) that 'God took the heart of His servant as a house, because it is the locus of gnostic not theoretical (*'irfānī lā naẓarī*) knowledge of Him'.[57]

Related to this post-Qur'anic development, the following divine hadith became commonly referenced in Sufism, even though its claim to authenticity was widely dismissed: 'My earth and my heaven contain Me not, but the heart of my believing servant contains Me.'[58] Also associated with Sufism, and likewise dismissed as inauthentic, was a prophetic hadith similar in meaning to the divine hadith, namely, 'The heart is God's House.'[59] In view of both of these hadiths, it was perhaps inevitable that the Ka'ba would become construed as a heart, at least in Sufism, although it should also be noted that elsewhere in Sufism the heart became tied to God's celestial Throne (*al-'Arsh*).[60]

Early, often quite allusive expressions of the Ka'ba as the human heart can be found, for example, in the teachings and sayings of al-Nūrī (d. 295/907),[61] Ibn 'Aṭā (d. 309/922)[62] and al-Niffarī (d. *c.*354/965).[63] Less allusive expressions can, however, also be found in this period, in the teachings and sayings of a number of influential Sufi figures. Al-Ḥallāj (d. 309/922), for example, says of the circumambulatory *ṭawāf* ritual: 'The important thing is to proceed seven times around the Ka'ba of one's heart.'[64] Al-Qushayrī (d. 465/1072) says, inter alia: '[T]he Ka'ba is the House of the Real in stone and the heart is the House of the Real in the innermost self.'[65] Al-Hujwīrī (d. *c.*467/1075) says: 'If [pilgrims] are bound to visit a stone which is looked at only once a year, surely they are more bound to visit the house (*khāna*) of the heart, where He may be seen three hundred and sixty times in a day and night.'[66] Al-Ghazālī says, with reference to the inner (*bāṭin*) dimensions of the Hajj: 'Do not think that the goal [of the *ṭawāf* ritual] lies in your bodily circumambulation of the House; the purpose is rather circumambulation of your heart through recollecting the Lord of the House.'[67] Lastly, with reference to the extralegal, Sufi dimensions of the Hajj (*hajj al-ṭarīqa*), 'Abd al-Qādir al-Jīlānī (d. 561/1166) speaks of circumambulating 'the Ka'ba of the heart'.[68]

In a slightly later period, especially in the work of Rūzbihān Baqlī (d. 605/1209), Ibn 'Arabī and Rūmī (d. 671/1273), unambiguously direct expressions of the Ka'ba as the human heart can be found.[69] Ibn 'Arabī, for example, reports God as saying: 'My Ka'ba is the heart of existence . . . Your sought-for heart contains Me. It is My House.'[70] Elsewhere, the mystic explains:

> When God created the land of your body, He placed within it [the] Ka'ba (*ja'ala fīhā ka'ba*), and that is your heart. He placed this cardio-house (*al-bayt al-qalbī*), the most noble of houses, in the believer; for He reported that the

> heavens, in which is the Frequented House, and the earth, in which is the Ka'ba, do not contain Him and are too constricted to hold Him, but that this heart [of the believer] contains Him.[71]

Rūmī says, for example: 'The heart is the intended Ka'ba. Why do you [pilgrims] bother with [the one of] clay?'[72] He then adds: 'You can circumambulate the Ka'ba one thousand times by foot. / The realisation of Truth (*qubūl-i Ḥaqq*) will not occur if you vex a [viz., your] heart.'[73] In a different work, he also says:

> The meaning (*maqṣūd*) of the Ka'ba is the heart of the prophets and saints, the locus of God's inspiration (*maḥall-i waḥy-i Ḥaqq*), of which the Ka'ba is but a branch. If there is no heart, what purpose is served by the Ka'ba?[74]

Underpinning this Sufi analogy between the Ka'ba and the heart, effectuating it, is the concept of enclosed interiority. In the words of Rūzbihān Baqlī: '[God] formed the heart like an oyster (*hamchūn ṣadafī*).'[75] In Sufi accounts of the human body, this enclosed interiority is what makes the heart vital, both somatically and spiritually. As the heart is described by al-Ghazālī:

> [The] term 'heart' (*qalb*) . . . is used with two meanings. One of them is the cone-shaped organ of flesh that is located at the left side of the chest. It is flesh of a particular sort within which there is a cavity (*tajwīf*), and in this cavity there is black blood that is the source and seat of the pneuma (*rūḥ*) . . . The second meaning is a numinous, spiritual, subtle substance, that has a dependency on the physical heart.[76]

As the heart is described by Sahl al-Tustarī:

> [The] heart has two cavities (*tajwīfān*), one of them is inward (*bāṭin*) and includes hearing and seeing; this is called the heart proper (*qalb al-qalb*). The other cavity is the outward (side) of the heart (*ẓāhir al-qalb*), and includes the intellect (*'aql*).[77]

Although the heart is not necessarily the end of the Sufi path, towards this numinous 'heart proper' the Sufi journeys, just as the pilgrim journeys towards the Ka'ba.[78] In a verse sometimes attributed to Jāmī (d. 898/1492), this understanding is expressed as follows: 'Offer the heart, because it is the greatest (*akbar*) Hajj. / One heart is better than a thousand Ka'bas.'[79] Rūmī, though, expresses the understanding better: 'Your body is like a camel which journeys to the Ka'ba of the heart.'[80]

In the foregoing manner, the Ka'ba entered Islamic thought. Preserved in this thought, this bodily incorporated Ka'ba, simultaneously gross and numinous, provides a third reason why the destruction of the Kaʿba never provoked the kind of apocalyptic anxiety one might have expected a ruined *axis mundi* to occasion.

The belly of the Kaʿba

Unrelated to Sufi texts, the Kaʿba is also paired with another enclosing organ: the *baṭn*, or belly, a term that in the Qurʾan and elsewhere can also mean womb.[81] This pairing is represented most clearly in the story relating the birth of the Prophet's cousin and future son-in-law, ʿAlī (d. 40/661), who was allegedly born inside the Kaʿba. The tradition is briefly mentioned by al-Masʿūdī (d. 345/956), but it receives its fullest exposition in eleventh/seventeenth-century Shiʿite sources.[82] There it is alleged that ʿAlī's heavily pregnant mother, Fāṭima bt. Asad, was outside the Kaʿba petitioning God for an easy birth, when the walls of the building miraculously parted and she entered through the gap. Remaining there in confinement, the tradition continues, with no one outside able to unlock the door, Fāṭima survived on dates from Paradise. After the fourth day, she exited, holding in her arms the infant ʿAlī.[83]

The parallel drawn in this tradition between Fāṭima's belly and the enveloping Kaʿba is surely not accidental. Not only is another Kaʿba birth recorded in the early sources, that of Ḥakīm b. Ḥizām, a companion of the Prophet;[84] but there are frequent early references to the Kaʿba as having a belly, or *baṭn*, and also a back, or *ẓahr*.[85] Of course, these references are metaphorical, intended to signify respectively the interior and exterior of the Kaʿba. Nevertheless, given the role played in Qurʾanic hermeneutics by the binary *bāṭin*/*ẓāhir* (inward/outward or hidden/apparent), which is derived from these two words for belly and back, the metaphor merits further investigation.

The metaphors we live by

In their book *Metaphors We Live By*, the cognitive scientist George Lakoff and the philosopher and cognitive linguist Mark Johnson argue that our conceptual system is metaphorical in nature, and that to overlook this fact is both natural and mistaken. Metaphor, they explain, is a mechanism of the mind. Metaphorisation, they continue, allows us to use what we know first-hand about our physical and social experience in order to understand other, more abstract subjects. Such metaphors are 'metaphors we live by': metaphors that shape our perceptions and actions without our ever noticing them.[86]

In a subsequent publication, *Philosophy in the Flesh*, the same authors argue for the bodily origin of this metaphorical conceptual system, for how the 'peculiar nature of our bodies shapes our very possibilities for conceptualisation and categorisation'.[87] As an example they discuss the way we project our bodies onto space:

> Bodily projections are especially clear instances of the way our bodies shape conceptual structure. Consider examples such as *in front of* and *in back of*. The most central senses of these terms have to do with the body. We have inherent fronts and backs [and] we project [them] onto objects . . . without inherent fronts [and backs] such as trees or rocks . . . The concepts *front* and *back* are body-based. They make sense only for beings with fronts and backs.[88]

This bodily projection means that abstract ideas which depend on the opposition of up and down, front and rear, right and left, inside and outside, and so forth – for example, feeling up, meaning happy, and stooping low, meaning acting dishonourably – are spatial in nature and bodily in origin.[89]

Applying Lakoff and Johnson's arguments to the Kaʿba, I tentatively suggest that the belly and back of the otherwise inanimate Kaʿba should be understood as the result of just such a bodily projection. (The projection would also account for the 'right and left hand', 'face' and 'rear' of the Kaʿba discussed in Chapter Two.) At some point in time, a body must have been projected onto the Kaʿba. Indeed, as I shall explain, that body must be understood as the origin of the Kaʿba, the building being its spatialised proxy.

Developing this suggestion, I shall argue in what follows below that the Kaʿba's belly and back represent (1) the primordial differentiation of space into an interior and an exterior, and (2) the origin of the binary concept of inside/outside that this differentiation gave rise to. So what? As I shall argue, because the differentiation of space happened in primordial time, long before the advent of Islam, that means that references in Islamic thought to the concept of inside/outside (*baṭn/ẓahr*) and the related concept of inward/outward (*bāṭin/ẓāhir*) are also references to the Kaʿba. Therein, I shall conclude, lies the fourth reason why destructions of the Kaʿba are not mourned in the way that destructions of the Temple are. Regardless of what physical Kaʿba structure stands or lies in ruin at Mecca, the bodily projected Kaʿba structure lives on in the structure of Islamic thought.

Given the argument's conjectural nature and reliance on Lakoff and Johnson's philosophy of embodied cognition and the still under-theorised ways that architecture helps makes concepts thinkable,[90] not everyone will be convinced by it. Hopefully, however, those same individuals will nevertheless concede that Terry Allen is correct when he writes that arguments not exclusively built on empirical data can 'give us ideas to critique and thus help us gain further insight'.[91] The same individuals might also turn to the work of Mitchell Schwarzer, who, without referring to cognitive philosophy, has argued for a relationship between the Jewish Temple and the Talmud, the collective memory of the former structuring the latter.[92]

Qurʾanic hermeneutics

According to a Qurʾanic verse, the Kaʿba is humanity's first house. The verse reads: 'The first House (*awwal Bayt*) established for mankind was that at [Mecca], a place of blessing and a guidance for all beings.'[93] Elsewhere in the Qurʾan, as noted in the Introduction, the Kaʿba is named the Ancient House (*al-Bayt al-ʿAtīq*). The verse asserts the Kaʿba's absolute architectural primordiality; the name echoes this primordiality, but does not denote it.

This Qurʾanic assertion of the House's architectural primordiality should be read to mean that the Kaʿba – as it is represented in the Qurʾan – is the result of the primordial projection of the body onto space: the moment when back and belly were first spatialised, simultaneously entering thought as the concept of inside/outside. Returning briefly to the parallel we saw earlier between the Kaʿba and Fāṭima bt. Asad's pregnant belly, it is hard to imagine a more iconic form of this concept than the Kaʿba, curtained and closed. The form almost bespeaks the Qurʾan's description of the womb: 'a threefold darkness'.[94]

There is nothing new about the idea of a building resulting from the projection of the body onto space; it dates from at least the time of Vitruvius.[95] There is also nothing culturally specific about the idea either, because the early Islamic sources attribute the design and construction of Islam's first house to Islam's first human, Adam, though with angelic assistance:

> Then God revealed to Adam: I have a sacred territory around My Throne. Go and build a house for Me there! . . . Adam said: My Lord! How could I do that? I do not have the strength to do it and do not know how. So God chose an angel to assist him, and he went with him toward Mecca . . . He built the House with (materials from) five mountains: Mount Sinai, the Mount of Olives, (Mount) Lebanon and al-Jūdī, and he constructed its foundations with (materials from Mount) Ḥirāʾ (near Mecca). When he finished with its construction, the angel went out with him to ʿArafāt.[96]

Given conceptual structure by their spatialised proxy the Kaʿba, belly and back, inside and outside, entered early Qurʾanic hermeneutics. As reported by al-Ṭabarī and others, the Prophet is alleged to have said: 'The Qurʾan was sent down in seven modes (*aḥruf*). Each mode has an exterior [literally, back (*ẓahr*)] and an interior [literally, belly (*baṭn*)].'[97] As reported by al-Qāḍī al-Nuʿmān (d. 363/974) and others, the Prophet is also alleged to have said: 'Not a verse of the Qurʾan has been revealed to me without it having an exterior [literally, back] and an interior [literally, belly].'[98]

On the basis of these and related hadiths, the Qurʾanic hermeneutic binary regarding a verse's symbolic, inward meaning and its literal, outward meaning developed.[99] This inward/outward (*bāṭin/ẓāhir*) binary derives, I argue, from the belly and back's spatialised proxy, the Kaʿba.[100]

The binary's importance to Islamic thought, not just Qurʾanic hermeneutics, can scarcely be overstated. According to Shahab Ahmed, it additionally allowed for (1) the inherent spatiality of revelation (*tanzīl, waḥy*) to be presented as the Qurʾanic categories of the Unseen (*al-Ghayb*) and the Seen (*al-Shahāda*), and (2) the transposition of this inherent spatiality 'into the exteriority and interiority of physical and social space'.[101]

There is, of course, no way of empirically proving the foregoing argument. However, given the generally negative view of the belly in the Qurʾan and Islamic thought, its pivotal place in Qurʾanic hermeneutics is perhaps a little strange. Its place there is perhaps only conceivable because of the belly's place at the Kaʿba, where, as we saw earlier, it is a term for the House's interior, its *baṭn*.

As noted above, Baṭn Makka is a toponym for the Kaʿba's precise location in Mecca: the 'Belly of Mecca'. As with the term used for the Kaʿba's interior, *baṭn al-Kaʿba*, this toponym surely precedes Islam. This is so, not just because Chabbi says that the toponym 'belongs to the very rich, ancient Arabic terminology of locations that are hollow and humid',[102] but because with the advent of the Qurʾan the belly receives a new toponymic usage, becoming a prime site of damnation and punishment.[103] In recurring phrases such as 'their bellies stuffed with hellish fruit' (Q 37:66, 56:53) and 'their bellies devouring nothing but fire' (Q 2:174, 4:10), the Qurʾan associates the belly with punishments in hell. This association is unquestionably uneven, however, because the Qurʾan also speaks positively of the belly. Honey, for example, described by the Qurʾan as 'a drink of . . . healing', is said to come from the bellies of bees (Q 16:69).

With the development of Islam, the belly even becomes a sign of fallen humanity. Before the Fall, Adam is said to have had an internal cavity (*jawf*), which distinguished him from God, who was solid (*al-Ṣamad*).[104] This cavity did not, however, function as a stomach. Only when Adam was cast out of Eden did it start functioning in that way, because hunger pangs struck him, as did the need to defecate. As al-Ḥasan al-Baṣrī (d. 110/728) relates this occurrence: 'When Adam came down into this world, the first thing he did was expel faeces.'[105]

Later in Islamic religious thought, at least as this thought is expressed by al-Ghazālī, the human body's interior as a whole, its *bāṭin*, is moralised negatively in opposition to its exterior, or *ẓāhir*. In al-Ghazālī's words:

> God made the repugnant parts (*maqābiḥ*) of the servant's body, which the eyes find repulsive, to be hidden in the servant's interior, covered over by the beauty of his exterior. In terms of cleanliness and filthiness (*qadhāra*), repulsiveness and beauty, how great [the difference] between the exterior of a servant and his interior![106]

It is hard to imagine the term 'belly' being used for sites of such importance as the Kaʿba's location and interior once it had been moralised so negatively. The nomenclature of those sites, therefore, is likely to have preceded the Qurʾan and Islam. The Qurʾanic hermeneutic binary that partly derives from the term 'belly' was possibly immune to this negativity because of the pedigree of its Kaʿba-based genealogy.[107]

Conclusion

This chapter began with a question, namely, how have the various destructions of the Kaʿba that have occurred or are alleged to have occurred throughout its history not occasioned the kind of apocalyptic fear and grief that were occasioned by the destructions of the Jewish Temple as recounted in the Bible? As the Muslims' *axis mundi*, one might have expected that when the Kaʿba was destroyed, the world it centred would be experienced as shaken, if not entirely thrown off true.

Four explanations were advanced in answer to this question. First, the signs of the apocalypse are established in prophetic hadiths, and none of the destructions of the Kaʿba fitted those signs. Second, the unearthly foundations of the Kaʿba are what count as the *axis mundi*, not what is erected upon them. Those foundations are the remains of the prototypical Kaʿba, and they endure, having never been destroyed. Third, in Sufism the Kaʿba is frequently spoken of as having two earthly forms: the base, stone Kaʿba of Mecca and the noble, corporeal Kaʿba of the heart. For the proponents of that division, so long as the corporeal one is preserved, what happens to the other one is of minimal concern. Fourth, on the basis of what I argued concerning the Kaʿba's function of facilitating abstract thought by having primordially structured fundamental, bodily derived concepts for that thought – for example, inside/outside, left/right and front/rear – the Kaʿba is as much an intellectual phenomenon as a material, ruin-prone object. Again, therefore, it is insignificant if the material Kaʿba falls into ruin, because the concept-facilitating Kaʿba lives on in Quraʾnic hermeneutics, for example.

CHAPTER FOUR

The Kaʿba as Beloved

This chapter concerns the principal ritual regarding the Kaʿba, the *ṭawāf*, or sevenfold circumambulation of the House, without which no pilgrimage to Mecca is valid. Although entering the Kaʿba is permissible, if restricted, no ritual is prescribed for the interior. Rather, the exterior of the Kaʿba is where the rituals are performed, principally the obligatory *ṭawāf*, but also the recommended pressing of one's body against the *Multazam*, a section of wall commonly identified as being between the door and the Black Stone. As I shall argue, in circling and hovering just outside the building in this way, the pilgrim temporarily fuses with Kaʿba; momentarily, the seeker and their goal, the 'lover' and the 'beloved', unite.

The chapter is in three parts. Part one describes the *ṭawāf* and looks at some of the meanings that have been attributed to the ritual. It examines an issue in Islamic studies of attributing meaning to ritual and relates it to a similar issue in Islamic architectural scholarship. This examination leads on to a discussion, first broached in the Introduction, of why the Kaʿba is all but absent in this scholarship and how this oversight is unjustifiable from the perspective of both Islamic tradition and Islamic architectural inscriptions. Part two refers to early, medieval and pre-modern pilgrims' experiential accounts of the *ṭawāf* so as to investigate, with regard to the Kaʿba, what Lindsay Jones calls the 'ritual-architectural event' of architecture. Ibn ʿArabī's account forms the core of this investigation. Part three takes its findings and, in the light of them, reviews an important and well-known academic work regarding the Kaʿba as a bride.

Part One: *Ṭawāf* and the Meaning of Architecture

The *ṭawāf*, from the Arabic verb *ṭawāfa*, 'to go about', is a ritual specific to the Kaʿba, where it involves the sevenfold circumambulation of the House's walls and semicircular *Ḥijr*. It is not limited in the number of times a pilgrim can perform it; rather, as the Moroccan traveller Ibn Baṭṭūṭa (d. 770/1369 or 778/1377) observed during his time in Mecca, some people perform it almost ceaselessly. This is an obsession that can end up in divorce, as he himself witnessed.[1]

Depending on when the *ṭawāf* is performed, its preconditions vary with respect to whether or not the pilgrim should be in their pilgrimage vestment, the *iḥrām*.[2] The one precondition that is all but invariable, however, is that the pilgrim must be ritually clean (*ṭāhir*), exactly as for the Islamic ritual prayer, to which the *ṭawāf* is compared. In the words of a hadith: 'The *ṭawāf* is a ritual prayer.'[3] Similarly, although one or two elements in its execution vary according to when it is performed, and the embellishments of this execution also vary from one authority to another (principally, what supplications should be uttered and where), among its few invariable rules are the following; first, each of its seven circuits begins and ends at the Black Stone corner; second, it is an anticlockwise movement; third, its orbit never gets sufficiently restricted in radius to allow the circling pilgrim to touch the sloping base of the Kaʿba, the *Shādharwān*;[4] fourth, for reasons that will be explained later, it never includes the semicircular *Ḥijr.*

As an example of how these rules are expressed and embellished by Islamic authorities (*fuqahāʾ*), quoted at length below is al-Ghazālī (d. 505/1111) from his chapter on the Hajj in his major work, *Iḥyāʾ ʿulūm al-dīn* ('Revival of the religious sciences'):

> If the pilgrim intends to start the *ṭawāf* . . . first he must observe the conditions of ritual prayer, such as the absence of all ritual defilement and filth on the clothing, body, and location, as well as the covering of nakedness . . . Then he is to put the House on his left and stand by the Black Stone . . . He should leave between him and the House a space of three strides so as not to be near to . . . the *Shādharwān* . . . Let him say . . . at the beginning of the *ṭawāf*: 'In the name of God. God is the most great. O God, I believe in You and have trust in Your Book and in fulfilment of Your Covenant and in following the Sunna of Your Prophet Muḥammad, the blessing and peace of God be upon him.' Then he begins the *ṭawāf*. As soon as he passes by the House, he says: 'O God, this House is Your House and this Sanctuary is Your Sanctuary, and this Security is Your Security, and this is the station of the one who seeks refuge in You from the Fire.' When reciting the [word] 'station' (*maqām*), he points with his eyes to the Station of Abraham. [He continues]: 'O God, Your House is great and Your Countenance is gracious and You are the most merciful of those who show mercy. Protect me from the Fire and Satan the Accursed, make my flesh and my blood inviolable against the Fire, and save me from the terror of the Day of Judgment, and make sufficient for me the provisions of this world and the hereafter.' Then he glorifies God and praises Him until he reaches the *ʿIrāqī* corner, where he says: 'O God, I seek refuge with You from idolatry and doubt and unbelief and hypocrisy and discord and immorality and the evil eye in respect of [my] family, [my] wealth and [my] children.' Then, when he reaches the [golden rainspout], the *Mīzāb*, he says: 'O God, shade us under Your Throne on the day when there is no shadow except yours. O God, offer me a drink from the cup of Muḥammad, the blessing and peace of God be upon him, a drink that will quench my thirst for ever.' And when he reaches the *Shāmī* corner, he says: 'O God, make this an accepted

pilgrimage and a praised one; and cause the endeavour therein to be rewarded, and sin to be forgiven, and let not the profit perish, O the Almighty, the Forgiver. O Lord, forgive, show mercy and pardon me whatever [sins] You know of. You are the most mighty, the most beneficent.' When he reaches the *Yamānī* corner, he says: 'O God, I seek refuge in You from unbelief, and I seek refuge in You from poverty, from the punishment of the grave and from the trial of life and death. I seek refuge in You from the disgrace of this world and of the hereafter.' And [while he is] between the *Yamānī* corner and the Black Stone, he says: 'Our Lord, grant us good in this world as well as good in the world to come, and protect us with Your mercy against the trial of the grave and the torment of the Fire.' And when he reaches the Black Stone, he says: 'O God, forgive me through Your mercy. I seek refuge in the Lord of this Stone from debt and poverty and from sadness and the torment of the grave.' With this, one circuit has been completed. He is to circumambulate seven times in the same manner and repeat the same invocations during each circuit.[5]

The meaning of ṭawāf

If the term *ṭawāf* is specific to the Kaʿba, circumambulation of an object deemed sacred is not unique to it, nor is it something performed by Muslims only at Mecca. Rather, it is widely attested to in pre-Islamic times;[6] it is practised by Muslims at numerous other sites in the Islamic world, although unlawfully in the eyes of most jurists;[7] and it is practised by members of other world religions at many more sites.[8]

As a general religious phenomenon, the origins of circumambulation are said to lie in the imitation of the apparent movement of the sun.[9] With specific regard to the *ṭawāf*, this explanation finds only limited support in Islamic tradition, where instead a different origin theory has greater traction. As recorded by al-Azraqī, the *ṭawāf* allegedly originated as the motion of angels about God's Throne (*al-ʿArsh*), in humble contrition at having angered God by questioning His decision to make Adam vice-regent on earth.[10] Begging and weeping, they circled and circled the Throne, until finally God forgave them and additionally instructed them to circle the celestial Kaʿba, the Frequented House.[11] Thereafter, Adam, and eventually humankind as a whole, imitated this angelic motion at the earthly Kaʿba.[12]

Notwithstanding the preponderance of this origin story in Islamic culture, a degree of support for the solar explanation of circumambulation can, however, be found in the work of the mystic Ibn ʿArabī, for whom the *ṭawāf* resembles the motion of the planetary spheres (*aflāk*).[13] Diverging from both these theories, some Western academics have supposed the origins of *ṭawāf* to lie in an ancient Semitic mourning rite.[14]

It is not hard to understand the range of these explanations if one puts oneself in the place of the anthropologist Abdellah Hammoudi when he was visiting the Sacred Mosque during the Hajj. In his memoirs of this visit, he explains that he was one day looking down at the circling pilgrims from the upper gallery of the Mosque, when he experienced the following:

> I could feel my legs trembling, and [my companion] started to weep. I was overcome by a feeling of slight vertigo, similar to what I feel when I look into bottomless water where one can guess at deep, savage currents beneath the surface calm. I was shaking, and my heart was beating unsteadily. I recognized the mounting anxiety, the feeling that gripped me at moments of extreme attraction, which I knew was dangerous. Perhaps this was the meaning, forgotten today, of the state of religious awe.[15]

Seeing such a sight and experiencing such a range of emotions, one might very well begin to speculate about the origins of this ritual and search for its meaning. Nevertheless, finding the putative meaning of the *ṭawāf* is not the aim of this chapter, for the reasons given immediately below.

The meaning of ritual

Prior to the modern period, Islamic authorities with little or no commitment to mysticism generally assert that the rituals of the Hajj, including the *ṭawāf*, are incomprehensible and unfathomable in their meaning.[16] For these authorities, the rituals belong to the non-rational rules of worship called *taʿabbudāt* and so have no symbolic, or referential, communicative content, being instead a demonstration of obedience.[17] As William Graham asserts regarding Islamic ritual in general: 'It is fundamentally aniconic, amythical, and commemorative or traditionalist in character.'[18]

An ethnographic instance of Graham's assertion is provided by al-Ghazālī in his aforementioned chapter on the Hajj. Al-Ghazālī writes:

> As for understanding [the Hajj], know that God assigned to it . . . rituals (*aʿmāl*) . . . whose meanings no minds can detect (*lā yahtadī ilā maʿānīhā al-ʿuqūl*), such as casting stones at the *Jamra* pillars and running to and fro repeatedly between [the Sanctuary's two hills] Ṣafā and Marwa.[19] By such rituals, complete bondage and servitude is shown (*yaẓharu kamāl al-riqq wa al-ʿubūdiyya*) . . . There is no motive to perform them except that doing so is the very command [of God] because it is a command that necessitates compliance only.[20]

Glossing the rationale behind al-Ghazālī's words, Marion Katz explains: 'Pure submission [to God's command] can only be diluted by one's understanding or approval of the commanded act.'[21]

The same rationale is also evident in the words of the jurist al-Sarakhsī (d. *c.*483/1090) regarding the pilgrimage ritual known as the *saʿy:* the running to and fro between the hills of the Sanctuary, Ṣafā and Marwa. As al-Sarakhsī explains, although some people have opined that the *saʿy* has a referential meaning, namely, Hagar's desperate search for water in the desert (because whenever Hagar lost sight of her infant, Ismaʿil, she would run until she could see him again), this opinion is unsound. The sounder opinion is to see the action as something the Prophet did and ordered his Companions to do, and thus something all Muslims do in obedient imitation.[22] Al-Sarakhsī concludes: 'We should not busy ourselves seeking a meaning in it, just as we do not busy ourselves seeking a meaning in the *ṭawāf* and *saʿy* being repeated seven times.'[23] Partly on the basis of this passage from al-Sarakhsī, the passage from al-Ghazālī, and from others,[24] the putative meaning of the *ṭawāf* will not be pursued in this chapter.

In addition to this reason for not pursuing the putative meaning of the *ṭawāf*, a second reason exists. Expecting this and other Islamic rituals to have an intended meaning is as debatable as expecting a building to have an intended meaning. With regard to the study of Islamic ritual, just such an expectation has been the predominant trend in scholarship of recent years.[25] The same is true with regard to the study of Islamic architecture, recent or otherwise.[26] This is problematic. What follows is an exploration of the problem.

The meaning of architecture

As argued by the philosopher Henri Lefebvre, a building has a *horizon of meaning*: a 'specific or indefinite multiplicity of meanings'.[27] These meanings are momentary, triggered by particular actions about and inside the building. They are also experiential, bound to the acting subject. Accordingly, what the architect or patron intended as the meaning of their building is just one of its meanings. Compounding matters, this intended meaning rarely survives beyond a certain period, in part because of the absence in Islamic culture of formal institutions that preserve this meaning and convey it across time and space.[28]

Lefebvre is not alone in arguing for this approach to the meaning of architecture. Lindsay Jones, for example, calls the momentary meaning generated by the acting subject the 'ritual-architectural event' of architecture. Adhering to the hermeneutical tradition of Continental philosophy, he explains this event as follows:

> [T]he locus of meaning resides neither in the building itself (a physical object) nor in the mind of the beholder (a human subject), but rather in the negotiation or the interactive relation that subsumes both building and beholder – in *the ritual-architectural event* in which buildings and human participants alike are involved.[29]

Because the ritual-architectural event is transformative of the acting subject, Jones argues, it allows for neither the disinterested viewing of architecture nor the aesthetic judgements that result from this approach to architecture.[30] For Jones, therefore, scholars of architecture who take buildings as autonomous objects to be viewed by autonomous subjects (themselves), and who suppose that meaning is inherent to buildings, miss what occasions the meaning of architecture.[31]

The curious invisibility of the Kaʿba

As Jones readily admits, there is nothing new about his approach to architecture.[32] Even so, to the best of my knowledge, such an approach has only once been adopted in the study of early to pre-modern Islamic architecture.[33] Although this dearth can partly be explained by the fact that texts recounting an individual's experience of this or that building are few and far between for the periods prior to modernity, it sheds additional light on why the Kaʿba has merited such little attention in Islamic architectural scholarship. When architecture is approached in the belief that meaning is inherent to it, tied to the intentions of the patron builders, the Kaʿba inevitably falls off the radar.[34] As noted in the Introduction, what is one to do with a building whose patron is said to be God and its builder Abraham or Adam? Grabar reveals exactly this predicament when he says, without apparent irony: '[The Kaʿba] is in a way an "uncreated" monument.'[35] The Kaʿba, we learn from Grabar, does not exist in an architectural way.

In another publication, the influential *The Formation of Islamic Art*, Grabar refers to the Kaʿba as 'but a parallelepiped without decoration or formally composed parts like doors and windows', one of the 'roughly mapped out and poorly constructed holy places' of pre- and early Islamic Central Arabia.[36] Admittedly, this judgement ostensibly pertains to the pre- and early Islamic Kaʿba, the period about which he is writing. However, because the judgement is explicitly tied to a photograph of the Kaʿba from the early twentieth century, and there is little or no reason to suppose that the Kaʿba of that period looked fundamentally different to earlier Islamic periods, the judgement is also a blanket judgement. It is echoed in the judgement that he and Ettinghausen propound in their survey textbook, where they write: '[The Kaʿba is] not too impressive as an architectural creation', as also mentioned in the Introduction.[37]

In these and other negative judgements, the currency and longevity of which should not be underestimated, lies another reason why the Kaʿba has received such little attention in Islamic architectural scholarship. The Kaʿba falls foul of the distinction, deeply embedded in the history of architectural scholarship, between architecture and building. Architecture has an aesthetic programme: it is designed, writes Sir Nikolaus Pevsner, 'with a view to aesthetic appeal'.[38] Building has function alone.[39]

It should go without saying that, unlike Grabar and Ettinghausen, pilgrims to Mecca have found the Kaʿba to be visually compelling.[40] Ibn Jubayr (d. 614/1217), for example, says this of his experience of seeing it: 'To look at the venerable House is terrifying. Souls know stupefaction; hearts and minds are lost.'[41] Even the explorer Richard Burton (d. 1890), who visited in disguise in 1853, found that 'the view was strange, unique'. He adds: 'Of all the worshippers who clung weeping to the curtain, or who pressed their beating hearts to the stone, none felt for the moment a deeper emotion than did [this pilgrim] from the far-north.'[42]

These and similar experiences help account for the following tradition, a disputed hadith: 'To gaze upon the inviolable House of God is an act of worship.'[43] In the light of this data, Grabar and Ettinghausen's opinion of the Kaʿba can only be considered parochial.

To emphasise this conclusion further, let us note that the huge, elaborate and decidedly impressive Süleymaniye Mosque in Istanbul is repeatedly compared in Ottoman sources to the Kaʿba; it is called, for example, the 'second Kaʿba', an epithet the sources also apply to the Hagia Sophia and the city's tenth/eighteenth-century Nuruosmaniye Mosque.[44] Another hallowed Ottoman mosque, the ninth/fifteenth-century Old Mosque, or *Eski Camii* in Edirne, is called the 'Kaʿba of Rūm'.[45] In Delhi, the earlier but no less hallowed Qutb Mosque is described as a 'second Kaʿba' in an inscription on one of its monumental doorways, the Alai Darwaza.[46] Similarly, an inscription over the doorway of the congregational mosque of Old Malda, Bengal, dating to 974/1567, refers to the building as the 'second Kaʿba'.[47] In Mashhad, the dome of the mid-ninth/fifteenth-century mosque known as the Masjid-i Shāh once carried an inscription comparing the building to the Kaʿba.[48] In the same century, at Ashtur in the district of Bidar, India, the mausoleum of Aḥmad Shāh Bahmanī (r. 825–39/1422–36) is compared to the Kaʿba, being called 'the Kaʿba of desires'.[49] In Lahore, the eleventh/seventeenth-century Wazir Khan Mosque has, on the right of the entrance, a *nastaʿlīq* faience panel in which the building is compared to the Kaʿba.[50] Indeed, in a chronogram of Lahore's Islamic foundation, the city as a whole is referred to as a Kaʿba.[51] In Agra in the same century, an inscription on the Motī Masjid calls the mosque 'this resplendent Kaʿba and second Frequented House'.[52] In Isfahan, the Safavid congregational mosque now called Masjid-i Imām is referred to as a 'second Kaʿba' in its foundation chronogram;[53] and in Ardabil, also in Iran, a tenth/sixteenth-century land register refers to the monumental tomb complex of the Safavid dynasty's eponymous founder, Shaykh Ṣafī al-Dīn (d. 735/1334), as the 'Kaʿba of hopes'.[54] In Fatimid panegyrics, the palace of the fourth/tenth-century city of Mahdia (*al-Mahdiyya*) in modern-day Tunisia is compared to the Kaʿba, as is the palace of *al-Manṣūriyya*.[55] In Norman Sicily, the Cappella Palatina is likened to the Kaʿba, indeed figured as the Kaʿba, with some of the rituals associated with the House perhaps also being performed there.[56] Finally, in Samarra, the ʿAbbasid palaces are related to aspects of the Kaʿba, with the court poet al-Buhṭurī (d. 284/897) referring to them as 'marvels constructed for the first of God's servants with the Corner [of the Kaʿba], [the Sanctuary's hill] Ṣafā, and the Station [of Abraham]'.[57]

Of course, the comparative gestures these extravagant, splendid buildings make or are reported to make in deference to the Kaʿba are a type of lip-service, a formality presumably transparent to many audiences reading them. Even so, these gestures were made; and they were made because at a profound level of the Islamic world the Kaʿba is architecture without compare.

An Islamic building

Returning once more to the subject of why the Kaʿba has received such little attention in Islamic architectural scholarship, a final reason is the widespread notion that the Kaʿba is not an Islamic but a pre-Islamic building and so cannot belong to the canon of Islamic art and architecture. As we have already had occasion to see in Chapter Three regarding the allegedly Abrahamic and earlier foundations of the Kaʿba, this reason is not altogether wrong. However, as we also saw there with regard to the reconstructions of the building by both Ibn al-Zubayr and al-Ḥajjāj b. Yūsuf in the first century of Islam, neither is it altogether correct.

More compellingly, the early Islamic sources represent Muḥammad helping to transform an early, pre-Islamic form of the Kaʿba (Figure I.1, a) into the cuboid form for which the main structure of the Islamic-period Kaʿba is known (Figure I.1, b). Insofar as we can be sure, the main structure of this rebuilt Kaʿba was a few metres shorter than that of the Islamic period Kaʿba (Figure I.1, c, d), but otherwise formally the same. In other words, in the early sources the future prophet of Islam is represented as a builder of the proto-Islamic Kaʿba. The sources report him, for example, transporting the stones required for the rebuilding; so committed is he to this labour, that his clothing rides up and he is reprimanded with the words: 'Muḥammad! Your modesty (*ʿawratuka*)!'[58] More tellingly, they report that it is he whom providence selects for the solemn honour of returning the Black Stone to its corner when the rebuilding is almost complete (Figure 4.1).[59]

Given the importance of the Black Stone to both the Kaʿba and the *ṭawāf*, Muḥammad's selection for this task cannot be considered mere happenstance, especially when taken in conjunction with another report

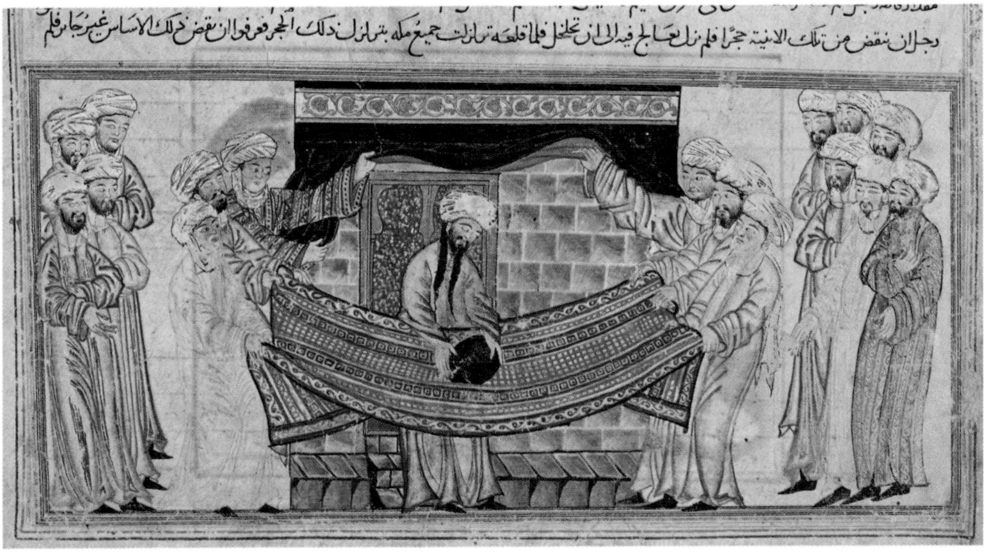

Figure 4.1 *The Prophet returns the Black Stone to the rebuilt Kaʿba. From the Arabic manuscript of the* Jāmiʿ al-tawārīkh *('Compendium of chronicles') by Rashīd al-Dīn (d.* 718/1318*), dated* 705/1306 *or* 714/1314. *Gold, gouache and ink on paper;* 33.5 × 44*cm (folio). Courtesy: The University of Edinburgh Library, Or. Ms* 20, *fol.* 45*r. © The University of Edinburgh.*

concerning the Black Stone. This reports states that when the Quraysh, Muḥammad's tribe, were dismantling what remained of the Kaʿba in order to build it anew, at the back of the Black Stone they found an inscription (*kitāb*) saying:

> I am God, Master of Mecca. I created [this Black Stone] on the day I created the earth and the heavens, the day I gave form to the sun and the moon. I surrounded it with seven angels, guardians of the pure religion. It will endure as long as the two mountains [of Mecca] endure, blessing its people with water and milk.[60]

The content of these and similar reports from the early Islamic sources suggest that they form part of an Islamic foundation legend that (1) promotes Muḥammad and his tribe as builders of the Kaʿba, (2) links the same people to the Kaʿba's first builders, Adam and Abraham, and (3) thereby heralds a new prophetic age.[61] The clearest indication of this foundation legend comes in another early report regarding the Quraysh's reconstruction of the Kaʿba. The report says that at this time there emerged from the base of the dismantled Kaʿba a goat-headed, white-bellied, black-backed serpent. Having just transported the stones required for the reconstruction, the people saw this fearsome creature and retreated in prayer, assuring God that they wanted only to build His House. Thereupon, a yellow-legged, white-bellied, black-backed bird appeared and carried off the serpent. The Prophet and his tribe could now build.[62] A new era had dawned.[63]

Part Two: Experiencing the *Ṭawāf*

That the exterior and not the interior of the Kaʿba is the focus of the *ṭawāf* ritual is clear from the obligatory and recommended rules for the ritual's performance discussed earlier. Never do the circling pilgrims go inside but remain outside, where they effectively trace the House's exterior by punctuating their revolutions with supplications uttered at the four corners. Should they happen to enter the gap between the Kaʿba itself and the semicircular *Ḥijr*, their *ṭawāf* is invalidated. Related to this proscription is another against the revolving pilgrims' touching or being near enough to touch the sloping base of the Kaʿba, the *Shādharwān*, including its imagined vertical elevation. This base, later clad with marble, is said to have formed the base of the Kaʿba's original walls at the time of its reconstruction by Muḥammad and his tribe, at which point the breadth of the building above the base was allegedly slightly reduced, thereby giving the base its slope.[64] This slope means that too great a proximity to the *Shādharwān* effectively places a pilgrim inside the Kaʿba and thus in violation of the Qurʾan's stipulation: 'Let [the pilgrims] turn about the Ancient House.'[65]

Samer Akkach describes well this exteriority of the circling pilgrims etching in space the Kaʿba's form. With reference to the supplications uttered at the House's four corners, he says: 'These utterances punctuate the continuity of the ritual revolution, marking four distinct points that correspond to the four directions of space determined by the four corners of the Kaʿba.'[66] In differentiating the Kaʿba's four near-cardinal directions this way, he argues, the pilgrims qualify space.[67] The historical diagram reproduced below visualises this process (Figure 4.2).

Anonymously created in Aceh, Indonesia, in the late thirteenth/nineteenth century by a 'humble mendicant for its owner, Teungku Imam Beutong', the diagram shows at its centre the Kaʿba in side view and the *Ḥijr* in top view.[68] In the form of text blocks that echo, or more precisely, reiterate the shape of the building, the appropriate supplicatory utterance for each different moment of the *ṭawāf* is given at each of the Kaʿba's corners, its golden rainspout and the Station of Abraham. This 'songline', if one might borrow that term from the indigenous Australians, begins with the pilgrim's statement of intention (*niyya*) at the bottom left-hand corner of the Kaʿba; immediately above it is the greeting for the Black Stone, and so forth. Other approximately thirteenth/nineteenth-century examples of the 'songline' exist, not all of them from South East Asia.[69]

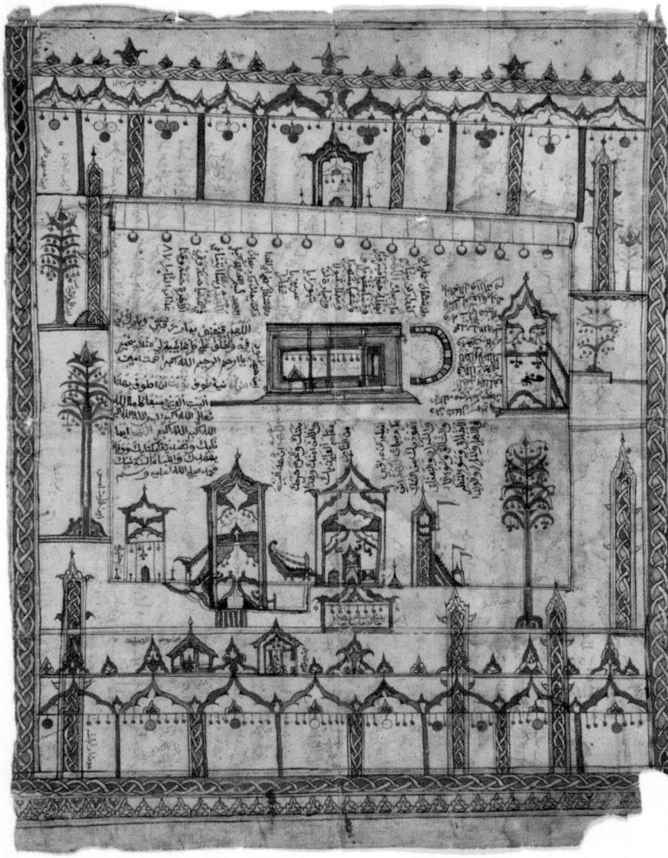

Figure 4.2 *Diagram of the Sacred Mosque from Aceh, Indonesia, with inscriptions in Malay and Arabic identifying the different parts of the Kaʿba's exterior and specifying the supplication to be uttered at each. Dated to before 1273/1876; gouache and ink on paper; 32.5 × 42.5cm. Courtesy: Collection Nationaal Museum van Wereldculturen, Amsterdam. Coll. no. TM-A-5992.*

Ibn ʿArabī's experience of the ṭawāf

Before the modern period, there are precious few experiential accounts of the *ṭawāf*.[70] Given the foregoing discussion of the meaning of architecture in which I argued that a building's meaning was tied to the person experiencing it, this paucity is a drawback. Fortunately, in the voluminous writings of the mystic Ibn ʿArabī there is a particularly detailed account of what he experienced when he performed the *ṭawāf* during his first visit to Mecca in 598/1202. His account will therefore form the core of this chapter's analysis of the experiential dimensions of the *ṭawāf*.

Ibn 'Arabī made three visits to Mecca, in 598/1202, 603/1207 and 610/1214 respectively, but whenever he performed the *ṭawāf* he started and stopped no differently to the circling pilgrim imagined in the above diagram.[71] Additionally, although his account of what he experienced when performing the *ṭawāf* is considerably more informative than any other account of the same ritual before the modern period, the fact that it relates extraordinary, supernatural phenomena is not exceptional, as the following historical review will show.

Long before Ibn 'Arabī's performance of the *ṭawāf*, al-Junayd (d. 298/910) had cautioned a pilgrim who had performed the *ṭawāf*, but had not experienced supernatural phenomena, as having not done the *ṭawāf* at all. Their exchange is reported as follows, with al-Junayd speaking first: '"When you performed the *ṭawāf* of the House did you see the immaterial beauty of God in the locus of transcendence (*maḥall-i tanzīh*)?" "No." "Then you have not performed the *ṭawāf*."'[72]

Abū al-Ḥasan al-Nūrī (d. 295/907), a contemporary of al-Junayd, would have needed no such cautioning when performing the *ṭawāf* – at least, not on the basis of this experience:

> I heard a voice proceeding from the midst of the Ka'ba, saying: 'Abū [al-Ḥasan], you would make yourself equal to Me. I change not from My attribute, but I keep My servants turning about and changing.'[73]

Bāyazīd Bisṭāmī (d. 234/848 or 261/875) would have needed no such cautioning either. He says of his *ṭawāf* experience: 'For a while I performed the *ṭawāf* about the House. When I attained the Truth (*Ḥaqq rasīdam*), I saw that the House was performing the *ṭawāf* about me.'[74]

As a brief aside to this review, Bāyazīd Bisṭāmī's experience of the Ka'ba circumambulating him is not unique to this mystic; rather, it is common to a number of mystics.[75] Included amongst these individuals is Abū Sa'īd b. Abī al-Khayr (d. 440/1049), who once told an audience that the celestial Ka'ba circumambulated him several times daily; he then proved it to them.[76] Included, too, is Sayyid Amīr Kulāl (d. 772/1371), whose companions once witnessed the Ka'ba circumambulating him; Rūmī (d. 671/1273), whose companions once saw the House circumambulating him, 'visibly and in certainty, without any doubt and conjecture';[77] and Rābi'a al-'Adawiyya (d. 175/801).[78] A Mughal miniature of the latter's experience is reproduced below (Figure 4.3).[79] In it, we see people in the Sacred Mosque, imagined as a Mughal fort, gesticulating in wonder and surprise that the Ka'ba should have risen off its base and gone about Rābi'a.

Also concerning the circumambulating Ka'ba, *pace* some interpretations the experience of the Ka'ba revolving about a mystic does not necessarily mean that the Ka'ba is thereby devalued, as if the mystic held him or

***Figure* 4.3** *Rābiʿa al-ʿAdawiyya prays at the Kaʿba, which has departed from its base in the Sacred Mosque and circled her. From a copy of the* Khamsa *('Quintet') by Mīr ʿAlī Shīr Nawāʾī (d. 906/1501). The Chaghatay text box reads: 'From weakness she had become so unable / [That] the Kaʿba was turning around her.' Dated to after* 1013/1605; *gold, gouache and ink on paper;* 23 × 34.4*cm (folio). Courtesy: Royal Collection Trust / © Her Majesty Queen Elizabeth II* 2016. *RCIN* 1005032.

herself to be more spiritual and less material than the building.[80] As I shall argue below in connection to the *ṭawāf* of Ibn ʿArabī, in performing the *ṭawāf* the pilgrim temporarily fuses with the building. This fusion means that, from the perspective of the Kaʿba, the building does indeed seem to be turning about the mystic; but from the perspective of the mystic, he or she seems to be turning about the Kaʿba. There is no hierarchy.

Returning to the review of supernatural phenomena occurring in relation to the *ṭawāf*, in the period known in Shiʿism as the Minor Occultation, commonly dated 260–329/874–941, at least two individuals are reported to have seen the Mahdi when performing the *ṭawāf*.[81] These reports note that the Mahdi took the form of a beautiful youth, a form that surely has significant resonance with the mysterious youth whom, as we shall read below, Ibn ʿArabī saw when performing the *ṭawāf*.

Approximately two centuries after these reports, Rūzbihān Baqlī (d. 605/1209), experienced a dream in which he was at the Sacred Mosque watching the Prophet perform the *ṭawāf* in the company of angels and other prophets. As he watched, so 'the Truth (*al-Ḥaqq*), glory be to Him, manifested Himself inside the Kaʿba, with the attributes of beauty, glory, and majesty'.[82] Elements of this experience are reminiscent, albeit in an inverted form, of the hadith in which the Prophet is said either to have dreamt of being at the Kaʿba or to have been asleep while circumambulating the Kaʿba, when he saw the Messiah performing the *ṭawāf*. Behind the Messiah, the hadith alleges, gripping the Messiah's shoulders, followed the false Messiah, the Antichrist al-Dajjāl.[83]

Lastly in this review, in the eleventh/seventeenth century the following supernatural events are recorded as occurring during the performance of the *ṭawāf*. One Mirzā Muḥammad al-Astarābādī (d. 1028/1619), a Shiʿite Muslim, is reported to have seen the Mahdi, again in the form of a beautiful youth, when performing the *ṭawāf*.[84] Muḥammad Maʿsūm (d. 1079/1668), son of the celebrated Mughal scholar and Sufi, Aḥmad Sirhindī (d. 1034/1624), is reported to have experienced feeling hugged by the Kaʿba and seeing the world illuminated by a light emitted from his body when performing the *ṭawāf*.[85] A few decades later, the Ottoman scholar and Sufi, İsmail Hakkı Bursevī (d. 1137/1725), spoke of how, when performing the *ṭawāf*, God told him: 'Greet the four caliphs; they are present here and now.'[86]

The foregoing examples of commonly shared experiences mean that Ibn ʿArabī's account cannot easily be dismissed as idiosyncratic and without bearing upon the *ṭawāf* of other pilgrims. As we shall shortly see, something truly extraordinary happened to Ibn ʿArabī when performing the *ṭawāf* during his first visit to Mecca. So transformative was this experience that he believed it occasioned the divine disclosure (pl. *futūḥāt*) of most of his magnum opus, *al-Futūḥāt al-makkiyya* ('The Meccan revelations').

'God,' he says 'disclosed to me most of what I have put down in this work when performing the *ṭawāf* of His House or [when] sitting staring at it.'[87] Notwithstanding this especially transformative *ṭawāf*, even a sober academic like the anthropologist Hammoudi, undertaking the Hajj to observe the Hajj, cannot help notice that something has altered in him as a result of having revolved about the House:

> Leaving the [Sacred Mosque], I couldn't help gazing at the black cube one last time . . . We [had] prayed turned toward it, but not within its walls, and we [had] revolved around it . . . A few moments later, going back to our lodgings, I felt clearly that something was missing. I missed the black cube I had left behind me. The memory I would preserve of it would be one of loss. It would thrust me into further wanderings, lead me onto unexpected paths. The black cube, and the image of the black cube, would remind me that I had lost something for all time and that it is written that I shall always seek it.[88]

Ibn 'Arabī's ṭawāf of 598/1202

> When I had arrived in Mecca . . . from time to time I would circumambulate His Ancient House. While I was circumambulating [it] and praising, glorifying, magnifying, and professing His unity, sometimes kissing and touching [the Black Stone and *Yamānī* corner] and sometimes cleaving to the *Multazam*, lo, perplexed at the Black Stone, I met the transient youth (*al-fatā al-fā'it*), the silent speaker, he who is neither living nor dying; the simple composite; the encompassing encompassed.[89]

Thus begins Ibn 'Arabī's account of the transformative experience he underwent when performing the *ṭawāf* during his first visit to Mecca in 598/1202. Although the miniature painting reproduced below (Figure 4.4) does not show Ibn 'Arabī's encounter with the 'transient youth', it does show his encounter with Niẓām: the woman who was to inspire another of Ibn 'Arabī's books, *Tarjumān al-ashwāq* ('The interpreter of ardent desires'). This encounter with Niẓām occurred in the same year as the encounter with the transient youth, also when he was performing the *ṭawāf*.[90]

The theophanic, mysterious and thus logically impenetrable aspects of Ibn 'Arabī's account of his experiences involving the transient youth, whose identity remains unclear but who is plausibly an epiphany of the Logos, have been discussed and interpreted by others.[91] So the aim of the present discussion is not to focus on those details, but to concentrate on the physical, bodily aspects of the account. These bodily aspects matter, not because they are transparent in meaning, if not in interpretation, but because they pertain to the corporeal, transformative effects of what we

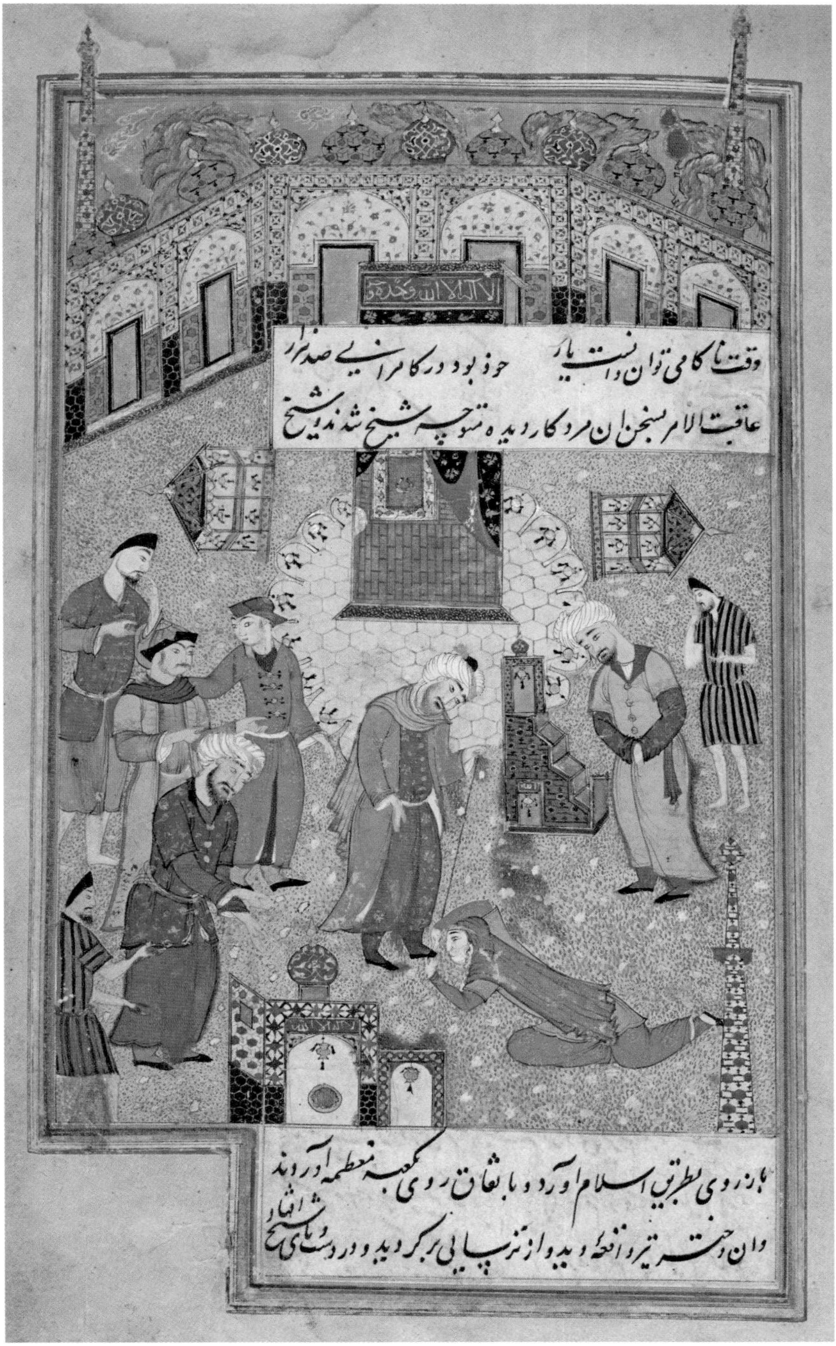

Figure 4.4 *Ibn ʿArabī encounters Niẓām at the Kaʿba. From a copy of* Majālis al-ʿushshāq *('Assemblies of the lovers') by Kamāl al-Dīn Ḥusayn Gāzargāhī (*fl. *tenth/sixteenth century), dated to* c.998/1590. *Gold and ink on paper; 18 × 27cm (folio). Courtesy: bpk / Museum für Islamische Kunst, Staatliche Museen zu Berlin / Georg Niedermeiser. I. 1986.229, fol. 84a (70158054).*

earlier called the ritual-architectural event of architecture, following the usage of Lindsay Jones. Additionally, although it would be nonsense to attribute to every circling pilgrim the theophanic quality of Ibn 'Arabī's experience, the sheer physicality of his experience is typical to most pilgrims, if only because performing the *ṭawāf* is widely regarded as bodily demanding.[92] This is especially so in the summer months and when the Sacred Mosque is full of other pilgrims trying to perform the same activity. This arduousness helps to explain why it is both legally permissible and commonplace for pilgrims to stop for a rest when performing the *ṭawāf*, subsequently resuming the ritual at the point and circuit number at which they had stopped.

Having now met this transient youth, Ibn 'Arabī thereafter keeps his company. In the next stage of the account, the youth takes the mystic out of himself:

> When . . . I had abutted the noble House . . . he seized me irresistibly from myself and spoke to me [this] dictum of scolding correction: 'Observe the inmost being (*sirr*) of the House before [its] evanescence! You will find it shining by way of [the pilgrims'] circling and performance of the *ṭawāf* about its stones. [This inmost being is] observing them behind its veils and screens.' Then I saw it shining, just as he had said.[93]

A moment of even greater physical intensity soon follows:

> I kissed [the youth's] right hand and wiped from his brow the perspiration of inspiration, and I said to him: 'Behold [this] petitioner of your company and seeker of your intimacy!' With gestures and riddles, he instructed me that it was not in his nature to address anyone except with signs. [He said:] 'When you know my sign, and have verified and understood it, you will know that the fluency of the fluent ones does not comprehend it and that its utterance is not disclosed by the eloquence of the eloquent ones.' I said to him: 'O messenger of good news, this is all a considerable good! But acquaint me with your code and instruct me how to turn your key! For truly, I want your eventide conversation and to belong to your family' . . . So he instructed [me] and then I knew. And he showed me the reality of his beauty, and I was frantic and fell to the floor. In an instant he had overcome me. When I got up from the swoon, my shoulder muscles shuddered in fear.[94]

Recovering from his collapse, Ibn 'Arabī is told by the youth:

> Circumambulate my vestige (*athar*) [viz., the Ka'ba] and look at me through the light of my moon until you have taken from my constitution what you will write in your book and what you will dictate to your copyists. Tell me the subtleties of what God (*al-Ḥaqq*) called upon you to witness in your circumambulation, things not seen by every circling pilgrim, so that I know your

> heart's creativity and your meaning (*himmataka wa maʿnāka*).[95] For I shall remember you according to what I learn from you there.[96]

Ibn ʿArabī does as he is instructed, and reports to the youth what he has learnt in circumambulating the House.

Ibn ʿArabī then performs the *ṭawāf* one last time, except that on this final occasion, after completing each of the requisite seven circuits, he and the youth undergo a bodily transformation (*taḥawwul*), so that by the end of this *ṭawāf* they have each gone through seven changes of form (*ṣūra*). The transformations in question are as follows: after completing the first circuit, Ibn ʿArabī assumes the form of death and the youth assumes the form of life; after completing the second circuit, Ibn ʿArabī assumes the form of blindness and the youth the form of vision; after the third, Ibn ʿArabī assumes the form of ignorance and the youth the form of knowledge; after the fourth, deafness and hearing; the fifth, muteness and speech; the sixth, negligence and will; the seventh, impotence and potency.[97]

Lastly in Ibn ʿArabī's account of his *ṭawāf*, as summarised here with regard to its physical aspects only, Ibn ʿArabī is instructed by the youth to enter the place where he would miraculously see written before him most of his aforementioned work, *al-Futūḥāt al-makkiyya*. He is told: 'Enter with me the Kaʿba of the *Ḥijr* (*Kaʿbat al-Ḥijr*)!'[98] Contrary to what both Fritz Meier and Henri Corbin misleadingly assert, this place is not the interior of the Kaʿba, but the interior of the semicircular *Ḥijr*.[99] Here, Ibn ʿArabī feels the youth's hand on his breast and hears him say: 'Lift my veils and read what my inscriptions (*suṭūr*) comprise!' To this command Ibn ʿArabī responds as follows:

> So I lifted his veils and observed his inscriptions. Then the light that had been deposited in him made visible to my eyes the concealed knowledge that he comprised and contained. The first inscription that I read and the first secret that I learnt I shall now relate in Chapter Two [of my book].[100]

The Kaʿba of the Ḥijr

Ibn ʿArabī refers to the location of this concluding event interchangeably as the 'Kaʿba of the *Ḥijr*' and the 'House of the *Ḥijr*'.[101] There is nothing strange or ambiguous about this designation, nothing that might make one think that Ibn ʿArabī had traversed the Kaʿba's doorway into the dark interior. As mentioned in the Introduction, the early Islamic sources allege that the *Ḥijr* was originally a contiguous part of the Kaʿba; most of it, they say, was incorporated within the Kaʿba's walls. When the Kaʿba was rebuilt by the pre-prophetic Muḥammad and his tribe, however, a lack of funds allegedly prevented the *Ḥijr* from once again being incorporated this way. Later, as Islam's prophet, Muḥammad is said to have regretted this state of affairs and wanted to remedy it by knocking down the Kaʿba and rebuilding it to include the *Ḥijr*; only his worry that doing so might wrong-foot the newly converted Meccans prevented him.[102] Nevertheless, he reportedly continued to conceive of the *Ḥijr* as an integral part of the Kaʿba's interior, because in a hadith he advised his wife ʿĀʾisha that she could satisfy her desire to enter and pray inside the Kaʿba by praying inside the *Ḥijr*. 'Pray in the *Ḥijr* if you want to enter the House', he is alleged to have said. 'It is a part (*qiṭʿa*) of the House, but your people fell short of it (*istaqṣarūhu*) when they [re-]built the Kaʿba and excluded it from the House.'[103]

Ibn ʿArabī likewise conceived of the *Ḥijr* as an integral part of the Kaʿba.[104] When he followed the youth there, in his mind he was therefore entering the Kaʿba. Architecturally speaking, however, he was doing no such thing. Rather, he was entering what might be termed the Kaʿba's 'phantom limb': an amputated body part still felt as present. The *Ḥijr* is empirically outside the main structure of the Kaʿba but perceived by Ibn ʿArabī, the Prophet and others as belonging inside. This perception is one reason why pilgrims performing the *ṭawāf* must avoid entering the *Ḥijr*; for as noted earlier, the *ṭawāf* is a ritual concerning the Kaʿba's exterior, not its interior.

At the Ḥijr *and* Multazam

Ibn ʿArabī had completed the *ṭawāf* when he entered the *Ḥijr*, and so he did not invalidate his performance of the ritual. Although it may not be customary (*sunna*) to enter the *Ḥijr* upon completing the *ṭawāf*, many pilgrims do so.[105] In part, this is because the prayer place of the elect (*akhyār*) is said to be below the Kaʿba's golden rainspout, the *Mīzāb*, which overhangs the *Ḥijr*.[106] Where it is customary to go after completing the *ṭawāf* is the *Multazam*, a section of the Kaʿba's walls commonly identified as being between the door and the Black Stone.[107] Against this section pilgrims press their cheeks, breasts, arms and sometimes even their bare bellies.[108] Thus does a pilgrim cleave (*yaltazim*) to the Kaʿba, in imitation of a practice that is said to have begun with Adam.[109] A photograph taken in approximately 1910 shows a white-clad, turbaned pilgrim in just such a state (Figure 4.5).

Whether pilgrims cleave to the *Multazam* upon completing the *ṭawāf*, enter the *Ḥijr*, or do both, I would argue that they achieve the same end: the expression of unification with the Kaʿba. My argument is in two stages. First, as illustrated by Ibn ʿArabī in the section of his account where he and the youth undergo seven changes of form, unification with the Kaʿba has itself been achieved by the performance of the *ṭawāf*.[110] For if the youth may indeed be taken as a divine emanation, as seems likely, he belongs to the Kaʿba, whence he has come. As such, he represents the Kaʿba. When he and Ibn ʿArabī go through their transformations, with each individual assuming

Figure 4.5 *A pilgrim cleaves to the* Multazam *of the Kaʿba in* c.1328/1910, *as others either perform the* ṭawāf, *cluster at the Black Stone, or emerge from the shallow basin* (khawḍ) *at the foot of the* Multazam. *The Swiss traveller John Lewis Burckhardt (d.* 1817*) calls this basin the* El Madjen, *explaining that it is where Abraham and Ismael kneaded the chalk and mud used to build the Kaʿba. One supposes, therefore, that he meant* al-Miʿjan *(kneading trough). However, given its location next to the* Multazam, *possibly he meant* al-Majann *(protector or shield). Courtesy: Library of Congress Prints and Photographs Division Washington, DC. LC-DIG-matpc-04658.*

the opposite form to the other, they are already locked together, fused, as a result of Ibn ʿArabī's having completed the first of the seven circuits.

Additional evidence for a fusion between pilgrim and building is found in a report in a Sufi commentary by Abū Ibrahīm Mustamlī Bukhārī (d. 434/1042) and in a poem by the Persian writer Muḥyī al-Dīn Lārī (d. 933/1526). In the first piece of evidence, an unnamed 'great' Sufi (*baʿḍ al-kubrā*) is cited as saying:

> One day I was sitting opposite the Kaʿba when I heard a lament from inside the House saying: 'O wall (*jidār*), move out of the way of My friends. Whoever visits Me by way of you, will circumambulate you. Whoever visits Me by way of Myself, will circumambulate Me.'[111]

Although at first glance this report seems to contradict my claim of a temporary fusion between the Kaʿba and the pilgrim, the unnamed Sufi is not saying that the pilgrim who visits God by circling the Kaʿba is thwarted in their intended union, because he acknowledges that the wall mediates their visit.[112] He says only that it is more efficacious to visit God immediately, bypassing the House, by which he means, presumably, by circling the corporeal Kaʿba of the heart.

In the second piece of evidence, Muḥyī al-Dīn Lārī poetically recalls his first performance of the *ṭawāf*. In verse six of this recollection, he says this of the split second before he, the reader imagines, became fused to the Kaʿba:

> [R]evolving, circling, and full of presence
> I became a moth, and He a luminous candle.[113]

Almost 500 years later in his guide to the Hajj, the Iranian revolutionary and sociologist, ʿAlī Sharīʿatī (d. 1977), would echo Lārī's verse when explaining the circumambulation ritual with these words: 'Tawaf: as a butterfly who encircles the candle until it burns; and its ashes are gone with the wind – disappearing in love and dying in light!'[114] The precise place of fusion for this butterfly, Muḥyī al-Dīn Lārī and Ibn ʿArabī is their and the Kaʿba's point of mutual contact, namely, the Kaʿba's tectonic frontiers: its walls, so doggedly reiterated by the pilgrims' sevenfold circuits about them.

Interestingly, on the basis of different but related evidence, Shalem has similarly argued for a fusion between the Kaʿba and the pilgrim:

> The juxtaposition between the stone and the skin – architecture and body – and the rubbing of the body on the surface of the [Kaʿba] converts the stone into flesh, at least in the imagination of the devotees, and the distinction between architecture and human body [is] seemingly annulled.[115]

In performing the *ṭawāf*, I have argued so far, the pilgrim becomes temporarily fused to the Kaʿba. In the second stage of my argument, I shall put it that the pilgrim's subsequent entrance into the *Ḥijr* and/or their cleaving to the *Multazam* are the supererogatory acts that express this temporary, liminal state.

Although in architectural studies a door is commonly considered the threshold of a building, in reality it is only a gap in a wall. The wall, rather, is the threshold, and the door is its point of traversal.[116] The *Ḥijr* is part of the threshold of the Kaʿba, because like a wall it is simultaneously inside and outside the Kaʿba. It is conceptually inside but empirically outside, and thus any occupant of the *Ḥijr* is at once inside and outside the Kaʿba. The cleaving pilgrim is likewise both inside and outside, for two reasons. The first reason is specific to the Kaʿba, namely, the existence of the *Shādharwān*, the Kaʿba's sloping base: any touching of it during the *ṭawāf* is said to place the circling pilgrim inside the building. The second reason is general to walls. As an extension of the Kaʿba's wall, the cleaving pilgrim takes the nature of a wall, namely, a liminal, uniting 'space between': between here and there, inside and outside. This functionality of a wall, at once uniting and reversing here and there, inside and outside, explains the opposing polarities of the transformations undergone by Ibn ʿArabī and the youth after each circuit of the House. The youth is from within the Kaʿba, Ibn ʿArabī is from without; the Kaʿba's edge is the frontier that unites and reverses them. Reversed, the cleaving pilgrim 'becomes' the Kaʿba. In that state, she embodies what Rūmī, Ibn ʿArabī's contemporary, says to pilgrims intent on reaching the Kaʿba: 'You are the Kaʿba, you!'[117]

Whether or not Ibn ʿArabī would agree with the foregoing interpretation of the *ṭawāf* that is premised on his account of the ritual, what is indisputable is the value he attributes to the action of cleaving to the Kaʿba. With reference to one of his subsequent visits to Mecca, he reports God as saying the following about this action: 'No one has made this House greater than other [Houses] except you, My servant, through your cleaving to it.'[118] Tying the cleaving action to the performance of *ṭawāf*, Ibn ʿArabī immediately adds, again in the words of God: 'While the houses of mortals grow dark, the Kaʿba is lit by your circling about it.'[119]

Part Three: The Kaʿba as Beloved

In an oft-cited article, the anthropologist William Young investigates a supposition by Richard Burton regarding the origins of covering the Kaʿba with a robe, the *Kiswa*. Burton supposed these origins lay in the ancient Christian custom of considering the community of the faithful, the church, as a bride.[120] By analysing the *Kiswa* as part of a symbolic system, specifically the Hajj rituals as practised at the turn of the twentieth century, Young finds value in the supposition, but modifies it to conclude that the Kaʿba is the bride, not the community of the faithful.[121] 'In Arab Muslim tradition,' he writes, 'it [is] the Ka'ba which [is] likened to a bride, the community of believers to a groom.'[122]

Young's conclusion is of interest to my argument regarding the circling pilgrim's union with the Ka'ba, because it implies a marriage of the bridal Ka'ba to the collective groom, the pilgrims.[123] This implication is highly suggestive, as proved by Elliot Wolfson's use of it to assert: '[C]ircumambulation [of the Ka'ba] has a hidden sexual connotation, as the circling of the square symbolically enacts the union of man and woman.'[124] The third and final part of this chapter explores Young's conclusion.

Before proceeding to that exploration, I should point out that although Wolfson's ostensibly extreme development of Young's conclusion is unwarrantedly gendered, in that it supposes the Ka'ba to be exclusively female and the union to be penetrative and necessarily heterosexual,[125] the following *ṭawāf*-related passage from the story of the lovers, 'Azīz and 'Azīza, in *The Thousand and One Nights* gives it some legitimacy:

> Then she undid her petticoat-trousers which slipped down to her anklets, and we fell to clasping and embracing and toying and speaking softly and biting and intertwining of legs and going round about the Holy House and the corners thereof (*ḥaml al-sīqān wa al-ṭawāf bi al-Bayt wa al-arkān*), till her joints became relaxed for love-delight and she swooned away (*dakhlat al-ghaybūba*).[126]

In contrast, however, some verses by the Persian poet Khāqānī Shirwānī (d. 595/1199) undermine Wolfson's interpretation. In a poem in which the Black Stone, and by extension the Ka'ba, is figured as an Indian bride, the poet says:

> That old and virginal Indian woman
> was given as a bridal present to God's creatures.
> People clasped her against their bosom
> and kissed her, but nobody perforated her.[127]

A bride awaiting marriage?

Although Wolfson's sexually explicit interpretation of the Ka'ba is certainly dubious, is Young correct when he concludes that the Ka'ba is a bride and implies that it awaits marriage to the pilgrims? There is some historical literature in support of his conclusion, including an Islamic tradition that speaks of the Ka'ba being conducted to the Rock of the Temple Mount on the Day of Resurrection 'like a bride conducted to her husband'.[128] For example, although

Young does not mention it, Burton himself quotes the following words by the poet ʿAbd al-Raḥīm al-Buraʿī (d. 803/1400): 'And Meccah's bride (i.e. the Ka'abah) is displayed with (miraculous) signs.'[129] Prior to al-Buraʿī, the traveller Ibn Jubayr had said this of his first visit to the Kaʿba:

> And so, at the time and on the day we have mentioned, we reached God's Sanctuary, the abode of God's Friend, Abraham. Thus we came upon the Kaʿba, the Sacred House, an unveiled bride conducted in solemn procession (like a bride to her groom) to the supreme felicity of heaven, encompassed by the deputations of the All-Merciful (*ʿarūs majluwwa mazfūfa ilā jannat al-Riḍwān maḥfūfa bi-wufūd al-Raḥmān*). We performed the *ṭawāf* of arrival . . . and at the *Multazam* we cleft to the Kaʿba's coverings.[130]

Significantly, however, neither of these two quotations restricts the bridal image to the period of the Hajj, as Young's conclusion inevitably tends to, given its basis in the rites of the Hajj.[131] More importantly, neither quotation references the *Kiswa* as the element that undergirds the image. For all that is interesting about his argument, Young overplays the alleged symbolism of the *Kiswa*, even though he acknowledges that non-Arab pilgrims would have had difficulty in recognising this symbolism.[132]

The literary topos of figuratively rendering the Kaʿba as a bride is a way to reach a conclusion that is similar to Young's but which is neither restricted to the Hajj nor dependent solely on the *Kiswa* and its alleged symbolism.[133] As evidenced in the above two quotations, this topos is well established in Arabic literature, and is especially so in Persian literature. It was explored by Anna Beelaert in her article, 'The Kaʿba as a Woman'.[134] In this article, the feminisation of the Kaʿba is as indubitable as it is wide in its temporal and geographic reach, being attested at least as early as Ibn Jubayr (d. 614/1217) from al-Andalus and the aforementioned poet Khāqānī (d. 595/1199) from Iran.[135]

Although this feminisation could take the form of the Kaʿba as bride, it also took the related form of the Kaʿba as beloved.[136] The latter form is most clearly exemplified in the Persian interpretations of the romantic legend of Laylā and Majnūn, in which Laylā is the unattainable beloved of the doomed lover Majnūn and thus in Sufism is a cipher for God.[137] As this legend was interpreted by Persian poets, notably Niẓāmī Ganjawī (d. *c.*613/1217) and Jāmī (d. 898/1492), at one point in Majnūn's life he gets taken to Mecca by his father, who hopes that in encountering the Kaʿba he would forget Laylā.

As Niẓāmī relates this encounter and the events leading up to it:

> The further away his moon, Laylā, shone in the sky, the higher Majnūn waved the banner of his love . . . His family and, above all, his father, had not given

> up hope that his dark night might end and a new morning dawn. Once more they took counsel, and, having talked for a long time without result, their thoughts finally converged on the Kaʿba, God's sanctuary in Mecca, visited every year by thousands and thousands of faithful pilgrims from near and far. 'Well,' they said, 'could it not happen after all that the Almighty One would come to our aid, that the door for which we have no key would suddenly open?' . . . [Arriving at the Kaʿba,] a strange thing happened. Majnūn darted forward like the head of a coiled snake, stretched out his hands towards the door of the temple, hammered against it and shouted: 'Yes, it is I, who knocks at this door today! I have sold my life for love's sake! Yes, it is I; may I always be love's slave! . . . I ask thee, my God, I beseech thee, in all the godliness of thy divine nature and all the perfection of thy kingdom: let my love grow stronger, let it endure, even if I perish. Let me drink from this well, let my eye never miss its light. If I am drunk with the wine of love, let me drink even more deeply.'[138]

As Jāmī relates the same encounter, speaking in the voice of Majnūn:

> I beheld the Kaʿba, and remembered your face.
> When I saw the black covering of the Kaʿba
> I stretched the hand of my desire towards your black tresses.
> When I seized the knocker of the Kaʿba with a hundred cravings
> I made a prayer for a musk-scented ringlet of your hair.
> The people in the sanctuary bowed their faces in humility to the Kaʿba
> I turned, amidst all, the face of my heart to you.
> In every stage I turned my footsteps to no other than you
> the *ṭawāf* and the *saʿy* I performed in search for you.[139]

In Niẓāmī's verse, the Kaʿba is as impregnable as Majnūn's love for Laylā: the shut Kaʿba is a figure, perhaps the figure, of his unassailable state. In Jāmī's verse, this figuration becomes less abstract: the Kaʿba's *Kiswa* is Laylā's hair, its door knocker one of her curls. Other examples of the same and similar figurative renderings could be cited,[140] but with regard to the subject matter of the present chapter, one rendering especially stands out: the analogy some Persian poets drew between the beloved's lips (*labān*) and the Kaʿba's threshold (*āsitāna*). The following are verses to that effect by Khāqānī:

> As long as the Black Stone and the threshold
> are the black mole and the lips of the Kaʿba,
> May I see you in eternal prosperity
> with the same dignity and power as the Kaʿba![141]

In the two ninth/fifteenth-century Persian miniatures reproduced below, we see Majnūn in pilgrimage vestment standing at the Kaʿba (Figures 4.6 and 4.7).[142] Having presumably performed the *ṭawāf*, it being

Figure 4.6 *Majnūn clasps the knocker of the Kaʿba. From a copy of the* Khamsa *by Niẓāmī (d. c.613/1217), dated 888/1483. Gouache, gold and ink on paper; 22.2 × 34.6cm (folio). Courtesy: Topkapı Palace Library. TSMK H.754, fol. 126r.*

Figure 4.7 *Majnūn clasps the knockers of the Kaʿba. From a copy of the* Khamsa *by Niẓāmī, dated 835/1431. Gouache, gold and ink on paper; 13.7 × 23.7cm (folio). Courtesy: The State Hermitage Museum, St Petersburg. Inv. no. VP-1000, fol. 175r. Photograph © The State Hermitage Museum. Photo by Vladimir Terebenin.*

the first thing pilgrims do upon their arrival in Mecca, Majnūn leans towards the threshold. With both hands he clasps the door's knocker (*Ḥalqa*) (Figure 4.6) or knockers (Figure 4.7), an action whose origins might lie in the pre-Islamic period when it is said that on the Kaʿba were crook-shaped rings (*ḥalaq amthāl lujum al-bahm*) used by people seeking refuge. In putting their hands through the rings, they were meant to be protected from persecution.[143] More likely, it is an action with a related meaning but whose origins lie in the early Islamic period, because in the early sources clasping the knocker is occasionally reported of leading individuals, where it signifies their pleading for God's aid.[144]

Clasping the Kaʿba's knocker or knockers, leaning towards its threshold, is Majnūn there united with his beloved? Angels circle overhead as if to say, yes. If they are right and he is, that might help explain the phrase 'Kaʿba of the lovers'.[145] In Ottoman Turkish, as *Kaʿbetü'l-ʿuşşāq*, this phrase is found in the foundation inscriptions of two tenth/sixteenth-century Ottoman mosques.[146] In Arabic, as *Kaʿbat al-ʿushshāq*, it forms part of an undated and otherwise Persian inscription in the entranceway to the museum devoted to Rūmī, the Mevlānā Museum in Konya, Turkey.[147] However, in a gloss on the appellation 'Sacred Mosque' in the Qurʾanic verse 'You will enter the Sacred Mosque in safety, God willing' (Q 48:27), Rūmī can hardly be said to be a proponent of the phrase except via some convoluted interpretive manoeuvres. He writes: 'In the view of the literalists (*ahl-i ẓāhir*), the "Sacred Mosque" is that Kaʿba to which people go. For lovers (*ʿāshshiqān*) and the elite, however, the "Sacred Mosque" is union (*wiṣāl*) with God.'[148]

Conclusion

This chapter has investigated the Kaʿba in terms of its exteriority. It has analysed the performance of the *ṭawāf* and what it occasions at the Kaʿba's boundaries that are circled and, in the distant fashion of an aboriginal songline, reiterated. Beginning with a description and discussion of the ritual of *ṭawāf*, the chapter subsequently focussed on Ibn ʿArabī's account of his performance of this ritual. On the basis of that account it was argued that the mystic had become temporarily conjoined to a divine emanation of the Kaʿba and thus simultaneously temporarily fused to the Kaʿba. This fusion, the argument continued, placed him in a liminal state, at once within and without the Kaʿba, which the mystic expressed by entering the *Ḥijr*.

The chapter has also argued that Ibn ʿArabī's experience of what happened to him at the Kaʿba when performing the *ṭawāf* is not dismissible as idiosyncratic. Rather, the customary cleaving of a pilgrim to the *Multazam* upon the completion of the *ṭawāf* should also be considered an expression of a momentary union with the Kaʿba. Cleaving to the Kaʿba's walls, pilgrims are almost literally fused to their journey's end. Finally, a discussion of the gendered Kaʿba in literature and art corroborated and developed aspects of this finding, with the pilgrims' goal figured as the bridal beloved.

CHAPTER FIVE

The House as Holder

Whereas the previous chapter investigated the Kaʿba in terms of its exteriority, this and the next chapter investigate it in terms of its interiority. Having drawn ever nearer to the Kaʿba, from the world born of the Kaʿba and the settlements and sites oriented to the Kaʿba, then to the Kaʿba's foundations and walls, we finally look inside. In this and the subsequent chapter, the book's final chapter, we examine how and what the House *houses* and thereby fulfils a basic function of architecture: to shelter and hold.

Counter-intuitively, the cloth that robes the Kaʿba's exterior, the *Kiswa*, forms a significant element of this inward-looking inquiry; for, as will be shown in the final chapter, in many verbal and visual representations of the Kaʿba it tells whether the House is empty or full. That is to say, in the second part of this inquiry into the sheltering function of the Kaʿba, I shall argue that a particular way of hanging the *Kiswa* annually signals when a superabundant, divine presence is imagined to be residing within the Kaʿba. This signalling forms a lesser-known function of the Kaʿba's robe.

The present chapter will focus on the first part of this inquiry. I shall argue that the total emptiness of the Kaʿba in terms of cultic content and its near emptiness in terms of material content are part of the House's function as a placeholder of the symbolic order of Islam. This function, I shall show, is similar to the function of zero in cultures historically stamped by visualising technologies based on linear perspective.

The chapter will proceed as follows: first, an account of what the early Islamic sources say the Kaʿba held before the advent of Islam, what they say this content was for, and what they allege the Prophet did with it upon his conquest of Mecca; second, a discussion of the sources' claim that the Prophet evacuated most of this content, and an analysis of diagrams of the Kaʿba which substantiate this claim; and third, an interpretation of the resultant emptied House as the placeholder of a void that is (1) functional in Islamic culture, anchoring the symbolic order of Islam, and (2) constitutive of the House's mystery.

Part One: Emptying the Pre-Islamic Kaʿba

With one notable exception, the early Islamic sources allege that in the pre-Islamic period the only god to be housed inside the Kaʿba was Hubal; the other gods of the Meccan pantheon were placed outside, about the Kaʿba.[1] The exception to this narrative is provided by al-Wāqidī (d. 207/822), who reports that the image of Hubal was located 'facing the Kaʿba, above [?] the door'.[2] This report would seem to imply that Hubal's image was not inside the Kaʿba, but on top of it, on its roof. Interestingly, that is where it would later also be located in a tenth/sixteenth-century miniature (Figure 5.1), contrary to the narrative the miniature illustrates, which specifies that Hubal's image was inside the Kaʿba.[3]

Al-Wāqidī's report would appear to be unique within the early sources regarding the location of Hubal's image. I am therefore inclined to discount it. Uri Rubin seems to make the same decision when he writes: 'The pre-Islamic deity of the Kaʿba was Hubal. His was the one and only statue situated inside the Kaʿba.'[4]

The early Islamic sources explain that Hubal was considered by the pre-Islamic Quraysh tribe of Mecca to be the greatest of their pantheon and that no expense was spared to mark this rank. Before the god's image, the sources state, rituals were performed.[5] In the words of Ibn al-Kalbī (d. 203/819 or 206/821):

> The Quraysh also had several idols (*aṣnām*) in and around the Kaʿba (*fī jawf al-Kaʿba wa ḥawlahā).* The greatest of these was Hubal. It was, as I was told, of red agate, in the form of a man with the right hand broken off. It came into the possession of the Quraysh in this condition, and they, therefore, made for it a hand of gold . . . It stood inside the Kaʿba. In front of it were seven divination arrows. On one of these arrows was written 'pure' (*ṣarīḥ*) and on another 'impure' (*mulṣaq*). Whenever the lineage of a newborn child was doubted, they would offer a sacrifice to [Hubal] and then shuffle the arrows and throw them. If the arrows showed the word 'pure', the child would be declared legitimate and the tribe would accept him. If, however, the arrows showed the words 'impure', the child would be declared illegitimate and the tribe would reject him . . . Whenever they disagreed concerning something, or purposed to embark upon a journey, or undertake some project, they would proceed to [Hubal] and shuffle the divination arrows before it. Whatever result they obtained they would follow and do accordingly.[6]

Notwithstanding the difficulty of distinguishing between cultic and votive material for this period, the pre-Islamic Kaʿba is also said to have housed material of a votive nature, in addition to its ritualistic, cultic content.[7] Thus the pre-Islamic Kaʿba is said to have housed, for example, the horns of a ram and perhaps even the head of a ram; two golden gazelles; swords; and armour.[8] These or some of these items were allegedly part of the Kaʿba's treasure (*kanz*), which was stored in a pit (*jubb*) or well (*biʾr*),[9] by or over which (*ʿalā*) Hubal allegedly stood.[10]

If these votive items were in fact stored there, whether they should count as part of the building's content is moot, because technically speaking they would have been underneath the building, not in it. What is less disputable is that when Mecca was captured by the Prophet and his army in 8/630, the town and its palladium simultaneously dropping their 'pre-Islamic' prefix, the early Islamic sources make almost no mention of them.[11] What the sources concentrate on, rather, is the smashing of the Kaʿba's idols.

The conquest of Mecca and the smashing of the idols

According to the early sources, in 8/630, eight years after being exiled from Mecca, the Prophet returned with an army and conquered the town.[12] Although a number of temples are said to have been looted and rid of their idols during the march there,[13] the ambition of the Prophet was the subjugation of Mecca.[14] This goal presumably also implied the control of the Sanctuary and the smashing of the Kaʿba's idols, because from the sources it could seem that the punitive motive alone was what mattered, not the religious motive.[15] As reported by al-Azraqī, the subjugation of Mecca reduced even the Devil to tears:

> It is said that the Devil (Iblīs) cried out in woe on three occasions: once when he was cursed [by God] and his form was changed from that of the angels; once when he saw the Prophet standing in prayer in Mecca; and once when the Prophet conquered Mecca and the Devil said to his progeny who had gathered by him, 'Abandon all hope that the community of Muḥammad will revert to idolatry (*shirk*) after this day of theirs.'[16]

There is no uniform narrative in the early Islamic sources for what is said to have taken place at the Kaʿba following the conquest of the town, with some sources, including al-Ṭabarī, not even mentioning the alleged smashing of the Kaʿba's idols.[17] This marked discrepancy between the sources is in part attributable to the fact that a significant element of what is commonly presented in the earliest extant written accounts, all of which date to the third/ninth century, is inflected by the debates about iconoclasm that were then current in the region.[18] Accordingly, these accounts cannot be taken at face value, contrary to what has mostly been done to date in Islamic art history, where they have been read as indicating the status of images at the beginnings of Islam.[19]

In view of the fact that much of what these frequently contradictory early accounts contain was subsequently reused by later Muslim authors, coalescing thereby into something approaching a canonical narrative, they are particularly important to examine.[20] For present purposes, however, the goal is not to attempt an exhaustive review of them, but to summarise the main narrative strands as they relate to the idolatrous, presumably ritualistic items that the Kaʿba allegedly sheltered.

The first narrative strand concerns the immediate exterior of the Kaʿba and the 300 or 360 idols that are said to have been placed around it, which the Prophet is said to have destroyed. As his actions are related by al-Bukhārī:

> The Prophet entered Mecca on the day of the conquest, and around the House there were 360 idols (sing. *nuṣub*). The Prophet started striking them with a stick that he had in his hand, saying: 'Truth has come and falsehood has perished [Q 17:81]. Truth has come and falsehood will neither start nor return.'[21]

The second narrative strand is more complicated and concerns the interior of the Kaʿba: how and when the Prophet entered it, and what he or others did once inside.[22] One form of the strand has the Prophet reaching the Kaʿba, performing the *ṭawāf*, requesting the door key, entering alone and finding inside a wooden dove (*ḥamāma*), which he destroys.[23] A second form of the strand has the Prophet remaining outside the Sacred Mosque, but deputising others to go to the Kaʿba, telling them to open and cleanse (*maḥā*) it of its idols, paintings (sing. *ṣūra*) and statues (sing. *timthāl*) alike.[24] A third, related form of the strand has the Prophet refusing to enter the Kaʿba until it has been cleansed of its idols.[25] A final form has the Prophet inside the Kaʿba either doing the cleansing himself or ordering another to do it.[26]

The third narrative strand concerns the representational nature of these idols which were allegedly cleansed from inside the Kaʿba. As just mentioned, one report alleges that a dove was represented. Another report, though not specific to the conquest of Mecca and additionally from the fourth/tenth century, alleges that personages from the ancestors of the Quraysh tribe were represented.[27] Considerably more numerous reports allege that a varying combination of angels, Abraham, Ishmael and Jesus with Mary were represented.[28]

The fourth and final narrative strand concerns what the Prophet is alleged to have done specifically with the representations of Abraham and Jesus with Mary. He is consistently said to have spared the latter from the cleansing process, and in one report also the former, as most commonly recounted, by placing his hand over them.[29] The strand's epilogue takes the form of the Kaʿba's destruction of 64/684 (see Chapter Three), at which time the spared images, specifically the one of Jesus with Mary, are reported to have gone up in smoke.[30] The narrator of this report, ʿAṭāʾ b. Abī Rabāḥ (d. 114/732), additionally asserts that by the time the image of Jesus and Mary came to be destroyed by the flames, it existed only as an all but obliterated trace.[31] This would suggest that the image of Jesus with Mary had not in fact been spared by the Prophet.

With reference to this fire, but as an aside, according to al-Masʿūdī (d. 345/956), when Ibn al-Zubayr came to restore the Kaʿba he used glass mosaics instead of images.[32] Although these mosaics remained there only until the Kaʿba's destruction of 72/692, if al-Masʿūdī's report is reliable they pre-date the glass mosaics of the Dome of the Rock by eight years.[33]

In summary of the foregoing narrative strands, as recalled in the third/ninth century the conquest of Mecca saw the purification of the Kaʿba of its idols: those immediately ringing the House's exterior and those occupying its interior. Possibly an image or two was allowed to remain inside, but in the fire of 64/684 they, too, were 'purified', bringing the cleansing to completion.

Although it might seem surprising that in these narrative strands no mention is made of the idol Hubal, two remarks are necessary. First, Hubal's destruction is reported by at least one of the third/ninth-century authors; in this report, the Prophet is said to have ordered the idol to be smashed in front of him.[34] Second, Hubal's relative insignificance in these early accounts is more than compensated for in later accounts, especially in the miniatures that sometimes illustrate these accounts. Thus, in the ninth/fifteenth-century semi-canonic Shiʿite narrative of the smashing of the Kaʿba's idols, Hubal is both mentioned and then smashed, thrown down by the Prophet's cousin and son-in-law, ʿAlī.[35] In a tenth/sixteenth-century Persian painting based on this narrative, ʿAlī is shown astride the Prophet's shoulders: from outside the Kaʿba, not inside, contrary to the original narrative and the section of that narrative copied out on the painting, he pulls down idols from the roof (Figure 5.1). As noted earlier, one of them is said in the original narrative to be Hubal.

In another tenth/sixteenth-century Ottoman painting, this time based on an eighth/fourteenth-century Turkish narrative, ʿAlī is once again shown outside the Kaʿba. He stands over a broken statue, captioned in the painting as Hubal, which he has just thrown to the ground (Figure 5.2).

Part Two: The Emptied Kaʿba

The Prophet's actions at the conquest of Mecca effectively emptied the building of its cultic contents. Ritually speaking, it now stood empty, never again to be used for ritually prescribed cultic purposes, a situation which has continued until today. To say that, however, is not simultaneously to say that in the early Islamic sources the building is represented as empty of all non-cultic content or that from the fifth/eleventh century onwards it had no physical content, for example, hanging lamps. It is also not to say that in these sources and periods its interior walls were free of decoration, that its interior would not be used for political rituals, and that worship would not occur there. What follows elucidates these qualifications.

Figure 5.1 *ʿAlī stands on the Prophet's shoulders for the smashing of the Kaʿba's idols. From a copy of* Rawḍat al-ṣafā *('The garden of purity') by Mīrkhwānd (d. 903/1498), dated to* c.998/1590. *Gold, tempera and ink on paper; 17 × 29.3cm. Courtesy: bpk / Museum für Islamische Kunst, Staatliche Museen zu Berlin / Wolfgang Selbach. I. 44/68 (000002284).*

Figure 5.2 *ʿAlī smashes the Kaʿba's idol, Hubal. From a copy of the* Siyer-i Nebī *('Biography of the Prophet') by Muṣṭafa Ḍarīr (*fl. *late eighth/fourteenth century), dated 1003/1595. Gold, gouache and ink on paper; 17 × 29cm (folio: 27 × 37.5cm). Courtesy: Topkapı Palace Library. TSMK H.1223, fol. 303a.*

The empty Kaʿba?

Beginning with the non-cultic content of the Kaʿba, the foregoing discussion of the Kaʿba at the time of the conquest of Mecca has indicated that the horns of a ram were likely left inside. On the basis of a report that the Prophet found a cache of gold in the Kaʿba's pit which he left there untouched, we might additionally presume that the Kaʿba's treasure was left inside, too.[36] However, according to the early sources, at some point in the first century of the Islamic period, this treasure, now contained in a treasury (*khizānat al-Kaʿba*), was removed to the house of Shayba b. ʿUthmān (*fl.* first/seventh century), a member of the Kaʿba's custodians, the Banū Shayba.[37] The sources do not elaborate upon its return to the Kaʿba.[38] Additionally, a report recounted by al-Azraqī says that it remained in the custodian's house for the next two years, suggesting that it might never have returned to the Kaʿba. The details are as follows. Referring to a throne sent to the Kaʿba by a conquered king of Tibet, al-Azraqī reports that this elaborate offering, complete with a crowned, golden idol at its zenith, was initially displayed in a public space in Mecca for three days of the pilgrimage season of 201/816. Thereafter it was sent for safe keeping in the Kaʿba's treasury, now located in the custodian's house. Two years later, it was removed from this house and melted down to pay for war preparations, leaving only the throne's silver dedication inscription and the idol's crown, both of which thus stayed, or perhaps *then* stayed (*fa-baqiya*) inside the Kaʿba until al-Azraqī's time.[39]

Was the Kaʿba's treasury ever returned to the Kaʿba? Certainly, in at least three pre-modern diagrams of the Sacred Mosque, a domed building is shown to the right of the Kaʿba, labelled 'treasury of the Kaʿba' (*makhzan al-Kaʿba*) (Figures 5.5, 5.9 and 5.10). This would imply that the treasure remained outside the Kaʿba. This domed building might, however, just be one of the two domed storage structures mentioned in the Introduction, the *Qubbatān*, which were used for storing quotidian items, for example, oil and carpets. They were probably not used for storing precious metals and jewels. A different suggestion regarding the Kaʿba's treasury is put forward by Rafique Jairazbhoy, who supposes it to have ended up in the space between the Kaʿba's ceiling and its roof.[40]

In view of this uncertainty regarding the treasury's whereabouts and the likelihood that what was stored in it was, almost by definition, closed off from sight, not to mention the early sources' assertion that not every precious item sent to the Kaʿba was housed in the Kaʿba, it would thus seem premature, *pace* Shalem, to talk of the 'display' of these precious items 'in' the Kaʿba.[41] Reservations about this claim are only strengthened when one comes to medieval accounts of the Kaʿba. For in these accounts, the jewels, precious metals, and so forth, that the early sources so clearly state belong to the Kaʿba, are, to the best of my knowledge, not referred to except as a limited number of objects that 'used to be' (*kānat*) in the Kaʿba, if they are mentioned at all.[42]

Wherever the treasury ended up being housed, associated with it or included in its contents were the precious objects which Muslim rulers and conquered kings, some of whom had subsequently embraced Islam, are reported to have gifted to the Kaʿba.[43] Gifts like those were firstly intended to honour the Kaʿba, and during the pilgrimage season a few of them were apparently suspended from the building's facade.[44] However, as the early sources make clear, the gifts were also meant to demonstrate the donors' obeisance to God: their submission to the precepts of Islam and recognition of the truth of Islam as the final religion.[45]

This second meaning of the gifts is exemplified by the alleged suspension of the 'Golden Book of the Zoroastrians' inside the Kaʿba, the Prophet having been gifted it by Bādhān, the recently converted Sasanian governor of Yemen.[46] This meaning thus indicates that the gifts to the

Ka'ba must also be understood as political in nature, which leads us to the next of the qualifications concerning the empty Ka'ba: political rituals within the Ka'ba. Before discussing them, however, a brief word must be said about the decorative nature of the Ka'ba's interior walls.

In the travel literature especially, the marble revetment used for the decoration is frequently described in detail.[47] Additionally, in the account of Nāṣir-i Khusraw (d. *c*.481/1088) six large *mihrab*-shaped frames immediately below the revetment of the western wall are described, each frame said to be made of burnished silver and nailed onto the wall.[48] Whether these frames and revetment should count as content and not decoration is, however, surely moot. Where the claim that they should count as content has some purchase is with regard to the marble plaques indicating where the Prophet is alleged to have stood on the occasions he prayed inside the Ka'ba, and the spot he faced as he did so.[49] Even so, regardless of whether or not these plaques count as part of the content of the Ka'ba, in the final analysis they are commemorative in nature, not cultic.

Returning now to the political rituals, if the historical purview of this study were weighted more towards recent times, it would be straightforward to show how the interior of the Ka'ba was used for political rituals. That is because, chief among them, is the admission of select world leaders into the Ka'ba's interior, invited there for a private tour.[50] As will be discussed in Chapter Six, because the Ka'ba is never permanently open, and in the modern period especially is opened only occasionally during the year, these visits by high-ranking dignitaries must be understood as predominantly political in nature.[51]

Fortunately, despite the fact that this book does not deal with the modern period, the early sources also reveal political uses of the Ka'ba's interior. Al-Ṭabarī, for example, reports how the Quraysh tribe wrote a document (*ṣaḥīfa*) in which they agreed to sanctioning of the Prophet and his growing number of followers. They allegedly hung this document inside the Ka'ba 'to make it even more binding upon themselves'.[52] Possibly in imitation of this action, the 'Abbasid caliph Harūn al-Rashīd (r. 170–93/786–809) is reported to have placed his succession plans within the Ka'ba.[53] These plans were probably hung from the building's ceiling, because when an opponent subsequently stripped (*naza'a*) them from the Ka'ba, the caliph al-Ma'mūn (r. 198–218/813–33) allegedly considered his actions to be a contemptuous violation (*istikhāff*) of the House, which he redressed by hanging a golden crown where once the plans had been.[54]

The placing of these documents within the Ka'ba seems to have been an attempt by the Quraysh tribe and Harūn al-Rashīd to guarantee the documents' legally binding content and to render this content inviolable in perpetuity.[55] If we are to take the chapter heading of the foregoing report about Harūn al-Rashīd to be of al-Azraqī's own choosing, namely, 'Copy of the *two* documents that were written inside the Ka'ba [and] which were witnessed', then we must also understand that the caliph's succession plans were additionally written inside the Kaʿba – again, as if to render them sacrosanct.[56]

The final qualification regarding the empty Kaʿba concerns worship there. As noted in Chapter Four, for the Islamic period there is no prescribed ritual for the interior of the Kaʿba, a prophetic hadith even specifying: 'We were not ordered with entering [the Kaʿba], only with circumambulating it.'[57] This does not, however, mean that worship (*ṣalāt*, *duʿāʾ*, and/or *takbīr*) does not and did not occur there both during and after the pilgrimage season, nor that it is proscribed from occurring there. On the contrary, there is plentiful evidence in the early sources of the Prophet and his companions worshipping inside the Kaʿba.[58] Equally, however, there is plentiful evidence of the Prophet discouraging worship, especially ritual prayer, there. As an example is the hadith we read in Chapter Four, in which the Prophet is alleged to have told his wife ʿĀʾisha to pray in the semicircular *Ḥijr* when she wanted to pray inside the Kaʿba. Other examples could be cited.[59]

Related to these examples of sanctioned worship inside the Kaʿba, there are also reports of unsanctioned worship there. Members of the medieval *ulema* recount in horror how the general populace (*al-ʿāmma*) would crowd into the Kaʿba to try to touch a particular spot high on one of the walls, which they called, with reference to the Qurʾan (Q 2:256, 31:22), the Firm Handhold (*al-ʿurwa al-wuthqā*). If Nāṣir-i Khusraw's reckoning is correct and the Kaʿba can hold 720 people, one gets a sense of this crowd's size.[60] Should these people have been unable to touch the Firm Handhold, then, as the *ulema* also complained, they would try to rub their bellies against a nail (*mismār*) in the floor, which they called the Navel of the World (*surrat al-dunyā*).[61] Both practices, condemned by the *ulema* as heretical innovations (sing. *bidʿa*), are said to have begun and ended in the seventh/thirteenth century.[62]

In view of the foregoing qualifications regarding the degree to which one can speak of an empty Kaʿba, the conclusion follows that it is (1) empty with regard to Islamic rituals prescribed for the interior – there are none, (2) empty, therefore, of ritual paraphernalia, (3) mostly empty of other items, and (4) for much of the year, mostly empty of political rituals. Perhaps, therefore, it is best to refer to the Kaʿba as either mostly empty or, with regard to the actions reported of the Prophet at the conquest of Mecca, liturgically empty. A third option is to consider it emptied, for that description speaks of the Prophet's actions at the time of the conquest and yet does not necessarily signify the evacuation of absolutely everything the House held.

Whichever of these descriptions one prefers, other than the aforementioned marbled walls, the three columns supporting the ceiling, and one or two other details, there is little else to see inside the Kaʿba, as travellers' eyewitness accounts amply testify. As ʿAlī Sharīʿatī, the aforementioned twentieth-century Iranian intellectual, playfully notes in his reflections on the Hajj: '[T]he Kaʿba is an empty cube – nothing else . . . There is nothing to view! An empty room (cube) is visible. Is that all?!! Is this the center of our faith, prayers, love, life and death?'[63] As Kishwar Rizvi more dramatically notes: 'What do we find when we crack the cube? There is nothing.'[64]

The following eyewitness account of the mostly empty interior of the Kaʿba comes from the seventh/twelfth-century Andalusian traveller, Ibn Jubayr. Other eyewitness accounts would also show the same relative emptiness of the Kaʿba; I have chosen Ibn Jubayr's because it is so minutely executed, the author having clearly been spared the pitch blackness that Eldon Rutter (d. after 1956) confronted when the door's inner curtain closed behind him.[65] Ibn Jubayr writes:

> The inside of the blessed House is overlaid with variegated marbles, and the walls are all variegated marbles (*rukhām mujazzaʿ*). [The ceiling] is sustained by three teak pillars of great height, four paces apart, and punctuating the length of the House, and down its middle. One of these columns, the first, faces the centre of the side enclosed by the two [southern] corners, and is three paces distant from it. The third column, the last, faces the side enclosed by the *Irāqī* and *Shāmī* corners. The whole circuit of the upper half of the House is plated with silver, thickly gilt, which the beholder would imagine, from its thickness, to be a sheet of gold. It encompasses the four sides and covers the upper half of the walls. The ceiling of the House is covered by a veil of coloured silk . . . The Kaʿba has five skylights (*maḍāw*[in]) of Irāqī glass, marvellously coloured (*badīʿ al-naqsh*).[66] One of them is in the middle of the ceiling, and at each corner is [one of the other skylights], one of which is not seen because it is beneath the vaulted passage described later. Between the pillars [hang] thirteen vessels, of silver save one that is gold. The first thing which he who enters at the door will find to his left is the corner outside which is the Black Stone. Here are two chests containing Qurʾans. Above them in the corner are two small silver doors like windows set in the [angle of the] corner, and more than a man's stature from the ground. In the corner which follows, the *Yamānī* corner, it is the same, but the doors have been torn out and only the wood to which they were attached remains. In the *Shāmī* corner it is the same and the small doors remain. It is the same in the *Irāqī* corner, which is to the right of him who enters. In the *Irāqī* corner is a door called the Door of Mercy (*Bāb al-Raḥma*),[67] from which ascent is made to the roof of the blessed House. It leads to a vaulted passage connecting with the roof of the House.[68]

Diagrams of the emptied Kaʿba

More concisely than Ibn Jubayr, a number of pre-modern diagrams of the Kaʿba also reveal the emptiness at the heart of the House. In manuscript copies of the popular compilation of prayers and blessings on the Prophet,

Dalāʾil al-khayrāt ('The waymarks of benefits') by Muḥammad al-Jazūlī (d. *c.*869/1465), it is common to find paired images of the Two Sanctuaries (*al-Ḥaramayn*): the Sacred Mosque in Mecca and the Prophet's Mosque in Medina. Their placement in this devotional text is especially the case with copies produced from the late twelfth/eighteenth century onwards.[69] Not always, but frequently, these diagrammatic images show the interiors of the structures that comprise the two sacred sites, with the exception of the Kaʿba. It is blacked out, its interior blocked to view.

In the first example of this phenomenon, taken from an early thirteenth/nineteenth-century copy of the devotional text, we see the two Mosques encircled by their minarets: four for Medina and seven for Mecca (Figure 5.3). In the diagram of the Prophet's Mosque on the left-hand page, the artist shows us inside the large domed burial chamber (*al-Ḥujra*), where we can see the tomb of the Prophet and the tombs of the two companions said to be buried alongside him. Immediately below this chamber, in a smaller, undomed chamber, the artist also shows us the tomb said to be Fatima's, the Prophet's daughter. Lastly, the artist shows

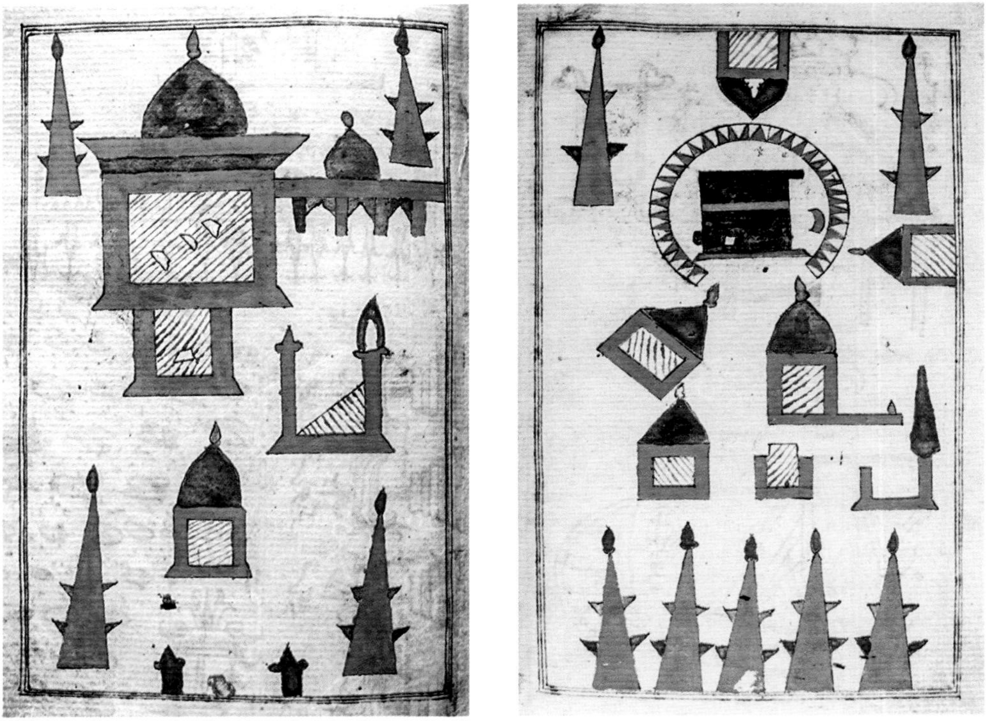

Figure 5.3 *Diagram of the Two Sanctuaries (*al-Ḥaramayn*), Mecca (R) and Medina (L). From a copy of* Dalāʾil al-khayrāt *('The waymarks of benefits') by Muḥammad al-Jazūlī (d.* c.869/1465*), produced in West Sumatra, and dated* 1229/1814*. Gold, gouache and ink on paper. Courtesy: Leiden University Library. MS Leiden, Or.* 1751*, ff.* 68*v*–69*r. Photo by J. J. Witkam.*

us the interior of the Mosque's domed treasury that stands in the courtyard. Turning next to the diagram of the Sacred Mosque on the right-hand page, although the artist shows us the interiors of the small domed edifices about the Kaʿba, all of which are unnamed but almost certainly include the pavilion housing the Zamzam well, the law school pavilions, the Mosque's treasury, and the Station of Abraham, the Kaʿba is blacked out and we are shown nothing.

We find the same phenomenon in two more pairs of diagrammatic images taken from other copies of the same devotional text (Figures 5.4 and 5.5).

An amplification of the phenomenon can be seen in Figures 5.6 and 5.7, in which lamps are shown hanging in the structures, as if to emphasise their interiors and to invite the viewer's eyes inside. The exception is the Kaʿba. Once more its interior is blocked to the eye, as if to indicate that the Kaʿba's architectural function to house and shelter is a function of its exterior only, where it 'houses' the world that unfolds centrifugally from it, a subject discussed in Chapter Two.[70] Unlike the Dome of the Rock

Figure 5.4 *Diagram of the Two Sanctuaries, Mecca (R) and Medina (L). From a copy of* Dalāʾil al-khayrāt *by al-Jazūlī, possibly produced in India. Thirteenth/nineteenth century; gouache and ink on paper. Courtesy: Leiden University Library. MS Leiden, Or. 22963, ff. 18v–19r. Photo by J. J. Witkam.*

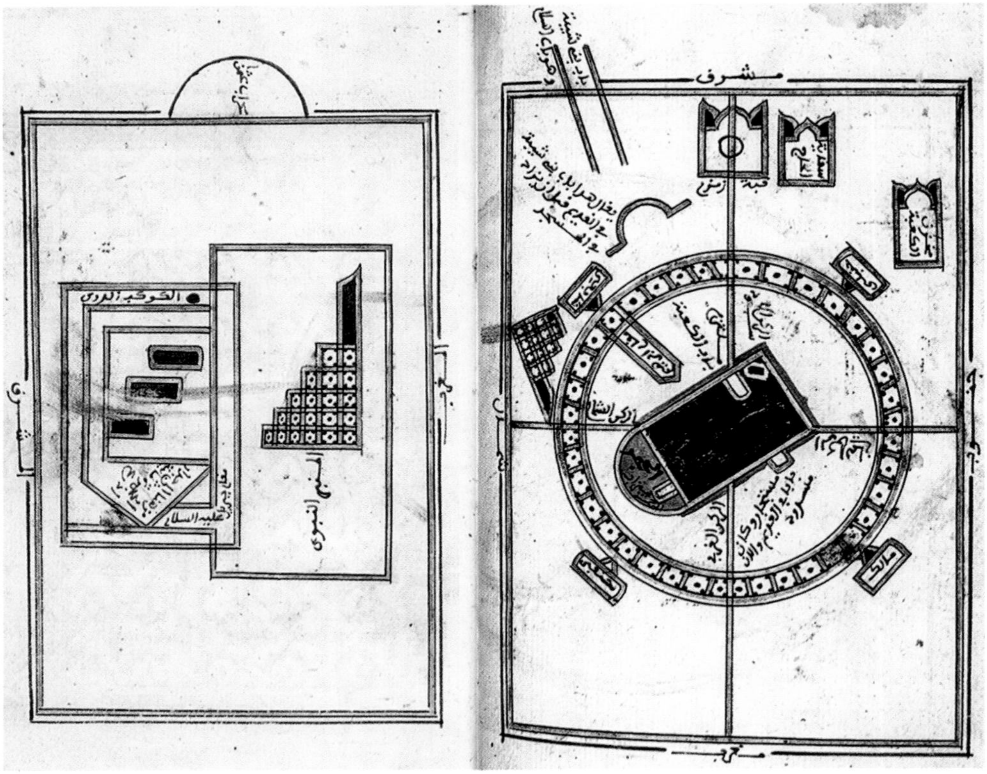

Figure 5.5 *Diagram of the Two Sanctuaries, Mecca (R) and Medina (L). From a copy of* Dalāʾil al-khayrāt *by al-Jazūlī, produced in North Africa in* 1048/1639. *Gold, gouache and ink;* 14.8 × 20.7*cm (folio). Courtesy: Chester Beatty Library. CBL Ar* 4223, *ff.* 3*v*–4*r*. *© The Trustees of the Chester Beatty Library, Dublin.*

in Jerusalem, another shrine-like, enclosed building to which the Kaʿba is often compared but whose diagrammatic representation commonly shows the Rock (*al-Ṣakhra*) and other internal content (Figure 5.8), the Kaʿba's curtained walls contain nothing.[71]

Importantly, the black paint used to depict the *Kiswa*'s curtaining of the Kaʿba's walls is not the cause of this image-based indication that the House houses in reverse, from outside. In other words, the objection that this image-based indication is merely the effect of the opacity of black paint does not hold. That is because in two almost negative versions of the foregoing pairs of diagrammatic images, both from the same devotional text, we do see inside the Kaʿba. In these two pairs of images, the Kaʿba's lack of housing, its emptiness, is now even more apparent, but the black paint that in the other pairs of diagrammatic images was used so extensively to depict the *Kiswa*, here is all but marginal (Figures 5.9 and 5.10). Here the eye is let in, but is again shown nothing.

Figure 5.6 *Diagram of the Two Sanctuaries, Mecca (R) and Medina (L). From a copy of* Dalāʾil al-khayrāt *by al-Jazūlī, possibly produced in Kashmir or Gujarat. Thirteenth/nineteenth century; gold, gouache and ink on paper. Courtesy: Leiden University Library. MS Leiden, Or. 14276, ff. 70v–71r. Photo by J. J. Witkam.*

Part Three: The Kaʿba as Placeholder

As noted in the Introduction, making architectural copies of the Kaʿba is a relatively common practice in Islamic culture, the origins of which allegedly date to pre-Islamic times. It is especially common in Sufism, where, as I have argued elsewhere, the practice exemplifies an aspect of Eliade's concept of the sacred centre.[72]

According to Eliade, a culture's sacred centre is inherently replicable. This replicability, he says, answers a human desire 'to find oneself always and without effort in the Centre of the World, at the heart of reality'.[73] In what remains of this chapter, I wish to argue that the replication of the Kaʿba can be understood not just in the religious terms of Eliade's concept, but also in the secular terms of another place-related concept, that of the placeholder. The argument I wish to make is that the Kaʿba is to Islam what the vanishing point of linear perspective is to modernity: the

Figure 5.7 *Diagram of the Two Sanctuaries, Mecca (R) and Medina (L). From a copy of* Dalāʾil al-khayrāt *by al-Jazūlī, produced in Iran. Early twelfth/eighteenth century; gold, gouache and ink on paper;* 20 × 11*cm (folio) Courtesy: bpk / Museum für Islamische Kunst, Staatliche Museen zu Berlin. I.*32/69 (00013668).

placeholder of a symbolic order, and something equally replicable. Just as the vanishing point has been interpreted by mathematicians as the visual equivalent of numerical zero, visual zero, so I shall interpret the Kaʿba as tectonic zero, the emptiness at the heart of the House forming part of this interpretation.

Following the anthropologist Webb Keane, I mean by modernity 'a conceptual orientation for actions' and 'an idea that has become a ubiquitous part of historical consciousness'.[74] 'Modernity,' writes Walter Mignolo, 'names a set of diverse but coherent narratives, since they belong to the same cosmology [. . . namely] the Western Christian version of humanity, complemented by secular . . . narratives of science, economic progress, political democracy and lately globalization.'[75] I neither mean to oppose modernity to Islam nor imply that they are mutually exclusive; the skyscrapers filling twenty-first-century Mecca prove that no such exclusivity exists. You can be in two places at once.

Figure 5.8 *Side elevation of the Aqsa Mosque (top) and plan of the Dome of the Rock (bottom), Jerusalem. From a copy of* Futūḥ al-Ḥaramayn *('Revelations of the two sanctuaries') by Muḥyī al-Dīn Lārī (d. 933/1526), dated 984/1577. Gold, gouache and ink. Courtesy: Bibliothèque Nationale de France. Supp. Pers. 1514, fol. 42v.*

Linear perspective and mathematical zero

In his award-winning book *The Dominion of the Eye: Urbanism, Art, and Power in Early Modern Florence*, Marvin Trachtenberg says this of trecento Florentine painters and urban planners:

> [T]recento painters shared with urban planners an intense engagement with the observer, with controlling the location and angle of vision and coordinating what is seen with where it is ideally seen from. This scopic desire led to the devising, respectively, of illusionistic and real spatial structures that fixed the ideal viewing point of both painting and monumental architecture, sometimes with extraordinary precision. Both media solicited the ambulatory viewer's immobility

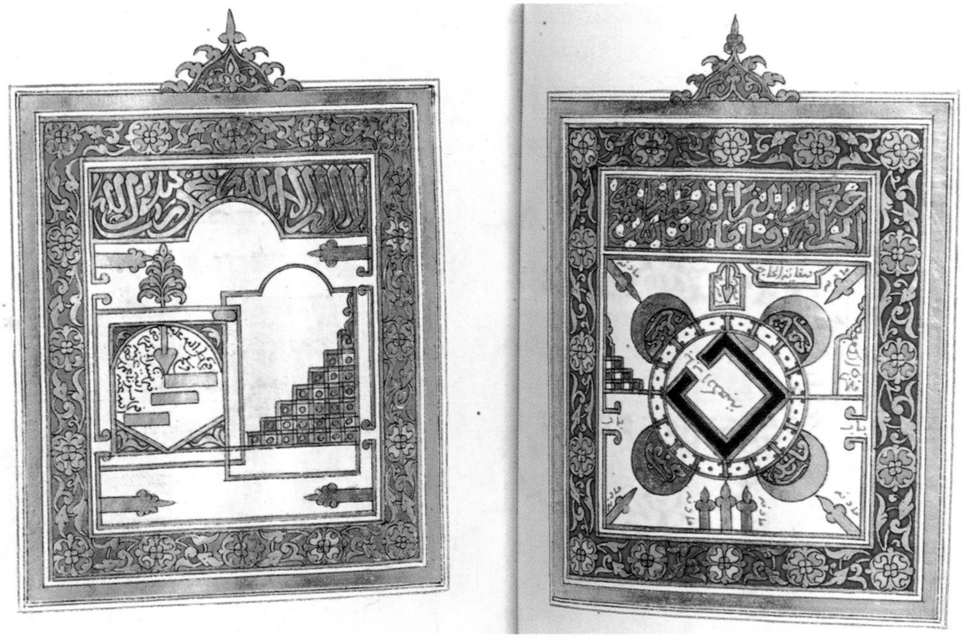

Figure 5.9 *Diagram of the Two Sanctuaries, Mecca (R) and Medina (L). From a copy of* Dalāʾil al-khayrāt *by al-Jazūlī, produced in North Africa. Thirteenth/nineteenth century; gold, gouache and ink on paper;* 14.5 × 13*cm (folio). Courtesy: The Aga Khan Museum. AKM* 535*, ff.* 16*v*–17*r.* © *The Aga Khan Museum.*

> at a particular station, where the spatially structured and structuring pictorial and scenographic image was ideally to be sensorially produced and visually consumed. Whether this new experience was essentially 'pictorial' or 'architectural' is rather moot.[76]

According to Trachtenberg, the Panopticon-like visuality that these urban practices gave rise to was deliberately produced and reproduced by the Florentine state as an instrument of authoritarian control.[77] It is not hard to see its apotheosis in Baron Haussmann's redevelopment of Paris in the mid-nineteenth century.[78] Although the following eyewitness account by a Tunisian visitor to Haussmann's Paris refers to the experience of seeing a photographic panorama of the redeveloped city at the Paris world fair of 1889, not the city itself, his words are nonetheless revealing. Echoing the experience of the imaginary warder at the centre of the Panopticon, this visitor writes: 'No different from reality . . . the observer sees himself at the centre of the city.'[79]

In Trachtenberg's book, a new origin story for the development of linear perspective is presented. Trachtenberg argues that the quattrocento invention of linear perspective in Florence was dependent on the trecento city's

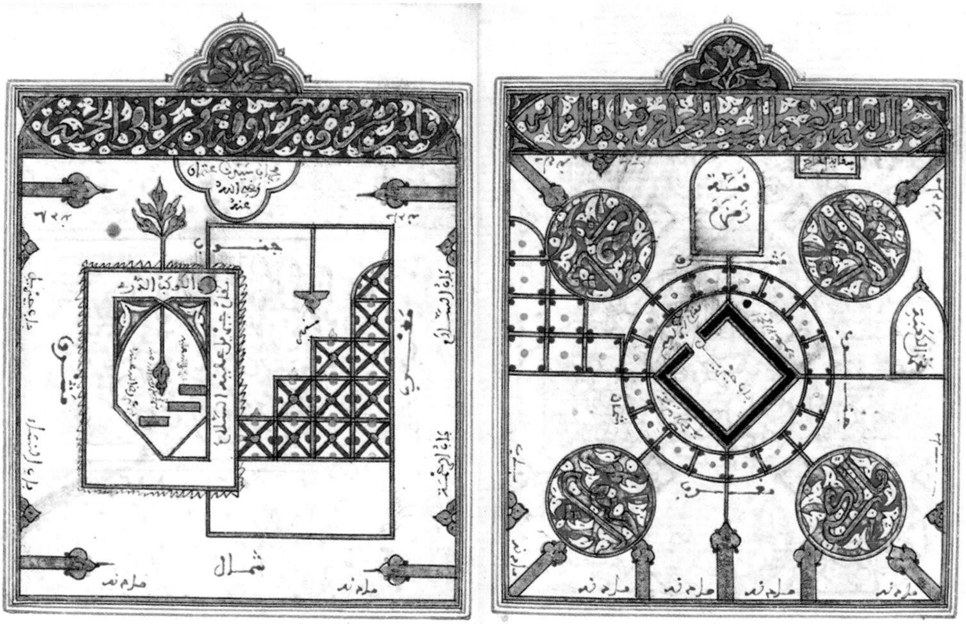

Figure 5.10 *Diagram of the Two Sanctuaries, Mecca (R) and Medina (L). From a copy of* Dalā᾿il al-khayrāt *by al-Jazūlī, produced in Morocco. Thirteenth/nineteenth century; 10.5 × 10cm (folio); gold, gouache and ink on paper. Courtesy: bpk/Staatsbibliothek zu Berlin. MS. OR. OCT 240, ff. 5v–6r (70156677, 70156678).*

incipient early modern visuality, and that the historical linkage between the two is provided by Brunelleschi's lost perspective-demonstration panels. These panels are said to have represented two of the city's principal monuments, the Palazzo Vecchio and Baptistery, which had been either built or reworked according to the principles of the aforementioned trecento practices. As such, Trachtenberg argues, the panels tie trecento urban visuality to the quattrocento invention of linear perspective and further cement the tie between urbanism and painting initiated in the trecento.[80]

In view of the fact that Brunelleschi's panels are lost and thus effectively mythical, perhaps it is as well not to side wholly with Trachtenberg's argument. The gist of the argument, however, seems more than likely, especially when it is recalled that the *sine qua non* of linear perspective is the construction of a vanishing point or points behind the picture plane. As Brian Rotman and other mathematicians have shown, this point is the visual equivalent of mathematical zero, a number that came to Europe via the Islamic world, but which only entered Europe in the medieval period, possibly at the hands of an Italian merchant and mathematician who had been schooled in North Africa, namely, Leonardo of Pisa, known as Fibonacci (d. *c.*1250).[81] Fibonacci's books on mathematics and, especially, geometry were pivotal for the planning techniques that gave rise to the new urbanism and visuality of trecento Florence and its satellites.[82]

The vanishing point and tectonic zero

'No rocket ship to the moon could ever have been invented, let alone be built and function, without the humble heritage of Renaissance linear perspective.'[83] If this assertion by Samuel Edgerton in his book subtitled *How Renaissance Linear Perspective Changed Our Vision of the Universe* sounds hyperbolic, there is no shortage of similar assertions by other scholars that could replace it. For example, reworking a phrase coined by the philosopher of science Alexandre Koyré, Bryan Wootton refers to linear perspective's invention as the beginning of the 'mathematization of the world' and thus the seed of the scientific revolution itself.[84] Panofsky indicates something similar when he speaks of the linear perspectival image as a 'construction that is itself comprehensible only for a quite specific, indeed specifically modern, sense of space, or if you will, sense of the world'.[85]

On the basis of these and similar assertions, I would submit that linear perspective's vanishing point has fair claim to being the placeholder of modernity: the mythic foundation site of the modern world. 'If we look closely,' writes Jean Baudrillard with reference to the thought of Hannah Arendt, 'we see that the real world begins, in the modern age, with . . . the invention of an Archimedean point outside the world (on the basis of the invention of the telescope by Galileo and the discovery of modern mathematical calculation).'[86] With reference to the thought of Jonathan Z. Smith, I would add that from this foundation site arises modernity's symbolic order. As Smith explains: 'Once an individual or culture has expressed its vision of its place, a whole language of symbols and social structures will follow.'[87]

Regardless of the acceptability of this submission, in discussing the vanishing point we are led to the possibility that the Kaʿba, the mythic foundation site of the Islamic world, is also a form of zero. My reasoning follows below.

As just noted, mathematicians have seen in the vanishing point the equivalent of mathematical zero, namely, visual zero. As this visual zero, the vanishing point is a meta-sign, what Rotman terms 'a sign-about-signs outside it'.[88] This meta-sign ties infinity to itself;[89] and from it unfolds a symbolic system for visualising what lies between. Norman Bryson explains well this visualising work of the vanishing point: '[It] is the anchor of a system which *incarnates* the viewer, renders him tangible and corporeal [as] a measurable, and above all a visible object in a world of absolute visibility.'[90] Like mathematical zero, visual zero is a sign of the void, 'the place where no thing is', and the placeholder of a symbolic system that it is outside.[91] The Kaʿba, I would argue, is visual zero's structural equivalent: tectonic zero, anchoring and partly structuring the symbolic order of Islam.[92] As we saw in the diagrammatic images of the Two Sanctuaries, similar to the vanishing point, the Kaʿba is outside this order; for in these images the Kaʿba is effectively invisible, blacked out from sight. The Kaʿba can indeed be described, but knowing it is altogether different; it constitutes a mystery. In my opinion, signifying the place where no thing is, place-holding the symbolic order of Islam, is the ultimate work of the Kaʿba.

Drawing on Schimmel's research on Islamic letter mysticism in order to put into more culturally specific terms this interpretation of the Kaʿba as the placeholder of a symbolic order that it is outside, my argument can be reframed as follows. The Kaʿba functions like the *primordial point* in Kabbalah, beyond which, as Schimmel notes, 'nothing may be known or understood'.[93] In Islamic letter mysticism, this point takes the form of the calligraphic point (*nuqṭa*), the dot which is the measure of all the letters in Arabic calligraphy. Beyond it, Schimmel explains, 'nothing can reach, as there would be no harmoniously shaped letters unless they could grow out of and be measured by the dot'.[94] The first of the letters arising from the dot is *alif*, 'a'. Unlike the dot, it has a numerical value: one. Next comes *bāʾ*, 'b', with a value of two, and so on.[95] With these letters comes the Qurʾan, the quintessence of which is contained in the dot, as al-Ḥallāj (d. 309/922) explains:

> The Qurʾan contains the [science] of everything. Now the science of the Qurʾan is in its initial letters! The science of the initial letters is in the *lām-alif*; the science of the *lām-alif* is in the *alif*, and that of the *alif* is in the point.[96]

Conclusion

This chapter, the first of two on the Kaʿba's sheltering and holding, or housing functions, has investigated the House's near emptiness of material content and total emptiness of cultic content. Commencing with an analysis of what the early Islamic sources say the Kaʿba housed before the advent of Islam, we saw how the Prophet set about emptying that content upon his conquest of Mecca. We saw that before the conquest the Kaʿba was relatively full of content, and that after the conquest it was all but empty. This emptied state we then found to be conventionally acknowledged in diagrammatic images of the Two Sanctuaries, wherein the depicted *Kiswa* prevented the viewers' eyes from looking inside, as if to signal there was nothing there to see. This emptiness of the Kaʿba I then interpreted as a void that was constitutive of the Kaʿba's mystery, its rational unknowability. This void, I suggested, was the 'content' of the Kaʿba; whence followed my interpretation of the Kaʿba as a placeholder, a tectonic zero, place-holding the symbolic order of Islam.

In the next chapter, we shall see that the otherwise empty House with nothing to see is, for a short period of the Islamic calendar, imagined as housing plenitude itself: divine presence. We shall find that so full is the Kaʿba with too much to see during this period, that paradoxically there remains nothing to see.

CHAPTER SIX

The House as Dwelling

In the previous chapter we discussed the content of the Kaʿba: what was housed there before and after the advent of Islam, and what is held there today. In the present chapter, we shall continue to inquire into the housing functions of the Kaʿba by looking at a little-known function of the robe that covers the House, the *Kiswa*. Referring to descriptions and depictions of the Kaʿba by travellers, pilgrims and miniaturists, I shall argue that a particular way of hanging the *Kiswa* signals when within the House a divine presence is imagined to dwell.

The chapter is in two parts and will proceed as follows. First, a history and description of the *Kiswa*, leading to an examination of the *Kiswa*'s relationship to the Kaʿba. Here we shall ask if the *Kiswa* is integral to the Kaʿba or an afterthought, and if it hides or reveals the Kaʿba. Second, an analysis of the dynamics of the *Kiswa*, of how the different ways it is hung in the course of the Islamic year serve either to animate the Kaʿba from without or to prompt the perception that the Kaʿba has been animated from within, quickened. The first type of animation will be seen to be figurative only, the elevated *Kiswa* breaking up the otherwise unbroken solidity of the Kaʿba's walls. Via a review of verbal and visual representations of the Kaʿba, the second type of animation will be seen to verge on the literal, and at times cross into it.

Part One: A History and Description of the *Kiswa*

The history of the *Kiswa* has been well treated in scholarship. A number of European-language publications cover the subject, meaning that only an overview will be provided here, taken from the most extensive of them.[1] In tandem with a description of the *Kiswa*, this overview will facilitate an examination of the relationship of the *Kiswa* to the Kaʿba, which is not straightforward.

From the *Kiswa*'s alleged origins in the fifth century CE as a gift from a Southern Arabian ruler wishing to honour the Kaʿba, to the animal skins and palm weavings that allegedly first comprised it, the pre-Islamic history of the *Kiswa* is mired in uncertainty and will not detain us. The situation is only a little clearer in the early Islamic period, where we confront marked inconstancies in the *Kiswa*'s usage. For example, it is said that in this period every time a new *Kiswa* was presented to the Kaʿba, it was laid on top of the old one, threatening thereby the stability of the Kaʿba. ʿUmar b. al-Khaṭṭāb (r. 13–23/634–44) allegedly put a partial stop to this practice, by having sections of the old *Kiswa*s removed. The practice, however, apparently resumed at some point after his death, and it was left to the early Umayyads to do more: to remove all the old covers before the re-robing. Even so, at some point soon afterwards the practice was apparently resumed, because the sources speak of it continuing, on and off, into the ʿAbbasid period, definitively ending only in the Mamluk era.[2]

In the early Islamic period we also confront the fact that during Umayyad and ʿAbbasid rule the *Kiswa* was replaced either annually or biannually, and sometimes even thrice-annually. The Mamluks definitively ended that inconstancy, too.[3] They had a new *Kiswa* annually manufactured in Cairo, sending it with great ceremony in a caravan to Mecca, along with a splendidly embroidered but otherwise empty *maḥmal*, or palanquin. This popular and much politicised dispatch and delivery of the *Kiswa* as part of the Egyptian Hajj caravan long outlived the Mamluks.[4] It ended for good in 1953, even though Egypt continued to make the *Kiswa* until 1962, when Saudi Arabia took over sole responsibility for the robe's manufacture.[5]

Most significant of all regarding the inconstant usages of the *Kiswa* in the early Islamic period is the colour chosen for the *Kiswa*. The practice of having a black *Kiswa* was only introduced by al-Nāṣir li-Dīn Allāh (r. 575–622/1180–1226), the last of the effective ʿAbbasid caliphs, probably in 622/1225. Before then the *Kiswa* had been made in a variety of uniform hues, including red, green, white and yellow. After then black has been the sole defining colour of the *Kiswa*, with the exception of the Wahhabis, who, according to Burton, temporarily reverted to red when they took control of Mecca at the start of the nineteenth century.[6] Of course, in order to be legible from a distance, the embroidered inscriptions and decorations in the panels and cartouches sewn onto the *Kiswa* are of another colour, and to them we now turn via a description of the *Kiswa*.[7]

The *Kiswa*, which in photographs can appear to be seamless, in fact comprises a number of sections that are sewn together only after they have been hung from the roof of the Kaʿba. These sections in turn comprise subsections, which in the past were sewn together on the floor of the Sacred Mosque, before being rolled into bolts and hauled up by ropes to the roof for hanging. The bolts are heavy, especially as the lampas-woven silk from which the *Kiswa* is made is often backed with a cotton calico material for extra durability.

Depending on the period in question, the exact number of sections the *Kiswa* comprises varies, but at least four comprise the part of the *Kiswa* that curtains the walls but not the door. These sections are sometimes collectively called the *Thawb* (garment). Another section, often called the *Burquʿ* (face veil), comprises the part of the *Kiswa* that curtains the door; it possibly originated as this discrete part in the seventh/thirteenth century.[8] It, too, is made up of subsections and is the most elaborately decorated area of the *Kiswa*, being extensively embroidered with Qurʾanic verses, pious formulae, and information concerning its date of manufacture and patron's name, all sewn in a mixture of silver wire, gilded silver wire and/or gold-plated silver wire.[9]

Onto the larger part of the *Kiswa*, the aforementioned *Thawb*, the *Ḥizām* (belt) is sewn. It is approximately 1m wide and runs around all four sides of the Kaʿba at a short but historically variable distance below the roof. It comprises a historically variable number of sections: calligraphic panels of Qurʾanic verses and pious formulae, and the date and name of its manufacture and patron. All are embroidered in a mixture of silver wire, gilded silver wire and/or gold-plated silver wire. The latter two wire types predominate in the embroidery, giving the *Ḥizām* its distinctive yellowish hue.

Onto the *Thawb* are also sewn at historically variable intervals calligraphic medallions (*jāmāt, dārāt, dawāʾir*) of Qurʾanic verses, embroidered in the same manner as the *Ḥizām*. The Qurʾanic verses and pious formulae chosen for them and the *Ḥizām* have changed over time, as have those for the *Burquʿ*.[10] Nevertheless, one especially common verse for the *Ḥizam* is: 'The first House established for mankind was that at [Mecca], a place of blessing and a guidance for all beings' (Q 3:96).[11]

Exactly when the *Ḥizām* and medallions first formed part of the *Kiswa* is uncertain. In terms of eyewitness accounts, Ibn Jubayr clearly observed the existence of both in 579/1183.[12] Before him, in the fourth/tenth century, Ibn ʿAbd Rabbih claims to have seen inscriptions on the *Kiswa*, although he does not say where they were located.[13] His claim is, however, corroborated by the early Islamic sources, above all by medieval historians citing from them.[14] From these same historians, al-Mūjān has presented evidence that the medallions existed as early the third/ninth century.[15]

From approximately the tenth/sixteenth century, the *Thawb* itself has also been a source of religious inscriptions, because repeatedly woven into it in a zigzag pattern are Qurʾanic verses and/or pious formulae.[16] Except in close-ups, like this book's cover, these inscriptions rarely show in photographs, being the same colour as the *Kiswa*. They also rarely get represented in painted depictions of the *Kiswa*, but one of the Persian miniatures that comprises the review of visual representations of the Kaʿba in part two below shows them (Figure 6.18). In contrast, non-calligraphic, medallion-like decorations frequently get depicted in miniatures; often they completely overwhelm the *Kiswa*, rendering the depiction fantastical. The same review contains a number of examples.

Lastly in this description of the *Kiswa*, non-calligraphic decoration has also sometimes formed part of it. In the fifth/eleventh century, Nāṣir-i Khusraw observed twelve decorative *mihrab*-shaped frames, *miḥrābhā*, embroidered onto it. He describes what he saw as follows: 'On four sides of the covering are woven coloured *mihrab*s geometrically decorated with gold thread. On each side are three *mihrab*s, a large one in the middle and a smaller one on either side.'[17] Although similarly shaped frames were also observed by Ibn Jubayr in the following century, by the eighth/fourteenth century *mihrab*-like frames seem to have been replaced by the calligraphic medallions.[18]

The relationship between the Kiswa *and the Ka'ba*

Whilst the parallels might seem obvious, it is problematic to relate the *Kiswa* to the veil, or *ḥijāb*, that is imposed on or chosen by many Muslim women.[19] That is because, unlike the veil, whose purpose includes hiding, the purpose of the *Kiswa* is not to hide the Ka'ba. Although technically speaking cover the Ka'ba is what the *Kiswa* does, this act of covering is similar to that of the skin of the human body, and one hardly talks of the skin as hiding the body. So closely does the *Kiswa* follow the contours of the Ka'ba before being fastened tight to the base, to the point of not covering the Black Stone but cutting around it, that thinking of the *Kiswa* in this way – as skin stretched over a body – is not inappropriate.[20] Significantly, the Qur'an uses the root of the Arabic word for *Kiswa*, k-s-w, to mean 'to robe (in a skin-like way)'. Referring to the creation of humankind, it says: 'We robed (*kasawnā*) the bones with flesh.'[21]

As an aside, it should be noted that tightening the *Kiswa* to such an extent that it cannot ripple in the wind was neither possible before the last century nor perhaps even desirable. As the Swiss traveller John Lewis Burckhardt (d. 1817) says of the rippling *Kiswa* during his visit to Mecca in 1229/1814:

> [T]he slightest breeze causes it to move in slow undulations, which are hailed with prayers by the congregation assembled around the building, as a sign of the presence of its guardian angels, whose wings, by their motion, are supposed to be the cause of the waving of the covering.[22]

Sometimes, the wind would do more than ripple but tear the *Kiswa*, ripping it off the building.[23] That might be interpreted as an ill omen, as happened in 644/1246, when it was taken to presage the end of the 'Abbasids and the coming of the Mongols.[24]

The *Kiswa* traces and thus reveals the Ka'ba's form; it does not hide it.[25] Although one correctly talks of the Ka'ba and the *Kiswa* as two discrete objects, in certain ways they form an inalienable unit, just like the body and its skin.[26] Apropos of this reading, Lisa Golombek memorably speaks of surface decoration in Islamic architecture 'as a "membrane" or fabric encasing the body of the architecture'.[27] Might there be a connection between Islamic architectural decoration and the *Kiswa*, the latter informing the former?

In view of the *Kiswa*'s relationship to the Ka'ba, and recalling the fact that honouring the Ka'ba is allegedly the reason for the *Kiswa*'s existence, robing the Ka'ba is a good description of the *Kiswa*'s covering function. That is because the notion of hiding is not strong in the term, whereas the notion of honouring is strong. By the same token, veiling the Ka'ba is not a good description of the *Kiswa*'s covering function, because as just explained, the *Kiswa* does not hide the Ka'ba but reveals it.

Should the skin analogy be found wanting, one can reach a similar conclusion regarding the inappropriateness of the veiling-as-hiding description of the *Kiswa*'s covering function by arguing as follows. In the same way that one does not see more of a person's identity when their clothes are removed, just more of their body, so one does not see more of the Ka'ba, more of its identity, when the *Kiswa* is removed or raised. Although Burckhardt and Burton both note that the Ka'ba is referred to as naked, *'uryāna*, at the moment when the old *Kiswa* is removed, that does not mean that the pilgrim who is in the Sacred Mosque then sees more of the Ka'ba's identity than the pilgrim who is not.[28] He or she sees only more of its body.

'Since we live in an *appearing* world,' conjectures Hannah Arendt, 'is it not much more plausible that the relevant and the meaningful in this world of ours should be located precisely on the surface?'[29] Showing what matters of the Ka'ba, the *Kiswa* is proof of her conjecture. The contrast with the Qur'anic hermeneutic principle *bāṭin/ẓāhir* (inward/outward), discussed in Chapter Three, could hardly be greater. With the *Kiswa*, all is apparent.

This interpretation of the robing and revealing but not veiling and hiding *Kiswa* we shall find amplified below. Against the interpretation, it should, however, be noted that Rūzbihān Baqlī (d. 605/1209) speaks of the veiled and hidden Ka'ba. In his Sufi interpretation of the Hajj rituals, he says that the Ka'ba is veiled in the following way: first, by the Sacred Mosque (but note, not by the *Kiswa*); second, by Mecca; and third, by the Sanctuary's two hills, Ṣafā and Marwa. These veilings, he explains, are an allegory of God, who is hidden behind veils in Paradise.[30]

The inalienable Kiswa?

In his writings on the origins and development of architecture, the nineteenth-century architect and critic Gottfried Semper (d. 1879) presents two observations relevant to the foregoing discussion of the relationship between the *Kiswa* and the Ka'ba. The first of these observations is that the use of animal skins, plant weavings and woven fabrics preceded the construction and use of tectonic walls for the isolation of space.[31] By 'the isolation of space' he means the creation of the enclosing booth, or 'pen', which he believes represents a critical moment in the formation of the concept of home, because it allowed for 'the *inner life* [to become] separated from the *outer life*'.[32] The second of Semper's observations is that, despite the subsequent development of tectonic walls, textiles were still used to dress them: to mask and dematerialise them.[33] As he explains this second observation: 'The denial of reality, of the material, is necessary if form is to emerge as a meaningful symbol, as an autonomous creation of man.'[34]

Applying Semper's observations in reverse order to the Ka'ba and *Kiswa* results in the following two interpretations: the form of the Ka'ba, so essential to the building's orienting functions, necessitates the *Kiswa*; the *Kiswa* first formed the House. As such, the *Kiswa* cannot be considered a supplement to the Ka'ba, an afterthought. Contrary to the report in the early Islamic sources that the *Kiswa* was first placed on the Ka'ba in the fifth century CE by a ruler wishing to honour it, it cannot be a later addition.

Another report in the early sources hints at the likely veracity of this interpretation, for it speaks of a very early stage of the Ka'ba's development, when the House was a rudimentary unroofed 'booth' (*'arīsh*), what Semper calls a pen. According to the report, this booth was robed. 'In the pre-Islamic period,' the report reads, 'the Ka'ba was built of loose stones (*raḍm laysa fīhā madar*). Its size was such that young goats could break into it. Its vestments (*thiyāb*) were placed on top of it, hanging down.'[35]

Related to this conjecture that the Ka'ba must always have been robed is Rubin's discussion of the term *'arīsh* that is used in the early sources for this booth. He writes:

> The term '*'arīsh*' has a profound ritual significance. This was, in fact, the word by which the Arabs used to refer to the Tabernacle which was built in the wilderness by the Children of Israel, in the time of Moses. The [early Islamic sources] seem to imply that the Ka'ba was originally built and treated like a similar sacred tabernacle, in which the dominant element was the *kiswa*.[36]

He adds that al-Azraqī and others report that the Ka'ba which Adam is said to have constructed was a tent (*khayma*): potentially a tabernacle-like structure, and something almost certainly made of skin or cloth.[37]

Part Two: The Dynamics of the *Kiswa*

With the notable exception of William Young's article discussed in Chapter Four, the dynamics of the Ka'ba have received little or no attention in scholarship. To that subject this part of the chapter is devoted. As I shall show, the *Kiswa*'s temporary but calendrically defined partial elevations in the course of the Islamic year do more than animate the otherwise unbroken solidity of the Kaʿba's exterior. Rather, they have been popularly imagined to signal when the Kaʿba is animated from within, alive. This signalling function of the *Kiswa* is as little known in scholarship as its honouring function is well known.

The elevated Kiswa

From medieval and early modern travel accounts, we know that the Kaʿba was regularly opened throughout the year. Precisely how often depends on the period in question; for example, at the time when Ibn Jubayr was visiting at the end of the sixth/twelfth century, it was opened weekly.[38] For the most part, the days when it was opened were times when members of the public were permitted to go inside, even if this permission was more in principle than in practice, because the large crowds and need for bribery made entrance impossible for many.[39] On the days when the Kaʿba was opened so that it could be washed (*ghusl*), however, the public was not admitted inside.[40] As with today's politically motivated invitations to tour the Kaʿba's interior, discussed in Chapter Five, it seems that the washing of the House was for a select few only.[41]

During the thirteenth/nineteenth century, one of the two times in the year when the Kaʿba was washed occurred immediately prior to the moment when the building was closed to everyone for approximately fifteen days.[42] That moment of closure, a day falling at the very end of the month of Dhū al-Qaʿda, seems to be more or less consistent in all the travel accounts, medieval and early modern, regardless of whether or not the Kaʿba was washed beforehand.[43] At that moment, the bottom of the *Kiswa* was either elevated, cut, covered or cut and replaced with a wrap (*izār*), so that it no longer reached to the ground (or was no longer exposed at the ground), but just low- to mid-door level.[44] The maximum height it reached from the ground this way was about three-and-a-half metres.

With the *Kiswa* elevated, cut, covered or cut and wrapped thus, the travel accounts relate that 'they [viz., the people] say the Kaʿba has entered the state of *iḥrām*'.[45] In the legal literature, the state of *iḥrām* is a ritually consecrated, temporary condition of taboo that pilgrims must be in for the Hajj rituals; *ghusl*, or the major ritual ablution, usually precedes it.[46] As just noted, *ghusl* is also the term commonly used for the washing of the Kaʿba. As noted in the Introduction, *iḥrām* is also the name given to the pilgrims' garb.

This shared terminological identity of the washed and *Kiswa*-elevated Kaʿba and the pilgrims' consecrated state is presumably not accidental, especially as Dhū al-Qaʿda is the month that precedes Dhū al-Ḥijja, the Hajj month. Nevertheless, come the twentieth century, it is also an identity that was viewed with scepticism by some authorities. For example, Ibrāhīm Rifʿat Bāshā (d. 1354/1935), who was often in charge of the Egyptian Hajj caravan during the first decade of that century, averred that the reason for cutting *Kiswa* and replacing the cut area with a wrap was not, as popularly believed, to put the Kaʿba into an *iḥrām* state. Rather, it was to allow the custodians of the Kaʿba, the Banū Shayba, to sell the offcut, and to keep the *Kiswa* clean from the hands of pilgrims reaching out to touch it.[47]

As Young notes, neither part of this official's explanation is convincing, most especially the first part, because if the practice were, as Young says, 'a ploy designed to satisfy the cupidity of the [Banū Shayba], it seems unlikely that the Muslim community would have permitted it to continue year after year'.[48] 'It seems preferable,' Young concludes, 'to accept the notion that this ritual put the Kaʿba in *iḥrām*, as if it were a pilgrim.'[49] Interestingly, Ibn Jubayr and Ibn Baṭṭūṭa both propound the second part of the official's explanation, but only with regard to the temporary elevation of the new *Kiswa* (see below); not the elevation that 'the people say' signifies that the Kaʿba is in its state of *iḥrām*.[50]

From the published engraving of the drawing made by Ali Bey (d. 1233/1818), we know how the Kaʿba looked when it was in this perceived state of *iḥrām*, at least for the early thirteenth/nineteenth century, the time when he was there (Figure 6.1). In this engraving, two depictions of the Kaʿba are presented, both based on Ali Bey's original drawings. The depiction on the left (numbered '1') shows the Kaʿba in its perceived state of *iḥrām*. The depiction on the right (numbered '2') shows the Kaʿba with its new *Kiswa* unfurled over it; for as reported by Ali Bey and others – medieval, early-modern and modern – when the Kaʿba comes out of its perceived state of *iḥrām* on or very close to the third day of the Hajj, the old *Kiswa* is replaced with a new one.[51] That third day is 10th Dhū al-Ḥijja, observed by non-pilgrims as the Feast of Sacrifice (*ʿĪd al-Aḍḥā*). It is also the day when the pilgrims come out of their state of *iḥrām*. In the medieval and early modern periods, the unfurling of the new *Kiswa* to replace the old one happened over a three- or four-day timespan; at the start of the twentieth century it happened in one day.[52]

As can be seen in the engraving, the shortened *Kiswa* of the Kaʿba in its perceived state of *iḥrām* is less elaborately arranged than the shortened *Kiswa* of the newly attired Kaʿba. In another thirteenth/nineteenth engraving of the newly attired Kaʿba, this time based on a drawing by Burton, we see the new *Kiswa* in a similarly elaborate shape, albeit more serrated than undulating (Figure 6.2). This rising-and-falling shape was achieved by means of ropes from the Kaʿba's roof.[53] It was a temporary shape only, lasting until the end of the pilgrimage season, when the bottom of the *Kiswa* was let all the way down, once again to skirt the building.[54] For much of that same period, the Kaʿba was once again open for public entry.[55]

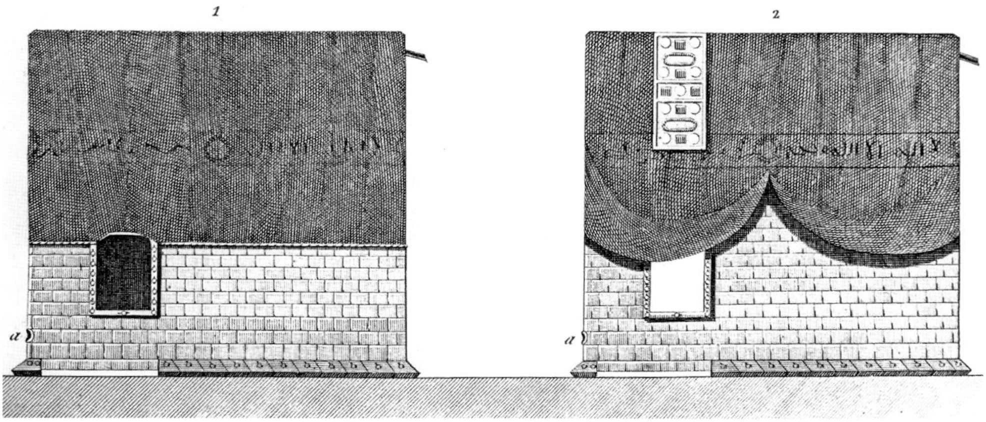

Figure 6.1 *The Ka'ba in its perceived state of* iḥrām *(L) and with its new* Kiswa *(R), as recorded by Ali Bey (d. 1233/1818) in 1221/1807. (Source: Ali Bey 1816, vol. 2, pp. 78–9.) Contrary to what one might have expected, the Ka'ba's door looks open in the image on the left and shut in the image on the right. As noted by the traveller Léon Roches (d. 1901), at the end of the month of Dhū al-Qa'da the Ka'ba was shut only after it had been washed. Perhaps that moment had not yet been reached when Ali Bey made his drawing, or perhaps in the process of preparing the engraving, the shadows and highlights became reversed.*

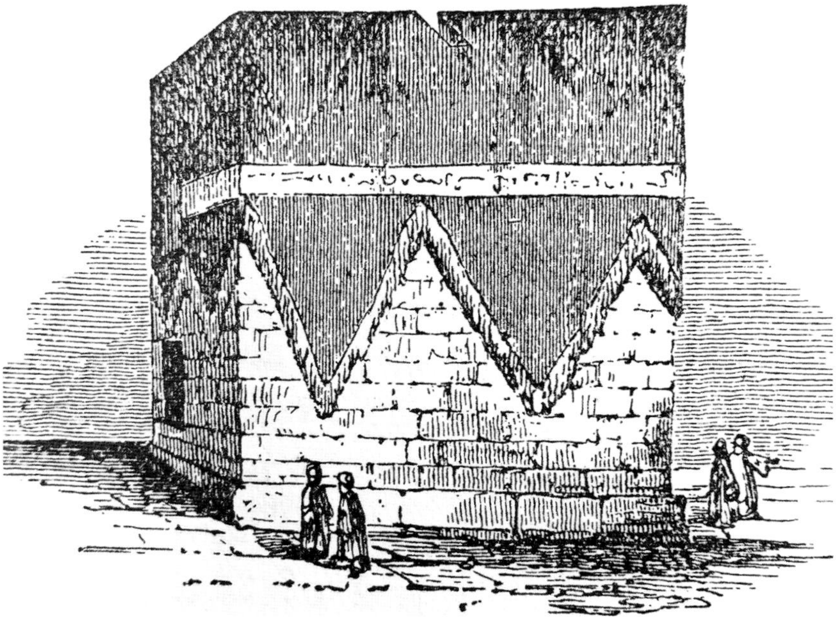

Figure 6.2 *The Ka'ba with its new* Kiswa*, as recorded by Richard Burton (d. 1890) in 1269/1853. (Source: Burton 1893, vol. 2, p. 212.)*

On the basis of both engravings, it is reasonable to assert that, visually speaking, elevating the *Kiswa* animates the Kaʿba. In this assertion, the verb 'to animate' is used figuratively only, the *Kiswa*'s risen shape serving to break the solidity of the Kaʿba's walls. At a certain point of the Islamic calendar, however, a less figurative use of the verb can also be said to apply to the Kaʿba. As I shall demonstrate, in this second usage the *Kiswa*'s dynamics again play a signal role; for as recorded in certain medieval and pre-modern verbal and visual representations of the Kaʿba, when elevated the *Kiswa* is imagined as indicating that the Kaʿba is animated from within, full of celestial life. To that demonstration the chapter now turns, commencing with the verbal representations.

Averring that the raised *Kiswa* is a signal of something is correct, as proved by the popular interpretation of the uniformly elevated cut, covered or cut and wrapped shape of the *Kiswa* as signalling when the Kaʿba is in its state of *iḥrām*. It is confirmed by Ibn Jubayr's additional reference to that same shape: 'It is as if this tucking up (*tashshmīr*) [of the *Kiswa*] were a signal (*iydhān*) to the people [journeying to Mecca] to hurry along, and a signal of the closeness of the moment of the awaited farewell to [the Kaʿba].'[56] Can more be said about the signal?

The living Kaʿba

In the medieval Arabic travel accounts, no terminological distinction is made between the uniformly elevated, cut, covered, or cut and wrapped shape of the old *Kiswa* that popularly signifies the *iḥrām*-state Kaʿba and the rising-and-falling shape of the new *Kiswa* at or after the Feast of Sacrifice. Rather, in both cases the phrase used to refer to the *Kiswa*'s elevated shape is: 'the Kaʿba's skirts are tucked up' (*shummirat adhyāl al-Kaʿba*).[57]

As Young points out, the passive verb of this phrase, *shummira*, does not just mean to be tucked up, but to be tucked up for a purpose, namely, 'to free the legs for quick walking or running'.[58] In its active form, that is how the verb is used, for example, in the post-Qurʾanic idiom 'war tucked up its garment from its shank' (*shammarat ʿan sāqihā*).[59] It is how the verb is used by the poet al-Mutanabbī (d. 354/965) to describe the miracles effected by his poetry. 'By way of [my poetry],' he boasts, 'the cripple takes flight (*mushammir*) and the tone-deaf sings like a bird.'[60] And it is how both the verb and phrase are used by Ibn ʿArabī to describe the moment when he believed the Kaʿba was freeing itself from its foundations to attack him for having shown insufficient respect to it:

> As perceived by the faculty of my imagination (*fīmā takhayyala lī*), I saw [the Kaʿba] tuck up its skirts (*shammarat adhyālahā*) and prepare to rise from its foundations (*qawāʿid*). It intended to repel me . . . and stop me from

> circumambulating it . . . As perceived by the faculty of my imagination, it [then] rose above the ground from its foundations, tucking up its skirts like one who tucks up his garments (*thiyāb*) before springing from his spot. Such did [the Kaʿba] seem to me: it had gathered up its veils (*jamaʿat sutūrahā*) to pounce at me.[61]

In the popular imagination recorded by the travellers and the mystical imagination of Ibn ʿArabī, the tucked-up *Kiswa* is the sign of an internally animated Kaʿba. In the popular imagination, the animation takes one of two forms. Either it takes the form of a pilgrim in a ritually consecrated state of taboo, off limits to all but God; this is signalled by the uniformly elevated, cut, covered or cut and wrapped shape of the old *Kiswa*. Or it takes the form of an unveiled bride; this is signalled by the rising-and-falling shape of the new *Kiswa*.[62] (Note, however, that as discussed in Chapter Four, imagining the Kaʿba as an unveiled bride is not restricted to the moment when the Kaʿba's new *Kiswa* is unfurled and tucked up; the image is not specific to the *Kiswa*'s dynamics.[63]) In the case of Ibn ʿArabī, the animation takes a divine form, because after the Kaʿba has girded itself to leap at the terrified mystic, God communicates with him using the Kaʿba as an oral conduit.[64]

In the visual imagination that underpins many Kaʿba-centric Persian miniatures, the animation also takes a divine form. To those miniatures we now turn.

The divinely animated Kaʿba? A review of Persian miniatures

In many Kaʿba-centric Persian miniatures, or Persian miniatures in which the Kaʿba is part of the narrative illustrated and not a topographical sign similar to its function in the Two Sanctuaries diagrammatic images discussed in Chapter Five, the Kaʿba is imagined as alive. Or so I would argue. That is because these miniatures show the *Kiswa* in its tucked-up shape: either its uniformly elevated 'taboo' shape or its rising-and-falling 'bridal' shape. I would further argue that because the events these miniatures illustrate have a cosmic signature, being cosmically significant for Islam and/or cosmically inspired, the Kaʿba is additionally imagined as divinely alive. The frequent inclusion of celestial phenomena, depicted as part of the events, would support that reading.

In brief, what I wish to argue is that in these Kaʿba-centric Persian miniatures the normally empty Kaʿba has been imagined as temporarily filled with a divine animating presence, which the tucked-up *Kiswa* signals. The following review presents the evidence for this argument.

Almost a century ago Ettinghausen noted the frequently extraordinary, painterly appearance of the *Kiswa* in Kaʿba-centric Persian miniatures.

Apart from saying that it was 'often shown in a raised position', he concluded nothing more.[65] Can more be concluded?

Review

Before commencing the review, I need to explain why I shall not be attending to the texts in which the miniatures are set. Following the lead of Marianna Shreve Simpson in her pioneering analysis of Persian Kaʿba-centric miniatures, I believe we must suppose that the painters of these and other Kaʿba-centric miniatures were 'transferring the imagery and iconography from one poetic text and episode to [an] other'.[66] They were not, in other words, paying attention to the specifics of the texts that their images illustrated, but creatively repeating an iconographic formula.[67] This claim can be buttressed by the fact that often included in these images are details not provided by the texts.[68] We have already seen an example of this in Chapter Five, in the miniature of the Prophet and ʿAlī smashing idols outside the Kaʿba, not inside it, contrary to both the text and the reproduced text block (Figure 5.1). Accordingly, because the loosely formulaic quality of the miniatures suggests that the texts they illustrate or accompany do not automatically hold the key to their interpretation, in the following review I am excluding them. Additionally, with reference to the miniatures in the review of the Prophet's miraculous heavenly ascension (*miʿrāj*), all of which include a vista of Mecca, I do not ask why Mecca is shown, not Jerusalem, the traditional locus of the ascension. This is not only because the question falls outside the scope of this review, but it has also been asked before.[69] I note only that, technically speaking, the ascension comprises two parts: the Prophet's night journey (*isrāʾ*) from Mecca to Jerusalem on the flying steed al-Burāq; and the ascension proper, as often narrated also on al-Burāq.[70] Because Mecca is the technical starting point of the ascension, its inclusion in the miniatures is therefore not particularly surprising.

Perhaps the clearest examples of what I am arguing is the imagined, divinely animated Kaʿba are the miniatures of the Prophet's ascension. A number of them exist.[71] Of the four known to me that accompany the prefaces of some copies of Niẓāmī's *Khamsa* ('Quintet'), three show the Kaʿba with its *Kiswa* elevated in such a way as to indicate it is in its perceived state of *iḥrām*. Celestial phenomena abound (Figures 6.3–6.6). As regards the cosmic significance of the Prophet's ascension for Islam, it could scarcely be greater.[72]

The last of these four ascension miniatures (Figure 6.6) is important, for it does not conform to what I propose is the convention for the representation of the *Kiswa* in Persian Kaʿba-centric miniatures, which is to depict it in its tucked-up form. This miniature is not, however, the exception that

Figure 6.3 *The Prophet rides over the Kaʿba upon the winged steed al-Burāq on his miraculous journey to the heavens* (miʿrāj)*. From a copy of the* Khamsa *('Quintet') by Niẓāmī (d.* c.613/1217*), dated* 900/1495*. Gold, gouache and ink on paper;* 17 × 24.3*cm (folio). Courtesy: The British Library. BL Or.* 6810*, fol.* 5*v. © The British Library Board.*

Figure 6.4 *The Prophet rides over the Kaʿba upon al-Burāq on his miraculous journey to the heavens. From a copy of the* Khamsa *by Niẓāmī, dated 813–14/1410–11. Gold, gouache and ink on paper; 12.7 × 18.4cm (folio). Courtesy: The British Library. BL Add. 27261, fol. 6r. © The British Library Board.*

***Figure 6.5** The Prophet rides over the Kaʿba upon al-Burāq on his miraculous journey to the heavens. From a copy of the* Khamsa *by Niẓāmī, dated* 866/1461. *Gold, gouache and ink on paper;* 20.4 × 31*cm (folio). Courtesy: Topkapı Palace Library. TSMK H.* 761, *fol.* 4*v.*

Figure 6.6 *The Prophet rides over the Kaʿba upon al-Burāq on his miraculous journey to the heavens. From a copy of the* Khamsa *by Niẓāmī, dated to c.910/1505. Gold, gouache and ink on paper; 19 x 28.7cm. Courtesy: The Keir Collection. Keir III.207. © The Keir Collection of Islamic Art on loan to the Dallas Museum of Art, K.1.2014.737.*

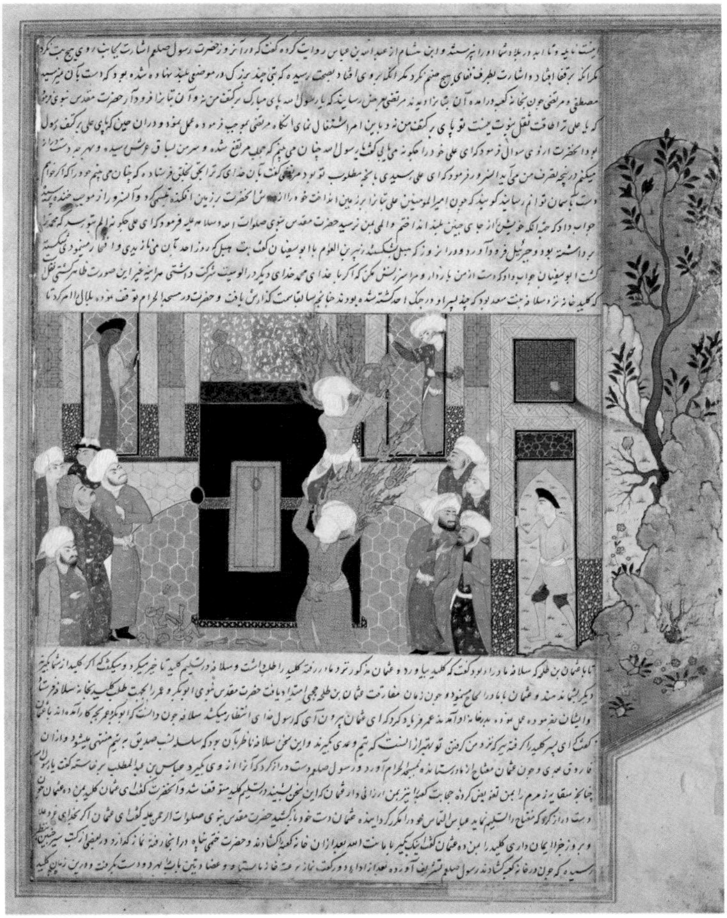

Figure 6.7 *ʿAlī stands on the Prophet's shoulders for the smashing of the Kaʿba's idols. From a copy of* Rawḍat al-ṣafā *('The garden of purity') by Mīrkhwānd (d.* 903/1498*), dated* 1003/1595*. Gold, gouache and ink on paper;* 25.4 × 35.5*cm (folio). Courtesy: Chester Beatty Library. CBL Per.* 254.83*. © The Trustees of the Chester Beatty Library, Dublin.*

proves the validity of my proposal; other Persian Kaʿba-centric miniatures exist that also do not conform to it. For example, although few events could be more cosmically significant for Islam than the smashing of the Kaʿba's idols, in a miniature of this moment from a copy of *Rawḍat al-ṣafā* ('The garden of purity') by Mīrkhwānd (d. 903/1498), the *Kiswa* is shown resolutely lowered (Figure 6.7). By way of contrast, in the miniature of the same event and from the same work that was reproduced in Chapter Five (Figure 5.1), the *Kiswa* is shown tucked up, rising and falling.

What I am proposing is an iconographical convention, not an iconographical rule. I would additionally ask the sceptical reader to consider the fact that until approximately the end of the twelfth/eighteenth century, diagrammatic paintings of the Sacred Mosque, such as those discussed in Chapter Five and especially those on wall tiles (for example, Figure 1.2), almost invariably show the *Kiswa* in its lowered state.[73] Why do Persian Kaʿba-centric miniatures not invariably do the same?[74]

Returning to the review and the subject of ascension miniatures that include the Kaʿba, four more are reproduced below (Figures 6.8–6.11).

Figure 6.8 *The Prophet rides over the Kaʿba upon al-Burāq on his miraculous journey to the heavens. From a copy of* Yūsuf wa Zulaykha *('Joseph and Zulaykha') by Jāmī (d. 898/1492), dated to c.993/1585. Gold, gouache and ink on paper; 26.5 × 41.5cm (folio). Courtesy: Topkapı Palace Library. TSMK H. 1084, fol. 11r.*

Figure 6.9 *The Prophet mounts al-Burāq outside the Kaʿba in preparation for his miraculous journey to the heavens. From a copy of* Yūsuf wa Zulaykha *by Jāmī, dated* 1011/1602. *Gold, gouache and ink on paper. Courtesy: The British Library. BL Or.* 1368, *fol.* 9*r.* © *The British Library Board.*

Figure 6.10 *The Prophet rides over the Kaʿba upon al-Burāq on his miraculous journey to the heavens. From an unidentified manuscript produced in Shiraz, dated to* c.1009/1600. *Gold, gouache and ink on paper;* 11.9 × 21.9*cm. Courtesy: Los Angeles County Museum of Art (www.lacma.org). The Edwin Binney, 3rd, Collection of Turkish Art at the Los Angeles County Museum of Art (M.*85.237.44*).*

None comes from Niẓāmī's *Khamsa* but texts by other authors. In the last of them (Figure 6.11), the *Kiswa* is shown elevated in the manner indicative of the Kaʿba's perceived state of *iḥrām*. In the others, it is shown elevated in the parted manner reminiscent of Ali Bey's and Richard Burton's drawings of the newly attired Kaʿba, the popularly perceived 'bridal' Kaʿba (Figures 6.1 and 6.2). Given the presence of jubilant angels over or about the Kaʿba, it is as if the *Kiswa* in these paintings had parted the sky.

Unrelated to the life of the Prophet are images of Iskandar, or Alexander the Macedonian conqueror, at the Kaʿba.[75] In Islamic culture, Iskandar is

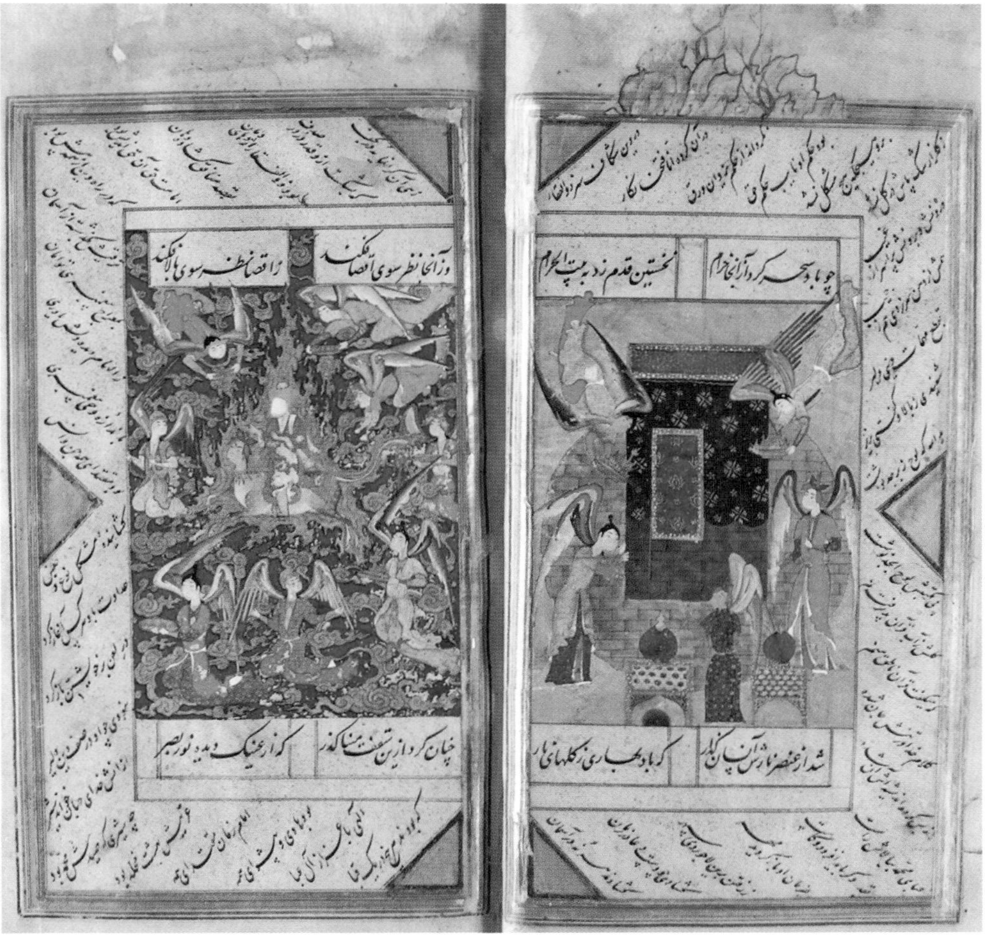

Figure 6.11 *The Prophet rides al-Burāq on his miraculous journey to the heavens, while angels worship at the Kaʿba. From a copy of* Shāhnāma-yi Ismāʿīl, *an epic panegyrising Shah Ismaʿil I (r. 907–30/1501–24), by Qāsimī (Mīrzā Muḥammad Qāsim Gunābādī, d.* c.*983/1575), dated to* c.*968/1560. Gold, gouache and ink on paper; 15 × 22.7cm (folio). Courtesy: Topkapı Palace Library. TSMK R. 1549, ff. 14v–15r.*

frequently presented as, inter alia, the ideal Muslim hero and archetypal king.[76] His visit to Mecca and his deference there to the Kaʿba, as related in both Firdawsī's *Shāhnāma* ('Book of kings') and Niẓāmī's *Khamsa*, therefore have a cosmic Islamic signature. Four miniatures of this visit are shown below (Figures 6.12–6.15). All depict the elevated *Kiswa*; the second (Figure 6.13) shows the Kaʿba in its popularly perceived state of *iḥrām*; the others show it in its 'bridal' state.

As we saw in Chapter Four, Majnūn also visits the Kaʿba: dressed in pilgrimage garb, he clasps the Kaʿba's knocker or knockers (Figures 4.6

Figure 6.12 *(L): Iskandar visits the Kaʿba. From a copy of the* Shāhnāma *('Book of kings') by Firdawsī (d.* c.411/1020*), dated* 843/1440. *Gold, gouache and ink on paper;* 8.5 × 14*cm. Courtesy: Director of the Turkish Institute of Manuscripts, Süleymaniye Manuscript Library. Hacı Beşir Ağa Collection* 00486, *fol.* 400*r.*

Figure 6.13 *(R): Iskandar visits the Kaʿba. From a copy of the* Khamsa *by Niẓāmī, dated to* c.896/1490. *Gold, gouache and ink on paper;* 15.6 × 22.8*cm (folio). Courtesy: Los Angeles County Museum of Art (www.lacma.org). The Nasli M. Heeramaneck Collection, gift of Joan Palevsky (M.*73.5.462*).*

and 4.7). In both of those Persian miniatures, the *Kiswa* is shown in the elevated manner indicative of the Kaʿba's perceived *iḥrām* state. Angels circle overhead through swirling clouds of gold. The miniature reproduced below of a pilgrim clasping the Kaʿba's knocker is clearly reminiscent of that iconography (Figure 6.16). The knocker-clasping pilgrim is surrounded by other pilgrims, some of whom might conceivably be greeting the Black Stone while performing the *ṭawāf.* The *Kiswa* is shown elevated in the manner suggestive of the Kaʿba's perceived state of taboo. Stationary and circling angels watch overhead through swirling clouds of gold. Similar to Majnūn in Chapter Four's two miniatures, this pilgrim would seem to have become united with his Beloved. A cosmic event, in other words.

Figure 6.14 *(L): Iskandar kneels in supplication at the Kaʿba, his crown on the ground beside him. From a copy of the* Shāhnāma *by Firdawsī, dated to* c.999/1590. *Gold, gouache and ink on paper;* 21.5 × 35*cm (folio). Courtesy: The British Library. I.O. ISLAMIC* 3540*, fol.* 381*r.* © *The British Library Board.*

Figure 6.15 *(R): Iskandar kneels in supplication at the Kaʿba, his crown on the ground beside him. From a copy of the the* Shāhnāma *by Firdawsī, dated to the mid-tenth/sixteenth century. Gold, gouache and ink on paper;* 24.2 × 37.5*cm (folio). Courtesy: The Nasser D. Khalili Collection of Islamic Art. MSS* 771. © *Nour Foundation.*

Importantly, not all miniatures of Majnūn at the Kaʿba show him as a pilgrim. Others show him as an ordinarily clad individual, surrounded by other ordinarily clad individuals. In those paintings, however, the *Kiswa* is still commonly shown tucked up (Figure 6.17).[77] The potential counter-argument that the Persian miniatures in this review represent the Kaʿba in its 'bridal' or perceived taboo state because the miniatures (1) illustrate events that are imagined to have occurred during the culmination of the Islamic year, the pilgrimage season, and so (2) they disinterestedly reflect the Hajj's realities, is therefore insufficient. In the miniature of Majnūn reproduced below (Figure 6.17), the pilgrimage season is almost certainly over, and to judge from the fact that Majnūn's hair shows no sign of having been trimmed close to the level of the skull, an obligation for men

Figure 6.16 *A pilgrim clasps a knocker of the Kaʿba. From the Miscellany of Iskandar Sultan (d.* 817/1414*), dated* 813–14/1410–11*. Gold, gouache and ink on paper;* 12.5 × 18.1*cm (folio). Courtesy: The British Library. BL Add.* 272621*, fol.* 363*r. © The British Library Board.*

Figure 6.17 *Majnūn clasps a knocker of the Kaʿba. From a copy of* Majālis al-ʿushshāq *('Assemblies of the lovers') by Kamāl al-Dīn Ḥusayn Gāzargāhī (*fl. *tenth/sixteenth century), dated to c.*1004/1595*. Gold, gouache and ink on paper. Courtesy: The British Library. I.O. ISLAMIC* 1138*, fol.* 192*v.*

Figure 6.18 *ʿAbd al-Muṭṭalib, the Prophet's grandfather, worships at the Kaʿba. From a copy of* Āthār al-muẓaffar *('Exploits of the victorious') by Niẓām Astarābādī (d. c.921/1515), dated 974/1567. Gold, gouache and ink on paper; 17.8 × 26cm (folio). Courtesy: The Morgan Library & Museum. MS G.72, recto. Gift of the Trustees of the William S. Glazier Collection, 1984. Photographic credit: The Pierpont Morgan Library, New York.*

exiting the state of *iḥrām*, he has not participated as a pilgrim during it. Why, then, is the *Kiswa* shown tucked up?

The penultimate image in this review is one of the Prophet's grandfather ʿAbd al-Muṭṭalib, considered a pagan in a number of Islamic traditions, worshipping at the Kaʿba in a manner not dissimilar to Islamic ritual prayer (Figure 6.18). Here the fact that the Kaʿba is shown in its perceived state of *iḥrām* is particularly fitting, given ʿAbd al-Muṭṭalib's alleged miraculous rediscovery of the Zamzam well, the sacred water of which is drunk by pilgrims, and his protection of the Kaʿba against an elephant-riding attacker.[78] Although the *Kiswa* is not elevated in the manner Ali Bey and Burton recorded, but covered at skirt-level with a plain cloth (*izār*), that is exactly how some travellers and visitors have reported the Kaʿba to look when in its perceived state of *iḥrām*.[79] Although no celestial phenomena are shown, the implication that ʿAbd al-Muṭṭalib was a Muslim *avant la lettre* is suggestive of cosmic forces at play.[80]

Figure 6.19 *ʿAlī stands atop the Kaʿba and throws down the idols, while the Prophet explains the exit of a black woman from the idol Nāyla. From a copy of* Āthār al-muẓaffar *by Niẓām Astarābādī, dated 974/1567. Gold, gouache and ink on paper; 17.8 × 26cm (folio). Courtesy: Chester Beatty Library. CBL Per 235, fol. 55a.*

Another miniature from the same tenth/sixteenth-century manuscript also shows the *Kiswa* covered this way, suggesting that in this period that is how the Kaʿba was put into its perceived state of *iḥrām* (Figure 6.19). The event this miniature illustrates is the smashing of the Kaʿba's idols, specifically the moment when the idol Nāyla (Arabic: Nāʾila) is hurled to the ground by ʿAlī. A black woman issues from the fragments, prompting the Prophet to explain: 'This is Nāyla. But she will never any more be worshipped in your country.'[81] The cosmic significance of this event hardly needs emphasising.

Conclusion

In this chapter, we have pursued two inquiries, both related to the *Kiswa*. First, an examination of the relationship between the *Kiswa* and the Kaʿba. Here we saw that the *Kiswa* revealed rather than hid the Kaʿba, and we concluded that the institution of the *Kiswa* was probably as ancient as the Kaʿba itself, because in important ways the two formed an inalienable unit. Second, an examination of the dynamics of the *Kiswa*, with a particular focus on the tucked-up *Kiswa* as a popularly perceived sign of the Kaʿba as alive. Here we looked at the terminology related to this perception and at Persian miniatures which depicted the tucked-up *Kiswa*. Regarding the miniatures, we argued that the tucked-up *Kiswa* meant that the Kaʿba had been imagined to be divinely animated from within: an active participant in the illustrated events and a House full of celestial life. We proposed that this was an iconographical convention only, not a rule.

This proposed convention requires further testing, as I do not claim to have looked at every Kaʿba-centric Persian miniature. Even so, did the Sufi al-Hujwīrī (d. *c.*467/1075) foresee it when he said: 'The blackest (*aẓlam*) thing in the world is the Beloved's House (*dār*) without the Beloved'?[82] Tucked up, the *Kiswa* presents less blackness to the eye.

Conclusion

This book has investigated the Kaʿba by examining six of its predominantly spatial effects, six actions that comprise but do not complete the work of the Kaʿba in the Islamic world. These effects were: the effect of the Kaʿba as *qibla*; the effect of the Kaʿba as *axis* and *matrix mundi*; the effect of the Kaʿba, specifically it foundations, as an architectural principle in the bedrock of the Islamic world; the effect of the Kaʿba as a circumambulated goal of pilgrimage and a site of spiritual union for mystics and Sufis; and the dual effects of the Kaʿba as a house that is imagined to shelter temporarily an animating force but which otherwise holds a void. To each effect a chapter was devoted, with the principal findings recapitulated at the chapter's end.

In the course of examining these effects, a number of secondary findings were made in addition to the principal ones, some equally more suggestive than conclusive. Unlike the principal findings, however, these findings were not repeated in summary form at each chapter's end. I am therefore devoting this Conclusion to them, not to another encapsulation of the book's principal findings. I kindly refer the reader to the chapters' conclusions should this decision prove disappointing.

From Chapter One, chief among the secondary findings was the likelihood that the Kaʿba played a ritual role for the proto-Muslim community of Believers from a very early period, contrary to revisionist claims. If, as argued, the earliest Islamic settlements were oriented to the Kaʿba, then its cultic importance already in the first half of the first Islamic century would seem to be beyond reasonable doubt. The possibility that this importance was due to the community's desire to remain participants in salvation history, an idea prompted by Neuwirth, remains compelling, I believe.

Also from Chapter One was the finding that whilst it was not uncommon for medieval and pre-modern sacrosanct leaders – caliphs and kings – to be personified as the Kaʿba, the Prophet was probably not personified that way before the Mughal period, when Qāsim-i Kāhī called him 'everyone's intended Kaʿba'.

From Chapter Two, a secondary finding of note was the possibility that the celestial Kaʿba, the Frequented House, was not a borrowing of Jewish Temple lore. If King was correct in interpreting the Meccan Kaʿba as a microcosm of the pre-Islamic universe, then he was likely also correct in surmising that Temple lore did not underpin the Islamic belief that the Kaʿba was a copy of the Frequented House.

From Chapter Three, a secondary finding of note was the possibility that the Qarmatians were imitating the Dhū al-Suwayqatayn prophecy when they sacked Mecca and partially destroyed the Kaʿba. Because their barbaric attack was intended as the harbinger of a new cosmic era, it was possibly modelled on that prophecy.

From Chapter Four, a secondary finding of note was the extent to which the canon of Islamic architecture comprised buildings of splendour whose epigraphic programmes, foundation documents and mentions in contemporary texts made comparisons to the Kaʿba. These comparisons could not be dismissed as just so much formulaic rhetoric, I argued, because at a profound level of the Islamic world the Kaʿba was architecture without compare.

Lastly in this summary, from Chapter Four, too, was the finding that the Kaʿba unequivocally counted as an Islamic building. This was not just because of the miraculous, Islamic-era-ushering events that the sources allege occurred when the Kaʿba was reconstructed by the Quraysh tribe and given the almost identical form to that of today. The Kaʿba also counted as Islamic because the future prophet of Islam is alleged to have been one of the builders of that reconstruction. Then, at a later date, as Islam's Prophet, he also harboured plans for its form.

As I bring this book to a close, I recall a conversation I had with a senior figure of Islamic art history when I was just beginning the book's research. 'But what is there to say about the Kaʿba?' asked this person incredulously on learning of my intentions. Although I hope that what I have written in this book represents an effective response to my interlocutor's incredulity, their question merits a moment of reflection. It can be explained, I think, by the pervasiveness in Islamic art history of a particular attitude to art, a subject touched upon in the Introduction and discussed at more length in Chapter Four. I am referring to the disinterested aesthetic attitude, which divorces aesthetic experience from religious experience.[1] Grabar unwittingly speaks of this divorce and his commitment to the attitude when he says with reference to the Kaʿba: 'There is no indication known to me in early Muslim writing or in pre-Islamic writing of an aesthetic reaction to the Kaʿba, of an interpretation of its holiness in terms of visual beauty.'[2] My incredulous interlocutor was, I believe, effectively echoing Grabar's words, but applying them to all periods of Islamic history.

The disinterested aesthetic attitude is a reason for the relative obscurity of the Kaʿba in Islamic architectural scholarship. Because the attitude has been shown by Gell and others to be a 'product of the religious crisis of the Enlightenment and the rise of Western science',[3] my book's final conclusion is this: the decolonisation of Islamic art history awaits completion.

Notes

Introduction

1. '[Religion is] orientation in the ultimate sense, that is, how one comes to terms with the ultimate significance of one's place in the world.' Long C. 1986, p. 7.
2. See, e.g., Wensinck and King 1954, p. 82; and Halevi 2007, pp. 320–1 n. 93; al-Jazīrī 2009, pp. 90, 93; Ibn Rushd 1989, vol. 1, p. 771; trans. Ibn Rushd 2000, vol. 1, pp. 541–2. Regarding interment only, there is a difference of opinion about the absolute obligation to have the corpse facing the *qibla*. See, e.g., al-Jazīrī 2009, p. 715; Halevi 2007, p. 4; and Ibn Rushd 1989, vol. 1, p. 384; trans. Ibn Rushd 2000 vol. 1, p. 259.
3. See, e.g., al-Bukhārī 1994, vol. 1, pp. 51–2 (*kitāb al-wuḍū', bāb lā tustaqbalu al-qibla bi-ghā'iṭ aw bawl*, #44).
4. See, e.g., Westermarck 1899, pp. 256–7.
5. Ibn al-Athīr 1963, vol. 4, p. 187; Ibn Ḥajar al-ʿAsqalānī 1998, vol. 12, p. 548 (#2998).
6. With regard to the survey texts, the only exception of note to this trend is the appendix in Michell 1978, specifically King G. and Lewcock 1978, pp. 209–10. With regard to architectural scholarship, to the best of my knowledge the only exceptions of note to this disregard are the following publications, not one of them being a monograph: Creswell 1958, pp. 1–3; Creswell 1969, vol. 1, pp. 1–5; Jairazbhoy 1962; Jairazbhoy 1986; Finster 1991; King G. 2002a; King G. 2002b; King G. 2004; Shalem 2005; Akkach 2005a, pp. 179–93; al-Mūjān 2010; Shalem 2013; and Shalem 2015. Lest the number of these publications suggest some kind of plenitude in Kaʿba architectural scholarship, in comparison it should be recalled that there are, for example, at least seven English-language monographs on the Dome of the Rock in Jerusalem. Four of them have been published this century, a number that rises to five when one counts book-length articles.
7. Q 22:29, 33.
8. Hegel 1979, p. 70; Hegel 1993, p. 11; and Heidegger 1971, pp. 44–5, respectively.
9. Rancière 2004, pp. 44–5.
10. Johnson 2013, p. 35 (italics as marked in the original).
11. Goodman 1985, p. 652.
12. Gell 1998, p. 6.
13. Layton 1991a, p. 92. Cf. Layton 1991b, pp. 451–2.
14. Appudarai 1986, p. 4.
15. Warnier 2006, pp. 190–1.

16. See, e.g., Mulder 2014, p. 91.
17. Grabar and Ettinghausen 1987, p. 18. In a later edition of this influential survey text, the authors tone down their opinion by refining the target of their judgement from the Kaʿba as 'an architectural creation' to the Kaʿba's 'architectural quality', a quality they consider the structure lacks. See Grabar et al. 2001, p. 3. This commonplace academic prejudice against indigenous traditions of Arabian art is addressed in King G. 1991; and Finster 1992.
18. See, e.g., Arazi 1984, pp. 206–12; Campo 1991b; Faroqhi 1994; Bianchi 2005; Marsham 2009, esp. pp. 124–5; McMillan 2011; Kennedy 2012, pp. 92–107; Munt 2013; Hendrickson 2016; Zadeh 2016; and al-Maqrīzī 2016.
19. Cf. 'Materializing the study of religion means asking how religion happens materially, which is not to be confused with asking the much less helpful question of how religion is expressed in material form. A materialized study of religion begins with the assumption that things, their use, their valuation, and their appeal are not something added to a religion, but rather are inextricable from it.' Birgit Meyer et al., 'The Origin and Mission of *Material Religion*', *Religion* 40 (2010), p. 209, as cited in Houtman and Meyer 2012, p. 7.
20. Norberg-Schulz 1988, p. 48.
21. Ibid.
22. Ahmed 2015, p. 410 n. 7.
23. Panofsky 1970, p. 65.
24. See in particular Radtke 1992; Ahmed 2015, esp. p. 94; and Knysh 2017, esp. pp. 7–14. In addition, see Knysh 1993; Calder 2007, pp. 233–4; McGregor 2009, pp. 79–83; and Homerin 2013, pp. 190–5.
25. On the polemics surrounding his thought during the first three centuries after his death, see Knysh 1999, *passim.*
26. Markiewicz 2019, pp. 250–71; Yılmaz 2018, pp. 200–6; and El-Rouayheb 2015, pp. 272–311, respectively.
27. In Islamic art history, Robert Hillenbrand has pioneered just this non-Sufism use of one of Ibn ʿArabī's texts. See Hillenbrand 2001a, vol. 1, p. 38. On the literary nature and antecedents of this text by Ibn ʿArabī, see de la Granja 1974.
28. See, e.g., Peters 1994b, pp. 13–14.
29. Lundquist 1983.
30. Points 10 and 12 of the typology are less at odds with what the early Islamic sources occasionally relate or imply about the Kaʿba, principally the pre-Islamic period Kaʿba.
31. Cassirer 1955, p. 100.
32. As also noted in Peters 1994b, p. 14.
33. On the names and locations of the principal boundary markers of the inner perimeter, see Ibn Duhaysh 1990, pp. 50–65.
34. See Abdul Ghani 2004, pp. 41–9. A serviceable but widely accessible diagram showing both perimeters is found in Aazam 2005, p. 313. A fuller diagram is found in Bindaqjī 1978, p. 51.
35. Chabbi 2002; and Chabbi 2010, pp. 38, 50–1. The classic work on pre-Islamic Arabian betyls remains Lammens 1920.
36. See Hawting 2001b. For a rare instance of the Qurʾan explicitly referring to the Kaʿba as 'the House', see Q 5:97: 'God has made the Kaʿba, the Sacred

House, a support for the people.' Hawting improbably suggests that this instance might incorporate a gloss. See Hawting 2001b, p. 79.

37. See Fahd 1966, pp. 132–6; and Chabbi 2010, pp. 36–40, 637–8.
38. Wensinck 1913, p. 584.
39. Cf. von Sivers 2003, pp. 5–9.
40. Cf. ibid. *passim*.
41. For a summary of what we know regarding the earlier periods, see Wensinck and Jomier 1954, pp. 318–19; and especially the text for which the diagrams were produced, namely, Finster 2011, pp. 229–31.
42. Ahmad 1954b, pp. 582–4.
43. Nāṣir-i Khusraw 1881, pp. 69–76; trans. Nāṣir-i Khusraw 1986, pp. 71–80.
44. Ahmad 1954a; and Ahmad 1954b, p. 579
45. Cf. Montgomery 2001, pp. 85–7; but note Zayde Antrim's discussion of Ibn Rusta in Antrim 2012, pp. 69–70
46. Ibn Rusta 1892, pp. 24–58.
47. As also conjectured in Antrim 2012, p. 70.
48. Montgomery 2001, p. 85.
49. Ibn ʿAbd Rabbih 1983, vol. 7, pp. 282–7; trans. Shafīʿ 1922.
50. Ibn ʿAbd Rabbih 1983, vol. 7, p. 286 (ll. 12–14); trans. Shafīʿ 1922, p. 428.
51. Shafīʿ 1922, p. 422.
52. Al-Jāḥiẓ 1938, vol. 3, p. 139 (*bāb dhikr khiṣāl al-Ḥaram*).
53. Ibn Rusta 1892, p. 57.
54. See, e.g., Bramón 1991, p. 62; and Ibn Baṭṭūṭa 1893, vol. 1, pp. 311–12; trans. Ibn Baṭṭūṭa 1958, vol. 1, p. 196.
55. What Nāṣir-i Khusraw observed regarding the dimensions and components of the Kaʿba, as well as what other earlier travellers observed or reported of the same, is usefully summarised in Jairazbhoy 1962, pp. 21–7.
56. Al-Mūjān 2010, p. 97. Cf. Burton 1893, vol. 2, pp. 319–25.
57. Abdul Ghani 2004, pp. 78–80.
58. *Pace* Al-Azmeh, who asserts: 'A cubical structure is the only possible meaning of *kaʿba* in Arabic.' Al-Azmeh 2014, p. 200 n. 116. For other etymologically derived meanings, see Fahd 1968, p. 204; Chabbi 2010, pp. 49–50; and Akkach 2005a, p. 191.
59. Finster 2010, p. 76.
60. Rabbat 1954, p. 175.
61. Zadeh 2016, p. 61. The explanation's specificities cannot account for the building skills of the Arabs described in King G. 1991, *passim*.
62. For an historical treatment of the enclosure, see Rubin 1986, pp. 100–15; and cf. Nevo and Koren 1990, pp. 29–33. A detailed panoramic view of the enclosure as it looked in 2015, by the photographer Wessam Hassanin, is available at <http://tinyurl.com/qd28mpu> (last accessed 18 April 2019).
63. See al-Azraqī 2003, vol. 1, p. 300 (#227); and Hawting 1982, p. 34. See also Chapter Four.
64. For further information, including the present inscriptions' content, see especially al-Mūjān 2010, pp. 94, 112, 132–7.
65. Abdul Ghani 2004, p. 83. For a positive account of the repairs, including a side-elevation of the now steel-tied and completely sealed ceiling and roof,

see al-Mūjān 2010, pp. 140–53. To judge from the panoramic photograph taken by Wessam Hassanin in 2015, this glass-covered aperture has gone. The photograph is available at at <http://tinyurl.com/q27syvr> (last accessed 18 April 2019). See below for additional sources regarding the repairs.

66. On these skylights, see Chapter Five.
67. Al-Mūjān 2010, p. 153.
68. Abdul Ghani 2004, p. 85. Photographs of the door are reproduced in al-Mūjān 2010, pp. 91, 138.
69. Al-Mūjān 2010, pp. 104–6, 151–2.
70. See, e.g., Wensinck and Jomier 1954, p. 318; and Chabbi 2010, pp. 48, 640.
71. For a thirteenth/nineteenth-century source mentioning the stone, see Tanındı 1983, p. 430.
72. Ibn Jubayr 1907, p. 99 (ll. 2–3); trans. Ibn Jubayr 1952, p. 94
73. Al-Kurdī al-Makkī 2000, vol. 3, p. 256.
74. Ibid.
75. This idea can be traced to at least Wellhausen 1887, p. 74.
76. Al-Mūjān 2010, p. 153. Photographs of the dais, the Black Stone, and the crowds, as well as a diagram, are available at <http://tinyurl.com/zurezgw> (last accessed 18 April 2019).
77. On this stone, the divine legend allegedly inscribed on it, and the possibility that it was indeed once bonded to the Kaʿba, see Kister 1971.
78. Ibid. pp. 479–80.
79. Abdul Ghani 2004, pp. 120–3; al-Mūjān 2010, pp. 128–31.
80. Kister 1971, p. 482.
81. See, e.g., Ibn Jubayr 1907, pp. 84–5; trans. Ibn Jubayr 1952, pp. 79–81. Cf. al-Muqaddasī 1906, p. 73; trans. al-Muqaddasī 1994, p. 67; Kister 1971, pp. 483–4; and Rubin 1986, p. 123.
82. Only the Hanafi law school pavilion is two-storey. The absence of a discrete pavilion for the Shafiʿi law school is explained by the fact that the Shafiʿis prayed behind the Station of Abraham. The upper storey of the Zamzam pavilion was also reserved for their use. See Milstein 2001, pp. 295–6; and al-Quʿayṭī 2007, p. 283.
83. Cf. Jairazbhoy 1962, p. 22, where similar posts are recorded for the fourth/tenth century.
84. The improbably small element to the left of the Banū Shayba Gate is the staircase.
85. For further information on the architectural elements of the Sacred Mosque, see Wensinck 1954b, pp. 708–9 (primarily regarding the modern period); and especially Milstein 2001, pp. 293–8 (regarding the tenth/sixteenth century).
86. For the first major period of construction, the second/eighth century, see Grabar 1985, pp. 4–5; and especially Peters 1994a, pp. 110–22; and Bloom 2013, pp. 58–64. For later periods, most especially that of the Ottomans, see Faroqhi 1994, pp. 92–126; and al-Quʿayṭī 2007, pp. 137–43, 168–327. For a detailed history of construction works related only to the Kaʿba from the second/eighth century until 2006, when an earlier version of al-Mūjān's book was published (in Arabic), see al-Mūjān 2010, pp. 81–163.
87. Bloom 2013, pp. 63, 305.

88. In addition to the sporadic coverage in some newspapers, see Sardar 2014, pp. 313–42; Ahmed 2015, pp. 532–7; and Mater 2016. For an account of the redevelopment by someone involved at a key moment of it, see Toulan 1993. On the viewpoint of the painting and the significance attributed to it in the development of the tradition of representing the Sacred Mosque from an elevated position, see Hickman 2012, pp. 25–6.
89. For further treatment of the painting, including a brief discussion and translation of each of its many inscriptions, see Tütüncü 2015.
90. All of these sites are highlighted and discussed in ibid.
91. For the ethical and bodily demands made of the pilgrim once in the state of *iḥrām*, see Wensinck 1954a, p. 1053; and Abdel Haleem 2013, p. 2.
92. A comparative chart listing the rituals required for both pilgrimages, and specifying when and where each is performed, is reproduced in Toorawa 2016, p. 223.
93. This point is well made in Chahanovich 2016. On what is currently known about this early history, see Kister 1990, pp. 18–29; Hawting 1993, pp. 36–8; Robinson 2005, pp. 95–6; and Donner 2010, pp. 199–201.
94. According to most juridical interpretations of the Hajj pilgrimage, the *ṭawāf al-wadāʿ*, or circumambulation of farewell, is not obligatory.
95. Other than, where applicable, the *ṭawāf al-qudūm*, in the course of the Hajj pilgrimage the *ṭawāf* is not performed in this state in any case. See Wensinck and Lewis 1954, pp. 35–6; and Toorawa 2016, p. 227.
96. On the popularity of the misconception, see O'Meara 2018, p. 143.
97. For the former assertion, see Hillenbrand 2001b, p. 8. For the latter assertion, see Rabbat 2002, p. 58. Perhaps the assertions stem from a comment by the early Islamic historian, al-Ṭabarī (d. 310/923), regarding the origin of the plan of the mosque of Kufa and other early mosques. Without mentioning the Kaʿba, he says that the Sacred Mosque was never emulated 'out of respect for its holiness'. See al-Ṭabarī 1960, vol. 4, pp. 44–5; trans. al-Ṭabarī 1989b, p. 69.
98. Cf. Al-Azmeh 2014, p. 222. But note Crone 1987, pp. 168–99.
99. On these four kaʿbas, see especially Ibn al-Kalbī 1924, pp. 44–5; trans. Ibn al-Kalbī 1952, pp. 38–40; Kister 1986, p. 44; Peters 1994b, pp. 13–14; and Al-Azmeh 2014, p. 222. Cf. Finster 1991, p. 55.
100. Al-Bukhārī 1994, vol. 4, p. 280 (*kitāb manāqib al-Anṣār, bāb dhikr Jarīr b. ʿAbd Allāh al-Bajallī*, #3822). The destruction of one other Kaʿba rival, not included among these four because it was destroyed immediately prior to the Prophet's time, is additionally alleged to have met with the Prophet's approval. See Kister 1986, pp. 43–4.
101. Al-Muqaddasī 1906, p. 122; trans. al-Muqaddasī 1994, p. 102. Cf. Northedge 2007, p. 231. One might be right to see in this report an ideologically motivated attempt to discredit a caliph who had so unsparingly forced upon his subjects the theological tenets of the Muʿtazilites.
102. Al-Muqaddasī 1906, p. 199; trans. al-Muqaddasī 1994, p. 168.
103. Al-Maqrīzī 1853, vol. 2, p. 453.
104. Ibn al-Wardī, *Taʾrīkh Ibn al-Wardī* (1969), vol. 2, p. 132, as cited in al-Harawī 2004, p. xxiv.

105. Mustawfī Qazwīnī 1915, vol. 2, p. 96.
106. Kaʿtī 2014, p. 234 (122); cf. Bloom and Blair 2009, vol. 3, p. 328.
107. See O'Meara 2020b.

Chapter One

1. Creswell 1958, p. 9, and Creswell 1969, vol. 1, p. 26; Wheatley 2001, p. 231.
2. See, e.g., Wensinck and King 1954, p. 82; Bashear 1991, pp. 268–73, 282; Hoyland 1997, p. 560; and Shtober 1999, pp. 87–90. On the pre-Islamic history of the equivalent of the *qibla* in Christianity and Judaism, see Landsberger 1957.
3. See, inter alios, Neuwirth 1993; Neuwirth 1996; Neuwirth 1998; and Neuwirth 2001b, p. 107. On the validity of identifying the Temple Mount with the Qurʾanic *al-Masjid al-Aqṣā* (Q 17:1), see Rubin 2008b, *passim*.
4. Neuwirth 2001b, p. 107.
5. Neuwirth 1998, p. 309.
6. See, e.g., Crone and Cook 1977, pp. 23–4; and Nevo and Koren 1990, pp. 25–34.
7. Ibn Khallikān 1977, vol. 4, pp. 232; trans. Ibn Khallikān 1843, vol. 2, p. 637. As noted by Neuwirth, the likelihood of this tradition long pre-dating the Ayyubid period is indicated by the number of early traditions for and against the merits of prayer in Jerusalem. See Neuwirth 1996, pp. 95–6. The traditions themselves are cited in Kister 1969, pp. 182–8.
8. See, e.g., Kimber 2001, pp. 325–6. For specific examples, see the traditions compiled in al-Ṭabarī 2001, vol. 2, pp. 8–9 (with respect to Q 2:142); but cf. the traditions indicating the Temple Mount was the *qibla* during the Prophet's Meccan period, as cited in Rubin 1987, p. 57; and Rubin 1990, p. 103.
9. Kister 1996, pp. 58–60; and Rubin 2008a, pp. 350–1. For the Kaʿba alone as the first *qibla*, see, e.g., al-Ṭabarī 2001, vol. 2, p. 9; and Rubin 1990, p. 102. For the Kaʿba in conjunction with the Temple Mount as the first *qibla*, see Ibn Hishām 1998, vol. 1, p. 264 (bāb 'Islām ʿUmar b. al-Khaṭṭāb'); trans. Ibn Hishām 1955, pp. 157–8. On the plausibility of this alleged conjunction, see Wensinck and King 1954, p. 82; and especially Neuwirth 2003, p. 379.
10. See, e.g., al-Ṭabarī 2001, vol. 2, pp. 6–8; and Duri 1989, p. 105.
11. Kister 1996, p. 59; Neuwirth 1993, p. 232; Neuwirth 2003, p. 379. Note, however, the other time periods given in Kimber 2001, p. 326.
12. Islamic tradition takes the designation *al-masjid al-ḥarām* of this Qurʾanic verse to be the Sacred Mosque (*al-Masjid al-Ḥarām*) of Mecca.
13. Q 2:144.
14. See Hawting 1982, pp. 36–8; and Hawting 2001b, pp. 77–8.
15. Al-Azraqī 2003, vol. 1, pp. 80–1 (#22); and especially al-Fākihī 1994, vol. 2, p. 274 (#1514), pp. 275–6 (#1517); and al-Ṭabarī M. 1970, p. 653; trans. Ibn Duhaysh 1990, pp. 23–5. For a discussion of the possible ideological motivations of traditions like these regarding the origins of the Sanctuary, see Webb 2013, pp. 10–12. The Frequented House is discussed at more length in Chapters Two and Three.
16. Al-Azraqī 2003, vol. 1, p. 116 (#73); and al-Ṭabarī M. 1970, p. 653; trans. Ibn Duhaysh 1990, pp. 23–5. On the inner perimeter, see the Introduction.

17. Some scholars have also argued that the implementation of the verse was not absolutely immediate, meaning that there was a short period when there was no Muslim *qibla*. See the references in Shtober 1999, p. 90 n. 18.
18. See Sharon 1988, pp. 230–2; and Sharon et al. 1996. This evidence is subsequently adduced in support of the claims advanced in Bashear 1991, p. 268.
19. Hoyland 1997, p. 565 n. 89; and Di Cesare 2017, p. 90 n. 44. Hoyland's interpretation of the site as a church would appear to be supported by the two differently oriented prayer apses of the Church of the Kathisma, Jerusalem. See Di Segni 2003, p. 248; and Avner 2010, p. 41. Nevertheless, note the doubt cast on Hoyland's interpretation in Shoemaker 2012, p. 341 n. 139.
20. Halevi 2007, p. 190.
21. Sharon 1988, p. 230; and especially Bashear 1991, pp. 273–82.
22. On the East-oriented *qibla*, see Andrae 1926, p. 4; Sharon 1988, pp. 229–30; Bashear 1991, pp. 271–2, 277–8; Sharon et al. 1996, pp. 113–14; and cf. Schimmel 1994, p. 62.
23. Sharon 1988, pp. 233. Cf. Sharon et al. 1996, p. 113.
24. For ʿAbd al-Malik's state-creation ambitions and interventions concerning the Qurʾan, see Robinson 2005, pp. 100–26.
25. Di Cesare 2017, pp. 89–90.
26. Al-Ṭabarī 2001, vol. 2, p. 6 (with respect to Q 2:142). Cf. Neuwirth 1998, p. 301; and Q 6:111.
27. *Pace* David King, who considers the term likely 'to derive from the name of the east wind, the *qabūl*'. See King 1954a, p. 181. The east wind's name derives, rather, from its sacred direction (see Chapter Two).
28. Ibn Manẓūr n.d., vol. 11, p. 25.
29. Al-Rāzī 2003, vol. 4, p. 26 (l. 11).
30. ʿAyn al-Quḍāt Hamadānī 1962, p. 321 (l. 14); trans. Ridgeon 2012, p. 9 (modified).
31. Baqlī 1970, p. 33 (l. 10); trans. Murata K. 2017, p. 93. In Sufi-related poetry, the material marker of the Islamic customary meaning of the term *qibla*, namely, the *mihrab* of a mosque, is not uncommonly figured as the eyebrows of the beloved's face. See Schimmel 1992a, pp. 46, 90. For the medieval Islamic mystical community known in external sources as the Ḥurūfiyya, the *mihrab* was actually a representation of the face. See Mir-Kasimov 2014, pp. 233–4.
32. Denny 2001, p. 159. For a third historical example of the physiognomic resonance of the term, see the description of mystical devotion to the Prophet and his descendants by the Moroccan hagiographer al-Ḥalabī al-Fāsī (d. 1120/1708): '[Souls that have tasted the remembrance of the Prophet] see nothing except that they see his face (*qubl*). They take witnessing his essence as their orientation in prayer (*qibla*).' Al-Ḥalabī al-Fāsī 1896, p. 4 (l. 8); trans. Kugle 2007, p. 58 (modified). Note, however, that the vowel markings in both the lithograph copy of al-Ḥalabī al-Fāsī's text referred to by Kugle and the new edition by Muḥammad Būkhunayfī (p. 91) render *qubl* as *qabla*; in other words, not as 'face' but 'before', as in '[the souls] see the remembrance of the Prophet before all else'.
33. ʿAntara b. Shaddād 1962, p. 171 (l. 8).

34. 'Wa antum li-hādhā al-dīn ka-al-qibla allatī / bi-hā an yaḍilla al-nās yahdī ḍalāluhā.' Al-Farazdaq 1936, vol. 2, p. 623 (l. 11); trans. Jamil 1999, p. 43. For an analysis of this and related verses, see Jamil 1999, pp. 43–4; Crone and Hinds 1986, pp. 28–34; and Milwright 2016, pp. 261–3.
35. See, inter alios, Crone and Hinds 1986, pp. 24–42; Al-Azmeh 1997, pp. 154–88; Darayee 2009, p. 81; and Canepa 2009, pp. 100–6, 124.
36. Al-Azmeh 1997, p. 159.
37. Abū Ḥayyān al-Tawḥīdī, *Kitāb al-Imtāʿ wa al-muʾānasa* (1953), vol. 3, p. 99, as cited in Al-Azmeh 1997, p. 160.
38. For the honorific use of the term, see below. For references to subjects circumambulating members of the ʿAbbasid dynasty as if they were the Kaʿba, see Jamil 1999, pp. 44–5; and the discussion in Milwright 2016, pp. 260–1 (which includes a reference to Umayyad subjects advised to circumambulate the palace of ʿAbd al-Malik). In the fourth/tenth century, the Qarmatians are also alleged to have circumambulated naked their supreme ruler, the temporarily visible Mahdi. See Hajnal 1998, p. 194.
39. Ali 2004, p. 9, with respect to the palaces of al-Jiṣṣ (al-Ḥuwayṣilāt), al-Iṣṭablāt and al-ʿĀshiq.
40. Ibid.
41. See, e.g., Ibn Hishām 1998, vol. 2, p. 65; trans. Ibn Hishām 1955, p. 202.
42. Schimmel 1994, p. 57. In a remarkable analysis of rabbinic toilet rules, Rachel Neis shows how a requirement to face away from the site of the Temple when relieving oneself – no matter where in Rabbinic Palestine and Babylonia one stood or squatted – helped enable the Temple to maintain its pivotal role in Judaism long after its destruction of 70 CE. Neis writes: 'Whether languishing in ruins, overtaken by a temple to Jupiter, lamented by Jewish pilgrims, or reshaped into a Christian center, the rabbinic temple could, when effected by bodily practices of toilet and prayer, remain standing.' Neis 2012, p. 368.
43. Ibn Ḥayyān, as cited in Hillenbrand 2001a, p. 38.
44. Northedge 2007, pp. 200–1, 233–5, with reference to the palaces of al-Iṣṭablāt and al-ʿĀshiq, the former more obviously oriented towards the *qibla* than the latter; and Enderlein and Meinecke 1992, p. 141, with reference to Mshatta. The ʿAbbasid palace-cum-city near Samarra, the Octagon of Qādisiyya, had a *qibla* orientation, as Northedge has shown; it could potentially have housed a counter-*qibla* audience hall. See Northedge 2007, pp. 88–90. If, as Marcus Milwright has suggested, the Dome of the Rock should be seen as 'representing qualities located in the person of [caliph] ʿAbd al-Malik', its location diametrically opposite the main *mihrab* of the Umayyad al-Aqsa Mosque might belong to the same counter-*qibla* pattern. See Milwright 2016, p. 263.
45. Koch 1993, p. 155; and cf. Koch 1997, pp. 137–8.
46. For Maḥmūd, see ʿUtbī 1858, p. 26. For al-Mustanṣir, see Muʾayyad fī al-Dīn Hibat Allāh b. Mūsā 1949, pp. 213, 229, 292; trans. Muʾayyad fī al-Dīn Hibat Allāh b. Mūsā 2011, pp. 73, 98, 189. For al-Nāṣir li-Dīn Allāh, see Mason 1972, p. 120; and Hartmann 1975, p. 102. For Abū al-Ḥasan ʿAlī, see Ibn al-Khaṭīb 1985, p. 101. For Dilshād Khātūn, see Wing 2016, pp. 141, 146 n. 83. For Tīmūr, see Moin 2012, p. 34. For Muḥammad Khudābanda, see Browne 1924, pp. 100–1 (an indirect reference only: '[T]hy gate is the *qibla* of the

Kings of the world'). For the Qajars, see Amanat 1997, p. 107. For Akbar, Jahangir, Aurangzeb and Qudsiyya Begum, see Badāʾūnī 1898, vol. 2, p. 266; Abū al-Faẓl b. Mubārak 1897, vol. 1, p. 138, p. 271; Jahāngīr 1909, vol. 1, pp. 194, 441; Manucci 1907, vol. 2, p. 346; and Sharma 2016, p. 145. For Shah Jahan, see Koch 1993, p. 155; and the V&A Museum's miniature portrait of him, on which a contemporary inscription reads, 'Blessed likeness of the *qibla*', available at: <http://tinyurl.com/y7pgakwh> (last accessed 18 April 2019).

47. Lowry 1987, p. 33.
48. Al-Azmeh 1997, p. 160.
49. Ibid.
50. Ibid. p. 162.
51. Ibid. p. 155
52. Ibn Sīrīn 1990, p. 68; Mavroudi 2002, p. 187, p. 202. In a seventh/thirteenth-century manual, however, to dream of the Kaʿba is to dream of the ruler's wife. See Schimmel 1998, p. 132.
53. Al-Qāḍī al-Nuʿmān 1995, vol. 2, pp. 230–2.
54. This argument would seem to be borne out by the fact that the Mughal emperors, Akbar and Aurangzeb, were both personified as the Kaʿba and honorifically titled as the *qibla*, and the same seems to be the case for the Ghaznavid ruler, Maḥmūd. See Abū al-Faẓl b. Mubārak 1897, vol. 1, p. 271; Sarkar 1917, p. 57; and ʿUtbī 1858, p. 26. According to the royal chronicle *Maasir-i Alamgiri* (completed in 1132/1720), one of Aurangzeb's rivalrous brothers sought forgiveness of the ruler by circumambulating him, 'the Kaʿba of the state', dressed in pilgrimage garb. See Mikkelson 2019, p. 248. The Nizārī Ismaʿili imams, Mustanṣir bi-Allāh II (d. 885/1480) and Mustanṣir bi-Allāh III (d. 904/1498), were likewise personified as the Kaʿba and taken as the *qibla*. See Virani 2007, pp. 112, 120, 130–2. Notwithstanding the comparisons drawn by the Persian poet Khāqānī Shirwānī (d. 595/1199) between the Prophet and the Kaʿba or aspects of the Kaʿba (e.g. the Black Stone), the earliest reference I have found to the Prophet being personified as the Kaʿba comes in a verse by the Mughal poet Qāsim-i Kāhī (d. 988/1580): '[He is] everyone's intended Kaʿba.' On these two poets and their references to the Kaʿba, see Schimmel 1982, p. 197; and Schimmel 1985, p. 204. For the verse quoted from Kāhī, see Hasan 1953, p. 185.
55. For example, Dilshād Khātūn (d. 752/1351), the Jalāyirid stateswoman, is eulogised as 'that lofty Kaʿba and that *qibla* of excellence'. She, however, was not the ruler; that was her husband, Shaykh Ḥasan Jalāyir (r. 740–57/1340–56). See Wing 2016, p. 146 n. 83. *Pace* Ebba Koch, who implies that referring to someone as the *qibla* is both an almost quotidian occurrence and not restricted to the court, I would argue that the honorific remained both highly charged and restricted in its use well into the Mughal period. See Koch 2010, p. 308 n. 37; and cf. Kinra 2015, p. 189. The use of it by Dūst Muḥammad (*fl.* 938–72/1531–64) in a royal album preface in which he calls the calligrapher Mīr ʿAlī Tabrīzī (*fl.* eighth/fourteenth century) the '*qibla* of the calligraphers' would conform to such usage. See Thackston 2001, p. 9. In Sufism, where the honorific is sometimes applied to revered masters (an occurrence increasingly common from the early modern period onwards), the usage is similarly restricted to a select group and not a public affair. For an early, medieval-period occurrence, see Farhādī 1996, p. 52.

56. Al-Ṭabarī 1960, vol. 7, p. 209; trans. al-Ṭabarī 1987b, pp. 88–9.
57. Cf. Cook M. 2013, p. 100. A more complex *qibla*-nesting tradition, as propounded in a commentary on a treatise attributed to the mystic Ibn ʿArabī, is cited in Akkach 2005a, p. 171.
58. Al-Ṭūsī 1992, vol. 2, p. 41 (*bāb al-qibla*, #139). Cf. ibid. vol. 2, p. 41 (#140); Herrera Casais and Schmidl 2008, p. 275; and Cook 2013, pp. 100, 111 n. 24.
59. Al-Bayhaqī 1925, vol. 2, p. 10. Cf. Cook 2013, p. 111 n. 25. For another version, see al-Azraqī 2003, vol. 1, p. 394 (#364).
60. King D. 1999, p. 48.
61. Wensinck and King 1954, p, 83. Cf. King D. 1999, p. 48.
62. Al-Bīrūnī, 'Kitāb Taḥdīd nihāyāt al-amākin li-taṣḥīḥ masāfāt al-masākin' (ed. Bulgakov and Aḥmad), *Majallat Maʿhad al-Makhṭuṭāt al-ʿArabiyya* 8 (1962), as reprinted in Sezgin 1992, pp. 35–7; cf. trans. al-Bīrūnī 1967, pp. 11–13.
63. Abū al-Yusr al-Bazdawī, *Risāla [fī samt al-qibla]*, as edited and translated in King D. 1983, pp. 5–6 (English), p. 37 (Arabic). See also the introduction of Ibn al-Haytham's (d. *c.*430/1040) treatise for scientifically determining the *qibla*, as cited in Dallal 1995, p. 152.
64. See, e.g., King D. 1999, pp. 48–54; King D. 2005; and King D. 2019. For a succinct discussion of the relevance and importance of the distinction drawn by King, see Rius 2009.
65. A representative example of this group is the Shāfiʿī law school judge Ibn al-Qāṣṣ (d. 335/946 or 336/947), author of *Dalāʾil al-qibla*, a work for determining the *qibla*. On this author and work, see Ducène 2001.
66. King D. 2005, pp. 165–6.
67. See, e.g., al-Tādilī b. al-Zayyāt 1997, p. 242 (#96), p. 375 (#195).
68. Haase 2007, p. 46.
69. A second instance of such placement is the *mihrab* of the mid-eleventh/sixteenth-century Solak Sinan Paşa Mosque, Üsküdar, Istanbul. See Erken 1971, p. 308; and cf. Maury 2013, p. 157 n. 23. A third, less certain instance is the *mihrab* of the Mosque of Hagia Sophia, Istanbul. See Maury 2013, p. 152. Regarding the twenty-first century, a mosque in Dearborn, Michigan, has in its *mihrab* a representation of the Kaʿba's door. See Gruber 2014, p. 248.
70. Maury 2013, esp. pp. 144, 151–3.
71. Gautier-van Berchem 1969, p. 238.
72. In some eighteenth- and nineteenth-century European histories of Islam, it is said that a piece of the Black Stone was set within the threshold of the caliphal palace of ʿAbbasid Baghdad, and that people greeted it by touching their foreheads against it. See, e.g., d'Herbelot 1781, vol. 1, p. 495 (with respect to 'Bab'); and Lebrecht 1840, p. 391. I have been unable to corroborate this claim, neither in primary nor later secondary sources. Assuming its veracity, did the palace take on thereby certain qualities of the Kaʿba?
73. The mosques in question are the Old Mosque, or *Eski Camii* of Edirne, completed in the first half of the ninth/fifteenth century; Sokullu Mehmet Paşa Mosque, completed in 979/1572; and the Sultan Ahmet I, or 'Blue' Mosque, completed in 1025/1616. For the first mosque, see Neçipoğlu 2005, p. 241; for the second, see Goodwin 1971, p. 274; and for the third, see Ring 1995, p. 337.
74. Basset and Lévi-Provençal 1922, pp. 419–21. For a plan of this *mihrab* and the prayer hall to which it belongs, see Nagy 2014, p. 134.

75. Basset and Lévi-Provençal 1922, p. 419.
76. Ibid. p. 419. For circumambulation of this *mihrab* outside the Hajj season, see Iványi 2016, pp. 68–9, 93.
77. Nagy 2014, p. 144; and especially Nagy 2019, pp. 279–82.
78. See, e.g., Lévi-Provençal 1928, pp. 173–4; Deverdun 2004, vol. 1, pp. 163–4, 181–2; Shatzmiller 1976, pp. 116–17; Crone and Cook 1977, p. 173 n. 26; Schimmel 1994, p. 58 (miracle); Suvorova 2004, p. 14 (miracle); Dallal 2010, pp. 3–9; Shahzad 2011, p. 167 (miracle); Cook 2013, p. 105; and Yılmaz 2018, p. 264. The role of state power in dictating the *qibla*'s angle is a theme in Kahera 2012, pp. 3–11.
79. See below for examples.
80. See, e.g., Kessler 1983; Kessler 1984; and Al-Harithy 2001, esp. pp. 77–9.
81. This practice can be dated to as early as the third/ninth century. See Northedge 2007, p. 114 n. 308; and especially Northedge and Kennet 2015, vol. 1, pp. 101, 110–11, 186, 190. The orientation of vernacular housing has been insufficiently researched, as noted decades ago by Elizabeth Fentress. See Fentress 1987, p. 43. Nevertheless, important exceptions to this oversight include: Bourdieu 1979, pp. 149–51; Donley 1982, pp. 68–70; Ben El Khadir and Lahbabi 1989, pp. 164, 166–70; and Campo 1991a, pp. 82–3.
82. Cf. Johns 1999, pp. 87–8, 110. *Pace* AlSayyad 1991, p. 57.
83. Evidence in support of this position will be presented in the course of the coming few pages, but for a succinct statement on the issue, see Whitcomb 2010.
84. For a discussion of the term *amṣār*, including an argument for broadening its conventionally accepted remit, see Whitcomb 1994; and Whitcomb 2012.
85. Al-Balādhurī 1987, p. 388; cf. trans. al-Balādhurī 1916, p. 435.
86. Al-Ṭabarī 1960, vol. 4, p. 44; trans. al-Ṭabarī 1989b, p. 69 (modified, but parenthetical interpolations as marked and explained in the original translation).
87. For an analysis of the discrepancy, and an attempt at its resolution, see Denoix 2008, pp. 121–2.
88. Di Cesare 2017, p. 87.
89. Cf. Djaït 1986, p. 199. But note Charles Wendell's comment that archery was not the province of the Arabs and the foundation act indicates, rather, a Persian influence. See Wendell 1971, pp. 109–10. Some scholars consider the archer to be a folktale. See, e.g., Johns 1999, p. 86.
90. Al-Ṭabarī 1960, vol. 4, p. 45; trans. al-Ṭabarī 1989b, p. 70.
91. Mustafa 1963; al-Janābī 1967.
92. AlSayyad 1991, pp. 58–65. More circumspect than AlSayyad, Fred Donner finds in the excavation reports evidence of 'clear efforts' to apply planning principles. See Donner 1981, p. 228. Hugh Kennedy is even more circumspect, saying only that 'it looks as if a rough and ready grid system was laid out'. See Kennedy 2010, p. 48.
93. Djaït 1986, pp. 120–1. See also his reconstructed map of the town in ibid. p. 302. Alastair Northedge considers his suggestion of orthogonality to be 'unlikely.' See Northedge 2017, p. 158.
94. Djaït 1986, p. 120.
95. Al-Ṭabarī 1960, vol. 4, p. 46; cf. trans. al-Ṭabarī 1989b, p. 72.

96. Cf. Bacharach 1991, p. 113.
97. Ibid. p. 113. Cf. Wheatley 2001, p. 229.
98. Johns 1999, p. 87. The report referenced by Johns in this citation is from al-Balādhurī 1987, p. 484; trans. al-Balādhurī 1924, p. 62.
99. Wheatley 2001, p. 228.
100. Al-Balādhurī 1987, p. 484; trans. al-Balādhurī 1924, pp. 61–2.
101. Ibn al-Athīr 1987, vol. 2, p. 373.
102. Kubiak 1987, p. 65. Note, however, that a few pages later he appears to contradict himself, because he writes: '[A]n ideal checkerboard pattern was adhered to in this area [of central plots] more than in any other part of the camp-town.' See ibid. p. 72.
103. Ibid. p. 129.
104. Whitcomb 2012, pp. 384–5.
105. Whitcomb 1994, p. 165. Cf. Whitcomb 2012, p. 384.
106. Whitcomb 2012, p. 385.
107. Note, however, Kennedy's clear support of Kubiak's arguments in Kennedy 2010, pp. 51–2.
108. Sheehan 2010, p. 86. See also ibid. pp. 1, 9.
109. Whitcomb 2012, p. 386. Note, however, Wheatley's more cautious approach to the question of orthogonality. He writes: 'Perhaps the question properly should be not, Were the *amṣār* laid out orthogonally? but rather, To what extent did some of them incorporate orthogonal elements?' Wheatley 2001, p. 268.
110. For the *qibla* orientation of ʿAnjar, which is almost identical to that of the Umayyad Mosque of Damascus, see Hillenbrand 1999, p. 61; and Finster 2008, p. 237 (Fig. 1). For Qaṣr al-Ḥayr al-Sharqī, specifically the so-called large enclosure, see Grabar et al. 1978, vol. 1, p. 40. For Mshatta and Qaṣr al-Ṭūba, see Enderlein and Meinecke 1992, pp. 141–2.
111. For a summary of these revisionist claims, see Shoemaker 2012, pp. 244–51.
112. Wheatley 1983, pp. 7–8.
113. Whitcomb's categorisation of Ayla as a *miṣr* and the date he assigns for its foundation are disputed and effectively dismissed in Northedge 2017, pp. 159, 161.
114. Whitcomb 2007, p. 23.
115. Whitcomb 2001, pp. 186–8.
116. Ibid. p. 188.
117. Cf. King D. 1995, p. 270.
118. King D. 1984a, p. 119.
119. Wendell 1971, pp. 112 n. 6, 117, 123. Cf. Le Strange 1900, p. 11. Note, however, the doubt cast upon this alleged orientation by Michelina Di Cesare, in Di Cesare 2018, pp. 79–91. That the name *al-Zawrāʾ* is related to the city's unexpected orientation would seem to be borne out in a reference by al-Yaʿqūbī (d. after 292/905) to an old name for Samarra: *al-Zawrāʾ Banī ʿAbbās*, or the 'Askew of the Banū ʿAbbās [tribe]'. For al-Yaʿqūbī this old name is credible, because '[in Samarra] all the *qibla*s of its mosques are skewed. Crookedness marks it (*fīhā izwirār*). There is not a straight *qibla* in it'. Al-Yaʿqūbī 1892, p. 268.

120. Hillenbrand 1988, p. 23. Cf. Hillenbrand 1994, pp. 392–5.
121. On the paradisiacal claims of Madīnat al-Zahrā᾿, see Fierro 2017, pp. 982–96.
122. Northedge 1994, p. 248.
123. Meinecke 1996, p. 164.
124. Northedge 2007, p. 200.
125. Meinecke 1996, pp. 164–7.
126. King D. 1984b, p. 79.
127. Ibid. p. 79. Note, however, the dismissal of this implicit suggestion in Kessler 1984, p. 107 n. 3. Note, too, King's more nuanced approach to the issue in his treatment of the orientation of the Great Mosque of Cordoba vis-à-vis the pre-Islamic street layout of Cordoba, which like Fatimid Cairo happened to have a *qibla* orientation, just not a mathematically determined one. See King D. 2018, *passim* (pp. 85–6 for Cairo).
128. King D. 2005, p. 175.
129. Bonine 1990, pp. 50–72. King cites this article in, e.g., King D. 1995, p. 273 n. 25.
130. Bonine 2008, p. 155. Cf. an earlier statement by Bonine: 'David King's statement that some Islamic cities were laid out in the direction of the *qibla* is indeed true for Morocco.' Bonine 1990, p. 70.
131. Bonine 1990, p. 70; Bonine 2008, p. 176.
132. King D. 1995, pp. 268–9.
133. Bonine 1990, p. 70.
134. In his later, second publication, Bonine effectively rewrites the above-cited conclusion, rendering it more cautious in tone. See Bonine 2008, p. 176.
135. Bonine 1990, pp. 55–6.
136. Al-Jaznā᾿ī 1991, p. 24; trans. al-Jaznā᾿ī 1923, p. 51. The objection will likely be raised that in the context of this historical narrative, *qibla* means 'south' only, a relatively common usage of the word, as discussed in Metcalfe 2012, pp. 46–9. This is a valid point. Even so, Fez remains an oriented foundation in this narrative, just a cardinally oriented one.
137. Akel Kahera presents this suggestion of a foundation desideratum in more definite terms. See Kahera 2012, pp. 12–15.
138. For Morocco, Bonine is emphatic about Marrakesh not having an orientation related to its earliest centre. See Bonine 1990, p. 58. More recently, however, Quentin Wilbaux has effectively thrown doubt on this assertion. See Wilbaux 2001, pp. 134–8.
139. Bonine 2008, pp. 156–61.
140. Ibid.
141. Ross 2006, esp. pp. 85–91.
142. See, e.g., Wheatley 1971, pp. 423–7; Eliade 1976, pp. 22–4; and Rykwert 1988, pp. 45–50.
143. Lévi-Provençal 1928, pp. 173–4.
144. Kahera 2012, p. 13. Cf. Neuwirth 2001a. The philosopher Emmanuel Levinas adds weight to Kahera's assertion when he talks of orientation as a leap 'outside-of-oneself toward the *other than oneself*'. See Levinas 1987, p. 90 (italics as marked in the original).

Chapter Two

1. See, e.g., Hjärpe 1979; Lewis J. 1982; Bennett 1994; and also Nasr 1996, even though he does not reference Eliade. Most recently, see O'Meara 2020b. On Eliade's notion of the sacred centre, see Eliade 1991.
2. King and Hawkins 1982.
3. King D. 1954a, p. 181.
4. King D. 1985, pp. 325–7. King accessibly expands on these findings, relating them to what is known of other oriented pre-Islamic buildings in Arabia and elsewhere, in King D. 1982, pp. 19–20. There he also speculates on the significance of the Kaʿba's lunar alignment, suggesting that the Prophet's ban on intercalation might explain why this alignment was later forgotten. See King D. 1982, p. 20.
5. King D. 1985, p. 327.
6. See, e.g., Wensinck 1916, p. 49; and the titles in Livne-Kafri 2008, p. 48 n. 7.
7. King D. 1985, p. 327.
8. Cited in Heinen 1982, p. 24 (Arabic); cf. trans. ibid. p. 157.
9. Cited in Schmidl 1999, p. 137.
10. On the prevalence of this Kaʿba-centred schema in the medieval period, see Schmidl 2007. On its popularity, see King D. 1954b, p. 840 (Fig. 2). On other wind schemas, see King D. 1954b, p. 839 (Fig. 1); and Forcada 1954.
11. See Aḥmad b. Mājid (*fl.* 865–905/1460–1500), *Taṣnīf qiblat al-Islām fī jamīʿ al-dunyā* ('Tabulating the *qibla* of Islam for all the world'), also known as *The Judges' Treasure*, in Ibn Mājid 1921, vol. 1, fol. 128v (ll. 15–16); trans. Ibn Mājid 1921, vol. 3, p. 210. The alternative title of the work is given in Ibn Mājid 1921, vol. 1, fol. 136v (l. 13).
12. Cf. ibid. vol. 1, fol. 128v (ll. 4–14); trans. Ibn Mājid 1921, vol. 3, pp. 209–10; and King D. 1985, pp. 320 ff.
13. King D. 1954a, pp. 183–5.
14. Cf. Gaudefroy-Demombynes 1923, p. 27 n. 1; and King D. 1954a, p. 185.
15. On this diagram and its maker, see Herrera Casais 2008; Herrera Casais 2013; and Kahlaoui 2018, pp. 207–25.
16. King D. 1999, p. 54 (italics as marked in the original).
17. Herrera Casais 2013, p. 461.
18. Herrera Casais and Schmidl 2008, p. 299.
19. Ibid. pp. 280–1.
20. Ibid. p. 281.
21. Ibn Isḥāq 1976, p. 73 (#79). Cf. Q 79:30. For additional references, see Wensinck 1916, p. 18.
22. Al-Ṭabarī 1960, vol. 1, p. 49; trans. al-Ṭabarī 1989a, p. 217 (modified). Cf. Wensinck 1916, p. 42.
23. Al-Azraqī 2003, vol. 1, p. 66 (#1). Cf. Wensinck 1916, p. 18.
24. Cf. Q 73:7.
25. Al-Azraqī 2003, vol. 1, p. 67 (#3). Cf. Wensinck 1916, p. 39. The designation *Umm al-qurā* (literally, Mother of the towns) is Qurʾanic: Q 6:92 and 42:7. Its translation as 'Metropolis' follows Wheeler 2006, p. 86; and Livne-Kafri 2008, p. 50.

26. Karen Pinto thinks this map might be Ilkhanid in origin. She compares it to an almost identical map in a ninth/fifteenth-century Timurid manuscript held at Heidelberg University Library: Cod. Heid. Orient. 118, ff. 258v–259r, available at <http://tinyurl.com/jqc7ntj> (last accessed 25 November 2018). Karen Pinto, personal communication, 27 November 2016.
27. The connection between the Kaʿba and the Dome of the earth, which in the medieval and pre-modern periods was also called the Dome of Arīn (most probably after the ancient city of Ujjayinī in India), is underscored by the mystic Ibn ʿArabī. In an early work, *The Night Journey*, he says he met the source of his inspiration, the mysterious youth (*al-fatā*ʾ), at Arīn. Later, in his magnum opus, *The Meccan Revelations*, he says he met him at the Kaʿba. See Chodkiewicz 2002, p. 20. For the connection between the Dome of the earth and Arīn, see Pellat 1954b; Miquel 1954; and especially Nazmi 2007, pp. 69–74.
28. Cf. Antrim 2012, pp. 37–8.
29. Ibn Sulaymān 2003, vol. 1, p. 359 (with respect to Q 6:92). Cf. al-Nahrawalī 1857, p. 18 (ll. 2–3); and the epithet's treatment in both Wensinck 1916, p. 38; and Livne-Kafri 2013, pp. 320–1.
30. As also noted in Vâlsan 1966, p. 221. On traditional childbirth in the medieval Arab world, see Guthrie 1995, pp. 157–61.
31. This apparent illogicality of there being more than one *axis mundi* in the Islamic world is not unique to Islamic culture. See Eliade and Sullivan 2005, vol. 3, p. 1501.
32. For Merv as *Umm al-qurā*, see al-Muqaddasī 1906, pp. 298–9; trans. al-Muqaddasī 1994, p. 243; and cf. Livne-Kafri 2008, p. 50 n. 25. Damascus is also referred to as *Umm al-qurā*, as noted in Livne-Kafri 2008, p. 50 n. 25. For Jerusalem as the world's navel, see Ibn al-Faqīh al-Hamadhānī 1885, p. 94 (l. 4); and Antrim 2012, pp. 40, 157 n. 36. Baghdad, too, is referred to as the world's navel, as detailed in Cooperson 1996, pp. 100–1; and contextually analysed in Olsson 2014, pp. 492–5.
33. Cf. Antrim 2012, p. 157 n. 36; and Wensinck 1916, p. 36. In both of these scholarly texts, all the references to Mecca as a navel come from sources written in the medieval and pre-modern periods.
34. I use the name Temple Mount, not Haram al-Sharif (*al-Ḥaram al-Sharīf*), because according to Kaplony's comprehensive investigations, the latter name is not found in the early Islamic sources. See Kaplony 2002, pp. 214–24, 384–6.
35. A tradition recorded by both Abū Bakr al-Wāsiṭī (*fl.* 410/1020) and Ibn al-Murajjā (*fl.* 429–39/1038–48), as cited in Kaplony 2002, p. 353 n. 2. Cf. Livne-Kafri 2008, pp. 51 n. 26, 53 n. 35. A minor variant of this tradition (the word 'under' is missing) is collected in a work from the same century: al-Iṣfahānī 1932, vol. 6, p. 3 (with respect to Kaʿb al-Aḥbār). For midrashic and earlier instances of a very similar image in Judaism, see Alexander 1999, pp. 114–16; Koltun-Fromm 2013, pp. 243–5; and Koltun-Fromm 2017, pp. 408–9.
36. This is not a scientific conclusion, for it was undertaken using only the searchable database *Al-Maktaba al-shāmila*.
37. Note, however, that in a specific edition of the exegesis by Muqātil b. Sulaymān (d. 150/767), there is this tradition: 'The Rock which is in the

Temple Mount is the centre of the entire world.' See Ibn Sulaymān 2002, vol. 2, p. 513 n. 1 (ll. 14–15); trans. Hasson 1996, p. 383. Although this tradition does not reference the image of the earth spreading out from under the Rock, it could be taken to imply that the Rock was the birthplace of the world. One could, of course, say the same thing for all the aforementioned navels in Islamic history. The tradition is similar to one misquoted by Kister, namely, 'The Rock is the navel of the universe', which Kister dates to the late first/seventh century. See Kister 1981, vol. 1. p. 185. It actually says: 'The Temple Mount is the navel of the world.' See Ibn al-Faqīh al-Hamadhānī 1885, p. 94 (l. 4).

38. Cf. Koltun-Fromm 2017, p. 418.
39. Ibn al-Faqīh al-Hamadhānī 1885, p. 97 (l. 2).
40. For citation details, see n. 35 above. On al-Wāsiṭī and the dating of his text, see Hasson 1981, vol. 1, p. 172. On the relationship between al-Wāsiṭī and al-Ramlī al-Zayyāt, see Mourad 2008, pp. 88–90.
41. Ibn Isḥāq 1976, p. 73 (#79); and al-Muqaddasī 1906, p. 75 (l. 14); trans. al-Muqaddasī 1994, p. 69, respectively.
42. Livne-Kafri 2013, p. 320.
43. King D. 1954a, p. 181. As Schmidl and Herrera Casais note, although names for three of the corners are attested in the early sources, only one of them conceivably pertains to divisions of the world: the *Yamānī* corner. See Herrera Casais and Schmidl 2008, p. 277 n. 10. As will be discussed below, this name is not, however, necessarily derived from the country, Yemen.
44. On this name, see Hawting 1982, p. 38.
45. Al-Bukhārī 1994, vol. 4, p. 187 (*kitāb al-manāqib, bāb al-manāqib*, #3499). This anonymous tradition is not asserted as a hadith by al-Bukhārī; rather, he gives it on his own authority. It is later cited by al-Muqaddasī (d. after 380/990); an anonymous fifth/eleventh-century author; and Ibn Manẓūr (d. 711/1312); although in all three cases the word 'left hand' is given as *shimāl*, not the etymologically implausible *yasār*. See respectively al-Muqaddasī 1906, p. 152; trans. al-Muqaddasī 1994, p. 248; Rapoport and Savage-Smith 2014, p. 436 (Arabic: p. 167); and Ibn Manẓūr n.d., vol. 15, p. 462 (with respect to *yaman*). For further discussion of the tradition, see below. On the etymological relationship between the name *al-Shām* and the word *shimāl*, see Chelhod 1973, p. 247.
46. In view of the foregoing discussion about whether the Kaʿba or the Temple generated the world, note that in the Syriac *Cave of Treasures* an equivalent four-wind schema is referenced, with Golgotha at its centre. See Toepel 2013, p. 557.
47. Abū Isḥāq al-Aṣbaḥī, *Kitāb al-Yawāqīt fī ʿilm al-mawāqīt* (unpublished), as cited in Schmidl 1999, p. 141 (my emphasis).
48. Ibid.
49. Ibn ʿArabī 1972, vol. 11, pp. 276–7; trans. Gilis 1982, p. 53.
50. Ibn ʿArabī 1972, vol. 11, p. 277; trans. Gilis 1982, p. 53.
51. An exception is Ibn ʿArabī, who counts the *Quṭb* as one of them. See Ibn ʿArabī 1972, vol. 11, p. 269; trans. Chodkiewicz 1993, p. 93.
52. Gilis 1982, pp. 53–5. Cf. Goldziher 1954, p. 772.

53. Ibn ʿArabī 1972, vol. 2, p. 401 (ll. 5–9); trans. Addas 1993, pp. 66–7. Cf. Chodkiewicz 1993, pp. 93, 100 n. 22.
54. Gilis 1982, pp. 40–62. Undermining this account of the four Pillars corresponding to the four corners of the Kaʿba, one should note that Ibn ʿArabī also speaks of the *Ḍurāḥ*: the allegedly divine model for the earthly Kaʿba which, some traditions say, Adam built on earth (see Chapter Three). This model, Ibn ʿArabī says, was a ternary structure, not a quaternary one. See Akkach 2005a, pp. 188–91.
55. Concerning Shiʿism, see Corbin 1986, pp. 65, 198–227. Concerning Sufism, see the Kaʿba-centric cosmology of the Naqshbandi shaykh Aḥmad Sirhindī (d. 1034/1624), in which a hierarchy of cosmic 'Realities' (*ḥaqāʾiq*) is set forth, culminating in the 'Reality of the Kaʿba' (*ḥaqīqat-i Kaʿba*). See Friedmann 2000, pp. 14–16.
56. See Friedman Y. 2010, p. 142.
57. See n. 6 above and especially the treatment and development of this view in Shoemaker 2012, pp. 241–57.
58. On Ibn al-Wardī and his work, see Bellino 2014. Bellino is wary of accepting his conventional death date of 861/1456, preferring to say that it was after 822/1419. See ibid. p. 257. On the form of *mappa mundi* associated with Ibn al-Wardī, see most recently Pinto 2016, pp. 32–3.
59. Other examples of the Ibn al-Wardī form include a late eleventh/seventeenth-century *mappa mundi*, reproduced in Seed 2014, p. 61 and available at <http://tinyurl.com/h575rdt> (last accessed 6 July 2017); and two earlier ones, reproduced in Pinto 2016, p. 36, and Pinna 1996, vol. 1, p. 151, respectively. Sometimes an image of the Kaʿba is not found at the *mappa mundi*'s centre, just its name or that of Mecca. See, e.g., Pinto 2016, pp. 217–18. Other examples of *mappae mundi* with a central Kaʿba, but not of the form associated with Ibn al-Wardī, are reproduced in Pinna 1996, vol. 1, p. 169; and Ducène 2002, pp. 124–5. See also Figs 2.5 and 2.11 in the present chapter.
60. Chekhab-Abudaya and Bresc 2013, p. 27; and Chekhab-Abudaya 2014, pp. 19–21.
61. See, for example, the almost identical map from the Topkapı Palace Library Ibn Ḥawqal manuscript, Ahmet 3346 (fol. 8b), securely dated to 479/1086, as reproduced in Antrim 2012, p. 116. See, too, the similar maps in Tibbets 1992, p. 119 (Figs 5.10 and 5.11); and Pinto 2016, pp. 238–40.
62. On this mountain range and its depiction in Islamic *mappae mundi*, see Pinto 2016, pp. 165–7.
63. On the distinction between (sacred) cosmography and (empirical) geography, at least as the distinction relates to medieval Christian *mappae mundi*, see Stone 1993, pp. 192–200; and Kupfer 2006. For historical evidence that the *mappae mundi* of the Ibn al-Wardī form were not taken seriously by all Muslims as empirical representations of the world, see Ducène 2011, p. 25. Something similar is said to be the case regarding medieval Christian *mappae mundi:* '[Their] significance was symbolic and theological right from the start.' Alexander 1999, p. 112.
64. Chekhab-Abudaya and Bresc 2013, p. 27; Chekhab-Abudaya 2014, p. 20. An early example of such a Creation tradition is found in al-Ṭabarī 1989a, p. 220.

65. Fahd 1959, pp. 252–5; and Heinen 1982, pp. 85–8, 143–5. Regarding Bahamūt (also called Balhūt) specifically, see Yāqūt b. ʿAbd Allāh al-Ḥamawī 1977, vol. 5, p. 23 (l. 20); Streck and Miquel 1954, p. 401; and especially Heinen 1982, pp. 116, 172, 235.
66. On the re-dating of this copy, see Savage-Smith 2013, p. 152.
67. See, e.g., Hillenbrand 1992, p. 87; and more contentiously Suleman 2013, esp. pp. 34–5.
68. Streck and Miquel 1954, p. 401.
69. The second image is on p. 311 of a 960/1553 copy of the same translated text of al-Qazwīnī, currently held at the Getty Research Institute: Acc. No. 2010.M.65, available at <http://tinyurl.com/zqe7xoe> (last accessed 13 April 2019).
70. This diagram has most recently been analysed in Savage-Smith 2016, pp. 234–8, and its legends translated in ibid. pp. 281–2. Possibly the legend 'the Red Light' is a scribal error (the Arabic letter 'th' miscopied as 'n'), so that it should instead read 'the Red Bull'. This would make sense, because in Islamic Creation traditions the cosmic bull (*thawr*) is sometimes located beneath the Green Rock (*al-Ṣakhra al-Khaḍrāʾ*). See, e.g., Heinen 1982, pp. 14 (Arabic), 145 (English).
71. Al-Azraqī 2003, vol. 1, p. 71 (#9); trans. Wensinck 1916, pp. 51–2 (modified).
72. Al-Azraqī 2003, vol. 1, p. 70 (#5). Cf. ibid. vol. 1, p. 91 (#36); and Wensinck 1916, p. 48.
73. Akkach 2005a, p. 183. For the few cosmographical traditions concerning the Kaʿba's alleged vertical relationship with the cosmos, i.e. the reports alleging that the Kaʿba is located at the point on earth closest to the heavens, see Wensinck 1916, pp. 14–15, 25.
74. Al-Qazwīnī 1848, p. 77. Cf. Wensinck 1916, pp. 25, 35; and von Grunebaum 1962, p. 33.
75. Cf. Chelhod 1973, p. 250. With respect to Mecca's cosmic awesomeness as a whole, see Wheatley 1971, pp. 428–9, 433; and Kister 1996, p. 41.
76. Kant 1992, pp. 366–8.
77. Casey 1997, p. 205 (italics as marked in the original).
78. See, especially, Casey 1993, pp. 71–105; but also Cassirer 1955, p. 90 (viz., 'Man's body and its parts are the system of references to which all other spatial distinctions are indirectly transferred'); Tuan 1977, p. 37 (viz., 'Cultures differ greatly in the elaboration of spatial schemata. [Yet] the vocabularies of spatial organization and value have certain common terms . . . ultimately derived from the structure and values of the human body'); and Hill 1982, p. 13 (viz., 'In all languages there appear to be pairs of lexical items that name asymmetrical axes of spatial orientation. [T]hey are ultimately anchored in the human body itself').
79. 'Lam afruq fī tilka al-ruʾya bayna jihātī bal kuntu mithla al-kura lā aʿqilu li-nafsī jiha illā bi-l-farḍ lā bi-l-wujūd.' Ibn ʿArabī 1852, vol. 2, p. 538 (l. 29, ch. 206).
80. Bashear 1989, pp. 329–32.
81. 'Al-Kaʿba murabbʿa fa-lā yamīn la-hā wa lā yasār.' Yāqūt b. ʿAbd Allāh al-Ḥamawī 1977, vol. 5, p. 447 (with respect to 'al-Yaman'). The squareness

of the Kaʿba plays a pivotal role in the tradition that asserts that the houses (sing. *bayt*) of the early inhabitants of Mecca were circular out of respect for the square (*murabbaʿ*) Kaʿba. See al-Azraqī 2003, vol. 1, pp. 390–1 (#352). Cf. Chelhod 1973, p. 249.

82. Yāqūt b. ʿAbd Allāh al-Ḥamawī 1977, vol. 5, p. 447.
83. Al-Azraqī 2003, vol. 1, p. 470 (#483–5). Cf. Gaudefroy-Demombynes 1923, pp. 211–12.
84. Yāqūt b. ʿAbd Allāh al-Ḥamawī 1977, vol. 5, p. 447.
85. See, e.g., al-Bukhārī 1994, vol. 2, p. 197 (*kitāb al-Ḥajj, bāb man lam yastalim illā al-Ruknayn al-Yamāniyayn*, #1609). Cf. Chelhod 1973, p. 250.
86. Ibn Qutayba 1995, pp. 197–8. The same tradition is also reported in al-Azraqī 2003, vol. 1, p. 447 (#420) and p. 450 (#428); and a variant of it is discussed in Al-Azmeh 2014, p. 219. Given this tradition, the question of why the Black Stone was not located on the *Yamānī* corner itself, as one might have expected, finds a speculative answer in the fact that the Black Stone 'looks out' from the Kaʿba towards the rising sun, which David King thinks was the *qibla* in pre-Islamic central Arabia. King explains that someone standing with their back against the Black Stone, looking towards the sunrise, occupies an axially calibrated location, in that 'on one's left (*shimal*) hand, the north *shamal* wind blows from *al-Sham*, Syria, [and] on one's right (*yamin*) hand, the south wind blows from *Yaman*, the Yemen'. King D. 1982, p. 20. On King's reading, the Black Stone would be the reason why the Kaʿba became conceptualised as a bilateral body. Interestingly, according to Chelhod, the Black Stone is a simulacrum of the rising sun. See Chelhod 1973, p. 248.
87. See, e.g., Campo 1991b, p. 75.
88. The references to these terms as they pertain to the Kaʿba are numerous in the Islamic sources, as a quick operation of the digital database *al-Maktaba al-shāmila* will reveal. Concerning hard copies of texts, see, inter alios, al-Azraqī 2003, vol. 1, pp. 483–9 (#522–40); and al-Fākihī 1994, vol. 1, pp. 170–3 (#247–56).
89. Cf. Bashear 1989, pp. 330–1. The admittedly inelegant translations 'front-comer' and 'rear-comer' follow Wright 1967, vol. 1, p. 185 (with respect to *faʿūl*).
90. The term *al-Burquʿ* (also *al-Burqaʿ*) is used for the door covering at least by the time of Ibn Baṭṭūṭa (d. 770/1369 or 778/1377). See Ibn Baṭṭūṭa 1893, vol. 1, p. 309 (l. 11); trans. Ibn Baṭṭūṭa 1958, vol. 1, p. 195. See Chapter Six for further treatment of this covering.
91. Shalem 2015, p. 176.
92. Jones 2000, vol. 2, p. 346 n. 29.
93. Ibid. vol. 2, p. 31 (italics as marked in the original).
94. Christian Norberg-Schulz, 'Meaning in Architecture' (1969), pp. 225–6, as cited Jones 2000, vol. 2, p. 30.
95. Susanne Langer, *Philosophy in a New Key: A Study in the Symbolism of Reason, Rite, and Art* (1960), p. 289, as cited Jones 2000, vol. 2, p. 29.
96. Ströker 1987, esp. pp. 20, 28. Jones refers to Ströker in Jones 2000, vol. 2, p. 28.
97. Lynch 1960, p. 125.
98. Steinbock 2007, p. 13.
99. Ibid. p. 16.

100. Ibid. p. 17.
101. Ibid. It remains to be proven that this description pertains to disorientation, not false orientation. False orientation would seem to be a more accurate way of conceptualising the nature of idolatry as recounted in the Qur᾿an and early Islamic sources, for example, not disorientation. On idolatry in those sources, see below.
102. On the term and its translation, see Hawting 1999, pp. 67–87; and Hawting 2001a, pp. 475–7.

Chapter Three

1. The various destructions of the Ka῾ba referred to in this chapter are not the ones that were allegedly anticipated but never realised by different invading rulers from pre-Islamic Southern Arabia. On those unrealised destructions, see de Prémare 2000; and Robin 2010.
2. Pellat 1954a, p. 607.
3. See, e.g., Elinson 2009, pp. 24–49.
4. Al-Azraqī 2003, vol. 1, p. 293 (#223); and al-Balādhurī 1996, vol. 7, p. 121, respectively.
5. See, e.g., al-Balādhurī 1996, vol. 5, pp. 357–69, vol. 7, pp. 120–8; and al-Azraqī 2003, vol. 1, pp. 289–320 (#215–55).
6. Cf. proposition 8b of Lundquist's temple typology: 'The destruction or loss of the temple is seen as calamitous and fatal to the community in which the temple stood.' Lundquist 1983, p. 212.
7. Al-Ṭabarī 1991, p. 225 (modified).
8. Cf. Hawting 2002, p. 14. For al-Jāḥiẓ, see Pellat 1952, pp. 316–19.
9. Note that in midrashic tradition, the destruction of the Temple is understood differently: Lamentations 4:11 becomes a description of 'the very condition for hope in the aftermath of the Destruction.' See Stern 1991, p. 40. On the 'cosmic disaster' occasioned by the Temple's destruction, see Smith J. 1969, pp. 117–18.
10. Note, however, that according to a historian of Saudi Arabia, after the repairs to the Ka῾ba had been completed following the first siege, that day was then observed 'as an anniversary for celebration for several centuries until gradually discontinued.' See al-Qu῾ayṭī 2007, p. 290. No sources are cited in support of this assertion.
11. On these practices, see Lazarus-Yafeh 1999, pp. 291–2.
12. See, e.g., al-Bukhārī 1994, vol. 2, p. 194 (*kitāb al-Ḥajj, bāb hadm al-Ka῾ba*, #1595–6). That these hadiths refer to the end of time is clarified in Ibn Ḥajar al-῾Asqalānī 2001, vol. 3, p. 660. On Dhū al-Suwayqatayn, see Cook 2002, pp. 78–9.
13. Ibn Ḥanbal 1995, vol. 11, pp. 628–9 (#7053).
14. Al-Azraqī 2003, vol. 1, p. 387 (#343). Se also ibid. vol. 1, p. 386 (#341).
15. Yavuz Demir translates the incomplete Ottoman Turkish text surrounding the image as follows: 'It is said that the group of Abyssinians were burned. That was described in the first edition in this manner: ῾Alī b. Abī Ṭālib, may God honour him, says that Basra's destruction will be by black men; Medina's

destruction by starvation; . . .' Yavuz Demir, personal communication, 21 April 2019.

16. 'Istamta'ū min hādhā al-Bayt fa-innahu qad hudima marratayni wa yurfa'u fī al-thālith.' Ibn Khuzayma 1980, vol. 4, pp. 128–9 (#2506). Cf. the slightly different wording in al-Ghazālī 1982, vol. 1, p. 242 (*kitāb asrār al-Ḥajj, bāb faḍīlat al-Bayt*); trans. Umar 1975, p. 35.
17. Ibn Khuzayma 1980, vol. 4, p. 129.
18. 'Idhā aradtu an ukharriba al-dunyā bada'tu bi-Baytī.' Al-Ghazālī 1982, vol. 1, p. 243; cf. trans. Umar 1975, p. 35. This report, I believe, originates with al-Ghazālī. Both of these hadiths run counter to a tradition which alleges that on the Day of Resurrection the Ka'ba will be conducted to the Rock of the Temple Mount 'like a bride conducted to her husband'. On that tradition, see Madelung 1986, pp. 141–4; Livne-Kafri 2006, p. 394; and especially Livne-Kafri 2013, pp. 311, 321–2. An alternative to it gives the Ka'ba's destination as the Prophet's tomb in Medina, not the Rock in Jerusalem. See Kister 1969, p. 191 n. 87.
19. Al-Ghazālī 1982, vol. 1, p. 242; trans. Umar 1975, pp. 34–5; Ibn Khuzayma 1980, vol. 4, p. 129.
20. On this attack, see e.g. al-Nahrawalī 1857, pp. 162–5; trans. Peters 1994a, pp. 123–5; de Goeje 1886, pp. 100–11; and Halm 1996, pp. 255 ff.
21. A similar observation is made in Lazarus-Yafeh 1999, p. 294.
22. Al-Nahrawalī 1857, p. 165. Cf. de Goeje 1886, pp. 100–11; and Halm 1996, p. 256.
23. Halm 1996, pp. 257–63, with minor additional information from Hajnal 1998; Daftary 1998, p. 48; Daftary 2007, pp. 149–50; and Moin 2014, p. 409.
24. Al-Ṭūsī n.d., p. 282. On the Banū Shayba, see Gaudefroy-Demombynes 1954a.
25. Al-Mufīd 1995, vol. 2, p. 383. Except for the destruction or otherwise of the Ka'ba, the Mahdi's actions in Shi'ite apocalyptic traditions are treated in Cook 2002, pp. 203–12.
26. Al-Nahrawalī 1857, pp. 163–4; trans. Peters 1994a, pp. 124–5; de Goeje 1886, pp. 105–11. As this book was going to press, I learnt of the argument that Abū Ṭāhir's hanging of the stolen Black Stone in Kufa also imitated an eschatological prophecy. See Friedman 2013, pp. 217, 225–6.
27. Al-Azraqī 2003, vol. 1, pp. 299–300 (#226). Cf. Hawting 1999, p. 110 n. 69.
28. Efendi 1987, p. 53.
29. For occasions of flooding as related in the early sources, see al-Balādhurī 1916, pp. 82–4. See, too, the discussion of the flood barrier known as the Wall (*Jidār*), which was allegedly erected by the ancient Jurhum tribe in the vicinity of the Ka'ba, in Rubin 1986, p. 99. For occasions of flooding as related in later histories of Mecca, see Peters 1994a, pp. 137–40; and especially the list of eighty-six flash floods (sing. *sayl*) occurring in Mecca from 1/622 to 1384/1964, as detailed in al-Kurdī al-Makkī 2000, vol. 2, pp. 243–55. One flood not included in this list occurred in 948/1541, when the Ka'ba collapsed, exactly as happened in the flood of 1039/1630. See Richardson 2012, p. 122.
30. On the geography of Mecca and the location of the Ka'ba, see Lammens 1924, pp. 180–2. The toponym Baṭn Makka appears in the Qur'an at Q 48:24. For further discussion of it, see below. According to Chabbi, only because the site of the Ka'ba is so prone to flooding was it ever considered to be sacred

and thus a suitable location for a betyl, the Black Stone. See Chabbi 1954, p. 441; and especially Chabbi 2010, pp. 33–7, 319–20.

31. The event and the reparations that followed are extensively treated in Faroqhi 1994, pp. 113–20; and al-Quʿayṭī 2007, pp. 289–96.
32. ʿʿAlāma min al-ʿalāmāt yawm al-qiyāma'. Sabri Paşa 2004, vol. 1, p. 450. On Sabri Paşa, see Toprakyaran 2001.
33. Al-Azraqī 2003, vol. 1, p. 385 (#339).
34. Sabri Paşa 2004, vol. 1, pp. 450 ff. Cf. Toprakyaran 2001, pp. 11–34.
35. Hawting 1982, *passim*.
36. Al-Azraqī 2003, vol. 1, p. 298 (#226); trans. Peters 1994b, p. 61.
37. Elsewhere in his history, al-Azraqī reports that the exposed foundations date to Adam's time. See al-Azraqī 2003, vol. 1, p. 79 (#20).
38. On the problem of translating the term *arkān* as it pertains to the Kaʿba, see Hawting 1978, pp. 91–6, 104–10; and Hawting 1982, pp. 38–47.
39. Al-Azraqī 2003, vol. 1, pp. 299–301 (#226–7). Cf. Peters 1994b, pp. 62–3, where some of the same passage is translated.
40. See, e.g., Ibn Hishām 1998, vol. 1, p. 157; trans. Ibn Hishām 1955, p. 84.
41. For flooding as the reason, see al-Azraqī 2003, vol. 1, p. 243 (#177); for fire, see ibid. vol. 1, pp. 240–2 (#176–7); and for the prevention of theft, see Ibn Hishām 1998, vol. 1, p. 157; trans. Ibn Hishām 1955, p. 84. Cf. Peters 1994a, p. 48.
42. As this event is reported by al-Azraqī, the stone in question was one of the Kaʿba's foundation stones. See al-Azraqī 2003, vol. 1, p. 246 (#177).
43. Ibn Hishām 1998, vol. 1, pp. 157–9; trans. Ibn Hishām 1955, pp. 84–5 (modified). As reported by al-Azraqī, the moment the crowbar was inserted into the two foundation stones, one of them emitted a blinding flash of light. See al-Azraqī 2003, vol. 1, p. 246 (#177).
44. Q 2:127. On the ambiguity of the verse regarding Ishmael's involvement in the construction activity, see Witztum 2009, pp. 26–7.
45. Q 16:26. On the different exegetical interpretations of *qawāʿid*, see Witztum 2009, p. 27.
46. Ibn Manẓūr n.d., vol. 11, p. 236.
47. This narrative thread finds a parallel in Islamic traditions concerning the (re) building of the Jewish Temple. See Livne-Kafri 2008, pp. 67, 70.
48. See, e.g., Ibn Sulaymān 2003, vol. 1, p. 78 (no mention of collapse); al-Ṭabarī 2001, vol. 1, pp. 631–4 (brief mention of collapse and frequent mention of elevation); al-Ṭabarsī 2005, vol. 1, p. 286 (no mention of elevation); al-Rāzī 2003, vol. 4, p. 59 (no mention of elevation).
49. For the confirmation that Abraham built on or raised the foundations of Adam's Kaʿba, see e.g. al-Azraqī 2003, vol. 1, pp. 107–8 (#60–2), p. 114 (#73). These and similar reports are discussed in Firestone 1990, pp. 85–91.
50. Al-Azraqī 2003, vol. 1, p. 73 (#11). Cf. ibid. vol. 1, p. 82 (#24); al-Ṭabarī 2001, vol. 1, p. 633; and Wensinck 1916 p. 42.
51. 'Fa-jaʿalahu mustaqbal al-Bayt al-Maʿmūr fa-lammā kāna zaman al-gharaq rufiʿa fī dībājatayn fa-huwa fīhumā ilā yawm al-qiyāma'. Al-Azraqī 2003, vol. 1, p. 93 (#41).
52. Ibid. vol. 1, p. 93 (#43).

53. Al-Ṭabarī 1989a, vol. 1, p. 302. See also ibid. vol. 1, p. 362, where al-Ṭabarī specifies that the Kaʿba which is elevated is the celestial Kaʿba: 'wa huwa al-Bayt al-Maʿmūr'.
54. McAuliffe 2001, pp. 407–9.
55. Al-Ghazālī 1982, vol. 3, p. 3; trans. al-Ghazālī 2010, p. 6. Cf. McAuliffe 2001, p. 409; Nasr 2002, p. 37; and Bashir 2011, pp. 43–5.
56. Sahl b. ʿAbd Allāh al-Tustarī, *Tafsīr al-Qurʾān al-ʿaẓīm* (1911), p. 59, as cited in Böwering 1980, pp. 252–3 (modified). Cf. another early Sufi, al-Nūrī (d. 295/907), who speaks of the heart as the locus of unification with God, as discussed in Karamustafa 2007, p. 15.
57. Ibn ʿArabī 1852, vol. 4, p. 7 (l. 18, ch. 405).
58. 'Mā wasiʿanī lā samāʾī wa lā arḍī wa lākin wasiʿanī qalb ʿabdī al-mūʾmin.' For an instance of its being referenced, see Ibn ʿArabī 1852, vol. 3, p. 281 (ll. 1–2, ch. 355). See also below. On the rejection of its authenticity, see e.g. Ibn Taymiyya 1997, vol. 18, p. 71 (122).
59. 'Al-qalb Bayt Allāh.' On its dismissal as inauthentic, see Ibn Taymiyya 1997, vol. 18, p. 71 (122); and al-Jarrāḥī 1932, vol. 2, pp. 99–100 (#1884–5).
60. Böwering 1980, p. 163.
61. Nwyia 1991, pp. 326–7.
62. Massignon 1922, vol. 1. p. 277.
63. Al-Niffarī 1935, pp. 55–7, 214. Cf. Nwyia 1991, pp. 331–2.
64. As cited in Massignon and Gardet 1954, p. 101.
65. Al-Qushayrī 2017, p. 311 (with respect to Q 3:97).
66. Al-Hujwīrī 1979, pp. 423–4; trans. al-Hujwīrī 1911, p. 327 (modified). He attributes the words to Muḥammad b. al-Faḍl (d. 319/931).
67. Al-Ghazālī 1982, vol. 1, p. 269 (*kitāb asrār al-Ḥajj, bāb bayān al-aʿmāl al-bāṭiniyya*); trans. Umar 1975, p. 116.
68. Al-Jīlānī 2007, p. 45; trans. al-Jīlānī 1992, p. 85
69. The celebrated Egyptian Sufi poet, Ibn al-Fāriḍ (d. 632/1235), belongs to this period, but although he does interpret the Kaʿba as the heart, he does so less explicitly. See, e.g., al-Qayṣarī 2004, p. 111 (v. 448); trans. Homerin 2011, p. 212.
70. 'Kaʿbatī hādhihī qalb al-wujūd . . . Baytī alladhī wasiʿanī huwa qalbuka al-maqṣūd.' Ibn ʿArabī 1972, vol. 1, pp. 226–7 (ll. 16 ff.). According to Cyrus Zargar, later in the same work Ibn ʿArabī relates the Kaʿba's corners to the 'various bestirrings (*khawatir*) that enter the heart, attributing undesirable Satanic bestirrings to the ʿIraqi Corner'. Zargar 2011, p. 142.
71. Ibn ʿArabī 1852, vol. 3, pp. 280–1 (ll. 37–8, ch. 355). For additional references, see Hirtenstein 2010, pp. 23–30. A number of these additional references clarify that although in the above citation Ibn ʿArabī says 'jaʿala fīhā kaʿba', which grammatically means God 'placed in the heart *a* kaʿba', the mystic means the Kaʿba of Mecca.
72. 'Dil-ast Kaʿba-yi maʿnī, tu gil che pindārī.' Rūmī 1958, vol. 6, p. 298 (l. 33,104, #3104).
73. Ibid.
74. Rūmī 1951, p. 165; trans. Rūmī 1999, p. 172 (#44). For instances from his *Mathnawī*, see Tosun 2012, pp. 139–40. For further discussion, see Subtelny 2010, pp. 206–8.

75. Baqlī 1972, p. 67 (l. 1). Regarding this Sufi's aforementioned interpretation of the Kaʿba as the heart, see Murata S. 1992, pp. 297–8.
76. 'Wa al-maʿnā al-thānī hūwa laṭīfa rabbāniyya rūḥāniyya la-hā bi-hādhā al-qalb al-jismānī taʿalluq.' Al-Ghazālī 1982, vol. 3, p. 3; trans. al-Ghazālī 2010, p. 5 (modified).
77. Recounted in Abū Ṭālib Muḥammad b. ʿAlī al-Makkī, *Qūt al-qulūb fī muʿāmalāt al-maḥbūb*, 4 vols (1932), vol. 1, p. 180, as cited in Böwering 1980, p. 252.
78. That the heart is not necessarily the end of the Sufi path is because the *sirr*, or the least gross (*kathīf*) and most spiritual (*alṭaf*) of the body's organs, is not always located inside the heart but beyond it. See Kamada 1983. For two clear instances of the *sirr* being located within the heart, see al-Tirmidhī 1958, pp. 38–9; trans. al-Tirmidhī and al-Sulamī al-Naysabūrī 2003, pp. 15–16; and Böwering 1980, p. 199.
79. As cited in translation in Maury 2013, p. 150 (modified). An early eleventh/seventeenth-century pilgrimage tile with this verse inscribed upon it is reproduced in ibid. p. 151. It is also curated on the David Collection's website: <http://tinyurl.com/y8des5gb> (last accessed 28 April 2019).
80. Rūmī 1958, vol. 6, p. 65 (l. 30,026, #2,828); trans. Rūmī 2009, p. 346 (#362, l. 10). See also Rūmī 1958, vol. 2, p. 65 (ll. 6,762–3, #648); trans. Nasr 2002, p. 35.
81. See, e.g., Q 3:35, 6:139 and 16:78.
82. Al-Masʿūdī 1861, vol. 4, p. 288.
83. Al-Majlisī 2008, vol. 35, p. 9. Cf. al-Baḥrānī 2007, pp. 94–5.
84. Al-Azraqī 2003, vol. 1, p. 262 (#205).
85. For *baṭn al-Kaʿba*, see e.g. al-Azraqī 2003, vol. 1, p. 187 (#142), pp. 408–14; and al-Ṭabarī 1960, vol. 8, p. 285; trans. al-Ṭabarī 1989c, p. 199. For *ẓahr al-Kaʿba*, see the birth of ʿAlī tradition discussed earlier; and Ibn Hishām 1998, vol. 1, p. 158; trans. Ibn Hishām 1955, p. 85. In this latter reference, it could seem that *ẓahr al-Kaʿba* was actually a specific wall of the Kaʿba. However, because the same term is also applied to the roof of the Kaʿba – see e.g. al-Azraqī 2003, vol. 1, p. 383 (#337) – this possibility must be discounted.
86. Lakoff and Johnson 1980, *passim*.
87. Lakoff and Johnson 1999, p. 19.
88. Lakoff and Johnson 1999, p. 34.
89. For further examples, see Lakoff and Johnson 1980, pp. 14–17.
90. Cf. '[B]uildings do not impose concepts of reality but make them thinkable.' See Piotrowski 2011, p. xvi.
91. Allen 1995.
92. Schwarzer 2001, *passim*.
93. Q 3:96. *Bakka*, not *Makka* (Mecca) is the location given in the verse. However, Islamic sources and most Western scholars agree that *Bakka* is an older name and/or an alternative spelling of *Makka*. See, e.g., al-Azraqī 2003, vol. 1, pp. 393–5 (#361, 366); al-Nawawī al-Shāfiʿī 1985, pp. 150–1; and Chabbi 2001, p. 337. In the sources, *Bakka* is additionally explained as the name of the sector of land on which the the Kaʿba stands, including (in some traditions) the Sacred Mosque, whereas *Makka* names the Sanctuary as a whole. On this explanation, *Bakka* is thus another name for the toponym, Belly of Mecca. See, e.g., al-Azraqī 2003, vol. 1, p. 395 (#365).

94. Q 39:6.
95. See especially Vidler 1990, pp. 3–10; and Rykwert 1996, pp. 26–67; but also Johnson 2001.
96. Al-Ṭabarī 1989a, p. 294.
97. Al-Ṭabarī 2001, vol. 1, pp. 16–17 (ch. *khuṭbat al-kitāb*). The translation of *aḥruf* follows Gilliot 2001, p. 320.
98. Al-Qāḍī al-Nuʿmān 1960, p. 30.
99. Poonawala 1954, p. 389; Berg 2001, pp. 157–8.
100. Cf. Lecerf 1954, with reference to *bāṭin* only.
101. Ahmed 2015, p. 377.
102. Chabbi 2010, p. 320.
103. Something similar seems to happen in the transition between classical antiquity and Christianity, especially Western Christianity. See Le Goff 1989, pp. 14–16; but note the interpretation in Sandnes 2002, pp. 24–60.
104. On Adam's cavity, see al-Ṭabarī 1989a, p. 262; and al-Thaʿlabī 2002, p. 45. On God's solidity, see al-Ṭabarī 2001, vol. 30, p. 420 (with respect to Q 112:2). Cf. Katz 2002, pp. 176–8.
105. As cited in translation in Gramlich 1997, p. 109.
106. Al-Ghazālī n.d., p. 72; cf. trans. al-Ghazālī 1992, p. 73. See also the 'unmentionable' place of the belly in a medieval hierarchy of the body in Kugle 2007, p. 82. In contrast to this religious condemnation of the belly, the litterateur al-Jāḥiẓ (d. 255/869) composed an essay on the superiority of the belly over the back, *Risāla fī tafḍīl al-baṭn ʿalā al-ẓahr*. As this partly ludicrous essay can be read as plainly homophobic, it is difficult to know what to make of its positive moralisation of the belly. See van Gelder 1991, pp. 204–6.
107. In the Qurʾan, the back (*ẓahr*) has less negative connotations. It is a means of carrying a burden (e.g. Q 6:31 and 43:13), and when something is cast behind the back, that action signifies rejection (e.g. Q 2:101 and 3:187).

Chapter Four

1. Ibn Baṭṭūṭa 1893, vol. 1, p. 356; trans. Ibn Baṭṭūṭa 1958, vol. 1, p. 221. Other perpetually circling pilgrims are described in Ibn Baṭṭūṭa 1893, vol. 1, pp. 280–2, 357–9.
2. See, e.g., Ibn Rushd 1989, vol. 1, pp. 579–86; trans. Ibn Rushd 2000, vol. 1, pp. 400–6. A clear summary in English is given in Long D. 1979, pp. 16, 21–2.
3. 'Innamā al-ṭawāf ṣalāt.' Ibn Ḥanbal 1995, vol. 27, p. 158 (#16612). Additional examples are given in Kister 1990, pp. 18–19. For atypical disagreement over the precondition of ritual purity, see Ibn Rushd 1989, vol. 1, p. 584; trans. Ibn Rushd 2000, vol. 1, p. 404.
4. Ibn Rushd 1989, vol. 1, pp. 579–83; trans. Ibn Rushd 2000, vol. 1, pp. 401–4; al-Nawawī al-Shāfiʿī 1985, pp. 73–4.
5. Al-Ghazālī 1982, vol. 1, p. 250 (*kitāb asrār al-Ḥajj, fī al-ṭawāf*); trans. Umar 1975, pp. 60–3 (modified). For other authoritative expressions in European languages of the rules of *ṭawāf* and their embellishment, see Burton 1893, vol. 2, pp. 165–7, 286–8; and especially Gaudefroy-Demombynes 1923, pp. 205–24.

6. Rubin 2011.
7. See the survey of this phenomenon in Iványi 2016, pp. 70–88. For instances of juridical condemnation of the practice, see Gaborieau 1994, p. 91; and Meri 2002, pp. 134–5. For an instance of a quasi-juridical counter-argument in favour of it outside Mecca, see Ernst 2009, p. 278.
8. Eck 2005, pp. 1795–8.
9. Ibid. p. 1795.
10. This decision, as well as the angels' complaint arising from it, is first recounted in the Qur'an (Q 2:30).
11. Al-Azraqī 2003, vol. 1, p. 69 (#5). A similar report is also related in al-Tirmidhī 1969, pp. 55–6.
12. Al-Azraqī 2003, vol. 1, p. 70; al-Tirmidhī 1969, p. 56; and, inter alios, al-Ṭabarī 1989a, p. 293; al-Thaʿlabī 2002, p. 147; and al-Ghazālī 1982, vol. 1, p. 269 (*kitāb asrār al-Ḥajj, bāb bayān al-aʿmāl al-bāṭiniyya*); trans. Umar 1975, p. 116.
13. Ibn ʿArabī 1972, vol. 11, p. 322 (l. 5, ch. 72). Cf. Gilis 1982, p. 169; and Fenton 1996, p. 183.
14. Wensinck 1917, pp. 43–4, 47; and less explicitly Goldziher 1966, vol. 1, p. 223. Cf. the parallel drawn by Ibn ʿArabī between the *ṭawāf* and the Islamic funerary prayer in Ibn ʿArabī 1972, vol. 1, p. 216 (l. 13, ch. 1).
15. Hammoudi 2006, pp. 156–7.
16. Cf. Lange 2015a, p. 268. For a convenient summary of Sufi interpretations of the Hajj rituals, see Masud 2006; and Tosun 2012. For a Fatimid interpretation, see al-Qāḍī al-Nuʿmān 1995, vol. 2, pp. 226–43; and, especially, the analysis of this interpretation in Velji 2016, pp. 98–104. For an account of some modern interpretations of the Hajj, see Katz 2004, pp. 125–6; and Bianchi 2005, pp. 23–36. Only two or three of these modern interpretations are mystically informed.
17. Reinhart 2014, pp. 76–92.
18. Graham 1983, p. 66. Cf. Reinhart 2016, p. 74.
19. For a description of these pilgrimage rituals and their locations, see, e.g., Hurgronje 2012, pp. 62–3, 100.
20. Al-Ghazālī 1982, vol. 1, pp. 265–6; trans. Umar 1975, pp. 104–7 (modified).
21. Katz 2004, p. 114.
22. Al-Sarakhsī 1989, vol. 4, pp. 13–14 (*kitāb al-manāsik*). Cf. Katz 2004, p. 113.
23. Al-Sarakhsī 1989, vol. 4, p. 14.
24. Katz 2004, *passim*.
25. Katz 2005, pp. 109–12. See also Powers 2004.
26. The titles alone of the following texts prove the claim: Tabbaa 1985; Grabar 1987b; Rabbat 1989; Khoury 1996; Mekeel-Matteson 1999.
27. Lefebvre 1991, p. 222.
28. Blair and Bloom 2012, p. 47.
29. Jones 2000, vol. 1, p. 41 (italics as marked in the original).
30. Jones 2000, vol. 1, p. 55. Cf. ibid. vol. 1, pp. 45–7, 86–103. The precise characteristics of the transformation to which Jones is referring are treated in Gadamer 2000, pp. 110–13.
31. Jones 2000, vol. 1, pp. 40, 45–6.

32. Ibid. vol. 1, p. 41.
33. Akkach 2005b.
34. The shortcomings of this way of thinking about buildings are well explained in ibid. pp. 120–3.
35. Grabar 1980, p. 8.
36. Grabar 1987a, p. 75. His assertion that the Kaʿba had no door is wrong, at least according to the early Islamic sources, with the possible exception of the earliest pre-Islamic years, when the Kaʿba was allegedly just a booth (*ʿarīsh*). See Finster 2011, pp. 229–30.
37. Grabar and Ettinghausen 1987, p. 18.
38. Nikolaus Pevsner, *An Outline of European Architecture* (1958), p. 23, as cited in Harries 1997, p. 4.
39. On this distinction and its attendant merits and demerits, see Harries 1997, *passim*.
40. Exceptionally, Nasser Rabbat notes visitors' aesthetic responses in Rabbat 2012, p. 1074.
41. 'Wa muʿāyanat al-Bayt al-karīm hawl^{un} yashʿuru al-nufūs min al-dhuhūl wa yaṭīshu al-afʾida wa al-ʿūqūl.' Ibn Jubayr 1907, p. 85 (l. 2); cf. trans. Ibn Jubayr 1952, p. 80. Cf. Shalem 2013, pp. 43–9, but note that when Ibn Jubayr is admiring the marbling and decoration of the interior of the *Ḥijr*, by definition he is not performing the *ṭawāf*.
42. Burton 1893, vol. 2, p. 161. For additional, pre-modern references to the compelling, awe-inspiring nature of beholding the Kaʿba, see Coşkun 1999, p. 236.
43. 'Al-naẓar ilā Bayt Allāh al-ḥarām ʿibāda.' As cited is in Efendi 1987, p. 52. A number of slightly different versions of this tradition exist. See, e.g., al-Fākihī 1994, vol. 1, p. 200 (#328).
44. Necĭpoğlu-Kafadar 1985, p. 106; Neçipoğlu 1992, p. 201; and Rüstem 2019, p. 154, respectively. Two other tenth/eighteenth-century mosques in Istanbul are compared in contemporary sources to the Frequented House, the Kaʿba's celestial prototype. See Rüstem 2019, pp. 176, 197.
45. Neçipoğlu 2005, p. 241.
46. Welch et al. 2002, p. 33. Cf. Blair 2013, p. 166.
47. Eaton 1993, p. 100.
48. Golombek and Wilber 1988, vol. 1, p. 336.
49. Yazdani 1947, p. 124 n. 1.
50. Mumtaz 2011. A detailed photograph of the panel is reproduced in Clévenot 2000, p. 154; and Burckhardt 2009, p. 59.
51. Latif 1892, p. 353.
52. Begley 1981, p. 12.
53. Munshī 1930, vol. 2, p. 1039.
54. Morton 1974, p. 34. See also Ḥusaynī al-Qumī 2004, vol. 2, p. 617 (v. 2); and the references to this verse in Rizvi 2010, pp. 51, 219 n. 78.
55. Ibn ʿIdhārī al-Marrākushī 1948, vol. 1, p. 184; trans. Ibn ʿIdhārī al-Marrākushī 1901, vol. 1, p. 262; Ibn Hāniʾ al-Andalusī 1933, pp. 147–8 (ll. 12–13); trans. Sanders 1994, p. 41.
56. Johns 2015, pp. 129–31.

57. Al-Buhturī 1963, vol. 3, p. 2006 (#768, l. 19); cf. trans. Scott-Meisami 2001, p. 76. Cf. Massignon 1975, vol. 1, p. 588. Other impressive buildings which are less formally compared to the Kaʿba could also be mentioned in this review. See Zarcone 2012, pp. 262–3. In the twentieth century, the Indian intellectual and poet, Muḥammad Iqbāl (d. 1357/1938), compared the Great Mosque of Cordoba to the Kaʿba. See Yaqin 2016, p. 146.
58. Al-Azraqī 2003, vol. 1, p. 239 (#174). Cf. the account of this or a similar event in the Hadith, in which some kind of divine intervention causes the Prophet to faint, preventing thereby the exposure of his modesty. See, e.g., al-Bukhārī 1994, vol. 4, p. 282 (*kitāb manāqib al-anṣār, bāb bunyān al-Kaʿba*, #3829).
59. See, e.g., al-Azraqī 2003, vol. 1, p. 241 (#176); and Ibn Hishām 1998, vol. 1, p. 160; trans. Ibn Hishām 1955, p. 86.
60. Ibn Hishām 1998, vol. 1, p. 159; trans. Ibn Hishām 1955, pp. 85–6 (modified).
61. Cf. Bashear 1992, pp. 373–4; Chabbi 2010, p. 173; and Hawting 2017, pp. 17, 20.
62. Al-Azraqī 2003, vol. 1, p. 240 (#174). Cf. the slightly different version of this event in Ibn Hishām 1998, vol. 1, p. 161; trans. Ibn Hishām 1955, pp. 86–7.
63. Cf. Canova 1994, p. 424.
64. See, e.g., al-Nawawī al-Shāfiʿī 1985, p. 73.
65. Q 22:29. See, e.g., al-Ghazālī 1982, vol. 1, p. 250; trans. Umar 1975, p. 61; and al-Nawawī al-Shāfiʿī 1985, pp. 73–4.
66. Akkach 2005a, p. 188.
67. Ibid.
68. The dedication is on the reverse side of the diagram. For further information, see Shatanawi 2014, pp. 220–2.
69. For South East Asia, see Witkam 2013, pp. 218–20. For Turkey, see Tanındı 1983, pp. 410, 430, with the diagram additionally available but incorrectly catalogued here: <http://tinyurl.com/yalu96ro> (last accessed 29 June 2019). The textual aspects of some medieval and later pilgrimage scrolls might also be said to approximate this songline. See Roxburgh 2008, vol. 2, p. 767.
70. Shortly before this book went to press, I came across an experiential account of the Kaʿba by an eleventh/seventeenth-century female pilgrim from Isfahan. See Babayan 2008.
71. In the course of his visits to Mecca, Ibn ʿArabī underwent a number of mystical experiences when performing the *ṭawāf*. This chapter focuses on the earliest of them, because it is the most detailed. A summary of the others is given in Addas 1993, pp. 211–17.
72. As cited in al-Hujwīrī 1979, p. 425; cf. trans. al-Hujwīrī 1911, p. 328.
73. As cited in ʿAṭṭār 1957, vol. 2, p. 44; trans. ʿAṭṭār 1966, p. 228. Al-Ḥallāj has a similar experience, as recounted in Massignon 1975, vol. 1, pp. 153, 589.
74. ʿAṭṭār 1957, vol. 1, p. 151.
75. In addition to the examples cited immediately below, see Gramlich 1965, vol. 2, p. 122.
76. Nicholson 1921, p. 62.
77. Bashir 2011, pp. 57–8; Aflākī 2002, p. 200.
78. ʿAṭṭār 1957, vol. 1, p. 77; trans. Smith M. 1974, pp. 8–9. In this account, we are told only that the Kaʿba went out to meet Rābiʿa on her approach to

Mecca. In the Mughal miniature of this meeting (Fig. 4.3), the caption states it circumambulated her.

79. The translation from the Chaghatay is by Yorgos Dedes.
80. Schimmel 1975, p. 242; and Ernst 1998, p. 129.
81. Ghaemmaghami 2012, p. 60.
82. Papan-Matin 2006, p. 118 (#205).
83. See, e.g., al-Bukhārī 1994, 4: 170–1 (*kitāb aḥādīth al-anbiyā'*, #3440–1).
84. Ghaemmaghami 2012, p. 63.
85. Reported in Muḥammad ʿUbayd Allāh, *Ḥasanāt al-Ḥaramayn* (n.d.), fol. 6b, as cited in Tosun 2012, p. 145.
86. İsmail Hakkı Bursevī, *Wāridāt-i ḥaqqiyya* (n.d.), fol. 210a, as cited in Tosun 2012, p. 145. Unable to read Ottoman Turkish, I have not pursued the likelihood that further references to the experiential aspects of the *ṭawāf* are available for this period. For more on this likelihood, see Coşkun 2000, p. 517; and Coşkun 2012, p. 80. Widely circulated on the Internet is a *ṭawāf*-based supernatural experience allegedly undergone by ʿAbd al-Qādir al-Jīlānī (d. 561/1166), which is said to be recounted in a work with the title *Azkārul abrār*. I have been unable to corroborate this account; it does not, for example, appear in Muḥammad Ghawthī Shaṭṭārī's eleventh/seventeenth-century Sufi biography, *Gulzār-i abrār*, translated into Urdu as *Adhkār-i abrār*.
87. Ibn ʿArabī 1972, vol. 1, p. 73 (ll. 1–2, ch. *Khuṭbat al-kitāb*). For a discussion of both this passage and the baselessness of the supposition that the *ṭawāf* in question occurred during a later visit to Mecca, see Chodkiewicz 2005, pp. 449, 458.
88. Hammoudi 2006, pp. 264–5.
89. Ibn ʿArabī 1972, vol. 1, p. 216 (ll. 6–11, ch. 1); cf. trans. Ibn ʿArabī 1996, p. 86, and Addas 1993, p. 201. Before this book went to press, I learned of a new complete translation of this chapter of Ibn ʿArabī's text. See Winkel 2014.
90. Addas 1993, pp. 208–9.
91. See most notably Meier 1955, pp. 155–68; Corbin 1969, pp. 277–81; and Chodkiewicz 2005, pp. 448–61. On the identity of the youth as an epiphany of the Logos, see Chodkiewicz 2005, p. 457. Regarding this identity, Addas asks: 'Is he the "personification of the Holy Spirit", as Michel Vâlsan has suggested in an unpublished study? Is he Ibn ʿArabī's own luminous double, his "celestial twin", as Henry Corbin believed? Or is he a dazzling theophany that manifested itself on the spot referred to by God as His House? These interpretations are by no means mutually contradictory.' Addas 1993, p. 202.
92. See, e.g., Wolfe 1997, p. 535.
93. Ibn ʿArabī 1972, vol. 1, p. 217 (ll. 5–8); cf. trans. Ibn ʿArabī 1996, p. 87.
94. Ibn ʿArabī 1972, vol. 1, p. 218 (ll. 4–14); cf. trans. Ibn ʿArabī 1996, pp. 88–9, and Addas 1993, p. 202.
95. My translation of *himma* follows Corbin 1969, pp. 220, 224–6.
96. Ibn ʿArabī 1972, vol. 1, p. 219 (ll. 7–10); cf. trans. Ibn ʿArabī 1996, p. 90.
97. Ibn ʿArabī 1972, vol. 1, pp. 224–5 (ll. 3 ff.); cf. trans. Ibn ʿArabī 1996, pp. 94–5.
98. Ibn ʿArabī 1972, vol. 1, p. 229 (l. 6); cf. trans. Ibn ʿArabī 1996, p. 100.

99. Meier 1955, p. 164; Corbin 1969, pp. 278, 280. In the footnotes to his text, Corbin amends his misleading assertion by specifying that the two enter the Kaʿba of the *Ḥijr.* See Corbin 1969, p. 388 n. 21. Even so, do his and Meier's assertions betray an unexamined belief that a building's sanctity necessarily increases the further one goes inside it, a belief which replicates the widespread Western philosophical prejudice that significance is tied to depth, not surface? For example, in referring to Rūzbihān Baqlī's visionary experiences of the Kaʿba, Carl Ernst misleadingly asserts that Rūzbihān saw the Prophet and his companions 'in the Kaʿba', whereas the Sufi says only that he saw them 'at (*bayna*) the Sacred Mosque . . . behind [the well of] Zamzam'. See Ernst 1998, p. 136; and Papan-Matin 2006, pp. 26–7 (#51).
100. Ibn ʿArabī 1972, vol. 1, p. 230 (ll. 10–13); cf. trans. Ibn ʿArabī 1996, p. 101; and Addas 1993, pp. 202–3.
101. Ibn ʿArabī 1972, vol. 1, p. 229 (ll. 6–7).
102. Al-Azraqī 2003, vol. 1, p. 300 (#227); Muslim 1994, vol. 5, pp. 98–102 (*kitāb al-Ḥajj, bāb naqḍ al-Kaʿba wa bināʾihā,* #1333). On the basis of one version of this hadith, whether all of the present-day *Ḥijr* would have been included in the Prophet's desired rebuilding of the Kaʿba or just most of it (viz., six cubits, or *adhruʿ*), is an open question. See Muslim 1994, vol. 5, p. 99. Different versions of the hadith are analysed in Hawting 2017, pp. 5–9, 13–16. On the role of ʿĀʾisha in transmitting her Prophet husband's suppressed desire to return the Kaʿba to its alleged Abrahamic form, a desire that would quickly become politicised after his death, see Geissinger 2005, pp. 154–8.
103. Al-Tirmidhī 1937, vol. 3, p. 216 (*kitāb al-Ḥajj, bāb mā jāʾ fī al-ṣalāt fī al-Ḥijr,* #876). Cf. Hawting 2017, pp. 9–11.
104. Ibn ʿArabī 1972, vol. 10, pp. 53–5 (ll. 10 ff., ch. 72). Cf. Gilis 1982, pp. 110–11; and Akkach 2005a , pp. 190–1.
105. See, e.g., al-Azraqī 2003, vol. 1, p. 439 (#406); and especially Knight 2009, pp. 260–2.
106. Ibid. vol. 1, p. 438 (#403).
107. Ibid. vol. 1, pp. 482–8 (#518–34); and especially al-Fākihī 1994, vol. 1, pp. 160–77 (#215–66), in which pages there is a section on cleaving to the Kaʿba at the rear of the building, not just at the *Multazam.* This section reflects the uncertainty in the sources on where exactly the *Multazam* is.
108. Al-Fākihī 1994, vol. 1, p. 169 (#242). See also Burton's personal account of the practice in Burton 1893, vol. 2, p. 169.
109. Al-Azraqī 2003, vol. 1, p. 84 (#27).
110. Cf. Charles-André Gilis's belief that Ibn ʿArabī viewed the *ṭawāf* as a way for a pilgrim to accede 'to the true Reality (*wujūd*) and escape his habitual state of non-existence (*ʿadam*) and illusion'. Gilis 1982, p. 181. Corbin believes something similar of the Sufi al-Jīlī (d. *c.*832/1428). Al-Jīlī, Corbin believes, viewed the *ṭawāf* as a means for a pilgrim to attain 'to his ipseity, his origin, his pre-eternal root. [The pilgrim] becomes the partner of this amazing dialogue pressed to the limits of his transconscience, in which the dualization of his being reveals his mystery to him, and in which, in his divine *Alter Ego*, his total individuality becomes fully visible to him.' Corbin 1969, pp. 387–8 n. 20.

111. 'Wa man zāranī bi-ka ṭāfa ḥawlaka wa man zāranī bi-yā ṭāfa ʿandī.' Mustamlī Bukhārī 1984, vol. 4, p. 1802 (ll. 5–7).
112. Note, however, that in the text to which Mustamlī Bukhārī's commentary pertains, *Kitāb al-Taʿarruf li-madhhab ahl al-taṣawwuf* ('The doctrine of the Sufis') by al-Kalābādhī (d. *c.*380/990), the mediating role of the wall is not mentioned. Rather, with reference to the wall, the unnamed Sufi says this: 'Whoever visits you by way of you, will circumambulate you.' See al-Kalabādhī 1934, p. 126 (ll. 4–5); trans. al-Kalabādhī 1935, p. 165.
113. Muḥyī al-Dīn Lārī, *Futūḥ al-Ḥaramayn* (1987), p. 49, as cited in a translation by Muhammad Isa Waley in Porter 2012, p. 55. The reader's inference regarding the verse's implicit suggestion of the poet's fusion to the Kaʿba would seem to be borne out by the shift from the rapt, slow-motion reverie of this verse to the rapid, jolting reality of the next three verses, as announced by the word 'suddenly' in the first of those three verses: 'Suddenly a thought grasped me by the collar / and my mind was stupefied with amazement. // Immense bewilderment came over me; / marvels took hold of my imagination. // What is this edifice full of might and splendour / at whose doors the heavenly sun is but dust?' Lārī 1987, p. 49 (vv. 7–9), as translated by Muhammad Isa Waley in a personal communication of 29 May 2014.
114. Sharīʿatī 1977, p. 41.
115. Shalem 2015, p. 184.
116. See O'Meara 2007, p. 19.
117. 'Kaʿba shumāyīd.' Rūmī 1958, vol. 2, p. 65 (#648, v. 3); trans. Schimmel 1992b, p. 148.
118. 'Bi-an talzamahu.' Ibn ʿArabī 1972, vol. 10, p. 292 (l. 2, ch. 72). For another instance of the first form of the verb *lazima* (to cleave) being used for the action of cleaving to the Kaʿba, instead of the more usual eighth form of the same verb, see the following tradition: 'ʿUthmān b. al-Aswad said, "Mujāhid saw a man standing [at the *Multazam*] making petitionary prayer, so he hit him with his hand and said, 'Cleave (*ilzam*)! Cleave!'"' ʿAbd al-Razzāq al-Ṣanʿānī 2000, vol. 5, p. 57 (#9115).
119. 'Taṭwāfukum bi-hā . . .' Ibn ʿArabī 1972, vol. 10, p. 292 (l. 3).
120. Burton 1893, vol. 2, p. 212.
121. Young 1993, pp. 288–96.
122. Ibid. p. 295.
123. Ibid. p. 296.
124. Wolfson 2009, p. 157.
125. That this exclusive gendering of the Kaʿba is historically unwarranted, see Dakake 2007, pp. 86–8; and Babayan 2008, pp. 262–4. That the union might not be penetrative, see immediately below. That the union might be homosexual, see the discussion of Ibn ʿArabī's *ṭawāf* above.
126. Macnaghten 1839, vol. 1, p. 586 (Night 118); trans. Burton 1885, vol. 2, p. 318. Note the identical Arabic wording of this passage in the recent, more widespread edition of *The Thousand and One Nights*, namely Ḥāṭūm 2008, vol. 1, p. 277. See, too, the discussion of this wording in El-Shamy 2005, p. 248. Burton's translation includes another sentence at the end of the passage:

'I entered the sanctuary.' This sentence, however, forms part of neither of my two Arabic editions. See Burton 1885, vol. 2, p. 318. For further discussion of Burton's translation and the kinaesthetic rapport between Islamic ritual prayer and intercourse related in the *Nights*, see Hoffmann 2009, pp. 67–71.

127. Khāqānī Shirwānī 1955, p. 129 (vv. 6–7); trans. Beelaert 2000, p. 150. In the absence of vocalisation, the verses can also be translated more lewdly as follows: 'The masses embraced and kissed her, but did not pierce her pudendum (*kusash nasufta*).' For a discussion of the verses, see Babayan 2008, pp. 262–3.
128. See Livne-Kafri 2013, p. 311.
129. 'Wa ʿarūs Makka bi-karāmāt tajallā.' As cited in both translation and in Arabic in Burton 1893, vol. 2, p. 212. According to Anna Beelaert, who also quotes Burton's translation, this 'half-verse is taken from a eulogy of the Prophet, and the image is not elaborated in the rest of the poem'. Beelaert 2000, p. 154.
130. Ibn Jubayr 1907, pp. 80–1; trans. Ibn Jubayr 1952, pp. 75–6 (modified). Later in his travel narrative, Ibn Jubayr writes: 'To the beholder the Kaʿba then presented the most comely sight, appearing as an unveiled bride (*ʿarūs juliyat*) in the finest green silk-brocade.' See Ibn Jubayr 1907, p. 179; trans. Ibn Jubayr 1952, p. 186.
131. Ibn Baṭṭūṭa also uses a bridal image for the Kaʿba (*ka-ʿarūs tujlā*), and once again the usage is not specific to the Hajj. Ibn Baṭṭūṭa 1893, vol. 1, p. 300 (l. 2); trans. Ibn Baṭṭūṭa 1958, vol. 1, p. 188.
132. 'Non-Arab pilgrims – from Indonesia, Pakistan, Turkey, Iran and elsewhere – may not have perceived the feminine traits of the Kaʿba, since they did not view it through the filters of Arab traditions and the Arabic language.' Young 1993, p. 300 n. 46.
133. In an addendum to his paper, published a year later, Young acknowledges that he did not know of this topos. See Young 1994, p. 363.
134. Anna Beelaert, 'The Kaʿba as a Woman: A Topos in Classical Persian Literature' (1989), pp. 107–23, revised and reprinted in Beelaert 2000, pp. 150–67. All subsequent references to this work are to the revised version.
135. Ibid. pp. 154–5. A recent figuration of the Kaʿba as a woman, by the Saudi novelist Rajāʾa ʿĀlim, is discussed in al-Tahawy 2017.
136. For an Arabic interpretation of the Kaʿba as beloved, see the ode *al-Tāʾiyya al-ṣughrā* by Ibn al-Fāriḍ (d. 632/1235), as translated and discussed in Homerin 2011, pp. 128–34.
137. In the course of his probing and provocative research into early Islamic poetry, Walter Chahanovich has suggested that the licentious (*ibāḥī*) poetry of ʿUmar b. Abī Rabīʿa (d. 93/712 or 103/721) and others – poetry which includes accounts of amorous flirtations at the Kaʿba with women performing the *ṭawāf* – was in creative tension with the chaste (*ʿudhrī*) poetry of the same period. Out of this latter poetry of unattainable love arose, he suggests, the Laylā and Majnūn legend, which was later so effectively interpreted by Persian poets. See Chahanovich 2016. In the pre-Islamic period, circumambulation of the Kaʿba naked is said to have been practised under certain conditions by a certain category of people, the *ḥilla*. See Watt 1954, p. 578.

138. Niẓāmī Ganjawī 1966, pp. 41–4. Cf. the discussion of this event and other Kaʿba-related events drawn from Niẓāmī's representation of Majnūn in Seyed-Gohrab 2003, pp. 230–4.
139. Jāmī 1962, p. 536 (#948, vv. 1–5); trans. Beelaert 2000, p. 166 (modified).
140. In addition to Beelaert's article, see Ritter 2003, p. 539.
141. Khāqānī Shirwānī 1959, p. 404 (vv. 20–1); trans. Beelaert 2000, p. 161.
142. For a discussion of the iconography of images of Majnūn at the Kaʿba, see Simpson 2010, pp. 140–6. See also Chapter Six.
143. Al-Azraqī 2003, vol. 1, pp. 249–50 (#178).
144. See, e.g., al-Nahrawalī 1857, p. 163 (l. 17); and Ibn Hishām 1998, vol. 1, p. 54; trans. Ibn Hishām 1955, p. 26. In these reports, the Kaʿba is related as having one knocker. In medieval travel accounts, four knockers are witnessed in Nāṣir-i Khusraw 1881, p. 72; trans. Nāṣir-i Khusraw 1986, p. 76; and two are witnessed in Ibn Jubayr 1907, p. 82; trans. Ibn Jubayr 1952, p. 78.
145. Although I have been unable to date this phrase, it is certainly pre-modern and most probably Persian in origin. Schimmel implies that it was in use before the seventh/thirteenth century. See Schimmel 1991, p. 165. Note, however, Chahanovich's tentative argument that a reference to the Kaʿba in Arabic poetry of the early Islamic period can sometimes be a conceit for the poet's romantic, carnal desires. See Chahanovich 2017.
146. Neçipoğlu 2005, pp. 263, 504.
147. Lewis 2008, p. 430.
148. Rūmī 1951, p. 100 (ll. 5–6); trans. Rūmī 1999, p. 104 (#23) (modified).

Chapter Five

1. See, e.g., Ibn Hishām 1998, vol. 1, p. 129; trans. Ibn Hishām 1955, p. 66; and al-Azraqī 2003, vol. 1, p. 187 (#142), p. 249 (#177). In the secondary literature, it has been claimed that the idols Isāf and Nāʾila were also placed inside the Kaʿba. See Elias 2012, p. 104. Pursuing the reference that buttresses this claim, I can find only that one of these two idols was positioned to 'cling to the Kaʿba', while the other was positioned 'by' or 'over' (*ʿalā*) the Zamzam well. See al-Azraqī 2003, vol. 1, p. 190 (#143–4).
2. 'Wujāha al-Kaʿba ʿalā bābihā'. Al-Wāqidī 1965, vol. 2, p. 832. Cf. Crone 187, pp. 187–8.
3. Mīrkhwānd 1959, vol. 2, p. 462; trans. Mīrkhwānd 1892, vol. 4, p. 599.
4. Rubin 1990, p. 103.
5. Al-Wāqidī 1965, vol. 2, p. 832 (l. 1); Ibn Hishām 1998, vol. 1, pp. 129–30; trans. Ibn Hishām 1955, pp. 66–7. See also Al-Azmeh 2014, pp. 215–16.
6. Ibn al-Kalbī 1924, pp. 27–8; trans. Ibn al-Kalbī 1952, pp. 23–4 (modified).
7. Regarding the obscure distinction between cultic and votive material for this period, cf. Hawting 1980, p. 46.
8. For the last three items, see e.g. al-Azraqī 2003, vol. 1, p. 555 (#657); and al-Masʿūdī 1861, vol. 3, p. 259. Cf. Rubin 1986, p. 117; and especially Wheeler 2006, pp. 24–46. For the ram's horns and head, see al-Azraqī 2003, vol. 1, p. 249 (#177), pp. 322–3 (#257–9); and Bashear 1990, p. 274. Cf. Rubin 1990, p. 104; and Rabbat 1993, pp. 71–3.

9. Al-Azraqī 2003, vol. 1, p. 345 (#263), p. 348 (#267); al-Ṭabarī 1987a, p. 51. Cf. Rubin 1986, p. 117. On this well or pit, see Hawting 1980, pp. 50–3.
10. For the well, see al-Azraqī 2003, vol. 1, p. 187 (#142). For the pit, see ibid. vol. 1, p. 249 (#177).
11. The one exception being the ram's horns, which the Prophet allegedly ordered to be concealed so as not to distract worshippers. See al-Azraqī 2003, vol. 1, p. 322 (#257).
12. See, e.g., Ibn Hishām 1998, vol. 4, pp. 34–40; trans. Ibn Hishām 1955, pp. 548–52; and al-Balādhurī 1916, pp. 65–6.
13. Al-Ṭabarī 1997, pp. 187–8.
14. Ibn Hishām 1998, vol. 4, pp. 28–30; trans. Ibn Hishām 1955, pp. 544–5.
15. Hawting 1986, p. 12.
16. Al-Azraqī 2003, vol. 1, p. 194 (#149). Cf. Hawting 1999, p. 69. The same report is also found in al-Wāqidī 1965, vol. 2, pp. 841–2.
17. As noted in Bashear 1992, p. 363. Cf. Hawting 1986, pp. 14–15. On al-Ṭabarī specifically, see his account of the conquest of Mecca in al-Ṭabarī 1997, pp. 181–2.
18. Bashear 1992, pp. 363–6.
19. As noted in ibid. pp. 361–2.
20. For the Sunni version of this quasi-canonical narrative, see e.g. Ibn Kathīr n.d., vol. 2, pp. 189–92; trans. Ibn Kathīr 1998, vol. 3, pp. 407–12. For the Shiʿi version, see below.
21. Al-Bukhārī 1994, vol. 5, p. 109 (*kitāb al-maghāzī, bāb ayna rakaza al-nabī al-rāya yawm al-fatḥ*, #4287). For a similar account, except with 300 not 360 idols (sing. *ṣanam*) about the Kaʿba, sixty of which were allegedly strengthened with lead, see al-Wāqidī 1965, vol. 2, p. 832 (ll. 1–5). Another tradition reports that the Devil had strengthened all 360 idols with lead. See, e.g., Ibn Hishām 1955, p. 552; and al-Azraqī 2003, vol. 1, p. 191 (#145).
22. Hawting plausibly contends that the events concerning the Kaʿba's exterior and those concerning its interior result from two different conceptions of the pre-Islamic cult which the early Islamic narrators were wrestling with. See Hawting 1986, pp. 3–5, 22.
23. Ibn Hishām 1998, vol. 4, p. 40; trans. Ibn Hishām 1955, p. 552; al-Azraqī 2003, vol. 1, p. 254 (#188).
24. Al-Wāqidī 1965, vol. 2, p. 834 (ll. 7–13).
25. Al-Bukhārī 1994, vol. 2, p. 195 (*kitāb al-Ḥajj, bāb man kabbara fī nawāḥī al-Kaʿba*, #1601); Mughulṭāy (*fl.* after 690/1290), *al-Zahr al-bāsim fī sīrat Abī al-Qāsim* (unpublished), fol. 317b, as cited in Bashear 1992, p. 366.
26. Al-Wāqidī 1965, vol. 2, p. 834 (ll. 20–1); and al-Azraqī 2003, vol. 1, pp. 248–9 (#177), respectively.
27. Al-Masʿūdī 1861, vol. 4, p. 126. The same author also mentions an image (*ṣūra*) of Ishmael riding a horse, and another of 'al-Fārūq', the latter personage being a possible reference to Jesus. See ibid. vol. 4, p. 126. For a discussion of this report, see Shahid 1989, p. 392; and Al-Azmeh 2014, pp. 335–8.
28. For angels, see e.g. Ibn Hishām 1998, vol. 4, p. 41. This (and the next) report is not provided in the source's English translation. For Abraham, see, e.g., Ibn Hishām 1998, vol. 4, p. 41. For Ishmael, see e.g. al-Azraqī 2003, vol. 1, p. 254 (#189). Even Isaac is said to have been represented. See Bashear 1992, p. 367. For Jesus and Mary, see, e.g., al-Azraqī 2003, vol. 1, p. 250 (#179).

29. For Abraham, see al-Wāqidī 1965, vol. 2, p. 834 (ll. 16–17). For Jesus with Mary, see e.g. al-Azraqī 2003, vol. 1, p. 251 (#181). Curiously, in the first of these two references, the one concerning Abraham, the Prophet is reported to have placed his hand over the image of Mary while simultaneously ordering that only the image of Abraham be spared.
30. Al-Azraqī 2003, vol. 1, p. 250 (#179). Cf. the discussion of this report in Bashear 1992, pp. 371–2.
31. Al-Azraqī 2003, vol. 1, p. 251.
32. Al-Masʿūdī 1861, vol. 5, p. 192.
33. Creswell 1969, vol. 1, p. 63.
34. 'Wa amara bi-Hubal fa-kusira wa huwa wāqif ʿalayhi.' Al-Wāqidī 1965, vol. 2, p. 832 (ll. 15–16). Cf. Hawting 1984, p. 241. *Pace* Geoffrey King's assertion that Ibn al-Kalbī reports Hubal being removed from the Kaʿba and destroyed, I can find no mention of this occurrence. See King G. 2004, p. 219.
35. Mīrkhwānd 1959, vol. 2, pp. 461–2; trans. Mīrkhwānd 1892, vol. 4, pp. 599–600.
36. Al-Azraqī 2003, vol. 1, p. 348 (#267); trans. Ibn al-Zubayr 1996, p. 166 (#175).
37. Al-Azraqī 2003, vol. 1, p. 327 (#262), vol. 2, p. 889. In the second of these references, the treasury is referred to as, or has become assimilated into, Mecca's treasury (*bayt māl Makka*).
38. Cf. Hawting 1980, p. 53.
39. Al-Azraqī 2003, vol. 1, pp. 326–7 (#262). But cf. Grabar's discussion of this throne, where he interprets al-Azraqī to mean that it was placed inside the Kaʿba, not the treasury, before being melted. Grabar 1987a, p. 57. As Grabar eschews references in his book, I am unable to see what page and edition of al-Azraqī's history he used for this interpretation.
40. Jairazbhoy 1986, p. 158.
41. Shalem 2005, esp. pp. 277–9.
42. See, e.g., ʿAbd al-Ḥamīd 1958, p. 16. Cf. Rabbat 1993, p. 72.
43. See, e.g., al-Azraqī 2003, vol. 1, pp. 324–6 (#261–2); al-Bīrūnī 1989, pp. 56–7; Ibn al-Zubayr 1996, p. 83 (#41), p. 186 (#236); and the summary in Grabar 1987a, p. 57.
44. Al-Azraqī 2003, vol. 1, p. 325 (#261); al-Bīrūnī 1989, p. 57.
45. See, e.g., al-Azraqī 2003, vol. 1, pp. 325–6 (#262); and al-Bīrūnī 1989, p. 56.
46. Al-Bīrūnī 1989, p. 56. On the contents of this legendary book, comprising some twelve thousand volumes, see Gutas 1998, p. 42.
47. See, e.g., Ibn Jubayr 1907, pp. 93–4; trans. Ibn Jubayr 1952, p. 89–91. See, too, the summary and discussion of a number of these descriptions in Jairazbhoy 1962, pp. 24–6; and the discussion of Ibn Jubayr's perception of the revetment in Flood 2016, pp. 173–4.
48. Nāṣir-i Khusraw 1881, p. 73; trans. Nāṣir-i Khusraw 1986, p. 77.
49. Jairazbhoy 1962, pp. 24–5; and especially Flood 1999, pp. 316–18.
50. See, e.g., al-Mūjān 2010, p. 157.
51. Cf. Sardar 2014, p. 341.
52. Al-Ṭabarī 1987a, p. 105.

53. Al-Azraqī 2003, vol. 1, pp. 334–40 (#262); al-Ṭabarī 1989c, p. 199. Cf. Gaudefroy-Demombynes 1923, p. 58; El-Hibri 1992, pp. 463–4; and Marsham 2009, pp. 220–2. Grabar mentions, again without references, a similar action that is said to have occurred in the late third/ninth century. See Grabar 1987a, p. 57.
54. Al-Azraqī 2003, vol. 1, pp. 343–4. The act of redress is translated in El-Hibri 2007, p. 104 n. 26.
55. Cf. Grabar 1987a, p. 58.
56. Al-Azraqī 2003, vol. 1, p. 334 (my emphasis). In contrast to this plausible political practice, the claim that the pre-Islamic Arabs used to hang their best poems inside the Kaʿba, the 'Suspended Odes' (*al-Muʿallaqāt*), has been considered implausible by some, including the fourth/tenth-century Egyptian grammarian al-Naḥḥās (d. 338/950). See Nicholson 1907, p. 102.
57. Al-Wāqidī 1965, vol. 3, p. 1100 (l. 13); trans. Hawting 1984, p. 234. Ibn Jubayr's report that when people were about to enter the House they would utter the Qurʾanic verse, 'Enter [here] in peace and security' (Q 15:46), is not a report of a prescribed ritual. See Ibn Jubayr 1907, p. 93; trans. Ibn Jubayr 1952, p. 89.
58. See, e.g., al-Bukhārī 1994, vol. 2, p. 195 (*kitāb al-Ḥajj, bāb al-ṣalāt fī al-Kaʿba*, #1598–9); and al-Azraqī 2003, vol. 1, pp. 375–83 (#320–36).
59. The subject is comprehensively covered in Hawting 1984, pp. 232–5. Apart from the Islamic sources, there are also reports of the existence of taboos (*muḥarramāt*) against entering the Kaʿba. See Burton 1893, vol. 2, p. 211; and cf. Gaudefroy-Demombynes 1923, p. 64.
60. Nāṣir-i Khusraw 1881, p. 76; trans. Nāṣir-i Khusraw 1986, p. 80
61. Al-Nawawī al-Shāfiʿī 1985, p. 134. For additional reports and discussion of these two practices, see Gaudefroy-Demombynes 1923, pp. 68–9; Kister 1969, 194; and Hawting 1984, p. 239. The people's (*al-nās*) crowding of the Kaʿba's doorway on the days when it was opened in 579/1183 is witnessed with some shock by Ibn Jubayr. See Ibn Jubayr 1952, pp. 89, 168–9, 186.
62. Gaudefroy-Demombynes 1923, p. 69. See also al-Quʿayṭī 2007, pp. 130–1.
63. Sharīʿatī 1977, p. 21.
64. Rizvi 2013.
65. Rutter 1928, vol. 1, p. 213. For other eyewitness accounts originally written in European languages, see especially Ali Bey 1816, vol. 2, pp. 76–7; Burton 1893, vol. 2, pp. 207–9; and Gaudefroy-Demombynes 1923, pp. 51–6.
66. Set within the double ceiling of the Kaʿba, these translucent skylights allowed for a degree of illumination within the building, not for sight out of it. Both Ibn Rusta and al-Azraqī (and others) refer to them as the *rawāzin*. See Ibn Rusta 1892, p. 30 (ll. 21–2); and al-Azraqī 2003, vol. 1, p. 405 (#382). Cf. Finster 1991, p. 55. Almost certainly they were not covered by glass, but marble or alabaster, exactly as per Ibn Rusta's fourth/tenth-century account. See Ibn Rusta 1892, p. 30 (l. 22).
67. As also noted by the translator of this account, this door is usually called the Door of Repentance (*Bāb al-Tawba*), as mentioned in the Introduction. See Ibn Jubayr 1952, p. 79.
68. Ibn Jubayr 1907, pp. 82–4; trans. Ibn Jubayr 1952, pp. 78–9 (modified). Cf. the much shorter account in Ibn Baṭṭūṭa 1893, vol. 1, pp. 310–11; trans. Ibn Baṭṭūṭa 1958, vol. 1, p. 195.

69. On this work and the development of the diagrammatic images many of its copies contain, see Witkam 2007, pp. 67–82, 295–9. Note, however, the early date of one of the image-pairs reproduced in Rusli 2016, p. 136 (Fig. 86), and the even earlier date of Fig. 5.5.
70. Cf. Aazam 2005, p. 319.
71. Concerning comparisons between the Kaʿba and the Dome of the Rock, see e.g. Busse 1988, pp. 236–46; and Milstein 1999, pp. 23–48.
72. O'Meara 2020b.
73. Eliade 1991, p. 55.
74. Keane 2002, p. 68; and Keane 2007, p. 26, respectively.
75. Mignolo and Walsh 2018, p. 139.
76. Trachtenberg 1997, pp. 181–4.
77. Ibid. p. 260
78. For a history of the intervening centuries regarding the role of perspective in urban design, see Benevelo 1993, pp. 124–71.
79. Al-Sanūsī 1891, p. 242 (ll. 13–14). Cf. the discussion of this remark in Mitchell 1988, p. 59. I also discuss it at more length in O'Meara 2020a.
80. Trachtenberg 1997, pp. 52–4; and more concisely in Trachtenberg 2002.
81. On mathematical zero and the vanishing point, see Rotman 1987, pp. 14–22; and Kaplan 1999, p. 99. On Fibonacci and zero, see Seife 2000, pp. 78–81; but note the much earlier date for the entrance of zero into Europe in Burnett 2010, p. 94. On the entrance of zero into the Islamic world, see n. 92 below.
82. Friedman D. 1988, pp. 125–30; Trachtenberg 1997, pp. 226–32.
83. Edgerton 2009, p. 171.
84. Wootton 2015, p. 200. Karsten Harries makes a similar argument in Harries 2001, pp. 14–16. Cf. Fred Kleiner's remark: 'Renaissance artists' interest in perspective reflects the emergence at this time of modern science itself.' Kleiner 2007, p. 232.
85. Panofsky 1997, p. 34. Cf. Kemp 2006, pp. 78–84.
86. Baudrillard 2009, p. 10. I pursue the subject of mythic foundation sites in O'Meara 2020a.
87. Smith J. 1970, p. 469.
88. Rotman 1987, p. 13.
89. As Harries notes: 'It is the conception of space as [an] infinite field that underlies . . . perspective construction.' Harries 2001, p. 66. On the relation between zero and infinity see Seife 2000, esp. pp. 40–61, 131–2.
90. Bryson 1983, p. 106 (italics as marked in the original).
91. Rotman 1987, p. 2.
92. Cf. Michel Chodkiewicz's interpretation of the Kaʿba as 'a zero point in time [and] space', in Chodkiewicz 2002, p. 23. On the transmission of zero from India to the Fertile Crescent in the first/seventh century, and Islam's rapid embrace of it commencing in the second half of the second/eighth century, see Seife 2000, pp. 71–4; and especially Kunitzsch 2003, pp. 3–4. On the first reference in this region to the Hindu numerical system (but without mention of zero), in a letter by Severus Sēbōkht, Archbishop of Qinnasrīn, Syria, in 42/662, see Reich 2000.
93. Schimmel 1987, p. 354.

94. Ibid. p. 355.
95. Ibid. p. 352.
96. As cited in ibid. p. 355. Cf. Akkach 2005a, pp. 101–5; and Böwering 2011, pp. 352–3.

Chapter Six

1. They are: Gaudefroy-Demombynes 1954b; Mortel 1988; Gouda 1989; al-Mūjān 2010; Shalem 2015; and Tezcan 2017.
2. In addition to the aforementioned sources of this historical summary, see al-Maqrīzī 2016, pp. 269–71.
3. Note, however, that on rare occasions thereafter, the *Kiswa* has still been replaced biannually. See, e.g., al-Mūjān 2010, p. 349.
4. On this caravan, the classic text remains Jomier 1953. More recently, see al-Mūjān 2010, pp. 314–33; and Porter 2013. For a theoretically informed analysis, see McGregor 2010.
5. Al-Mūjān 2010, pp. 326, 337, 348–9.
6. Burton 1893, vol. 2, p. 215. Cf. Wensinck 1913, p. 587.
7. As with the foregoing historical summary, this description is taken from secondary sources only, primarily al-Mūjān 2010. Where other sources are used, they will be referenced accordingly.
8. On its probable first appearance there, allegedly at the instigation of the Mamluk consort and later ruler, Shajarat al-Durr (d. 655/1257), see Gaudefroy-Demombynes 1918, p. 334. Note, however, that the Prophet is alleged to have used a curtain over the Kaʿba's door at the time of his conquest of Mecca, so as to shield him from view once inside the building. See al-Yaʿqūbī 2010, vol. 1, p. 379 (l. 2); and cf. Gaudefroy-Demombynes 1923, pp. 65–6. For more on the *Burquʿ*, see most recently Sardi 2013, pp. 170–1; Nassar 2013, pp. 176–7; and especially al-Mūjān 2010, pp. 251, 284–9; and Tezcan 2017, pp. 69–74.
9. For a detailed description of the exact content of specific 'face veils', see al-Mūjān 2010, pp. 284–5, 399–402, 407–8.
10. For a detailed description of the exact content of specific belts and medallions, see al-Mūjān 2010, pp. 280–4, 398–9, 405–7. Regarding the variable content of the *Burquʿ*, see the previous note.
11. See, e.g., Ibn Jubayr 1907, p. 83; trans. Ibn Jubayr 1952, p. 79; and al-Mūjān 2010, pp. 243, 283, 398, 405.
12. Ibn Jubayr 1907, pp. 83, 179; trans. Ibn Jubayr 1952, pp. 79, 185.
13. Ibn ʿAbd Rabbih 1983, vol. 7, p. 285; trans. Shafiʿ 1922, p. 427. Cf. al-Mūjān 2010, pp. 242–6.
14. Al-Mūjān 2010, p. 242.
15. Ibid. p. 246.
16. This subject is especially well treated in Tezcan 2007; and Tezcan 2017, pp. 163–72.
17. Nāṣir-i Khusraw 1881, p. 74; trans. Nāṣir-i Khusraw 1986, pp. 77–8 (modified).
18. Ibn Jubayr 1907, p. 83; cf. trans. Ibn Jubayr 1952, p. 79 (where *maḥārīb* is erroneously translated as 'pulpits'). See also al-Mūjān 2010, p. 246.

19. For recent examples of scholarship drawing the parallel, see El Guindi 1999, p. 95; Winter 2004, p. 148; and Wolfson 2009, p. 153. The parallel only works if, like the informants of the anthropologist Aida Kanafani, one holds that the *ḥijāb* functions 'by covering what is considered ugly and by enhancing what is considered beautiful'. See Kanafani, *Aesthetics and Ritual in the United Arab Emirates* (1983), p. 72, as cited in Stillman 2003, p. 150. In scholarship, it is not uncommon to find the name *Kiswa* translated as 'veil'. See, e.g., Tezcan and Delibaş 1986, p. 13; and al-Maqrīzī 2016, p. 18.
20. Leaving the Black Stone and part of the *Yamānī* corner uncovered by the *Kiswa* is a practice that dates to at least the fourth/tenth century, if one is to believe Ibn ʿAbd Rabbih. See Ibn ʿAbd Rabbih 1983, vol. 7, p. 285; trans. Shafīʿ 1922, p. 427. For the fastening and tightening of the *Kiswa*, see Ibn Jubayr 1907, pp. 92–3; trans. Ibn Jubayr 1952, p. 88.
21. Q 23:14.
22. Burckhardt 1829, vol. 1, pp. 256–7.
23. See, e.g., al-Maqrīzī 2016, pp. 338–9; and cf. Mortel 1988, p. 39.
24. Ibn Kathīr 2010, vol. 15, p. 259.
25. The artists Christo and Jeanne-Claude produced a similar effect in 1995, when for two weeks they wrapped Berlin's Reichstag building.
26. That it is obviously correct to refer to the *Kiswa* and the Kaʿba as two discrete items is underlined by the aforementioned ceremonial Hajj caravan from Egypt, which carried the *Kiswa* to the Kaʿba.
27. Golombek 1988b, p. 39.
28. Burckhardt 1829, vol. 1, p. 256; and Burton 1893, vol. 2, pp. 211–12 n. 3, respectively. Burckhardt's remark that the *Kiswa* is removed from the Kaʿba for a period of fifteen days, is taken by Burton to mean exactly that. Understandably, he thinks that in Burckhardt's time the Kaʿba was left 'naked' for that length of time. However, Burckhardt's observation is contrary to all that we know of this *Kiswa* replacement process, which is effectively an established ritual (see below). Reading Burckhardt's text in the light of what we know from other travellers' accounts, it seems clear that he is saying the Kaʿba is left in its perceived state of *iḥrām* (see below), the *Kiswa* being elevated to signify this state, for fifteen days. See Burckhardt 1829, vol. 1, p. 255.
29. Hannah Arendt, *The Life of the Mind: Thinking* (1978), p. 27, as cited in Andrews 2014, p. 99 (italics as marked in the original). With regard to Islamic material culture, I pursue this conjecture at more length in O'Meara 2019.
30. See Masud 2006, p. 288.
31. Semper 1989, pp. 103, 254–5.
32. Ibid. p. 254 (italics as marked in the original).
33. In substantiating her celebrated concept of the 'draped universe of Islam', but without referencing Semper's observations, Golombek has shown how the tectonic walls of Islamic architecture so often seem to imitate textiles. See Golombek 1988a, p. 34; and especially Golombek 1988b, pp. 39–44.
34. Semper 1989, pp. 255–7. As Harry Mallgrave explains Semper's words: '[By dressing the wall,] the wall and (by spatial extension) architecture gain their essential artistic meaning through the denial of their material basis.' Mallgrave 1989, p. 40.

35. 'Kānat thiyābuhā tūḍa'u 'alayhā tasdulu sadl[an].' Ibn Ḥajar al-'Asqalānī 2001, vol. 3, p. 633 (*kitāb al-Ḥajj, bāb faḍl Makka wa bunyānihā*, #1586). Cf. al-Azraqī 2003, vol. 1, p. 239 (#174), where the term *kiswa* is used instead of *thiyāb* (vestments); and 'Abd al-Razzāq al-Ṣan'ānī 2000, vol. 5, p. 71 (*bāb bunyān al-Ka'ba*, #9166), where the term *'arīsh* (booth) is used to describe the rudimentary form of the Ka'ba, but no mention is made of vestments or a *kiswa*.
36. Rubin 1986, pp. 98–9. Cf. Peters 1986, pp. 6–7; and Nevo and Koren 1990, p. 28.
37. Rubin 1986, p. 99 n. 4.
38. Ibn Jubayr 1907, p. 93; trans. Ibn Jubayr 1952, p. 88. For a period-based review of the days when the Ka'ba has customarily been opened since the sixth/twelfth century, see Gaudefroy-Demombynes 1923, pp. 59–61. When Eldon Rutter visited in 1925, it was opened 'to men on seven fixed days of the year, and to women on seven others'. See Rutter 1928, vol. 1, p. 216.
39. On the crowds, see e.g. Ibn Jubayr 1952, pp. 89, 137, 168–9, 186; and Ali Bey 1816, vol. 2, p. 54. On the bribery and the crowds, see Burton 1893, vol. 2, pp. 209–10; and especially Peters 1994b, pp. 238–40.
40. Note, however, that Peters cites a report by the Frenchman, Léon Roches (d. 1901), which indicates that at least in this traveller's time the Ka'ba was open for public entry until the moment of washing proper. See Peters 1994b, p. 240.
41. See, e.g., Ali Bey 1816, vol. 2, pp. 58–9. For what happens today, see al-Mūjān 2010, p. 418.
42. For the washing, see Ali Bey 1816, vol. 2, p. 58; Peters 1994b, pp. 239–40; al-Batanūnī 1911, p. 108; and Rutter 1928, vol. 1, p. 216. For the closure, see Ibn Jubayr 1907, p. 165 (l. 14); trans. Ibn Jubayr 1952, p. 169; Ibn Baṭṭūṭa 1893, vol. 1, p. 395 (ll. 7–8); trans. Ibn Baṭṭūṭa 1958, vol. 1, p. 242; and Peters 1994b, p. 240. For the minimally varying number of days this period of total closure could comprise, see the references to the reopening of the Ka'ba in n. 55 below, as well as the three preceding references in the present note (the first two of which state when the Ka'ba was due to be re-opened).
43. Ibn Jubayr mentions only one occasion of washing: 30 Rajab/18 November. He does not mention a washing prior to the Ka'ba's total closure. See Ibn Jubayr 1952, p. 138.
44. Ibn 'Abd Rabbih 1983, vol. 7, p. 285, cf. trans. Shafi' 1922, p. 427 (covered); Ibn Jubayr 1907, p. 165; trans. Ibn Jubayr 1952, p. 169 (elevated); Ibn Baṭṭūṭa 1893, vol. 1, p. 395; trans. Ibn Baṭṭūṭa 1958, vol. 1, p. 242 (elevated); Ali Bey 1816, vol. 2, p. 60 (cut); al-Batanūnī 1911, p. 108 (covered); and Young 1993, p. 294 (cut and covered). Cf. Gaudefroy-Demombynes 1954b, p. 14; and Young 1993, pp. 293–4.
45. 'Fa-yaqūlūna uḥrimat al-Ka'ba.' Ibn Jubayr 1907, p. 165 (l. 13); trans. Ibn Jubayr 1952, p. 169. The identical terminology and similar phrasing are used in Ibn Baṭṭūṭa 1893, vol. 1, p. 395 (l. 6); trans. Ibn Baṭṭūṭa 1958, vol. 1, p. 242; Ali Bey 1816, vol. 2, p. 60 (l. 10); and al-Batanūnī 1911, p. 108 (l. 20). Ibn 'Abd Rabbih does not use the identical terminology, but terminology in the same Hajj-specific semantic field. See Ibn 'Abd Rabbih 1983, vol. 7, p. 285; trans. Shafi' 1922, p. 427.

46. See Wensinck 1954a, p. 1052.
47. Ibrāhīm Rifʿat Bāshā, *Mirʾāt al-Ḥaramayn* (1925), vol. 1, p. 265, as cited in Young 1993, p. 294.
48. Young 1993, p. 294.
49. Ibid.
50. Ibn Jubayr 1907, p. 179 (ll. 19–20); trans. Ibn Jubayr 1952, pp. 185–6; and Ibn Baṭṭūṭa 1893, vol. 1, p. 402 (l. 7); trans. Ibn Baṭṭūṭa 1958, vol. 1, p. 247.
51. Ali Bey 1816, vol. 2, p. 78; Ibn ʿAbd Rabbih 1983, vol. 7, p. 285; trans. Shafiʿ 1922, p. 427; Ibn Jubayr 1907, p. 179; trans. Ibn Jubayr 1952, p. 185; Ibn Baṭṭūṭa 1893, vol. 1, pp. 401–2; trans. Ibn Baṭṭūṭa 1958, vol. 1, p. 247; Burton 1893, vol. 2, p. 211. Cf. Young 1993, p. 295. For some slight variations regarding the precise day when the Kaʿba has in the past come out of its perceived state of *iḥrām*, see al-Mūjān 2010, p. 428. Today, that day is 9 Dhū al-Ḥijja. See al-Mūjān 2010, p. 428.
52. Ibn Jubayr 1907, p. 179; trans. Ibn Jubayr 1952, p. 185; Ibn Baṭṭūṭa 1893, vol. 1, p. 402; trans. Ibn Baṭṭūṭa 1958, vol. 1, p. 247; Young 1993, p. 295; al-Mūjān 2010, p. 428.
53. Burton 1893, vol. 2, p. 212. Cf. Ali Bey 1816, vol. 2, p. 78. In the modern period, ropes are still used. See al-Mūjān 2010, p. 428.
54. This termination date is implied but not explicitly stated in travel accounts. See, e.g., Ibn Jubayr 1907, p. 179; trans. Ibn Jubayr 1952, pp. 185–6; Ibn Baṭṭūṭa 1893, vol. 1, p. 402; trans. Ibn Baṭṭūṭa 1958, vol. 1, p. 247; and Ali Bey 1816, vol. 2, p. 78. Because these travellers all add that one purpose of elevating the *Kiswa* on the second occasion, the Feast of Sacrifice, is to protect it from people's sullying and/or stealing hands, this conjectured termination date seems reasonable. Today, the *Kiswa* is completely let down on 10 Muḥarram. See al-Mūjān 2010, p. 428.
55. Ibn Jubayr 1907, p. 180; trans. Ibn Jubayr 1952, p. 186; Ibn Baṭṭūṭa 1893, vol. 1, pp. 402–3; trans. Ibn Baṭṭūṭa 1958, vol. 1, p. 247; Burton 1893, vol. 2, p. 206.
56. Ibn Jubayr 1907, p. 165 (ll. 15–16); cf. trans. Ibn Jubayr 1952, p. 169.
57. See, e.g., Ibn Jubayr 1907, p. 165 (l. 11), p. 179 (l. 19); trans. Ibn Jubayr 1952, pp. 169, 185; and Ibn Baṭṭūṭa 1893, vol. 1, p. 395 (l. 4), p. 402 (l. 7); trans. Ibn Baṭṭūṭa 1958, vol. 1, pp. 242, 247.
58. Young 1993, p. 294.
59. As cited in Lange 2015b, p. 79 n. 21.
60. Al-Mutanabbī 2005, p. 237.
61. Ibn ʿArabī 1972, vol. 10, pp. 295–7 (ll. 6 ff., ch. 72); cf. trans. Addas 1993, p. 212. For a contextual analysis of this event, see Gril 1995, pp. 40–6.
62. See, e.g., Ibn Jubayr 1907, p. 179 (l. 21, viz., 'ka-annahā ʿarūs juliyat'); trans. Ibn Jubayr 1952, p. 186. Cf. Young 1993, pp. 294–6.
63. See, e.g., Ibn Baṭṭūṭa 1893, vol. 1, p. 300; trans. Ibn Baṭṭūṭa 1958, vol. 1, p. 188.
64. Ibn ʿArabī 1972, vol. 10, p. 296 (ll. 3–7).
65. Ettinghausen 1934, p. 126.
66. Simpson 2010, p. 145
67. Cf. ibid. pp. 142–5. For an example not included in Simpson's text, see Fig. 6.15, which shows Iskandar at the Kaʿba from a tenth/sixteenth-century copy of Firdawsī's *Shāhnāma*, and then compare it to the image

of worshippers at the Kaʿba from a tenth/sixteenth-century copy of Jāmī's *Haft Awrang*, available at: <http://tinyurl.com/y8vr40md> (last accessed 27 May 2019). The iconography is similar. Compare, too, Figs 4.6 and 4.7 (Chapter Four) with Simpson 2010, p. 139 (Fig. 2).

68. See, e.g., Simpson 2010, pp. 145–6; Milstein 2018, p. 61; and especially Balafrej 2019, pp. 111–22.
69. See Gruber 2005, pp. 257–63. On the bipartite structure of the ascension, see Colby 2008, pp. 14–16.
70. See Colby 2008, pp. 14–16.
71. Miniatures of the ascension scene that do not include the Kaʿba are, of course, to be found in numerous copies of Niẓāmī's *Khamsa* ('Quintet'). See Dodkhudoeva 1985, pp. 106–7, 123, 203, 235. On Niẓāmī's use of the ascension story, see de Fouchécour 2000; and Gruber 2005, pp. 257–62.
72. The literature is extensive. For a summary, see O'Meara 2012, p. 2
73. For examples of tile paintings, see Erdmann 1959, pp. 192–7; and especially Maury 2013, pp. 143–59.
74. The issue is different for Ottoman miniatures. See, e.g., Fig. 5.2.
75. Iskandar's visit to the Kaʿba provides the principal narrative of the Persian Kaʿba-centric miniatures comprising Marianna Shreve Simpson's aforementioned article. See Simpson 2010, *passim*.
76. See ibid. p. 127; and Milstein 2018, pp. 49, 61, respectively
77. In addition to Internet-based searches, see Ettinghausen 1934, Figs 6, 9 (unpaginated).
78. Ibn Rāshid 2014, pp. 3–5; Chabbi 1954, pp. 441–2; and Rubin 2007, respectively. Cf. Hawting 1980, pp. 44–6.
79. See, e.g., al-Batanūnī 1911, p. 108; and Young 1993, p. 294.
80. Cf. Rubin 2007.
81. Mīrkhwānd 1959, vol. 2, p. 462; trans., Mīrkhwānd 1892, vol. 4, p. 599. Cf. Hawting 1999, pp. 68–9, 109. Contrary to what has been said of this image (Gruber 2015, p. 308), the Prophet has not been marginalised because of the pro-ʿAlid politics and ideology of the period and place where the image was produced, namely, Safavid Iran. The Prophet, rather, occupies a central position in the miniature. As he holds forth on the meaning of Nāyla's exit, his gesturing, 'speaking' hand is additionally at the painting's epicentre.
82. Al-Hujwīrī 1979, p. 424 (ll. 12–13); trans. al-Hujwīrī 1911, p. 327 (modified).

Conclusion

1. Gell 1998, p. 97; and cf. Dubuisson 2015, pp. 302–4.
2. Grabar 1987a, p. 75.
3. Gell 1998, p. 97. Cf. Mignolo and Vazquez 2013.

Bibliography

Aazam, Ziad (2005). 'To, Around and From the Centre: How the Kabah Continues to Integrate the Society and its Rituals', in *Proceedings of the 5th International Space Syntax, Delft University of Technology, Delft, June 13–17, 2005*, edited by Akkelies van Nes. Delft: Techne Press, pp. 309–22, <http://tinyurl.com/jfou6aj> (last accessed 6 June 2017).

ʿAbd al-Ḥamīd, Saʿd Zaghlūl (ed.) (1958). *Kitāb al-Istibṣār fī ʿajāʾib al-amṣār: waṣf Makka wa al-Madīna wa Miṣr wa bilād al-Maghrib*. Alexandria: Maṭbaʿat Jāmiʿat al-Iskandariyya.

ʿAbd al-Razzāq al-Ṣanʿānī, Abū Bakr al-Yamanī al-Ḥimyarī (2000). *Al-Muṣannaf wa fī ākhirihi Kitāb al-Jāmiʿ li-Maʿmar b. Rāshid al-Azadī*, edited by Ayman Naṣr al-Dīn al-Azharī, 12 vols. Beirut: Dār al-Kutub al-ʿIlmiyya.

Abdel Haleem, Muhammad (2013). 'The Religious and Social Importance of Hajj', in *The Hajj: Collected Essays*, edited by Venetia Porter and Liana Saif. London: The British Museum Press, pp. 1–5.

Abdul Ghani, Muhammad Ilyas (2004). *The History of Makkah Mukarramah*, translated by Afzal Hoosen Elias. Medina: Al-Rasheed Printers.

Abū al-Faẓl b. Mubārak (1897). *The Akbarnāma of Abu-l-Faẓl*, translated by Henry Beveridge, 3 vols. Calcutta: Asiatic Society.

Addas, Claude (1993). *Quest for the Red Sulphur: The Life of Ibn ʿArabī*, translated by Peter Kingsley. Cambridge: The Islamic Texts Society.

Aflākī, Shams al-Dīn Aḥmad (2002). *The Feats of the Knowers of God = Manāqib al-ʿārifīn*, translated by John O'Kane. Leiden: Brill.

Ahmad, Sayyid Maqbul (1954a). 'Ibn Rusta', in *Encyclopaedia of Islam, Second Edition*, edited by P. Bearman, Th. Bianquis, C. E. Bosworth, E. van Donzel and W. P. Heinrichs, 12 vols. Leiden: Brill, vol. 3, pp. 920–1.

—— (1954b). 'Jughrāfiyā', in *Encyclopaedia of Islam, Second Edition*, edited by P. Bearman, Th. Bianquis, C. E. Bosworth, E. van Donzel and W. P. Heinrichs, 12 vols. Leiden: Brill, vol. 2, pp. 575–90.

Ahmed, Shahab (2015). *What is Islam? The Importance of Being Islamic*. Princeton: Princeton University Press.

Akkach, Samer (2005a). *Cosmology and Architecture in Premodern Islam: An Architectural Reading of Mystical Ideas*. Albany: SUNY Press.

—— (2005b). 'The Poetics of Concealment: Al-Nabulusi's Encounter with the Dome of the Rock', *Muqarnas* 22: 110–27.

Al-Azmeh, Aziz (1997). *Muslim Kingship: Power and the Sacred in Muslim, Christian, and Pagan Polities*. London: I. B. Tauris.

—— (2014). *The Emergence of Islam in Late Antiquity: Allāh and His People*. Cambridge: Cambridge University Press.

Al-Harithy, Howayda (2001). 'The Concept of Space in Mamluk Architecture', *Muqarnas* 18: 73–93.

Alexander, Philip (1999). 'Jerusalem as the *Omphalos* of the World: On the History of a Geographical Concept', in *Jerusalem: Its Sanctity and Centrality to Judaism, Christianity, and Islam*, edited by Lee Levine. New York: Continuum, pp. 104–19.

Ali, Samer (2004). 'Praise for Murder? Two Odes by al-Buhturī surrounding an Abbasid Patricide', in *Writers and Rulers: Perspectives on their Relationship from Abbasid to Safavid Times*, edited by Beatrice Gruendler and Louise Marlow. Wiesbaden: Reichert Verlag, pp. 1–38.

Ali Bey (1816). *The Travels of Ali Bey in Morocco, Tripoli, Cyprus, Egypt, Arabia, Syria, and Turkey, Between the Years 1803 and 1807*, 2 vols. Philadelphia: Printed for John Conrad, at the Shakespeare Buildings.

Allen, Terry (1995). 'Imagining Paradise in Islamic Art'. Sebastopol: Solipsist Press, <http://tinyurl.com/yxjfas45> (last accessed 4 April 2018).

Alpers, Svetlana (1982). 'Art History and its Exclusions: The Example of Dutch Art', in *Feminism and Art History: Questioning the Litany*, edited by Norma Broude and Mary Garrard. New York: Harper & Row, pp. 183–99.

AlSayyad, Nezar (1991). *Cities and Caliphs: On the Genesis of Arab Muslim Urbanism*. New York: Greenwood Press.

Amanat, Abbas (1997). *Pivot of the Universe: Nasir al-Din Shah Qajar and the Iranian Monarchy*. London: I. B. Tauris.

Andrae, Tor (1926). *Der Ursprung des Islams und Christentum*. Upsala: Almqvist & Wiksell.

Andrews, Jorella (2014). *Showing Off: A Philosophy of Image*. London: Bloomsbury.

ʿAntara b. Shaddād (1962). *Sharḥ dīwān ʿAntara b. Shaddād*, edited by ʿAbd al-Munʿim ʿAbd al-Raʾūf Shalabī. Cairo: Al-Maktaba al-Tijāriyya al-Kubrā.

Antrim, Zayde (2012). *Routes and Realms: The Power of Place in the Early Islamic World*. Oxford: Oxford University Press.

Appudarai, Arjun (ed.) (1986). *The Social Life of Things: Commodities in Cultural Perspective*. Cambridge: Cambridge University Press.

Arazi, Albert (1984). 'Matériaux pour l'étude du conflit de préséance entre la Mekke et Médine', *Jerusalem Studies in Arabic and Islam* 5: 177–237.

ʿAṭṭār, Farīd al-Dīn (1957). *Kitāb-i Tadhkirat al-awliyāʾ bā muqaddama-yi Mīrzā Muḥammad Khān Qazwīnī*, 2 vols in 1. [Tehran]: Kitābkhāna-yi Markazī.

—— (1966). *Muslim Saints and Mystics: Episodes from the Tadhkirat al-Auliyaʾ ('Memorial of the Saints')*, translated by Arthur John Arberry. London: Routledge & Kegan Paul Ltd.

Avner, Rina (2010). 'The Dome of the Rock in Light of the Development of Concentric Martyria in Jerusalem: Architecture and Architectural Iconography', *Muqarnas* 27: 31–49.

al-Azraqī, Muḥammad b. ʿAbd Allāh (2003). *Akhbār Makka wa mā jāʾa fīhā min al-āthār*, edited by ʿAbd al-Malik b. ʿAbd Allāh b. Duhaysh, 2 vols. Mecca: Maktabat al-Asadī.

ʿAyn al-Quḍāt Hamadānī, ʿAbd Allāh b. Muḥammad (1962). *Tamhīdāt*, edited by ʿAfīf ʿUsayrān. Tehran: Dānishgāh-i Tihrān.

Babayan, Kathryn (2008). '"In Spirit We Ate of Each Other's Sorrow": Female Companionship in Seventeenth Century Safavi Iran', in *Islamicate Sexualities: Translations Across Temporal Geographies of Desire*, edited by Kathryn Babayan and Afsaneh Najmabadi. Cambridge, MA: Harvard Middle Eastern Monographs, pp. 239–74.

Bacharach, Jere (1991). 'Administrative Complexes, Palaces, and Citadels: Changes in the Loci of Medieval Muslim Rule', in *The Ottoman City and Its Parts: Urban Structure and Social Order*, edited by Irene Bierman, Rifaʿat Abou-El-Haj and Donald Preziosi. New Rochelle: Aristide D. Caratzas, pp. 111–28.

Badāʾūnī, ʿAbd al-Qādir b. Mulūk Shāh (1898). *Muntakhabu-t-tawarikh: Translated from the Original Persian and Edited by George Ranking (vol. 1), W. H. Lowe (vol. 2) and Sir Wolseley Haig (vol. 3)*, 3 vols. Calcutta: Asiatic Society of Bengal.

al-Baḥrānī, Hāshim b. Sulaymān al-Ḥusaynī (2007). *Nuzhat al-abrār wa manār al-anẓār fī khalq al-jannah wa al-nār*, edited by Fāris Ḥassūn Karīm. Qum: Maktabat Fadak li-Iḥyāʾ al-Turāth.

al-Balādhurī, Aḥmad b. Yaḥyā (1916). *The Origins of the Islamic State, Vol. 1: Being a Translation from the Arabic, Accompanied with Annotations, Geographic and Historic Notes, of the Kitāb Futūḥ al-buldān*, translated by Philip Khūri Ḥitti. New York: Columbia University.

—— (1924). *The Origins of the Islamic State, Vol. 2: Being a Translation from the Arabic, Accompanied with Annotations, Geographic and Historic Notes, of the Kitāb Futūḥ al-buldān*, translated by Francis Clark Murgotten. New York: Columbia University.

—— (1987) *Futūḥ al-buldān*, edited by ʿAbd Allāh Anīs al-Ṭabbāʿ. Beirut: Maktabat al-Maʿārif.

—— (1996). *Kitāb Jumal min al-Ansāb al-ashrāf*, edited by Suhayl Zakkār and Riyāḍ al-Ziriklī, 13 vols. Beirut: Dar al-Fikr.

Balafrej, Lamia (2019). *The Making of the Artist in Late Timurid Painting*. Edinburgh: Edinburgh University Press.

Baqlī, Rūzbihān b. Abī Naṣr (1970). *Kitāb-i ʿAbhar al-ʿāshiqīn*, edited by Jawād Nūrbakhsh. Tehran: Intishārāt-i Khānaqāh-i Niʿmatullāhī.

—— (1972). *Risālat al-quds wa Risāla-yi ghalaṭāt al-sālikīn*, edited by Jawād Nūrbakhsh. Tehran: Intishārāt-i Khānaqāh-i Niʿmatullāhī.

Bashear, Suliman (1989). 'Yemen in Early Islam: An Examination of Non-Tribal Traditions', *Arabica* 36 (3): 327–61.

—— (1990). 'Abraham's Sacrifice of his Son and Related Issues', *Der Islam* 67 (2): 243–77.

—— (1991). '*Qibla Musharriqa* and Early Muslim Prayer in Churches', *The Muslim World* 81 (3–4): 267–82.

—— (1992). 'The Images of Mecca: A Case-Study in Medieval Iconography', *Le Muséon: Revue d'Études Orientales* 105 (1–2): 361–77.

Bashir, Shahzad (2005). *Fazlallah Astarabadi and the Hurufis*. Oxford: Oneworld Publications.

—— (2011). *Sufi Bodies: Religion and Society in Medieval Islam*. New York: Columbia University Press.

Basset, Henri and Évariste Lévi-Provençal (1922). 'Chella: une nécropole mérinide', *Hespéris: Archives Berbères et Bulletin de l'Institut des Hautes-Études Marocaines* 2: 1–92, 255–316, 385–425.

al-Batanūnī, Muḥammad Labīb (1911). *Al-Riḥla al-ḥijāziyya*. Cairo: Maṭbaʿat al-Jamāliyya.
Baudrillard, Jean (2009). *Why Hasn't Everything Already Disappeared?*, translated by Chris Turner. London: Seagull Books.
al-Bayhaqī, Abū Bakr b. al-Ḥusayn b. ʿAlī (1925). *Kitāb al-Sunan al-kubrā wa fī dhaylihi al-Jawhar al-naqī li-l-ʿallāma ʿAlāʾ al-Dīn b. ʿAlī b. ʿUthmān al-Mārdīnī al-shahīr bi-Ibn al-Turkumānī*, 10 vols. Hyderabad: Maṭbaʿat Majlis Dāʾirat al-Maʿārif al-Niẓāmiyya.
Beelaert, Anna Livia (2000). *A Cure for the Grieving: Studies on the Poetry of the 12th-Century Persian Court Poet Khāqānī Shirwānī*. Leiden: Nederlands Instituut voor het Nabije Oosten.
Begley, Wayne Edison (1981). 'The Symbolic Role of Calligraphy on Three Imperial Mosques of Shāh Jahān', in *Kalādarśana: American Studies in the Art of India*, edited by Joanna Williams. Leiden: Brill, pp. 7–18.
Bellino, Francesca (2014). 'Sirāj al-Dīn ibn al-Wardī and the *Kharīdat al-ʿajāʾib*: Authorship and Plagiarism in a Fifteenth-century Arabic Cosmography', *Eurasian Studies* 12: 257–96.
Ben El Khadir, Mohamed and Abderrafih Lahbabi (1989). *Architectures régionales: un parcours à travers le nord marocain*. Casablanca: Imprimerie Najah El Jadida.
Benevelo, Leonardo (1993). *The European City*, translated by Carl Ipsen. Oxford: Blackwell.
Bennett, Clinton (1994). 'Islam', in *Sacred Place*, edited by Jean Holm with John Bowker. London: Pinter Publishers, pp. 88–114.
Berg, Herbert (2001). 'Polysemy in the Qurʾān', in *Encyclopaedia of the Qurʾān*, edited by Jane Dammen McAuliffe, 6 vols. Leiden: Brill, vol. 4, pp. 155–8.
Bianchi, Robert (2005). *Guests of God: Pilgrimage and Politics in the Islamic World*. Oxford: Oxford University Press.
Bindaqjī, Ḥusayn Ḥamza (1978). *Atlas of Saudi Arabia*. Oxford: Oxford University Press.
al-Bīrūnī, Abū al-Rayḥān Muḥammad b. Aḥmad (1967). *The Determination of the Coordinates of Positions for the Correction of Distances Between Cities: A Translation from the Arabic of al-Bīrūnī's Kitāb Taḥdīd nihāyāt al-amākin li-taṣḥīḥ masāfāt al-masākin*, translated by Jamil Ali. Beirut: American University of Beirut.
—— (1989). *The Book Most Comprehensive in Knowledge on Precious Stones: al-Beruni's Book on Mineralogy = Kitāb al-Jamāhir fī maʿrifat al-jawāhir*, translated by Hakim Mohammad Said. Islamabad: Pakistan Hijra Council.
Blair, Sheila (2013). 'Inscribing the Hajj', in *The Hajj: Collected Essays*, edited by Venetia Porter and Liana Saif. London: The British Museum Press, pp. 160–8.
Blair, Sheila and Jonathan Bloom (2012). 'Cosmophilia and its Critics: An Overview of Islamic Ornament', in *Beiträge zur Islamischen Kunst und Archäologie: Band 3*, edited by Lorenz Korn and Anja Heidenreich. Wiesbaden: Reichert Verlag, pp. 39–54.
Bloom, Jonathan (2013). *The Minaret*. Edinburgh: Edinburgh University Press.
Bloom, Jonathan and Sheila Blair (eds) (2009). *The Grove Encyclopedia of Islamic Art and Architecture*, 3 vols. New York: Oxford University Press.
Bonine, Michael (1990). 'The Sacred Direction and City Structure: A Preliminary Analysis of the Islamic Cities of Morocco', *Muqarnas* 7: 50–72.

—— (2008). 'Romans, Astronomy and the *Qibla*: Urban Form and Orientation of Islamic Cities of Tunisia', in *African Cultural Astronomy: Current Archaeoastronomy and Ethnoastronomy Research in Africa*, edited by Jarita Holbrook, R. Thebe Medupe and Johnson Urama. Berlin: Springer, pp. 145–78.

Bourdieu, Pierre (1979). *Algeria 1960: Essays*, translated by Richard Nice. Cambridge: Cambridge University Press.

Böwering, Gerhard (1980). *The Mystical Vision of Existence in Classical Islam: The Qur'anic Hermeneutics of the Ṣūfī Sahl At-Tustarī (d. 283/896)*. Berlin: Walter de Gruyter.

—— (2011). 'Sulamī's Treatise on the Science of the Letters (*'Ilm al-Ḥurūf*)', in *In the Shadow of Arabic: The Centrality of Language to Arabic Culture: Studies Presented to Ramzi Baalbaki on the Occasion of His Sixtieth Birthday*, edited by Bilal Orfali. Leiden: Brill, pp. 339–97.

Bramón, Dolors (1991). *El mundo en el siglo XII: estudio de la versión castellana y del 'original' árabe de una geografía universal, 'El tratado de al-Zuhrī'*. Sabadell: Editorial AUSA.

Browne, Edward (1924). *A Literary History of Persia, Vol. 4: A History of Persian Literature in Modern Times, AD 1500–1924*. Cambridge: University Press.

Bryson, Norman (1983). *Vision and Painting: The Logic of the Gaze*. New Haven: Yale University Press.

al-Buhṭurī, al-Walīd b. 'Ubayd (1963). *Dīwān al-Buhṭurī*, edited by Ḥasan Kāmil al-Ṣayrafī. Cairo: Dār al-Ma'ārif.

al-Bukhārī, Abū 'Abd Allāh b. Ismā'īl (1994). *Ṣaḥīḥ al-Bukhārī*, edited by 'Abd al-'Azīz b. 'Abd Allāh b. Bāz, 8 vols in 5. Beirut: Dār al-Fikr.

Burckhardt, John Lewis (1829). *Travels in Arabia: Comprehending an Account of those Territories in Hedjaz which the Mohammedans Regard as Sacred*, edited by William Ouseley, 2 vols. London: Henry Colburn.

Burckhardt, Titus (2009). *Art of Islam: Language and Meaning*, rev. ed., translated by J. P. Hobson. Bloomington: World Wisdom.

Burnett, Charles (2010). 'Fibonacci's "Method of the Indians"', in *Numerals and Arithmetic in the Middle Ages*, edited by Charles Burnett. Farnham: Ashgate Publishing Limited, XI: 87–97.

Burton, Richard (1885). *A Plain and Literal Translation of the Arabian Nights Entertainments, Now Entituled The Book of the Thousand Nights and a Night: with Introduction, Explanatory Notes on the Manners and Customs of Moslem Men, and a Terminal Essay upon the History of The Nights*, 10 vols. Printed by the Burton Club for Private Subscribers only.

—— (1893). *Personal Narrative of a Pilgrimage to Al-Madina & Meccah*, edited by Isabel Burton, 2 vols. London: Tylston and Edwards.

Busse, Heribert (1988). 'Jerusalem and Mecca, the Temple and the Kaaba: An Account of their Interrelation in Islamic Times', in *Pillars of Smoke and Fire: The Holy Land in History and Thought*, edited by Moshe Sharon. Johannesburg: Southern Book Publishers, pp. 236–46.

Calder, Norman (2007). 'The Limits of Islamic Orthodoxy', in *Defining Islam: A Reader*, edited by Andrew Rippin. London: Equinox Publishing, pp. 222–36.

Campo, Juan Eduardo (1991a). *The Other Sides of Paradise: Explorations into the Religious Meanings of Domestic Space in Islam*. Columbia: University of South Carolina Press.

—— (1991b). 'Authority, Ritual, and Spatial Order in Islam: The Pilgrimage to Mecca', *Journal of Ritual Studies* 5 (1): 65–91.

Canepa, Matthew (2009). *The Two Eyes of the Earth: Art and Ritual of Kingship between Rome and Sasanian Iran*. Berkeley: University of California Press.

Canova, Giovanni (1994). 'Il serpente della Kaʿba: una nota sulla Mecca preislamica', *Annali di Ca' Foscari: Rivista della Facoltà di Lingue e Letterature straniere dell'Università di Ca' Foscari* 33 (3): 421–5.

Casey, Edward (1993). *Getting Back Into Place: Toward a Renewed Understanding of the Place-World*. Bloomington: Indiana University Press.

—— (1997). *The Fate of Place: A Philosophical History*. Berkeley: University of California Press.

Cassirer, Ernst (1955). *The Philosophy of Symbolic Forms, Vol. 2: Mythical Thought*, translated by Ralph Mannheim. New Haven: Yale University Press.

Chabbi, Jacqueline (1954). 'Zamzam', in *Encyclopaedia of Islam, Second Edition*, edited by P. Bearman, Th. Bianquis, C. E. Bosworth, E. van Donzel and W. P. Heinrichs, 12 vols. Leiden: Brill, vol. 11, pp. 440–2.

—— (2001). 'Mecca', in *Encyclopaedia of the Qurʾān*, edited by Jane Dammen McAuliffe, 6 vols. Leiden: Brill, vol. 3, pp. 337–41.

—— (2002). 'Aux origines de La Mecque: le regard de l'historien', *Clio (www.clio.fr)* November, <http://tinyurl.com/y6lef4qr> (last accessed 8 January 2017).

—— (2010). *Le seigneur des tribus: l'islam de Mahomet*. Paris: CNRS Éditions.

Chahanovich, Walter Sasson (2016). 'Kissing at the Kaʿbah: Ghazal Poetry and Early Arabo-Islamic Conceptualizations of the Sacred and the Sensual', unpublished paper presented at the conference *Mots du désir*, Institut du Monde Arabe, Paris, 6–7 May 2016.

—— (2017). 'The Mecca of Love and Lewdness: Identifying a Conceit in the Poetry of ʿUmar b. Abī Rabīʿa, al-ʿArjī, Abū Nuwās, and Ibn al-Rūmī', unpublished paper.

Chekhab-Abudaya, Mounia (2014). *Mémoires du Hajj: le pèlerinage à La Mecque vu à travers les arts de l'Islam, la production intellectuelle et matérielle de l'époque médiévale à l'époque contemporaine*. Paris: Les Cahiers de l'Islam.

Chekhab-Abudaya, Mounia and Cécile Bresc (2013). *Hajj – The Journey Through Art: Exhibition Album*. Milan: Skira.

Chelhod, Joseph (1973). 'A Contribution to the Problem of the Pre-eminence of the Right, Based upon Arabic Evidence', in *Right & Left: Essays on Dual Symbolic Classification*. Chicago: University of Chicago Press, pp. 239–62.

Chodkiewicz, Michel (1993). *Seal of the Saints: Prophethood and Sainthood in the Doctrine of Ibn ʿArabī*, translated by Liadain Sherrard. Cambridge: The Islamic Texts Society.

—— (2002). 'Toward Reading the *Futūhāt Makkiya*', in *The Meccan Revelations: Ibn al-ʿArabi*, edited by Michel Chodkiewicz, translated by William Chittick, James Morris, Cyrille Chodkiewicz and Denis Gril, 2 vols. New York: Pir Press, vol. 2, pp. 3–55.

—— (2005). 'Le paradoxe de la Kaʿba', *Revue de l'Histoire des Religions* 222 (4): 435–61.

Clévenot, Dominique (2000). *Splendors of Islam: Architecture, Decoration and Design*. New York: Vendome Press.

Colby, Frederick (2008). *Narrating Muhammad's Night Journey: Tracing the Development of the Ibn ʿAbbās Ascension Discourse*. Albany: SUNY Press.

Cook, David (2002). *Studies in Muslim Apocalyptic*. Princeton: Darwin Press.

Cook, Michael (2013). 'Why Incline to the Left in Prayer? Sectarianism, Dialectic, and Archaeology in Imāmī Shīʿism', in *Law and Tradition in Classical Islamic Thought: Studies in Honor of Professor Hossein Modarressi*, edited by Michael Cook, Najam Haider, Intisar Rabb and Asma Sayeed. New York: Palgrave Macmillan, pp. 99–124.

Cooperson, Michael (1996). 'Baghdad in Rhetoric and Narrative', *Muqarnas* 13: 99–113.

Corbin, Henry (1969). *Alone with the Alone: Creative Imagination in the Sūfism of Ibn ʿArabī*, translated by Ralph Manheim. Princeton: Princeton University Press.

—— (1986). *Temple and Contemplation*, translated by Philip and Liadain Sherrard. London: KPI Limited.

Coşkun, Menderes (1999). 'Ottoman Pilgrimage Narratives and Nabi's *Tuhfetü'l-Haremeyn*', unpublished PhD dissertation. Durham: Durham University.

—— (2000). 'Pilgrimage Narratives in Arabic and Persian Literature', in *The Great Ottoman-Turkish Civilisation*, edited by Kemal Cicek, 4 vols. Ankara: Yeni Turkiye, vol. 2, pp. 510–25.

—— (2012). 'Ottoman Attitudes towards writing about Pilgrimage Experience', *Millî Folklor* 24 (95): 72–82.

Creswell, Keppel Archibald Cameron. (1958). *A Short Account of Early Muslim Architecture*. Harmondsworth: Penguin Books.

—— (1969). *Early Muslim Architecture*, 2nd ed., 2 vols. Oxford: Clarendon Press.

Crone, Patricia (1987). *Meccan Trade and the Rise of Islam*. Oxford: Blackwell.

Crone, Patricia and Michael Cook (1977). *Hagarism: The Making of the Islamic World*. Cambridge: Cambridge University Press.

Crone, Patricia and Martin Hinds (1986). *God's Caliph: Religious Authority in the First Centuries of Islam*. Cambridge: Cambridge University Press.

Daftary, Farhad (1998). *A Short History of the Ismailis: Traditions of a Muslim Community*. Edinburgh: Edinburgh University Press.

—— (2007). *The Ismāʿīlīs: Their History and Doctrines*, 2nd ed. Cambridge: Cambridge University Press.

Dakake, Maria (2007). '"Guest of the Inmost Heart": Conceptions of the Divine Beloved among early Sufi Women', *Comparative Islamic Studies* 3 (1): 72–97.

Dallal, Ahmad (1995). 'Ibn al-Haytham's Universal Solution for Finding the Direction of the Qibla by Calculation', *Arabic Sciences and Philosophy* 5: 145–93.

—— (2010). *Islam, Science, and the Challenge of History*. New Haven: Yale University Press.

Daryaee, Touraj (2009). *Sasanian Persia: The Rise and Fall of an Empire*. London: I. B. Tauris.

Denny, Frederick Mathewson (2001). 'Face', in *Encyclopaedia of the Qurʾān*, edited by Jane Dammen McAuliffe, 6 vols. Leiden: Brill, vol. 2, pp. 158–9.

Denoix, Sylvie (2008). 'Founded Cities of the Arab World from the Seventh to the Eleventh Centuries', in *The City in the Islamic World*, edited by Salma Jayyusi, 2 vols. Leiden: Brill, vol. 2, pp. 115–42.

Deverdun, Gaston (2004). *Marrakech: des origines à 1912*, 2 vols. Casablanca: Éditions Frontispice.

Di Cesare, Michelina (2017). 'A *Qibla Musharriqa* for the First al-Aqṣā Mosque? A New Stratigraphic and Chronological Reading of Hamilton's Excavation, and some considerations on the Introduction of the Concave *Miḥrāb*', *Annali dell'Università degli Studi di Napoli 'L'Orientale. Sezione orientale* 77: 66–96.
—— (2018). 'A Reconstructive Hypothesis of the Palace-Mosque Complex in the Round City of al-Manṣūr in Baghdād', in *Mantua Humanistic Studies: Volume 2*, edited by Riccardo Roni. Mantova: Universitas Studiorum, pp. 53–95.
Di Segni, Leah (2003). 'Christian Epigraphy in the Holy Land: New Discoveries', *ARAM Periodical* 15: 247–67.
Djaït, Hichem (1986). *Al-Kūfa: naissance de la ville islamique*. Paris: Editions G.-P. Maisonneuve et Larose.
Dodkhudoeva, Larisa Nazarovna (1985). *Poėmy Nizami v srednevekovoĭ miniatiūrnoĭ zhivopisi*. Moscow: Izd-vo 'Nauka', Glav. red. vostochnoĭ lit-ry.
Donley, Linda (1982). 'House Power: Swahili Space and Symbolic Markers', in *Symbolic and Structural Archaeology*, edited by Ian Hodder. Cambridge: Cambridge University Press, pp. 63–73.
Donner, Fred (1981). *The Early Islamic Conquests*. Princeton: Princeton University Press.
—— (2010). 'Umayyad Efforts at Legitimation: The Umayyads' Silent Heritage', in *Umayyad Legacies: Medieval Memories from Syria to Spain*, edited by Antoine Borrut and Paul Cobb. Leiden: Brill, pp. 187–211.
Dubuisson, Daniel (2015). 'Visual Culture and Religious Studies: A New Paradigm', *Method and Theory in the Study of Religion* 27: 299–311.
Ducène, Jean-Charles (2001). 'Le *Kitāb Dalāʾil al-qibla* d'Ibn al-Qāṣṣ: analyse des trois manuscrits et des emprunts d'Abū Ḥāmid al-Gharnāṭī', *Zeitschrift für Geschichte der Arabisch-islamischen Wissenschaften* 14: 169–87.
—— (2002). 'La carte circulaire du *Kitāb Dalāʾil al-qibla* d'Ibn al-Qāṣṣ: représentation du monde et toponymie originales', *Folia Orientalia* 38: 115–46.
—— (2011). 'L'Afrique dans les mappemondes circulaires arabes médiévales: typologie d'une représentation', *Cartes et géomatique* 2010: 19–35.
Duri, Abdul Aziz (1989). 'Jerusalem in the Early Islamic Period: 7th–11th Centuries AD', in *Jerusalem in History*, edited by K. J. Asali. Buckhurst Hill: Scorpion Publishing, pp. 105–28.
Eaton, Richard M. (1993). *The Rise of Islam and the Bengal Frontier, 1204–1760*. Berkeley: University of California Press.
Eck, Diana (2005). 'Circumambulation', in *Encyclopedia of Religion, Second Edition*, edited by Lindsay Jones, 15 vols. London: Macmillan Reference USA, vol. 3, pp. 1795–8.
Edgerton, Samuel (2009). *The Mirror, the Window, and the Telescope: How Renaissance Linear Perspective Changed Our Vision of the Universe*. Ithaca: Cornell University Press.
Efendi, Caʿfer (1987). *Risāle-i miʿmāriyye: An Early Seventeenth-century Ottoman Treatise on Architecture*, translated by Howard Crane. Leiden: Brill.
El Guindi, Fadwa (1999). *Veil: Modesty, Privacy and Resistance*. Oxford: Berg.
El-Hibri, Tayeb (1992). 'Harun al-Rashid and the Mecca Protocol of 802: A Plan for Division or Succession?', *International Journal of Middle East Studies* 24 (3): 461–80.

—— (2007). *Reinterpreting Islamic Historiography: Hārūn al-Rashīd and the Narrative of the ʿAbbāsid Caliphate*. Cambridge: Cambridge University Press.

El-Rouayheb, Khaled (2015). *Islamic Intellectual History in the Seventeenth Century: Scholarly Currents in the Ottoman Empire and the Maghreb*. New York: Cambridge University Press.

El-Shamy, Hasan (2005). 'A "Motif Index of Alf Laylah wa Laylah": Its Relevance to the Study of Culture, Society, the Individual, and Character Transmutation', *Journal of Arabic Literature* 36 (3): 235–68.

Eliade, Mircea (1959). 'Sacred Space and Making the World Sacred', in *The Sacred and the Profane: The Nature of Religion*, edited and translated by Willard R. Trusk. New York: Harcourt, pp. 20–65.

—— (1976). 'The World, the City, the House', in *Occultism, Witchcraft, and Cultural Fashions: Essays in Comparative Religions*, edited by Mircea Eliade. Chicago: University of Chicago Press, pp. 18–31.

—— (1991). 'Symbolism of the "Centre"', in *Images and Symbols: Studies in Religious Symbolism*, edited by Mircea Eliade, translated by Philip Mairet. Princeton: Princeton University Press, pp. 27–56.

Eliade, Mircea and Lawrence Sullivan (2005). 'Center of the World', in *Encyclopedia of Religion, Second Edition*, edited by Lindsay Jones, 15 vols. London: Macmillan Reference USA, vol. 3, pp. 1501–5.

Elias, Jamal (2012). *Aisha's Cushion: Religious Art, Perception, and Practice in Islam*. Cambridge, MA: Harvard University Press.

Elinson, Alexander (2009). *Looking Back at al-Andalus: The Poetics of Loss and Nostalgia in Medieval Arabic and Hebrew Literature*. Leiden: Brill.

Enderlein, Volkmar and Michael Meinecke (1992). 'Graben, Forschen, Präsentieren: Probleme der Darstellung vergangener Kulturen am Beispiel der Mschatta-Fassade', *Jahrbuch der Berliner Museen* 34: 137–72.

Erdmann, Kurt (1959). 'Kaʿbah-Fliesen', *Ars Orientalis* 3: 192–7.

Erken, Sabih (1971). 'Türk Çiniciliğinde Kâbe Tasvirleri', *Vakıflar Dergisi* 9: 297–320.

Ernst, Carl (1998). 'Vertical Pilgrimage and Interior Landscape in the Visionary Diary of Rūzbihān Baqlī (d. 1209)', *The Muslim World* 88 (2): 129–40.

—— (2009). 'An Indo-Persian Guide to Sufi Shrine Visitation', in *Tales of God's Friends: Islamic Hagiography in Translation*, edited by John Renard. Berkeley: University of California Press, pp. 269–85.

Ettinghausen, Richard (1934). 'Die bildliche Darstellung der Kaʿba im Islamischen Kulturkreis', *Zeitschrift der Deutschen Morgenländischen Gesellschaft* 87 (3/4): 111–37.

Fahd, Toufic (1959). 'La naissance du monde selon l'Islam', in *Sources orientales, Vol. 1: La naissance du monde*. Paris: Éditions du Seuil, pp. 237–79.

—— (1966). *La divination arabe: études religieuses, sociologiques et folkloriques sur le milieu natif de l'Islam*. Leiden: E. J. Brill.

—— (1968). *Le panthéon de l'Arabie centrale à la veille de l'hégire*. Paris: Librarie Orientalise Paul Geuthner.

al-Fākihī, Abū ʿAbd Allāh Muḥammad Isḥāq (1994). *Akhbār Makka fī qadīm al-dahr wa ḥadīthihi*, edited by ʿAbd al-Malik b. ʿAbd Allāh b. Duhaysh, 6 vols in 3. Beirut: Dār Khiḍr.

al-Farazdaq, Hammām b. Ghālib (1936). *Sharḥ dīwān al-Farazdaq*, edited by ʿAbd Allāh Ismāʿīl al-Ṣāwī, 2 vols. Cairo: Maṭbaʿat al-Ṣāwī.

Farhādī, ʿAbd-ul-Ghafūr Ravān (1996). *ʿAbdullāh Anṣārī of Herāt (1006–1089): An Early Ṣūfī Master*. Richmond: Curzon Press.

Faroqhi, Suraiya (1994). *Pilgrims and Sultans: The Hajj under the Ottomans 1517–1683*. London: I. B. Tauris.

Fenton, Paul (1996). 'Le symbolisme du rite de la circumambulation dans le judaïsme et dans l'islam: étude comparative', *Revue de l'Histoire des Religions* 213 (2): 161–89.

Fentress, Elizabeth (1987). 'The House of the Prophet: African Islamic Housing', *Archeologia Medievale* 14: 43–68.

Fierro, Maribel (2004) (2017). 'Madīnat al-Zahrāʾ, Paradise and the Fatimids', in *Roads to Paradise: Eschatology and Concepts of the Hereafter in Islam*, edited by Sebastian Gunther and Todd Lawson, 2 vols. Leiden: Brill, vol. 2, pp. 979–1009.

Finster, Barbara (1991). 'Cubical Yemeni Mosques', *Proceedings of the Seminar for Arabian Studies* 21: 49–68.

—— (1992). 'Review of *A Short Account of Early Muslim Architecture*', *Journal of Islamic Studies* 3 (2): 310–14.

—— (2008). 'ʿAnjar: Spätantik oder frühislamisch?', in *Residences, Castles, Settlements: Transformation Processes from Late Antiquity to Early Islam in Bilad al-Sham: Proceedings of the International Conference held at Damascus, 5–9 November 2006*, edited by Karin Bartl and Abd al-Razzaq Moaz. Rahden: Verlag Marie Leidorf, pp. 229–42.

—— (2010). 'Arabia in Late Antiquity: An Outline of the Cultural Situation in the Peninsula at the Time of Muhammad', in *The Qurʾān in Context Historical and Literary Investigations into the Qurʾānic Milieu*, edited by Angelika Neuwirth, Nicolai Sinai and Michael Marx. Leiden: Brill, pp. 61–114.

—— (2011). 'Mecca and Medina in the Early Islamic Period', in *Roads of Arabia: The Archaeological Treasures of Saudi Arabia*, edited by Ute Franke, Joachim Gierlichs, Sophia Vassipoulou and Lucia Wagner, translated by Linda Schilcher and Michael Marx. Tübingen: Ernst Wasmuth, pp. 224–35.

Firestone, Reuven (1990). *Journeys in Holy Lands: The Evolution of the Abraham-Ishmael Legends in Islamic Exegesis*. Albany: SUNY Press.

Flood, Finbarr Barry (1999). 'Light in Stone: The Commemoration of the Prophet in Umayyad Architecture', in *Bayt al-Maqdis: Jerusalem and Early Islam*, edited by Jeremy Johns. Oxford: Oxford University Press, pp. 311–59.

—— (2016). '"God's wonder": Marble as Medium and the Natural Image in Mosques and Modernism', *West 86th: A Journal of Decorative Arts, Design History, and Material Culture* 23 (2): 168–219.

Forcada, Miquel (1954). 'Rīḥ', in *Encyclopaedia of Islam, Second Edition*, edited by P. Bearman, Th. Bianquis, C. E. Bosworth, E. van Donzel and W. P. Heinrichs, 12 vols. Leiden: Brill, vol. 8, pp. 526–7.

de Fouchécour, C.-H. (2000). 'The Story of the Ascension (*Miʿraj*) in Nizamis's Work', in *The Poetry of Nizami Ganjavi: Knowledge, Love, and Rhetoric*, edited by Kamran Talattof and Jerome Clinton. Basingstoke: Palgrave, pp. 179–88.

Friedman, David (1988). *Florentine New Towns: Urban Design in the Late Middle Ages*. Cambridge, MA: The MIT Press.

Friedman, Yaron (2010). *The Nuṣayrī-ʿAlawīs: An Introduction to the Religion, History, and Identity of the Leading Minority in Syria*. Leiden: Brill.

—— (2013). '"Kūfa is Better": The Sanctity of Kūfa in Early Islam and Shīʿism in particular', *Le Muséon* 126 (1–2): 203–37.

Friedmann, Yohanan (2000). *Shaykh Aḥmad Sirhindī: An Outline of His Thought and a Study of His Image in the Eyes of Posterity*, paperback ed. New Delhi: Oxford University Press.

Gaborieau, Marc (1994). 'Le culte des saints musulmans en tant que rituel: controverses juridiques', *Archives de Sciences Sociales des Religions* 85: 85–98.

Gadamer, Hans-Georg (2000). *Truth and Method*, 2nd rev. ed., translated by Joel Weinsheimer and Donald Marshall. New York: Continuum.

Gaudefroy-Demombynes, Maurice (1918). 'Notes sur la Mekke et Médine', *Revue de l'Histoire des Religions* 77: 316–44.

—— (1923). *Le pèlerinage à la Mekke: étude d'histoire religieuse*. Paris: Paul Geuthner.

—— (1954a). 'Shayba', in *Encyclopaedia of Islam, Second Edition*, edited by P. Bearman, Th. Bianquis, C. E. Bosworth, E. van Donzel and W. P. Heinrichs, 12 vols. Leiden: Brill, vol. 9, pp. 389–91.

—— (1954b). 'Le voile de la Kaʿba', *Studia Islamica* 2: 5–21.

Gautier-van Berchem, Marguerite (1969). 'The Mosaics of the Dome of the Rock in Jerusalem and of the Great Mosque in Damascus', in Keppel Archibald Cameron Creswell, *Early Muslim Architecture*, 2nd ed., 2 vols. Oxford: Clarendon Press, vol. 1, pp. 213–322.

Geissinger, Aisha (2005). 'The Portrayal of the Hajj as a Context for Women's Exegesis: Textual Evidence from al-Bukhari's (d. 870) "*al-Ṣāḥīḥ*"', in *Ideas, Images, and Methods of Portrayal: Insights into Classical Arabic Literature and Islam*, edited by Sebastian Günther. Leiden: Brill, pp. 153–79.

Gell, Alfred (1998). *Art and Agency: An Anthropological Approach*. Oxford: Clarendon Press.

Ghaemmaghami, Omid (2012). 'Numinous Vision, Messianic Encounters: Typological Representations in a Version of the Prophet's *ḥadīth al-ruʾyā* and in Visions and Dreams of the Hidden Imam', in *Dreams and Visions in Islamic Societies*, edited by Özgen Felek and Alexander Knysh. Albany: SUNY Press, pp. 51–76.

al-Ghazālī, Abū Ḥāmid (n.d.). *Al-Maqṣad al-asnā fī sharḥ asmāʾ Allāh al-ḥusnā*. Casablanca: Dār al-Furqān.

—— (1982). *Iḥyāʾ ʿulūm al-dīn wa bi-dhaylihi Kitāb al-Mughnī ʿan ḥaml al-asfār fī al-asfār fī takhrīj mā fī al-Iḥyāʾ min al-akhbār li-ʿalāmat Zayn al-Dīn Abī al-Faḍl ʿAbd al-Raḥīm al-Ḥusayn al-ʿIrāqī*, 4 vols. Beirut: Dār al-Maʿrifa.

—— (1992). *The Ninety-Nine Beautiful Names of God*, translated by David Burrell and Nazih Daher. Cambridge: The Islamic Texts Society.

—— (2010). *The Marvels of the Heart: Kitāb Sharḥ ʿajāʾib al-qalb, Book 21 of the Iḥyāʾ ʿulūm al-dīn, The Revival of the Religious Sciences*, translated by Walter James Skellie. Louisville: Fons Vitae.

Gilis, Charles-André (1982). *La doctrine initiatique du pèlerinage à la Maison d'Allâh*. Paris: Les Editions de l'Oeuvre.

Gilliot, Claude (2001). 'Traditional Disciplines of Qur'ānic Studies', in *Encyclopaedia of the Qur'ān*, edited by Jane Dammen McAuliffe, 6 vols. Leiden: Brill, vol. 5, pp. 318–39.

de Goeje, Michael Jan (1886). *Mémoire sur les Carmathes du Bahraïn et les Fatimides*, 2nd ed. Leiden: Brill.

Goldziher, Ignaz (1954). 'Awtād', in *Encyclopaedia of Islam, Second Edition*, edited by P. Bearman, Th. Bianquis, C. E. Bosworth, E. van Donzel and W. P. Heinrichs, 12 vols. Leiden: Brill, vol. 1, p. 772.

—— (1966). *Muslim Studies (Muhammedanische Studien)*, edited by S. M. Stern, translated by C. R. Barber and S. M. Stern, 2 vols. London: George Allen & Unwin.

Golombek, Lisa (1988a). 'The Draped Universe of Islam', in *Content and Context of Visual Arts in the Islamic World: Papers from a Colloquium in Memory of Richard Ettinghausen, Institute of Fine Arts, New York University, 2–4 April* 1980, edited by Priscilla Soucek. University Park: Pennsylvania State University Press, pp. 25–38.

—— (1988b). 'The Function of Decoration in Islamic Architecture', in *Theories and Principles of Design in the Architecture of Islamic Societies*, edited by Margaret Bentley Sevcenko. Cambridge, MA: Aga Khan Program for Islamic Architecture, pp. 35–45.

Golombek, Lisa and Donald Wilber (1988). *The Timurid Architecture of Iran and Turan*, 2 vols. Princeton: Princeton University Press.

Goodman, Nelson (1985). 'How Buildings Mean', *Critical Inquiry* 11 (4): 642–53.

Goodwin, Godfrey (1971). *A History of Ottoman Architecture*. London: Thames & Hudson.

Gouda, Abdelaziz (1989). 'Die Kiswa der Ka'ba in Makka', unpublished PhD dissertation. Berlin: Freie Universität.

Grabar, Oleg (1980). 'Symbols and Signs in Islamic Architecture', in *Architecture as Symbol and Self-Identity: Proceedings of Seminar Four in the Series Architectural Transformations of the Islamic World, held in Fez, Morocco, October 9–12, 1979*, edited by Jonathan Katz. Philadelphia: The Aga Khan Award for Architecture, pp. 1–11.

—— (1985). 'Upon Reading al-Azraqi,' *Muqarnas* 3: 1–7.

—— (1987a). *The Formation of Islamic Art*, rev. ed. New Haven: Yale University Press.

—— (1987b). 'The Date and Meaning of Mshatta', *Dumbarton Oaks Papers* 41: 243–7.

Grabar, Oleg, Renata Holod, James Knustad and William Trousdale (1978). *City in the Desert: Qasr al-Hayr East: An Account of the Excavations Carried out at Qasr al-Hayr East on Behalf of the Kelsey Museum of Archaeology at the University of Michigan, with the help of Harvard University and the Oriental Institute, the University of Chicago*, 2 vols. Cambridge, MA: Distributed for the Center for Middle Eastern Studies of Harvard University by Harvard University Press.

Grabar, Oleg and Richard Ettinghausen (1987). *Islamic Art and Architecture 650–1250*. Harmondsworth: Penguin Books.

Grabar, Oleg, Richard Ettinghausen and Marilyn Jenkins-Madina (2001). *Islamic Art and Architecture 650–1250*, 2nd ed. New Haven: Yale University Press.

Graham, William (1983). 'Islam in the Mirror of Ritual', in *Islam's Understanding of Itself*, edited by Richard Hovannisian and Speros Vryonis. Malibu: Undena Publications, pp. 53–71.

Gramlich, Richard (1965). *Die schiitischen Derwischorden Persiens*, 3 vols. Wiesbaden: Kommissionsverlag Steiner.

—— (1997). *Weltverzicht: Grundlagen und Weisen islamischer Askese*. Wiesbaden: Otto Harrassowitz Verlag.

de la Granja, F. (1974). 'A propósito de una embajada cristiana en la corte de ʿAbd al-Raḥmān III', *Al-Andalus* 39: 391–406.

Gril, Denis (1995). 'Love Letters to the Kaʿba: A Presentation of Ibn ʿArabi's *Tāj al-Rasāʾil*', *Journal of the Muhyiddin Ibn ʿArabi Society* 17: 40–54.

Gruber, Christiane (2005). 'The Prophet Muhammad's Ascension (*miʿrāj*) in Islamic Art and Literature 1300–1600', unpublished PhD dissertation. Philadelphia: University of Pennsylvania.

—— (2014). 'Islamic Architecture on the Move', *International Journal of Islamic Architecture* 3 (2): 241–64.

—— (2015). 'Curse Signs: The Artful Rhetoric of Hell in Safavid Iran', in *Locating Hell in Islamic Traditions*, edited by Christian Lange. Leiden: Brill, pp. 297–335.

Gutas, Dimitri (1998). *Greek Thought, Arabic Culture: The Graeco-Arabic Translation Movement in Baghdad and Early ʿAbbāsid Society (2nd–4th/8th–10th centuries)*. London: Routledge.

Guthrie, Shirlie (1995). *Arab Social Life in the Middle Ages: An Illustrated Study*. London: Saqi Books.

Haase, Claus-Peter (ed.) (2007). *A Collector's Fortune: Islamic Art from the Collection of Edmund de Unger*. Munich: Hirmer.

Hajnal, István (1998). 'The Pseudo Mahdī Intermezzo of the Qarāmiṭa in Baḥrayn', *The Arabist: Budapest Studies in Arabic* 19–20: 187–201.

al-Ḥalabī al-Fāsī, Aḥmad b. ʿAbd al-Ḥayy (1896). *Kitāb al-Durr al-nafīs wa al-nūr al-anīs fī manāqib al-Imām Idrīs b. Idrīs*. Fez: al-Maṭbaʿat al-ʿĀmira.

Halevi, Leor (2007). *Muhammad's Grave: Death Rites and the Making of Islamic Society*. New York: Columbia University Press.

Halm, Heinz (1996). *The Empire of the Mahdi: The Rise of the Fatimids*, translated by Michael Bonner. Leiden: Brill.

Hammoudi, Abdellah (2006). *A Season in Mecca: Narrative of a Pilgrimage*, translated by Pascale Ghazaleh. New York: Hill and Wang.

al-Harawī, ʿAlī b. Abī Bakr (2004). *A Lonely Wayfarer's Guide to Pilgrimage: ʿAlī b. Abī Bakr al-Harawī's* Kitāb al-Ishārāt ilā maʿrifat al-ziyārāt, translated by Josef Meri. New Jersey: Darwin Press.

Harries, Karsten (1997). *The Ethical Function of Architecture*. Cambridge, MA: The MIT Press.

—— (2001). *Infinity and Perspective*. Cambridge, MA: The MIT Press.

Hartmann, Angelika (1975). *An-Nāṣir li-Dīn Allāh (1180–1225): Politik, Religion, Kultur in der Späten ʿAbbāsidenzeit*. Berlin: De Gruyter.

Hasan, Hadi (1953). 'Qasim-i Kahi: His Life, Time and Works', *Islamic Culture* 27: 99–131, 161–194, 199–224.

Hasson, Isaac (1981). 'Muslim Literature in Praise of Jerusalem: *Faḍā'il Bayt al-Maqdis*', in *The Jerusalem Cathedra: Studies in the History, Archaeology, Geography and Ethnography of the Land of Israel*, edited by Lee Levine, 3 vols. Jerusalem: Yad Izhak Ben-Zvi Institute for the Study of Eretz Israel, vol. 1, pp. 168–84.

—— (1996). 'The Muslim View of Jerusalem: Qur'ān and Ḥadīth', in *The History of Jerusalem: The Early Muslim Period, 638–1099*, edited by John Prawer and Haggai Ben-Shammai. Jerusalem: Yad Izhak Ben-Zvi Institute for the Study of Eretz Israel, pp. 349–85.

Ḥāṭūm, 'Afīf Nāyif (ed.) (2008). *Alf layla wa layla*, 2 vols. Beirut: Dār Ṣādir.

Hawting, Gerald (1978). 'Aspects of Muslim Political and Religious History in the 1st/7th Century, with Special Reference to the Development of the Muslim Sanctuary', unpublished PhD dissertation. London: SOAS, University of London.

—— (1980). 'The Disappearance and Rediscovery of Zamzam and the "Well of the Ka'ba"', *Bulletin of the School of Oriental and African Studies* 43: 44–54.

—— (1982). 'The Origins of the Muslim Sanctuary at Mecca', in *Studies on the First Century of Islamic Society*, edited by G. H. A. Juynboll. Carbondale: Southern Illinois University Press, pp. 23–47, 202–11.

—— (1984). '"We were not ordered with entering it but only with circumambulating it": *Ḥadīth* and *Fiqh* on Entering the Ka'ba', *Bulletin of the School of Oriental and African Studies* 47 (2): 228–42.

—— (1986). 'Al-Ḥudaybiyya and the Conquest of Mecca: A Reconsideration of the Tradition about the Muslim Takeover of the Sanctuary', *Jerusalem Studies in Arabic and Islam* 8: 1–25.

—— (1993). 'The Ḥajj in the Second Civil War', in *Golden Roads: Migration, Pilgrimage, and Travel in Mediaeval and Modern Islam*, edited by Ian Netton. Richmond: Curzon Press, pp. 31–42.

—— (1999). *The Idea of Idolatry and the Emergence of Islam: From Polemic to History*. Cambridge: Cambridge University Press.

—— (2001a). 'Idolatry and Idolaters', in *Encyclopaedia of the Qur'ān*, edited by Jane Dammen McAuliffe, 6 vols. Leiden: Brill, vol. 2, pp. 475–80.

—— (2001b). 'Ka'ba', in *Encyclopaedia of the Qur'ān*, edited by Jane Dammen McAuliffe, 6 vols. Leiden: Brill, vol. 3, pp. 75–80.

—— (2002). *The First Dynasty of Islam: The Umayyad Caliphate AD 661–750*, 2nd ed. London: Routledge.

—— (2017). '"A Plaything for Kings": 'Ā'isha's *ḥadīth*, Ibn al-Zubayr and Rebuilding the Ka'ba', in *Islamic Studies Today: Essays in Honor of Andrew Rippin*, edited by Majid Daneshgar and Walid Saleh. Leiden: Brill, pp. 3–21.

Hegel, Georg Wilhelm Friedrich (1979). *Introduction to Aesthetics: Being the Introduction to the Berlin Aesthetics Lectures of the 1820s*, translated by T. M. Knox. Oxford: Clarendon Press.

—— (1993). *Introductory Lectures on Aesthetics*, edited by Michael Inwood, translated by Bernard Bosanquet. Harmondsworth: Penguin Books.

Heidegger, Martin (1971). *Poetry, Language, Thought*, translated by Albert Hofstadter. New York: Harper & Row.

Heinen, Anton (1982). *Islamic Cosmology: A Study of as-Suyūṭī's* al-Hay'a as-sanīya fī l-hay'a as-sunnīya, *with Critical Edition, Translation, and Commentary*. Beirut: Orient-Institut der Deutschen Morgenländischen Gesellschaft.

Hendrickson, Jocelyn (2016). 'Prohibiting the Pilgrimage: Politics and Fiction in Mālikī *Fatwās*', *Islamic Law and Society* 23: 161–238.

d'Herbelot, Barthelemy (1781). *Bibliothèque orientale, ou Dictionnaire universel, contenant tout ce qui fait connoître les peuples de l'Orient; leurs histoires & traditions, tant fabuleuses que véritables; leurs religions & leurs sectes; leurs gouvernements, loix, politique, moeurs, coutumes; & les révolutions de leurs empires*, 6 vols. Paris: Moutard.

Herrera Casais, Mónica (2008). 'The Nautical Atlases of ʿAlī al-Sharafī', *Suhayl: International Journal for the History of the Exact and Natural Sciences in Islamic Civilisation* 8: 223–63.

—— (2013). 'Geografía sagrada islámica en dos atlas náuticos tunecinos del siglo XVI', in *Mediterráneos: An Interdisciplinary Approach to the Cultures of the Mediterranean Sea*, edited by Sergio Carro Martín, Arturo Echavarren, Esther Fernández Medina, Daniel Riaño Rufilanchas, Katja Šmid and Jesús Téllez Rubio. Newcastle upon Tyne: Cambridge Scholars Publishing, pp. 457–73.

Herrera Casais, Mónica and Petra Schmidl (2008). 'The Earliest Known Schemes of Islamic Sacred Geography', in *Islamic Thought in the Middle Ages: Studies in Text, Transmission and Translation, in Honour of Hans Daiber*, edited by Anna Akasoy and Wim Raven. Leiden: Brill, pp. 275–99.

Hickman, Bill (2012). 'Note on a Nineteenth Century Painting of the Sacred Precinct in Mecca', *Journal of Ottoman Studies* 39: 17–28.

Hill, Clifford (1982). 'Up/Down, Front/Back, Left/Right: A Contrastive Study of Hausa and English', in *Here and There: Cross-Linguistic Studies on Deixis and Demonstration*, edited by Jürgen Weissenborn and Wolfgang Klein. Amsterdam: Jon Benjamins Publishing Company, pp. 13–42.

Hillenbrand, Robert (1988). 'The Symbolism of the Rayed Nimbus in Early Islamic Art', in *Kingship*, edited by Emily Lyle. Edinburgh: Traditional Cosmology Society, pp. 1–52.

—— (1992). 'The Uses of Space in Timurid Painting', in *Timurid Art and Culture: Iran and Central Asia in the Fifteenth Century*, edited by Lisa Golombek and Maria Subtelny. Leiden: Brill, pp. 76–102.

—— (1994). *Islamic Architecture: Form, Function and Meaning*. Edinburgh: Edinburgh University Press.

—— (1999). 'ʿAnjar and Early Islamic Urbanism', in *The Idea and Ideal of the Town Between Late Antiquity and the Early Middle Ages*, edited by Gian Petro Broglio and Bryan Ward-Perkins. Leiden: Brill, pp. 59–98.

—— (2001a). '"The Ornament of the World": Medieval Cordoba as a Cultural Centre', in *Studies in Medieval Islamic Architecture*, edited by Robert Hillenbrand, 2 vols. London: Pindar Press, vol. 1, pp. 21–49.

—— (2001b). 'The Legacy of the Dome of the Rock', in *Studies in Medieval Islamic Architecture*, edited by Robert Hillenbrand, 2 vols. London: Pindar Press, vol. 1, pp. 1–20.

Hirtenstein, Stephen (2010). 'The Mystic's Kaʿba: The Cubic Wisdom of the Heart According to Ibn ʿArabī', *Journal of the Muhyiddin Ibn ʿArabi Society* 48: 19–43.

Hjärpe, Jan (1979). 'The Symbol of the Centre and its Religious Function in Islam', in *Religious Symbols and Their Functions: Based on Papers Read at the Symposium on Religious Symbols and their Functions held at Åbo on the 28th–30th August*

1978, edited by Haralds Biezais. Stockholm: Almqvist & Wiksell International, pp. 30–40.

Hoffmann, Thomas (2009). 'The Intercourse of Prayer: Notes on an Erotic Passage in The Arabian Nights and the Islamic Ritual Prayer', in *Religion, Ritual, Theatre*, edited by Bent Holm, Bent Flemming Nielsen and Karen Vedel. Frankfurt: Peter Lang, pp. 63–76.

Homerin, Th. Emil (2011). *Passion Before Me, My Fate Behind: Ibn al-Fāriḍ and the Poetry of Recollection*. Albany: SUNY Press.

—— (2013). 'Sufism in Mamluk Studies: A Review of Scholarship in the Field', in *Ubi sumus? Quo vademus?: Mamluk Studies, State of the Art*, edited by Stephan Conermann. Göttingen: V&R Unipress, pp. 187–210.

Houtman, Dick and Birgit Meyer (eds) (2012). *Things: Religion and the Question of Materiality*. New York: Fordham University Press.

Hoyland, Robert G. (1997). *Seeing Islam as Others Saw It: A Survey and Evaluation of Christian, Jewish, and Zoroastrian Writings on Early Islam*. Princeton: The Darwin Press.

al-Hujwīrī, ʿAlī b. ʿUthmān al-Jullābī (1911). *The Kashf al-Maḥjūb: The Oldest Persian Treatise on Sūfism*, translated by Reynold Alleyne Nicholson. Leiden: Brill.

—— (1979). *Kashf al-maḥjūb*, edited by Valentin Alekseevič Žukovskij. Tehran: Ṭuhūrī.

Hurgronje, Christiaan Snouck (2012). *The Mecca Festival*, edited and translated by Wolfgang Behn. Wiesbaden: Harrassowitz Verlag.

Ḥusaynī al-Qumī, Aḥmad Ibrāhīmī (2004). *Khulāṣat al-tawārīkh*, edited by Iḥsān Ishrāqī, 2 vols. Tehran: Dānishgāh-i Tihrān.

Ibn ʿAbd Rabbih, Aḥmad b. Muḥammad (1983). *Al-ʿIqd al-farīd*, edited by Mufīd Muḥammad Qumayḥa, 9 vols in 8. Beirut: Dār al-Kutub al-ʿIlmiyya.

Ibn ʿArabī, Muḥyī al-Dīn (1852). *Al-Futūḥāt al-makkiyya*, 4 vols. Cairo: Dār al-Ṭibāʿa.

—— (1972). *Al-Futūḥāt al-makkiyya*, edited by ʿUthmān Yaḥyā, 14 vols. Cairo: al-Hayʾa al-Miṣriyya al-ʿĀmma li-l-Kitāb.

—— (1996). *Las iluminaciones de La Meca: textos escodigos*, translated by Victor Pallejà de Bustinza. Madrid: Ediciones Siruela.

Ibn al-Athīr, ʿIzz al-Dīn (1987). *Al-Kāmil fī al-taʾrīkh*, edited by Abu al-Fidāʾ ʿAbd Allāh al-Qāḍī, 10 vols. Beirut: Dār al-Kutub al-ʿIlmiyya.

Ibn al-Athīr, Majd al-Dīn al-Mubārak b. Muḥammad (1963). *Al-Nihāya fī gharīb al-ḥadīth wa al-athar*, edited by Ṭāhir Aḥmad al-Zāwī and Maḥmūd Muḥammad al-Ṭanāḥī, 5 vols. Cairo: ʿĪsā al-Bābī al-Ḥalabī.

Ibn Baṭṭūṭa (1893). *Voyages d'Ibn Batoutah: texte arabe, accompagné d'une traduction*, translated by C. Defrémery and B. R. Sanguinetti, 4 vols. Paris: Imprimerie Nationale.

—— (1958). *The Travels of Ibn Baṭṭūṭa, AD 1325–1354*, translated by H. A. R. Gibb, 5 vols. Cambridge: Published for the Hakluyt Society at the University Press.

Ibn Duhaysh (Bin Dehaish), ʿAbd al-Malik b. ʿAbd Allāh (1990). 'The Holy Haram of Makkah and the Boundary Marks Surrounding It', unpublished PhD dissertation. Lucknow: Lucknow University. Available (with revised pagination) at <http://tinyurl.com/y3qk9t6k> (last accessed 14 April 2019).

Ibn al-Faqīh al-Hamadhānī, Aḥmad b. Muḥammad (1885). *Mukhtaṣar Kitāb al-Buldān*, edited by Michael Jan de Goeje. Leiden: Brill.

Ibn Ḥajar al-ʿAsqalānī, Aḥmad b. ʿAlī (1998). *Al-Maṭālib al-ʿāliya bi-zawāʾid al-masānīd al-thamāniya*, edited by ʿAbd Allāh b.ʿAbd al-Muḥsin b. Aḥmad al-Tuwayjirī, 19 vols. Riyad: Dār al-ʿĀṣima.

—— (2001). *Fatḥ al-bārī fī sharḥ Ṣaḥīḥ al-Bukhārī*, edited by ʿAbd al-ʿAzīz b. ʿAbd Allāh b. Bāz and Muḥammad Fuʾād ʿAbd al-Bāqī, 15 vols. Cairo: Dār Miṣr li-l-Ṭibāʿa.

Ibn Ḥanbal, Aḥmad (1995). *Musnad al-Imām Ibn Ḥanbal*, edited by Shuʿayb al-Arnāʾūṭ and ʿĀdil al-Murshid, 50 vols. Beirut: Muʾassasat al-Risāla.

Ibn Hāniʾ al-Andalusī, Muḥammad (1933). *Tabyīn al-maʿānī fī sharḥ dīwān Ibn Hāniʾ*, edited by Zāhid ʿAlī. Cairo: Maṭbaʿat al-Maʿārif wa Maktabatiha bi-Miṣr.

Ibn Hishām, Muḥammad ʿAbd al-Malik (1955). *The Life of Muhammad: A Translation of Isḥāq's Sīrat Rasūl Allāh*, translated by A. Guillaume. London: Oxford University Press.

—— (1998). *Al-Sīra al-nabawiyya*, edited by Saʿīd Muḥammad al-Laḥḥām, 4 vols. Beirut: Dār al-Fikr.

Ibn ʿIdhārī al-Marrākushī (1901). *Histoire de l'Afrique et de l'Espagne, intitulée* Al-Bayano'l-Mogrib, edited by G. S. Colin and Évariste Lévi-Provençal, 2 vols. Algiers: Imprimerie Orientale P. Fontana et cie.

—— (1948). *Al-Bayān al-mughrib fī akhbār al-Andalus wa al-Maghrib*, edited by G. S. Colin and Évariste Lévi-Provençal, 2 vols. Leiden: E. J. Brill.

Ibn Isḥāq, Muḥammad (1976). *Sīrat Ibn Isḥāq [riwāyat Yūnus b. Bukayr], al-musammāh bi-Kitāb al-Mubtadaʾ wa al-mabʿath wa al-maghāzī*, edited by Muḥammad Ḥamīd Allāh. Rabat: Maʿhad al-Dirāsāt wa al-Abḥāth li-l-Taʿrīb.

Ibn Jubayr (1907). *Riḥlat Ibn Jubayr*, edited by William Wright and Michael Jan de Goeje. Leiden: Brill.

—— (1952). *The Travels of Ibn Jubayr*, translated by Roland Broadhurst. Jonathan Cape: London.

Ibn al-Kalbī, Hishām b. Muḥammad (1924). *Kitāb al-Aṣnām*, edited by Aḥmad Zakī. Cairo: Maṭbaʿat Dār al-Kutub al-Miṣriyya.

—— (1952). *The Book of Idols: Being a Translation from the Arabic of the* Kitāb al-Aṣnām *by Hishām Ibn-al-Kalbī*, translated by Nabih Amin Faris. Princeton: Princeton University Press.

Ibn Kathīr, Abū Fidāʾ Ismāʿīl (n.d.). *Al-Sīra al-nabawiyya*, edited by Aḥmad ʿAbd al-Shāfī, 2 vols. Beirut: Dar al-Kutub al-ʿIlmiyya.

—— (1998). *The Life of the Prophet Muḥammad: Al-Sīra al-Nabawiyya*, translated by Trevor Le Gassick, 4 vols. Reading: Garnet Publishing.

—— (2010). *Al-Bidāya wa al-nihāya*, edited by Muḥyī al-Dīn Dīb Mistū, 20 vols in 11. Damascus: Dār Ibn Kathīr.

Ibn Khallikān, Aḥmad b. Muḥammad (1843). *Ibn Khallikan's Biographical Dictionary*, translated by William Mac Guckin de Slane, 2 vols. Paris: Oriental Translation Fund of Great Britain and Ireland.

—— (1977). *Wafayāt al-aʿyān wa anbāʾ abnāʾ al-zamān*, edited by Iḥsān ʿAbbās, 8 vols. Beirut: Dār al-Ṣadir.

Ibn al-Khaṭīb, Lisān al-Dīn (1985). *Nufādat al-jirāb fī ʿulālat al-ightirāb: [al-juzʾ al-thānī]*, edited by Aḥmad Mukhtār al-ʿAbbādī. Casablanca: Dār al-Nashr al-Maghribiyya.

Ibn Khuzayma, Abū Bakr Muḥammad b. Isḥāq (1980). *Ṣaḥīḥ Ibn Khuzayma*, edited by Muṣṭafā al-Aʿẓamī, 4 vols. Beirut: al-Maktab al-Islāmī.

Ibn Mājid, Aḥmad Shihāb al-Dīn (1921). *Instructions nautiques et routiers arabes et portugais des XVe et XVIe siècles: reproduits, traduits et annotés*, edited by Gabriel Ferrand, 3 vols. Paris: Librarie Orientaliste Paul Geuthner.

Ibn Manẓūr, Muḥammad b. Mukarram (n.d.). *Lisān al-ʿarab*, 18 vols. Beirut: Iḥyāʾ al-Turāth al-ʿArabī.

Ibn Qutayba, ʿAbd Allāh b. Muslim (1995). *Taʾwīl mukhtalaf al-ḥadith*, edited by Muḥammad ʿAbd al-Raḥīm. Beirut: Dār al-Fikr.

Ibn Rāshid, Maʿmar (2014). *The Expeditions: An Early Biography of Muḥammad = Kitāb al-Maghāzī*, edited and translated by Sean Anthony. New York: New York University Press.

Ibn Rushd, Abū al-Walīd Muḥammad b. Aḥmad (1989). *Bidāyat al-mujtahid wa nihāyat al-muqtaṣid*, edited by Ṭaha ʿAbd al-Raʾūf Saʿd, 2 vols. Beirut: Dār al-Jīl.

—— (2000). *The Distinguished Jurist's Primer: Bidāyat al-Mujtahid wa Nihāyat al-Muqtaṣid*, translated by Imran Ahsan Khan Nyazee, 2 vols. Reading: Garnet Publishing.

Ibn Rusta, Aḥmad b. ʿUmar (1892). *Al-Mujallad al-sābiʿ min Kitāb al-Aʿlāq al-nafīsa*, edited by Michael Jan de Goeje. Leiden: E. J. Brill.

Ibn Sīrīn, Muḥammad (1990). *Muntakhab al-kalām fī tafsīr al-aḥlām*. Beirut: Dār al-Fikr al-Lubnānī.

Ibn Sulaymān, Abū al-Ḥasan Muqātil (2002). *Tafsīr Muqātil b. Sulaymān*, edited by ʿAbd Allāh Maḥmūd Shaḥāta, 5 vols. Beirut: Muʾassasat al-Taʾrīkh al-ʿArabī.

—— (2003). *Tafsīr Muqātil b. Sulaymān*, edited by Aḥmad Farīd, 3 vols. Beirut: Dār al-Kutub al-ʿIlmiyya.

Ibn Taymiyya, Aḥmad (1997). *Majmūʿat al-fatāwā li-shaykh al-Islām Taqī al-Dīn Aḥmad b. Taymiyya al-Ḥarrānī*, edited by ʿĀmir al-Jazzār and Anwār al-Bāz, 37 vols. Alexandria: Dār al-Wafāʾ.

Ibn al-Zubayr, Aḥmad b. al-Rashīd (1996). *Book of Gifts and Rarities = Kitāb al-Hadāyā wa al-tuḥaf: Selections Compiled in the Fifteenth century from an Eleventh-Century Manuscript on Gifts and Treasures,* translated by Ghāda al-Hijjāwī al-Qaddūmī. Cambridge, MA: Distributed for the Center for Middle Eastern Studies of Harvard University by Harvard University Press.

al-Iṣfahānī, Aḥmad b. ʿAbd Allāh Abū Nuʿaym (1932). *Ḥilyat al-awliyāʾ wa ṭabaqāt al-asfiyāʾ*, 10 vols in 5. Cairo: Maktabat al-Khānjī.

Iványi, Tamás (2016). 'On Circumambulation in Chellah and Elsewhere: on Popular Traditions, Legal Prohibitions', *The Arabist: Budapest Studies in Arabic* 37: 65–98.

Jahāngīr, Emperor of Hindustan, 1569–1627 (1909). *The Tūzuk-i-Jahāngīrī, or Memoirs of Jahāngīr*, edited by Henry Beveridge, translated by Alexander Rogers, 2 vols. London: Royal Asiatic Society.

al-Jāḥiẓ, ʿUthmān ʿAmr b. Baḥr (1938). *Al-Ḥayawān*, edited by ʿAbd al-Salām Muḥammad Hārūn, 7 vols. [Cairo]: Maktabat Muṣṭafā al-Bābī al-Ḥalabī.

Jairazbhoy, Rafique Ali (1962). 'The History of the Shrines at Mecca and Medina', *The Islamic Review* 50 (1–2): 19–34, <http://tinyurl.com/jqsns9m> (last accessed 16 April 2019).

—— (1986). 'The Architecture of the Holy Shrine in Makkah', in *Hajj in Focus*, edited by Zafarul-Islam Khan and Yaqub Zaki. London: The Open Press, pp. 151–69.

Jāmī, ʿAbd al-Raḥmān b. Aḥmad (1962). *Dīwān-i kāmil-i Jāmī*, edited by Hāshim Raḍī. Tehran: Intishārāti-i Pīrūz.

Jamil, Nadia (1999). 'Caliph and *Quṭb*: Poetry as a Source for Interpreting the Transformation of the Byzantine Cross on Steps on Umayyad Coinage', in *Bayt al-Maqdis: Jerusalem and Early Islam*, edited by Jeremy Johns. Oxford: Oxford University Press, pp. 11–57.

al-Janābī, Kāẓim (1967). *Takhṭīṭ madīnat al-Kūfa ʿan al-maṣādir al-taʾrīkhiyya wa al-athariyya*. Baghdad: [Dār al-Jumhūriyya].

al-Jarrāḥī, Ismāʿīl b. Muḥammad al-ʿAjlūnī (1932). *Kashf al-khafāʾ wa muzīl al-ilbās ʿammā ishtahara min al-aḥādīth ʿalā alsinat al-nās*, 2 vols. Cairo: Maktabat al-Qudsī.

al-Jazīrī, ʿAbd al-Raḥmān (2009). *Islamic Jurisprudence According to the Four Sunni Schools, Vol. 1: Modes of Islamic Worship*, translated by Nancy Roberts. Louisville: Fons Vitae.

al-Jaznāʾī, ʿAlī (1923). *Zahrat el-âs (La fleur du myrte): traitant de la fondation de la ville de Fès par Abou-l-Hasan ʿAli El-Djaznâi*, translated by Alfred Bel. Algiers: Jules Carbonel.

—— (1991). *Janā zahrat al-ās fī bināʾ madīnat Fās*, edited by ʿAbd al-Wahhāb b. Manṣūr. Rabat: Al-Maṭbaʿa al-Malakiyya.

al-Jīlānī, ʿAbd al-Qādir (1992). *The Secret of Secrets*, translated by Tosun Bayrak. Cambridge: Islamic Texts Society.

—— (2007). *Sirr al-asrār wa maẓhar al-anwār fīmā yaḥtāju ilayhi al-abrār*, edited by Aḥmad Farīd al-Mazīdī. Beirut: Dar al-Kutub al-ʿIlmiyya.

Johns, Jeremy (1999). 'The "House of the Prophet" and the Concept of the Mosque', in *Bayt al-Maqdis: Jerusalem and Early Islam*, edited by Jeremy Johns. Oxford: Oxford University Press, pp. 59–112.

—— (2015). 'Arabic Inscriptions in the Cappella Palatina: Performativity, Audience, Legibility and Illegibility', in *Viewing Inscriptions in the Late Antique and Medieval World*, edited by Antony Eastmond. Cambridge: Cambridge University Press, pp. 124–47.

Johnson, Mark (2001). 'Architecture and the Embodied Mind,' *OASE Journal for Architecture* 58: 75–96, <http://tinyurl.com/y6tsbmoy> (last accessed 30 June 2019).

—— (2013). 'Identity, Bodily Meaning, and Art', in *Art and Identity: Essays on the Aesthetic Creation of Mind*, edited by Tone Roald and Johannes Lang. Amsterdam: Rodopi, pp. 15–38.

Jomier, Jacques (1953). *Le maḥmal et la caravane égyptienne des pèlerins de La Mecque, XIIIe–XXe siècles*. Cairo: Institut Français d'Archéologie Orientale.

Jones, Lindsay (2000). *The Hermeneutics of Sacred Architecture: Experience, Interpretation, Comparison*, 2 vols. Cambridge, MA: Harvard University Center for the Study of World Religions.

Kahera, Akel Isma'il (2012). *Reading the Islamic City: Discursive Practices and Legal Judgment*. Lanham: Lexington Books.

Kahlaoui, Tarek (2018). *Creating the Mediterranean: Maps and the Islamic Imagination*. Leiden: Brill.

al-Kalabādhī, Abū Bakr Muḥammad b. Isḥāq (1934). *Kitāb al-Taʿarruf li-madhhab ahl al-taṣawwuf*, edited by Arthur John Arberry. Cairo: Maktabat al-Khānjī.

—— (1935). *The Doctrine of the Ṣūfis = Kitāb al-Taʿarruf li-madhhab ahl al-taṣawwuf*, translated by Arthur John Arberry. Cambridge: Cambridge University Press.

Kamada, Shigeru (1983). 'A Study of the Term *Sirr* (Secret) in Sufi *Laṭāʾif* Theories', *Orient: Report of the Society for Near Eastern Studies in Japan* 19: 7–28.

Kant, Immanuel (1992). *Theoretical Philosophy, 1755–1770*, edited and translated by David Walford with Ralf Meerbote. Cambridge: Cambridge University Press.

Kaplan, Robert (1999). *The Nothing That Is: A Natural History of Zero*. Oxford: Oxford University Press.

Kaplony, Andreas (2002). *The Ḥaram of Jerusalem: Temple, Friday Mosque, Area of Spiritual Power*. Stuttgart: Franz Steiner Verlag.

Karamustafa, Ahmet (2007). *Sufism: The Formative Period*. Edinburgh: Edinburgh University Press.

Kaʿtī, Maḥmūd (et al.) (2014). *Taʾrikh al-fattāsh*. Damascus: Resalah Publishers.

Katz, Marion (2002). *Body of Text: The Emergence of the Sunnī Law of Ritual Purity*. Albany: SUNY Press.

—— (2004). 'The Ḥajj and the Study of Islamic Ritual', *Studia Islamica* 98/99: 95–129.

—— (2005). 'The Study of Islamic Ritual and the Meaning of *Wuḍūʾ*', *Der Islam* 82 (1): 106–45.

Keane, Webb (2002). 'Sincerity, "modernity", and the Protestants', *Cultural Anthropology* 17 (1): 65–92.

—— (2007). *Christian Moderns: Freedom and Fetish in the Mission Encounter*. Berkeley: University of California Press.

Kemp, Martin (2006). *Seen|Unseen: Art, Science, and Intuition from Leonardo to the Hubble Telescope*. Oxford: Oxford University Press.

Kennedy, Hugh (2010). 'How to Found an Islamic City', in *Cities, Texts and Social Networks, 400–1500: Experiences and Perceptions of Medieval Urban Space*, edited by Caroline Goodson, Anne Lester and Carol Symes. Farnham: Ashgate, pp. 45–63.

—— (2012). 'Journey to Mecca: A History', in *Hajj: Journey to the Heart of Islam*, edited by Venetia Porter. London: The British Museum Press, pp. 68–135.

Kessler, Christel (1983). 'Mecca-Oriented Architecture Within an Urban Context: On a Largely Unexplored Building Practice of Mediaeval Cairo', in *Arab Architecture, Past and Present: An Exhibition Presented by the Arab–British Chamber of Commerce at the Royal Institute of British Architects, London, 24th January–17th February 1984*, edited by Anthony Hutt. Durham: Centre for Middle Eastern & Islamic Studies, University of Durham, pp. 13–20.

—— (1984). 'Mecca-Oriented Urban Architecture in Mamluk Cairo: The Madrasa-Mausoleum of Sultan Shaʿban II', in *In Quest of an Islamic Humanism: Arabic and Islamic Studies in Memory of Mohamed al-Nowaihi*, edited by A. H. Green. Cairo: The American University in Cairo Press, pp. 97–108.

Khāqānī Shirwānī, Afḍal al-Dīn Badīl b. ʿAlī (1955). *Mathnawī tuḥfat al-ʿIrāqīn*, edited by Yaḥyā Qarīb. Tehran: Chāpkhāna-yi Sipihr.

—— (1959). *Dīwān Khāqānī Shirwānī*, edited by Ḍiyāʾ al-Dīn Sajjādī. Tehran: Zawwār.

Khoury, Nuha (1996). 'The Meaning of the Great Mosque of Cordoba in the Tenth Century', *Muqarnas* 13: 80–98.

Kim, Hyung-Jun (2010). 'Praxis and Religious Authority in Islam: The Case of Ahmad Dahlan, Founder of Muhammadiyah', *Studi Islamika: Indonesian Journal for Islamic Studies* 17 (1): 69–92.

Kimber, Richard (2001). 'Qibla', in *Encyclopaedia of the Qur'ān*, edited by Jane Dammen McAuliffe, 6 vols. Leiden: Brill, vol. 4, pp. 325–8.

King, David (1954a). 'Makka (4): As the Centre of the World', in *Encyclopaedia of Islam, Second Edition*, edited by P. Bearman, Th. Bianquis, C. E. Bosworth, E. van Donzel and W. P. Heinrichs, 12 vols. Leiden: Brill, vol. 6, pp. 180–7.

—— (1954b). 'Al-Maṭlaʿ', in *Encyclopaedia of Islam, Second Edition*, edited by P. Bearman, Th. Bianquis, C. E. Bosworth, E. van Donzel and W. P. Heinrichs, 12 vols. Leiden: Brill, vol. 6, pp. 839–40.

—— (1982). 'Faces of the Kaaba: It's a Primitive Observatory, Weather Vane, and Pointer to God', *The Sciences (The New York Academy of Sciences)* 22 (5): 16–20.

—— (1983). 'Al-Bazdawī on the *Qibla* in Early Islamic Transoxania', *Journal for the History of Arab Science* 7 (1–2): 3–38.

—— (1984a). 'Architecture and Astronomy: The Ventilators of Medieval Cairo and their Secrets', *Journal of the American Oriental Society* 104 (1): 97–133.

—— (1984b). 'The Astronomy of the Mamluks: A Brief Overview', *Muqarnas* 2: 73–84.

—— (1985). 'The Sacred Direction in Islam: A Study of the Interaction of Religion and Science in the Middle Ages', *Interdisciplinary Science Reviews* 10 (4): 315–28.

—— (1995). 'The Orientation of Medieval Islamic Religious Architecture and Cities', *Journal for the History of Astronomy* 26: 253–74.

—— (1999). *World-Maps for Finding the Direction and Distance to Mecca: Innovation and Tradition in Islamic Science*. Leiden: Brill.

—— (2005). 'The Sacred Geography of Islam', in *Mathematics and the Divine: A Historical Study*, edited by Teun Koetsier and Luc Bergmans. Amsterdam: Elsevier Science, pp. 161–78.

—— (2018). 'The Enigmatic Orientation of the Great Mosque of Córdoba', *Suhayl: International Journal for the History of the Exact and Natural Sciences in Islamic Civilisation* 16–17: 33–111.

—— (2019). 'Finding the *Qibla* by the Sun and Stars: A Survey of the Sources of Islamic Sacred Geography'. Published online only, at <http://tinyurl.com/yyydcysh> (last accessed 10 May 2019).

King, David and Gerald Hawkins (1982). 'On the Astronomical Orientation of the Kaaba', *Journal for the History of Astronomy* 13: 102–9.

King, Geoffrey (1991). 'Creswell's Appreciation of Arabian Architecture', *Muqarnas* 8: 94–102.

—— (2002a). 'The Prophet Muḥammad and the Breaking of the *Jāhiliyyah* Idols', in *Studies on Arabia in Honour of G. Rex Smith*, edited by John Healey and Venetia Porter. Oxford: Oxford University Press on behalf of the University of Manchester, pp. 91–122.

—— (2002b). 'The Sculptures of the Pre-Islamic Haram at Makka', in *Cairo to Kabul: Afghan Studies Presented to Ralph Pinder-Wilson*, edited by Warwick Ball and Leonard Harrow. London: Milisende, pp. 144–50.

—— (2004). 'The Paintings of the Pre-Islamic Kaʿba', *Muqarnas* 21: 219–29.
King, Geoffrey and Ronald Lewcock (1978). 'Arabia', in *Architecture of the Islamic World: Its History and Social Meaning*, edited by George Michell. London: Thames & Hudson, pp. 209–11.
Kinra, Rajeev (2015). *Writing Self, Writing Empire: Chandar Bhan Brahman and the Cultural World of the Indo-Persian State Secretary*. Oakland, CA: University of California Press.
Kister, Meir Jacob (1969). '"You shall only set out for three mosques": A Study of an Early Tradition', *Le Muséon* 82: 173–96.
—— (1971). 'Maqām Ibrāhīm: A Stone with an Inscription', *Le Muséon* 84: 477–91.
—— (1981). 'A Comment on the Antiquity of Traditions Praising Jerusalem', in *The Jerusalem Cathedra: Studies in the History, Archaeology, Geography and Ethnography of the Land of Israel*, edited by Lee Levine, 3 vols. Jerusalem: Yad Izhak Ben-Zvi Institute for the Study of Eretz Israel, vol. 1, pp. 185–6.
—— (1986). 'Mecca and the Tribes of Arabia: Some Notes on their Relations', in *Studies in Islamic History and Civilization in Honour of Professor David Ayalon*, edited by Moshe Sharon. Leiden: Brill, pp. 33–57.
—— (1990). 'On "Concessions" and Conduct: A Study in Early *Ḥadīth*', in *Society and Religion from Jāhiliyya to Islam*, edited by Meir Jacob Kister. Aldershot: Variorum, XIII: pp. 1–37.
—— (1996). 'Sanctity Joint and Divided: On Holy Places in the Islamic Tradition', *Jerusalem Studies in Arabic and Islam* 20: 18–65.
Kleiner, Fred (2007). *Gardner's Art Through the Ages: A Concise Western History*, 4th ed. Boston: Cengage.
Knight, Michael Muhammad (2009). *Journey to the End of Islam*. New York: Soft Skull Press.
Knysh, Alexander (1993). '"Orthodoxy" and "Heresy" in Medieval Islam: An Essay in Reassessment', *Muslim World* 83 (1): 48–67.
—— (1999). *Ibn ʿArabī in the Later Islamic Tradition: The Making of a Polemical Image in Medieval Islam*. Albany: SUNY Press.
—— (2017). *Sufism: A New History of Islamic Mysticism*. Princeton: Princeton University Press.
Koch, Ebba (1993). 'Diwan-i ʿAmm and Chihil Sutun: The Audience Halls of Shah Jahan', *Muqarnas* 11: 143–65.
—— (1997). 'Hierarchical Principles of Shah-Jahani Painting', in *King of the World: The Padshahnama: An Imperial Mughal Manuscript from the Royal Library, Windsor Castle*, edited by Milo Cleveland Beach, Ebba Koch and Wheeler Thackston. London: Azimuth Editions and Sackler Gallery, pp. 130–62.
—— (2010). 'The Mughal Emperor as Solomon, Majnun, and Orpheus, or the Album as a Think Tank for Allegory', *Muqarnas* 27: 277–311.
Koltun-Fromm, Naomi (2013). 'Rock Over Water: Pre-Historic Rocks and Primordial Waters from Creation to Salvation in Jerusalem', in *Jewish and Christian Cosmogony in Late Antiquity*, edited by Lance Jenoot and Sarit Kattan Gribetx. Tübingen: Mohr Seibeck, pp. 239–54.
—— (2017). 'Jerusalem Sacred Stones from Creation to Eschaton', *Journal of Late Antiquity* 10 (2): 405–31.

Kubiak, Wladyslaw (1987). *Al-Fustat: Its Foundation and Early Urban Development*. Cairo: The American University in Cairo Press.

Kugle, Scott (2007). *Sufis and Saints' Bodies: Mysticism, Corporeality and Sacred Power in Islam*. Chapel Hill: University of North Carolina Press.

Kunitzsch, Paul (2003). 'The Transmission of Hindu-Arabic Numerals Reconsidered', in *The Enterprise of Science in Islam: New Perspectives*, edited by Jan Hogendijk and Abdelhamid Sabra. Cambridge, MA: The MIT Press, pp. 3–21.

Kupfer, Marcia (2006). 'Mappaemundi: Image, Artefact, Social Practice', in *The Hereford World Map: Medieval World Maps and their Context*, edited by P. D. A. Harvey. London: The British Library, pp. 253–67.

al-Kurdī al-Makkī, Muḥammad Ṭāhir (2000). *Al-Taʾrīkh al-qawīm li-Makka wa Bayt Allāh al-karīm*, 6 vols in 3. Beirut: Dār Khiḍr.

Lakoff, George and Mark Johnson (1980). *Metaphors We Live By*. Chicago: University of Chicago Press.

—— (1999). *Philosophy in the Flesh: The Embodied Mind and its Challenge to Western Thought*. New York: Basic Books.

Lammens, Henri (1920). 'Le culte des bétyles et les processions religieuses chez les Arabes préislamites', *Bulletin d'Institut Français d'Archéologie Orientale* 17: 39–101.

—— (1924). 'La Mecque à la veille de l'Hégire', *Mélanges de l'Université Saint-Joseph* 9 (3): 1–439.

Landsberger, Franz (1957). 'The Sacred Direction in Synagogue and Church', *Hebrew Union College Annual* 28: 181–203.

Lange, Christian (2015a). *Paradise and Hell in Islamic Traditions*. Cambridge: Cambridge University Press.

—— (2015b). 'Revisiting Hell's Angels in the Quran', in *Locating Hell in Islamic Traditions*, edited by Christian Lange. Leiden: Brill, pp. 74–99.

Lārī, Muḥyī al-Dīn (1987). *Futūḥ al-Ḥaramayn*, edited by ʿAlī Muḥaddith. Tehran: Intishārāt-i Iṭṭilāʿāt.

Latif, Syad Muhammad (1892). *Lahore: Its History, Architectural Remains and Antiquities: With an Account of its Modern Institutions, Inhabitants, Their Trade, Customs, &c.* Lahore: New Imperial Press.

Layton, Robert (1991a). *The Anthropology of Art*, 2nd ed. Cambridge: Cambridge University Press.

—— (1991b). 'Art and Agency: A Reassessment', *Journal of the Royal Anthropological Institute* 9 (3): 447–63.

Lazarus-Yafeh, Hava (1999). 'Jerusalem and Mecca', in *Jerusalem: Its Sanctity and Centrality to Judaism, Christianity, and Islam*, edited by Lee Levine. New York: Continuum, pp. 287–99.

Le Goff, Jacques (1989). 'Head or Heart? The Political Use of Body Metaphors in the Middle Ages', in *Fragments for a History of the Human Body: Part Three*, edited by Michel Feher, Ramona Naddaff and Nadia Tazi. New York: Zone, pp. 13–26.

Le Strange, Guy (1900). *Baghdad during the Abbasid Caliphate from Contemporary Arabic and Persian Sources*. Oxford: Clarendon Press.

Lebrecht, Fürchtegott Schemaja (1840). 'An Essay on the State of the Khalifate of Bagdad [*sic*] during the Latter Half of the Twelfth Century: In illustration of the episode in R. Benjamin's Itinerary pp. 54–59,' in *The Itinerary of Rabbi*

Benjamin of Tudela, Vol. 2: Notes and Essays, edited and translated by A. Asher. London: A. Asher & Co, pp. 318–92.

Lecerf, J. (1954). 'Baṭn', in *Encyclopaedia of Islam, Second Edition*, edited by P. Bearman, Th. Bianquis, C. E. Bosworth, E. van Donzel and W. P. Heinrichs, 12 vols. Leiden: Brill, vol. 1, p. 1102.

Lefebvre, Henri (1991). *The Production of Space*, translated by Donald Nicholson-Smith. Oxford: Blackwell.

Lévi-Provençal, Évariste (1928). *Documents inédits d'histoire almohade: fragments manuscrits du 'legajo' 1919 du fonds arabe de l'Escurial*. Paris: Paul Geuthner.

Levinas, Emmanuel (1987). *Collected Philosophical Papers of Emmanuel Levinas*, translated by Alphonso Lingis. Dordrecht: Martinus Nijhoff Publishers.

Lewis, Franklin (2008). *Rumi: Past and Present, East and West: The Life, Teachings, and Poetry of Jalāl al-Din Rumi*, rev. ed. Oxford: Oneworld Publications.

Lewis, James (1982). 'Some Aspects of Sacred Space and Time in Islam', *Studies in Islam* 19 (3): 167–78.

Livne-Kafri, Ofer (2006). 'Jerusalem in Early Islam: The Eschatological Aspect', *Arabica* 53 (3): 382–403.

—— (2008). 'Jerusalem: The Navel of the Earth in Muslim Tradition', *Der Islam* 84 (1): 46–72.

—— (2013). 'Women and Feminine Images in Muslim Traditions of the End', *Arabica* 60 (3–4): 306–31.

Long, Charles (1986). *Significations: Signs, Symbols, and Images in the Interpretation of Religion*. Philadelphia: Fortress Press.

Long, David (1979). *The Hajj Today: A Survey of the Contemporary Makkah Pilgrimage*. Albany: SUNY Press.

Lowry, Glenn (1987). 'Urban Structures and Functions', in *Fatehpur-Sikri: Selected Papers from the International Symposium on Fatehpur-Sikri held on October 17–19, 1985, at Harvard University*, edited by Glenn Lowry and Michael Brand. Bombay: Marg Publications, pp. 25–48.

Lundquist, John (1983). 'What is a Temple? A Preliminary Typology', in *The Quest for the Kingdom of God: Studies in Honor of George E. Mendenhall*, edited by H. B. Huffman, F. A. Spina and A. R. W. Green. Winona Lake, IN: Eisenbrauns, pp. 205–19.

Lynch, Kevin (1960). *The Image of the City*. Cambridge, MA: The MIT Press.

Macnaghten, William (ed.) (1839). *The Alif Laila, or Book of the Thousand Nights and One Night, Commonly Known as 'The Arabian Nights' Entertainments'; Now, for the First Time, Published Complete in the Original Arabic, from an Egyptian Manuscript Brought to India by the Late Major Turner*, 4 vols. Calcutta: W. Thacker and Co.

Madelung, Wilferd (1986). 'Apocalyptic Prophecies in Ḥimṣ in the Umayyad Age', *Journal of Semitic Studies* 31 (2): 141–85.

al-Majlisī, Muḥammad Bāqir b. Muḥammad (2008). *Biḥār al-anwār al-jāmiʿa li-durar akhbār al-aʾimma al-aṭhār*, edited by [Lajna min al-ʿulamāʾ], 110 vols in 66. Beirut: Muʾassasat al-Aʿlamī li-l-Maṭbūʿāt.

Mallgrave, Harry Francis (1989). 'Introduction', in Gottfried Semper, *The Four Elements of Architecture and Other Writings*, translated by Harry Francis Mallgrave and Wolfgang Herrman. Cambridge: Cambridge University Press, pp. 1–44.

al-Maqrīzī, Taqī al-Dīn Aḥmad b. ʿAlī (1853). *Kitāb al-Mawāʿiẓ wa al-iʿtibār bi-dhikr al-khiṭaṭ wa al-āthār*, 2 vols. Cairo: Dār al-Ṭibāʿa al-Miṣriyya.

—— (2016). *Caliphate and Kingship in a Fifteenth-Century Literary History of Muslim Leadership and Pilgrimage = Al-Dhahab al-masbūk fī dhikr man ḥajja min al-khulafāʾ wa al-mulūk*, edited and translated by Jo van Steenbergen. Leiden: Brill.

Markiewicz, Christopher (2019). *The Crisis of Kingship in Late Medieval Islam: Persian Emigres and the Making of Ottoman Sovereignty*. Cambridge: Cambridge University Press.

Marsham, Andrew (2009). *Rituals of Islamic Monarchy: Accession and Succession in the First Muslim Empire*. Edinburgh: Edinburgh University Press.

Manucci, Niccolao (1907). *Storia do Mogor, or Mogul India 1653–1708*, translated by William Irvine, 4 vols. London: John Murray.

Mason, Herbert (1972). *Two Statesmen of Medieval Islam: Vizir Ibn Hubayra (499–560 AH/1105–1165 AD) and Caliph an-Nāṣir li Dīn Allāh (553–622 AH/1158–1225 AD)*. The Hague: Mouton.

Massignon, Louis (1922). *La passion d'al-Hosayn-Ibn-Mansour al-Hallaj, martyr mystique de l'Islam, exécuté à Bagdad le 26 mars 922: étude d'histoire religieuse*, 2 vols. Paris: Paul Geuthner.

—— (1975). *La Passion de Husayn Ibn Mansûr Hallâj: martyr mystique de l'islam, exécuté à Bagdad le 26 mars 922: étude d'histoire religieuse, nouv. ed.*, 4 vols. Paris: Éditions Gallimard.

Massignon, Louis and Louis Gardet (1954). 'Al-Ḥallāj', in *Encyclopaedia of Islam, Second Edition*, edited by P. Bearman, Th. Bianquis, C. E. Bosworth, E. van Donzel and W. P. Heinrichs, 12 vols. Leiden: Brill, vol. 3, pp. 99–104.

Masud, Muhammad Khalid (2006). 'Sufi Understanding of Hajj Rituals', in *El sufismo y las normas del Islam: trabajos del IV Congreso Internacional de Estudios Jurídicos Islámicos: derecho y sufismo*, edited and translated by Alfonso Carmona. Murcia: Editora Regional de Murcia, pp. 271–90.

al-Masʿūdī, ʿAlī b. al-Ḥusayn (1861). *Maçoudi: les prairies d'or*, translated by C. Barbier de Meynard and Pavet de Courteille, 9 vols. Paris: Imprimerie Impériale.

Mater, Ahmed (2016). *Desert of Pharan: Unofficial Histories Behind the Mass Expansion of Mecca*, edited by Catherine David. Zurich: Lars Müller Publishers.

Maury, Charlotte (2013). 'Depictions of the Haramayn on Ottoman Tiles: Content and Context', in *The Hajj: Collected Essays*, edited by Venetia Porter and Liana Saif. London: The British Museum, pp. 143–59.

Mavroudi, Maria (2002). *A Byzantine Book on Dream Interpretation: The Oneirocriticon of Achmet and its Arabic Sources*. Leiden: Brill.

McAuliffe, Jane Dammen (2001). 'Heart', in *Encyclopaedia of the Qurʾān*, edited by Jane Dammen McAuliffe, 6 vols. Leiden: Brill, vol. 2, pp. 406–10.

McGregor, Richard (2009). 'The Problem of Sufism', *Mamluk Studies Review* 13 (2): 69–83.

—— (2010). 'Dressing the Kaʿba from Cairo: The Aesthetics of Pilgrimage to Mecca', in *Religion and Material Culture: The Matter of Belief*, edited by David Morgan. London: Routedge, pp. 247–61.

McMillan, M. E. (2011). *The Meaning of Mecca: The Politics of Pilgrimage in Early Islam*. London: Saqi Books.

Meier, Fritz (1955). 'The Mystery of the Kaʿba: Symbol and Reality in Islamic Mysticism', in *The Mysteries: Papers from the Eranos Yearbooks*, translated by Ralph Manheim. London: Routledge & Kegan Paul, pp. 149–68.

Meinecke, Michael (1996). 'Ar-Raqqa am Euphrat: Imperiale und religiöse Strukturen der islamischen Stadt', *Mitteilungen der Deutschen Orient-Gesellschaft zu Berlin* 128: 157–72.

Mekeel-Matteson, Carolanne (1999). 'The Meaning of the Dome of the Rock', *The Islamic Quarterly* 43 (3): 149–85.

Meri, Josef (2002). *The Cult of Saints among Muslims and Jews in Medieval Syria*. Oxford: Oxford University Press.

Metcalfe, Alex (2012). 'Orientation in Three Spheres: Medieval Mediterranean Boundary Clauses in Latin, Greek and Arabic', *Transactions of the Royal Historical Society* 22: 37–55.

Michell, George (ed.) (1978). *Architecture of the Islamic World: Its History and Social Meaning*. London: Thames & Hudson.

Mignolo, Walter and Rolando Vazquez (2013). 'Decolonial AestheSis: Colonial Wounds/Decolonial Healings', *Social Text Online*, <http://tinyurl.com/y58apejx> (last accessed 10 January 2019).

Mignolo, Walter and Catherine Walsh (2018). *On Decoloniality: Concepts, Analytics, Praxis*. Durham, NC: Duke University Press.

Mikkelson, Jane (2019). 'The Way of Tradition and the Path of Innovation: Aurangzeb and Dara Shukuh's Struggle for the Mughal Throne', in *The Empires of the Near East and India: Source Studies of the Safavid, Ottoman, and Mughal Literate Communities*, edited by Hani Khafipour. New York: Columbia University Press, pp. 240–60.

Milstein, Rachel (1999). 'The Evolution of a Visual Motif: The Temple and the Kaʿba', *Israel Oriental Studies* 19: 23–48.

—— (2001). '*Kitāb Shawq-Nāma*: An Illustrated Tour of Holy Arabia', *Jerusalem Studies in Arabic and Islam* 25: 275–345.

—— (2006). '*Futuh-i Haramayn*: Sixteenth-century Illustrations of the Hajj Route', in *Mamluk and Ottoman Studies in Honour of Michael Winter*, edited by David Wasserstein and Ami Ayalon. London: Routledge, pp. 167–94.

—— (2018). 'Picturing the Archetypal King: Iskandar in Islamic Painting', in *Romance and Reason: Islamic Transformations of the Classical Past*, edited by Roberta Casagrande-Kim, Samuel Thrope and Raquel Ukeles. Princeton: Princeton University Press, pp. 48–63.

Milwright, Marcus (2016). *The Dome of the Rock and its Umayyad Inscriptions*. Edinburgh: Edinburgh University Press.

Miquel, André (1954). 'Istiwāʾ', in *Encyclopaedia of Islam, Second Edition*, edited by P. Bearman, Th. Bianquis, C. E. Bosworth, E. van Donzel and W. P. Heinrichs, 12 vols. Leiden: Brill, vol. 4, p. 273.

Mir-Kasimov, Orkhan (2014). '*Ummīs* versus Imāms in the Ḥurūfī Prophetology: An Attempt at a Sunnī/Shīʿī Synthesis?', in *Unity in Diversity: Mysticism, Messianism and the Construction of Religious Authority in Islam*, edited by Orkhan Mir-Kasimov. Leiden: Brill, pp. 221–46.

Mīrkhwānd, Muḥammad b. Khāwandshāh (1892). *The Rauzat-us-safa, or, Garden of Purity: Containing the Histories of Prophets, Kings, and Khalifs by Muhammad bin Khâvendshâh bin Mahmûd, Commonly Called Mirkhond*, edited by Forster Fitzgerald Arbuthnot, translated by Edward Rehatsek, 5 vols. London: Royal Asiatic Society of Great Britain and Ireland.

—— (1959). *Tārīkh-i rawḍat al-ṣafā*, 10 vols. [Tehran]: Markazī-i Khayyām Pīrūz.

Mitchell, Timothy (1988). *Colonising Egypt*. Cambridge: Cambridge University Press.

Moin, Ahmed Azfar (2012). *The Millennial Sovereign: Sacred Kingship and Sainthood in Islam*. New York: Columbia University Press.

—— (2014). 'Messianism, Heresy and Historical Narrative in Mughal India', in *Unity in Diversity: Mysticism, Messianism and the Construction of Religious Authority in Islam*, edited by Orkhan Mir-Kasimov. Leiden: Brill, pp. 393–413.

Montgomery, James (2001). 'Ibn Rusta's Lack of "Eloquence", the Rūs, and Samanid Cosmography', *Edebiyat* 12: 73–93.

Mortel, Richard (1988). 'The *Kiswa*: Its Origins and Development from Pre-Islamic Times until the End of the Mamluk Period', *Ages (al-ʿUṣūr): A Semi-Annual Journal of Historical, Archaeological and Civilizational Studies* (Riyadh) 3 (2): 30–46.

Morton, A. H. (1974). 'The Ardabīl Shrine in the Reign of Shāh Ṭahmāsp I', *Iran* 12: 31–64.

Mourad, Suleiman Ali (2008). 'The Symbolism of Jerusalem in Early Islam', in *Jerusalem: Idea and Reality*, edited by Suleiman Ali Mourad and Tamar Mayer. London: Routledge, pp. 86–102.

Muʾayyad fī al-Dīn Hibat Allāh b. Mūsā (1949). *Dīwān al-Muʾayyad fī al-Din dāʿī al-duʿāt*, edited by Muḥammad Kāmil Ḥusayn. Cairo: Dār al-Kitāb al-Miṣrī.

—— (2011). *Mount of Knowledge, Sword of Eloquence: Collected Poems of an Ismaili Muslim Scholar from Fatimid Egypt: A Translation from the Original Arabic of al-Muʾayyad al-Shīrāzī's Dīwān*, translated by Mohamed Adra. London: I. B. Tauris.

al-Mufīd, Muḥammad b. Muḥammad (1995). *Al-Irshād fī maʿrifat ḥujaj Allāh ʿalā al-ʿibād*, 2 vols. Beirut: Muʾassasat Āl al-Bayt li-Iḥyāʾ al-Turāth.

al-Mūjān (Al Mojan), Muḥammad b. Ḥusayn (2010). *The Honorable Kabah: Architecture and Kiswah*, translated by Ghassan Rimlawi. Mecca: Al-Kawn Center.

Mulder, Stephennie (2014). 'Seeing the Light: Enacting the Divine at Three Medieval Syrian Shrines', in *Envisioning Islamic Art and Architecture: Essays in Honor of Renata Holod*, edited by David Roxburgh. Leiden: Brill, pp. 89–109.

Mumtaz, Kamil Khan (2011). 'Reading Masjid Wazir Khan', *Islamic Arts and Architecture*, 12 October, <http://tinyurl.com/6sjyc2w> (last accessed 20 June 2018).

Munshī, Iskandar Beg (1930). *History of Shah ʿAbbas the Great = Tārīkh-i ʿālam-ārā-yi ʿAbbāsī*, translated by Roger Savory. Boulder, CO: Westview Press.

Munt, Harry (2013). 'The Official Announcement of an Umayyad Caliph's Successful Pilgrimage to Mecca', in *The Hajj: Collected Essays*, edited by Venetia Porter and Liana Saif. London: The British Museum Press, pp. 15–20.

al-Muqaddasī, Muḥammad b. Aḥmad (1906). *Kitāb Aḥsan al-taqāsīm fī maʿrifat al-aqālīm*, edited by Michael Jan de Goeje. Leiden: Brill.

—— (1994). *The Best Divisions for Knowledge of the Regions: A Translation of Aḥsan al-Taqāsīm fī Maʿrifat al-Aqālīm*, translated by Basil Collins. Reading: Garnet.

Murata, Kazuyo (2017). *Beauty in Sufism: The Teachings of Ruzbihan Baqli*. Albany: SUNY Press.

Murata, Sachiko (1992). *The Tao of Islam: A Sourcebook on Gender Relationships in Islamic Thought*. Albany: SUNY Press.

Muslim, Abū al-Ḥusayn b. al-Ḥajjāj (1994). *Ṣaḥīḥ Muslim bi-sharḥ al-Nawāwī*, edited by ʿIṣṣām al-Ṣabābṭī, 11 vols. Cairo: Dār al-Ḥadīth.

Mustafa, Muhammad Ali (1963). 'Preliminary Report on the Excavations in Kufa during the Third Season', *Sumer* 19: 36–65.

Mustamlī Bukhārī, Abū Ibrāhīm Ismāʿīl b. Muḥammad (1984). *Sharḥ-i al-Taʿarruf li-madhhab al-taṣawwuf*, edited by Muḥammad Rawshan, 4 vols. Tehran: Intishārāt-i Asāṭīr.

Mustawfī Qazwīnī, Ḥamd Allāh (1915). *The Geographical Part of the Nuzhat-al-Qulub: Composed by Ḥamd-Allāh Mustawfī of Qazwīn in 740 (1340)*, edited and translated by Guy Le Strange, 2 vols. Leiden: Brill.

al-Mutanabbī, Abū al-Ṭayyib Aḥmad b. al-Ḥusayn (2005). *Dīwān al-Mutanabbī*. Beirut: Dār Ṣādir.

Nagy, Péter (2014). 'Sultans' Paradise: The Royal Necropolis of Shāla, Rabat', *Al-Masaq: Journal of the Medieval Mediterranean* 26 (2): 132–46.

—— (2019). 'The Kaʿba, Paradise, and Ibn al-Khaṭīb in Shālla (Rabat): The "Work" of the Fourteenth-Century Marīnid Funerary Complex', *Miscelánea de Estudios Árabes y Hebreos (Sección Árabe-Islam)* 68: 257–87.

al-Nahrawalī, Quṭb al-Dīn (1857). *Die Chroniken der Stadt Mekka, Vol. 3: Quṭb al-Dīn's Geschichte der Stadt Mecca und ihres Tempels*, edited by Ferdinand Wüstenfeld. Leipzig: F. A. Brockhaus.

Nāṣir-i Khusraw (1881). *Sefer nameh: relation du voyage de Nassiri Khosrau en Syrie, en Palestine, en Égypte, en Arabie, et Perse, pendant les années de l'Hégire 437–444 (1035–1042)*, translated by Charles Schefer. Paris: Ernest Leroux.

—— (1986). *Nāṣer-e Khosraw's Book of Travels = Safarnāma*, translated by Wheeler Thackston. Albany: Bibliotheca Persica.

Nasr, Seyyed Hossein (1996). 'To Live in a World with No Center – and Many', *Cross Currents: The Journal of the Association for Religion and Intellectual Life* 46 (3): 318–25.

—— (2002). 'The Heart of the Faithful is the Throne of the All-Merciful', in *Paths to the Heart: Sufism and the Christian East*, edited by James Cutsinger. Bloomington: World Wisdom, pp. 32–45.

Nassar, Nahla (2013). '*Dar al-Kiswa al-Sharifa*: Administration and Production', in *The Hajj: Collected Essays*, edited by Venetia Porter and Liana Saif. London: The British Museum Press, pp. 175–83.

al-Nawawī al-Shāfiʿī, Muḥyī al-Dīn (1985). *Kitāb Matn al-īḍāḥ fī manāsik*. Beirut: Dār al-Kutub al-ʿIlmiyya.

Nazmi, Ahmad (2007). *The Muslim Geografical* [sic] *Image of the World in the Middle Ages: A Source Study*. Warsaw: Academic Publishing House Dialog.

Nead, Lynda (1992). *Female Nude: Art, Obscenity, and Sexuality*. Abingdon: Routledge.

Necĭpoğlu-Kafadar, Gülru (1985). 'The Süleymaniye Complex in Istanbul: An Interpretation', *Muqarnas* 3: 92–117.

Neçipoğlu, Gülru (1992). 'The Life of an Imperial Monument: Hagia Sophia after Byzantium', in *Hagia Sophia: From the Age of Justinian to the Present*, edited by Robert Mark and Ahmet Çakmak. Cambridge: Cambridge University Press, pp. 195–225.

—— (2005). *The Age of Sinan: Architectural Culture in the Ottoman Empire*. London: Reaktion Books.

Neis, Rachel (2012). '"Their Backs toward the Temple and Their Faces toward the East": The Temple and Toilet Practices in Rabbinic Palestine and Babylonia', *The Journal for the Study of Judaism* 43 (3): 328–68.

Neuwirth, Angelika (1993). 'Erste Qibla – Fernstes Masğid? Jerusalem im Horizont des historischen Muhammad', in *Zion: Ort der Begegnung: Festschrift für Laurentius Klein zur Vollendung des 65. Lebensjahres*, edited by Angelika Neuwirth, Ferdinand Hahn, Frank-Lothar Hossfeld and Hans Jorissen. Bodenheim: Beltz Athenäum, pp. 227–70.

—— (1996). 'The Spiritual Meaning of Jerusalem in Islam', in *City of the Great King: Jerusalem from David to the Present*, edited by Nitza Rosovsky. Cambridge, MA: Harvard University Press, pp. 95–102.

—— (1998). 'Face of God – Face of Man: The Significance of the Direction of Prayer in Islam', in *Self, Soul and Body in Religious Experience*, edited by Albert Baumgarten, Jan Assmann, Gedaliahu Stroumsa and Guy Stroumsa. Leiden: Brilll, pp. 305–10.

—— (2001a). 'Geography', in *Encyclopaedia of the Qur'ān*, edited by Jane Dammen McAuliffe, 6 vols. Leiden: Brill, vol. 2, pp. 293–313.

—— (2001b). 'Spatial Relations', in *Encyclopaedia of the Qur'ān*, edited by Jane Dammen McAuliffe, 6 vols. Leiden: Brill, vol. 5, pp. 104–8.

—— (2003). 'From the Sacred Mosque to the Remote Temple: Sūrat al-Isrā' Between Text and Commentary', in *With Reverence for the Word*, edited by Jane Dammen McAuliffe, Barry Walfish and Joseph Goering. New York: Oxford University Press, pp. 376–407.

Nevo, Yehuda and Judith Koren (1990). 'The Origins of the Muslim Descriptions of the Jāhilī Meccan Sanctuary', *Journal of Near Eastern Studies* 49 (1): 23–44.

Nicholson, Reynold Alleyne (1907). *A Literary History of the Arabs*. New York: Charles Scribner's Sons.

—— (1921). *Studies in Islamic Mysticism*. Cambridge: Cambridge University Press.

al-Niffarī, Muḥammad b. ʿAbd al-Jabbār (1935). *The Mawāqif and Mukhātabāt of Muḥammad Ibn ʿAbdi ʾl-Jabbār Al-Niffarī*, edited and translated by Arthur John Arberry. London: Luzac & Co.

Niẓāmī Ganjawī (1966). *The Story of Layla and Majnun*, translated by R. Gelpke. London: Bruno Cassirer.

Norberg-Schulz, Christian (1988). *Architecture: Meaning and Place: Selected Essays*. New York: Electa/Rizzoli.

Northedge, Alastair (1994). 'Archaeology and New Urban Settlement in Early Islamic Syria and Iraq', in *The Byzantine and Early Islamic Near East, Vol. 2: Land Use and Settlement Patterns*, edited by Geoffrey King and Averil Cameron. Princeton: The Darwin Press, pp. 231–65.

—— (2007). *The Historical Topography of Samarra: Samarra Studies I*, 2nd rev. ed. London: The British School of Archaeology in Iraq.
—— (2017). 'Early Islamic Urbanism', in *A Companion to Islamic Art and Architecture, Vol. 1: From the Prophet to the Mongols*, edited by Finbarr Barry Flood and Gülru Necipoğlu. Oxford: Blackwell, pp. 155–76.
Northedge, Alastair and Derek Kennet (2015). *Archaeological Atlas of Samarra: Samarra Studies II*, 3 vols. London: The British Institute for the Study of Iraq.
Nwyia, Paul (1991). *Exégèse coranique et langage mystique: nouvel essai sur le lexique technique des mystiques musulmans*, 2nd ed. Beirut: Dar el-Machreq.
Olsson, Joshua (2014). 'The World in Arab Eyes: A Reassessment of the Climes in Medieval Islamic Scholarship', *Bulletin of the School of Oriental and African Studies* 77 (3): 487–508.
O'Meara, Simon (2007). *Space and Muslim Urban Life: At the Limits of the Labyrinth of Fez*. Abingdon: Routledge.
—— (2012). 'The Space Between Here and There: The Prophet's Night Journey as an Allegory of Islamic Ritual Prayer', *Middle Eastern Literatures* 15 (3): 1–8.
—— (2018). 'The Kaaba of New York', in *Taking Offense: Religion, Art, and Visual Culture in Plural Configurations*, edited by Birgit Meyer, Christiane Kruse and Anne-Marie Korte. Paderborn: Wilhelm Fink, pp. 140–60.
—— (2019). 'Haptic Vision: Making Surface Sense of Islamic Material Culture', in *The Routledge Handbook of Sensory Archaeology*, edited by Robin Skeates and Jo Day. Leiden: Brill, pp. 906–33.
—— (2020a). 'Out of Sight in Morocco, or How to See the Jinn in the Modern-day Museum', in *Festschrift in Honor of Dale F. Eickelman*, edited by Allen Fromherz and Nadav Samin. Leiden: Brill (forthcoming).
—— (2020b). 'Mecca and other Cosmological Centres in the Sufi Universe', in *Handbook of Sufi Studies, Vol. 2: Sufi Cosmology*, edited by Christian Lange and Alexander Knysh. Leiden: Brill (forthcoming).
Panofsky, Erwin (1970). 'Iconography and Iconology: An Introduction to the Study of Renaissance Art', in Erwin Panofsky, *Meaning in the Visual Arts*. Harmondsworth: Penguin Books, pp. 51–81.
—— (1997). *Perspective as Symbolic Form*, translated by Christopher Wood. New York: Zone Books.
Papan-Matin, Firoozeh (in collaboration with Michael Fishbein) (2006). *The Unveiling of Secrets (Kashf al-asrār): The Visionary Autobiography of Rūzbihān al-Baqlī (1128–1209 AD)*. Leiden: Brill.
Pellat, Charles (1952). 'Un document important pour l'histoire politico-religieuse de l'Islâm: la "Nâbita" de Djâhiz', *Annales de l'Institut d'Études Orientales* 10: 302–25.
—— (1954a). 'Marthiya (1)', in *Encyclopaedia of Islam, Second Edition*, edited by P. Bearman, Th. Bianquis, C. E. Bosworth, E. van Donzel and W. P. Heinrichs, 12 vols. Leiden: Brill, vol. 6, pp. 603–8.
—— (1954b). 'Al-Qubba', in *Encyclopaedia of Islam, Second Edition*, edited by P. Bearman, Th. Bianquis, C. E. Bosworth, E. van Donzel and W. P. Heinrichs, 12 vols. Leiden: Brill, vol. 5, p. 297.
Peters, Francis Edward (1986). *Jerusalem and Mecca: The Typology of the Holy City in the Near East*. New York: New York University Press.

—— (1994a). *Mecca: A Literary History of the Muslim Holy Land*. Princeton: Princeton University Press.

—— (1994b). *The Hajj: The Muslim Pilgrimage to Mecca and the Holy Places*. Princeton: Princeton University Press.

Pinna, Margherita (1996). *Il Mediterraneo e la Sardegna nella cartografia musulmana: dall'VIII al XVI secolo*, 2 vols. Nuoro: Istituto Superiore Regionale Etnografico.

Pinto, Karen (2016). *Medieval Islamic Maps: An Exploration*. Chicago: The University of Chicago Press.

Piotrowski, Andrzej (2011). *Architecture of Thought*. Minneapolis: University of Minnesota Press.

Poonawala, I. (1954). 'Al-Ẓāhir wa'l-Bāṭin', in *Encyclopaedia of Islam, Second Edition*, edited by P. Bearman, Th. Bianquis, C. E. Bosworth, E. van Donzel and W. P. Heinrichs, 12 vols. Leiden: Brill, vol. 11, pp. 389–90.

Porter, Venetia (2012). *The Art of Hajj*. London: British Museum Press.

—— (2013). 'The *Mahmal* Revisited', in *The Hajj: Collected Essays*, edited by Venetia Porter and Liana Saif. London: The British Museum Press, pp. 195–205.

Powers, Paul (2004). 'Interiors, Intentions, and the "Spirituality" of Islamic Ritual Practice', *Journal of the American Academy of Religion* 72 (2): 425–59.

de Prémare, Alfred-Louis (2000). '"Il voulut détruire le temple": l'attaque de la Kaʿba par les rois yéménites avant l'islam: *akhbār* et histoire', *Journal Asiatique* 288 (2): 261–367.

al-Qāḍī al-Nuʿmān, Abū Ḥanīfa (1960). *Kitāb Asās al-taʾwīl*, edited by ʿArīf Tamīr, 3 vols. Beirut: Dār al-Thaqāfa.

—— (1995). *Taʾwīl al-Daʿāʾim*, edited by ʿArīf Tamīr, 3 vols in 2. Beirut: Dār al-Aḍwāʾ.

al-Qayṣarī, Dāwūd b. Maḥmūd (2004). *Sharḥ Tāʾiyyat Ibn al-Fāriḍ al-kubrā*. Beirut: Dār al-Kutub al-ʿIlmiyya.

al-Qazwīnī, Zakarīyā b. Muḥammad (1848). *El-Cazwini's Kosmographie, Vol. 2: Kitāb Āthār al-bilād*, edited by Ferdinand Wüstenfeld. Göttingen: Verlag der Dieterichschen Buchhandlung.

al-Quʿayṭī, Sulṭān Ghālib (2007). *The Holy Cities, the Pilgrimage and the World of Islam: A History from the Earliest Traditions until 1925 (1344H)*. Louisville: Fons Vitae.

al-Qushayrī, Abū al-Qāsim ʿAbd al-Karīm (2017). *Laṭāʾif al-Ishārāt, Subtle Allusions: Great Commentaries on the Qurʾān, Part 1: Sūras 1–4*, translated by Kristin Zahra Sands. Louisville: Fons Vitae.

Rabbat, Nasser (1954). 'Shadirwān', in *Encyclopaedia of Islam, Second Edition*, edited by P. Bearman, Th. Bianquis, C. E. Bosworth, E. van Donzel and W. P. Heinrichs, 12 vols. Leiden: Brill, vol. 9, pp. 175–6.

—— (1989). 'The Meaning of the Umayyad Dome of the Rock', *Muqarnas* 6: 12–21.

—— (1993). 'The Dome of the Rock Revisited: Some Remarks on al-Wasiti's Accounts', *Muqarnas* 10: 67–75.

—— (2002). 'In the Beginning was the House: On the Image of the Two Noble Sanctuaries of Islam', *Thresholds* 25: 56–9.

—— (2012). 'The Kaʿba: A Primordial Locus of Memory', in *The Challenge of the Object: 33rd Congress of the International Committee of the History of Art,*

Nuremberg, 15th – 20th July 2012, edited by Georg Ulrich Grossmann and Petra Krutisch. Nürnberg: Germanisches Nationalmuseum, pp. 1073–4.

Radtke, Bernd (1992). 'Between Projection and Suppression: Some Considerations Concerning the Study of Sufism', in *Shīʿa Islam, Sects and Sufism: Historical Dimensions, Religious Practice and Methodological Considerations*, edited by Frederick de Jong. Utrecht: M. Th. Houtsma Stichting, pp. 70–82.

Rancière, Jacques (2004). *The Politics of Aesthetics: The Distribution of the Sensible*, translated by Gabriel Rockhill. London: Continuum.

Rapoport, Yossef and Emilie Savage-Smith (eds) (2014). *An Eleventh-Century Egyptian Guide to the Universe: The Book of Curiosities*. Leiden: Brill.

al-Rāzī, Fakhr al-Dīn (2003). *Al-Tafsīr al-kabīr aw Mafātīh al-ghayb*, edited by ʿImād Zakī al-Bārūdī, 32 vols in 16. Cairo: Al-Maktaba al-Tawfīqiyya.

Reich, Edgar (2000). 'Ein Brief des Severus Sēḇōḵt', in *Sic itur ad astra: Studien zur Geschichte der Mathematik und Naturwissenschaften: Festschrift für den Arabisten Paul Kunitzsch zum 70. Geburtstag*, edited by Menso Folkerts and Richard Lorch. Wiesbaden: Harrassowitz Verlag, pp. 479–89.

Reinhart, A. Kevin (2014). 'Ritual Action and Practical Action: The Incomprehensibility of Muslim Devotional Action', in *Islamic Law in Theory: Studies in Jurisprudence in Honor of Bernard Weiss*, edited by A. Kevin Reinhart and Robert Gleave. Leiden: Brill, pp. 55–104.

—— (2016). 'What to Do with Ritual Texts: Islamic *fiqh* Texts and the Study of Islamic Ritual', in *Islamic Studies in the Twenty-first Century: Transformations and Continuities*, edited by Léon Buskens and Annemarie van Sandwijk. Amsterdam: Amsterdam University Press, pp. 67–86.

Richardson, Kristina (2012). *Difference and Disability in the Medieval Islamic World: Blighted Bodies*. Edinburgh: Edinburgh University Press.

Ridgeon, Lloyd (2012). 'The Controversy of Shaykh Awḥad al-Dīn Kirmānī and Handsome, Moon-Faced Youths: A Case Study of *Shāhid-Bāzī* in Medieval Sufism', *Journal of Sufi Studies* 1: 3–30.

Ring, Trudy (ed.) (1995). *International Dictionary of Historic Places, Vol. 3: Southern Europe*. Chicago: Fitzroy Dearborn Publishers.

Ritter, Hellmut (2003). *The Ocean of the Soul: Man, the World and God in the Stories of Farīd al-Dīn ʿAṭṭār*, translated by John O'Kane. Leiden: Brill.

Rius, Mónica (2009). 'Finding the Sacred Direction: Medieval Books on the *Qibla*', in *Cosmology Across Cultures: ASP Conference Series, Vol. 409: Proceedings of the Conference held on 8–12 September, 2008, at Parque de las Ciencias, Granada, Spain*, edited by José Alberto Belmonte Rubiño-Martín, Juan Antonio, Francisco Prada and Anxton Alberdi. San Francisco: Astronomical Society of the Pacific, pp. 177–82.

Rizvi, Kishwar (2010). *The Safavid Dynastic Shrine: Architecture, Religion and Power in Early Modern Iran*. London: I. B. Tauris.

—— (2013). 'Art Through Time, A Global View: Expert Perspective: Kaʿba', *Annenberg Learner*, <https://tinyurl.com/wult6zm> (last accessed 13 April 2020).

Robin, C. J. (2010). 'L'Arabie à la veille de l'Islam: la campagne d'Abraha contre La Mecque ou la guerre des pèlerinages', in *Les sanctuaires et leur rayonnement dans le monde méditerranéen, de l'Antiquité à l'époque moderne*, edited by Juliette de La Genière, André Vauchez and Jean Leclant. Paris: De Boccard, pp. 213–42.

Robinson, Chase (2005). *ʿAbd al-Malik*. Oxford: Oneworld Publications.

Ross, Eric (2006). *Sufi City: Urban Design and Archetypes in Touba*. Rochester: Rochester University Press.

Rotman, Brian (1987). *Signifying Nothing: The Semiotics of Zero*. Stanford: Stanford University Press.

Roxburgh, David (2008). 'Pilgrimage City', in *The City in the Islamic World*, edited by Salma Jayyusi, 2 vols. Leiden: Brill, vol. 2, pp. 753–74.

Rubin, Uri (1986). 'The Kaʿba: Aspects of its Ritual Functions and Position in Pre-Islamic and Early Islamic Times', *Jerusalem Studies in Arabic and Islam* 8: 97–131.

—— (1987). 'Morning and Evening Prayers in Early Islam', *Jerusalem Studies in Arabic and Islam* 10: 40–64.

—— (1990). '*Ḥanīfiyya* and Kaʿba: An Inquiry into the Arabian Pre-Islamic Background of *dīn Ibrāhīm*', *Jerusalem Studies in Arabic and Islam* 13: 85–112.

—— (2007). 'ʿAbd al-Muṭṭalib b. Hāshim', in *Encyclopaedia of Islam, Third Edition*, edited by Kate Fleet Gudrun Krämer, Denis Matringe, John Nawas and Everett Rowson. Leiden: Brill Online, <http://dx.doi.org.ezproxy.soas.ac.uk/10.1163/1573-3912_ei3_SIM_0156> (last accessed 20 April 2019).

—— (2008a). 'Between Arabia and the Holy Land: A Mecca–Jerusalem Axis of Sanctity', *Jerusalem Studies in Arabic and Islam* 34: 345–62.

—— (2008b). 'Muḥammad's Night Journey (*isrāʾ*) to al-Masjid al-Aqṣā: Aspects of the Earliest Origins of the Islamic Sanctity of Jerusalem', *Al-Qanṭara* 29 (1): 147–64.

—— (2011). 'Circumambulation', in *Encyclopaedia of Islam, Third Edition*, edited by Kate Fleet Gudrun Krämer, Denis Matringe, John Nawas and Everett Rowson. Leiden: Brill Online, <http://referenceworks.brillonline.com.proxy.library.uu.nl/entries/encyclopaedia-of-islam- 3/circumambulation-COM_25135> (last accessed 30 September 2013).

Rūmī, Jalāl al-Dīn (1951). *Kitāb-i Fīhi mā fīh: az guftār-i mawlānā Jalāl al-Dīn Muḥammad mashhūr bi-Mawlawī*, edited by Badīʿ al-Zamān Furūzānfar. Tehran: Intishārāt-i Dānishgāh-i Tihrān.

—— (1958). *Kullīyāt-i Shams, yā Dīwān-i kabīr: mushtamil bar qaṣāʾid wa ghazalīyāt wa muqaṭṭaʿāt-i fārsī wa ʿarabī wa tarjīʿāt wa mulammaʿāt: az guftār-i mawlānā Jalāl al-Dīn Muḥammad mashhūr bi-Mawlawī*, edited by Badīʿ al-Zamān Furūzānfar, 10 vols in 9. Tehran: Intishārāt-i Dānishgāh-i Tihrān.

—— (1999). *Signs of the Unseen: The Discourses of Jalaluddin Rumi*, translated by Wheeler Thackston. Boston: Shambhala.

—— (2009). *Mystical Poems of Rumi*, edited by Ehsan Yarshater, translated by Arthur John Arberry. Chicago: University of Chicago Press.

Rusli, Nurul Iman (2016). *Dalaʾil al-Khayrat: Prayer Manuscripts from the 16th–19th Centuries*. Kuala Lumpur: Islamic Arts Museum Malaysia.

Rüstem, Ünver (2019). *Ottoman Baroque: The Architectural Refashioning of Eighteenth-Century Istanbul*. Princeton: Princeton University Press.

Rutter, Eldon (1928). *The Holy Cities of Arabia*, 2 vols. London: G. P. Putnam's Sons.

Rykwert, Joseph (1988). *The Idea of a Town: The Anthropology of Urban Form in Rome, Italy, and the Ancient World*. Cambridge, MA: The MIT Press.

—— (1996). *The Dancing Column: On Order in Architecture*. Cambridge, MA: The MIT Press.

Sabri Paşa, Eyüp (Ayyūb Ṣabrī Pāshā) (1884). *Mirat ül-Harameyn, Vol. 1: Mirat-ı Mekke*. Istanbul: Bahriye Matbaası.

—— (2004). *Mawsūʿat mirʾāt al-Ḥaramayn al-sharīfayn wa Jazīrat al-ʿArab*, translated by Mājida Makhlūf, Ḥusayn Majīd al-Miṣrī and ʿAbd al-ʿAzīz ʿIwaḍ, 5 vols. Cairo: Dār al-Āfāq al-ʿArabiyya.

Sanders, Paula (1994). *Ritual, Politics, and the City in Fatimid Cairo*. Albany: SUNY Press.

Sandnes, Karl Olav (2002). *Belly and Body in Pauline Epistles*. Cambridge: Cambridge University Press.

al-Sanūsī, Muḥammad b. ʿUthmān (1891). *Istitlāʿāt al-bārisiyya fī maʿriḍ 1889*. [Tunis]: n.pub.

al-Sarakhsī, Muḥammad b. Aḥmad (1989). *Kitāb al-Mabsūṭ li-Shams al-Dīn al-Sarakhsī*, 30 vols in 15. Beirut: Dār al-Maʿrifa.

Sardar, Ziauddin (2014). *Mecca: The Sacred City*. London: Bloomsbury.

Sardi, Maria (2013). 'Weaving for the Hajj under the Mamluks', in *The Hajj: Collected Essays*, edited by Venetia Porter and Liana Saif. London: The British Museum Press, pp. 169–74.

Sarkar, Jadunath (1917). *Anecdotes of Aurangzib and Historical Essays*. Calcutta: M. C. Sarkar & Sons.

Savage-Smith, Emilie (2013). 'The Most Authoritative Copy of ʿAbd al-Rahman al-Sufi's Tenth-Century *Guide to the Constellations*', in *'God is Beautiful; He Loves Beauty': The Object in Islamic Art and Culture*, edited by Sheila Blair and Jonathan Bloom. New Haven: Yale University Press, pp. 122–55.

—— (2016). 'In Medieval Islamic Cosmography, Where is Paradise?', in *The Cosmography of Paradise: The Other World from Ancient Mesopotamia to Medieval Europe*, edited by Alessandro Scafi. London: The Warburg Institute, pp. 227–44.

Schimmel, Annemarie (1975). *Mystical Dimensions of Islam*. Chapel Hill: The University of North Carolina Press.

—— (1982). *As Through a Veil: Mystical Poetry in Islam*. New York: Columbia University Press.

—— (1985). *And Muhammad Is His Messenger: The Veneration of the Prophet in Islamic Piety*. Chapel Hill: The University of North Carolina Press.

—— (1987). 'The Primordial Dot: Some Thoughts about Sufi Letter Mysticism', *Jerusalem Studies in Arabic and Islam* 9: 350–6.

—— (1991). 'Sacred Geography in Islam', in *Sacred Places and Profane Spaces: Essays in the Geographics of Judaism, Christianity, and Islam*, edited by Jamie Scott and Paul Simpson-Housley. New York: Greenwood Press, pp. 163–75.

—— (1992a). *A Two Colored Brocade: The Imagery of Persian Poetry*. Chapel Hill: University of North Carolina Press.

—— (1992b). *I Am Wind, You are Fire: The Life and Work of Rumi*. Boston: Shambhala.

—— (1994). *Deciphering the Signs of God: A Phenomenological Approach to Islam*. Albany: SUNY Press.

—— (1998). *Die Träume des Kalifen: Träume und ihre Deutung in der islamischen Kultur*. Munich: C. H. Beck.

Schmidl, Petra (1999). 'Zur Bestimmung der Qibla mittels der Winde', in *Der Weg der Wahrheit: Aufsätze zur Einheit der Wissenschaftsgeschichte: Festgabe zum 60. Geburtstag von Walter G. Saltzer*, edited by Peter Eisenhardt, Frank Linhard and Kaisar Petanides. Georg Olms Verlag: Hildesheim, pp. 135–46.

—— (2007). *Volkstümliche Astronomie im islamischen Mittelalter: Zur Bestimmung der Gebetszeiten und der Qibla bei al-Aṣbaḥī, Ibn Raḥīq und al-Fārisī*, 2 vols. Leiden: Brill.

Schwarzer, Mitchell (2001). 'The Architecture of Talmud', *Journal of the Society of Architectural Historians* 60 (4): 474–87.

Scott-Meisami, Julie (2001). 'The Palace-Complex as Emblem: Some Samarran Qaṣīdas', in *A Medieval Islamic City Reconsidered: An Interdisciplinary Approach to Samarra*, edited by Chase Robinson. Oxford: Oxford University Press, pp. 69–78.

Seed, Patricia (2014). *The Oxford Map Companion: One Hundred Sources in World History*. New York: Oxford University Press.

Seife, Charles (2000). *Zero: The Biography of a Dangerous Idea*. London: Penguin Books.

Semper, Gottfried (1989). *The Four Elements of Architecture and Other Writings*, translated by Harry Francis Mallgrave and Wolfgang Herrman. Cambridge: Cambridge University Press.

Seyed-Gohrab, Ali Ashgar (2003). *Laylī and Majnūn: Love, Madness, and Mystic Longing in Niẓāmī's Epic Romance*. Brill: Leiden.

Sezgin, Fuat (ed.) (1992). *Islamic Geography*, Vol. 26. Frankfurt am Main: Institut für Geschichte der Arabisch-Islamischen Wissenschaften.

Shafīʿ, Muḥammad (1922). 'A Description of the Two Sanctuaries of Islam by Ibn ʿAbd Rabbihi', in *A Volume of Oriental Studies Presented to Edward G. Browne on his 60th Birthday*, edited by T. W. Arnold and Reynold Alleyne Nicholson. Cambridge: University Press, pp. 416–38.

Shahid, Irfan (1989). *Byzantium and the Arabs in the Fifth Century*. Washington: Dumbarton Oaks Research Library and Collection.

Shahzad, Ghafer (2011). 'Historiography of Architecture: Extent and Restraints of Conjecture', in *Historiography of Architecture of Pakistan and the Region*, edited by Pervaiz Vandal. Lahore: THAAP, pp. 161–72.

Shalem, Avinoam (2005). 'Made for the Show: The Medieval Treasury of the Kaʿba in Mecca', in *The Iconography of Islamic Art: Studies in Honour of Robert Hillenbrand*, edited by Bernard O'Kane. Edinburgh: Edinburgh University Press, pp. 269–83.

—— (2013). 'The Four Faces of the Kaʿba in Mecca', in *Architecture and Pilgrimage, 1000–1500: Southern Europe and Beyond*, edited by Paul Davies, Deborah Howard and Wendy Pullan. Farnham: Ashgate, pp. 39–58.

—— (2015). 'The Body of Architecture: The Early History of the Clothing of the Sacred House of the Kaʿba in Mecca', in *Clothing the Sacred: Medieval Textiles as Fabric, Form, and Metaphor*, edited by Mateusz Kapustka and Warren Woodfin. Emsdetten: Edition Imorde, pp. 173–87.

Sharīʿatī, ʿAlī (1977). *Hajj*, translated by Ali Behzadnia and Najla Denny. [Houston]: Free Islamic Literatures.

Sharma, Sudha (2016). *The Status of Muslim Women in Medieval India*. New Delhi: Sage Publications India Pvt Ltf.

Sharon, Moshe (1988). 'The Birth of Islam in the Holy Land', in *Pillars of Smoke and Fire: The Holy Land in History and Thought*, edited by Moshe Sharon. Johannesburg: Southern Book Publishers, pp. 225–35.

Sharon, Moshe, Uzi Avner and Dov Nahlieli (1996). 'An Early Islamic Mosque Near Be'er Ora in the Southern Negev: Possible Evidence for an Early Eastern *Qiblah?*', *'Atiqot* 30: 107–14.

Shatanawi, Mirjam (2014). *Islam at the Tropenmuseum*. Arnhem: LM Publishers.

Shatzmiller, Maya (1976). 'Les premiers mérinides et le milieu religieux de Fès: l'introduction des médersas', *Studia Islamica* 43: 109–18.

Sheehan, Peter (2010). *Babylon of Egypt: The Archaeology of Old Cairo and the Origins of the City*. Cairo: The American University in Cairo Press.

Shoemaker, Stephen (2012). *The Death of a Prophet: The End of Muhammad's Life and the Beginnings of Islam*. Philadelphia: University of Pennsylvania Press.

Shtober, Shimon (1999). '"*Lā yajūz an yakūn fī al-ʿālam li-llāhi qiblatayn*": Judaeo-Islamic Polemics Concerning the *Qibla* (625–1010)', *Medieval Encounters* 5 (1): 85–98.

Simpson, Marianna Shreve (2010). 'From Tourist to Pilgrim: Iskandar at the Kaʿba in Illustrated Shahnama Manuscripts', *Iranian Studies* 43 (1): 127–46.

Smith, Jonathan Zittell (1969). 'Earth and Gods', *The Journal of Religion* 49 (2): 103–27.

—— (1970). 'The Influence of Symbols upon Social Change: A Place on Which to Stand', *Worship* 44 (8): 457–74.

Smith, Margaret (1974). *Rabiʿa the Mystic and Her Fellow-Saints in Islam*. Amsterdam: Philo Press.

Smith, Martyn (2008). *Religion, Culture, and Sacred Space*. New York: Palgrave Macmillan.

Steinbock, Anthony (2007). *Phenomenology and Mysticism: The Verticality of Religious Experience*. Bloomington: Indiana University Press.

Stern, David (1991). *Parables in Midrash: Narrative and Exegesis in Rabbinic Literature*. Cambridge, MA: Harvard University Press.

Stillman, Yedida (2003). *Arab Dress: A Short History from the Dawn of Islam to Modern Times*. Leiden: Brill.

Stone, Jon (1993). 'The Medieval Mappaemundi: Toward an Archaeology of Sacred Cartography', *Religion* 23: 197–216.

Streck, M. and André Miquel (1954). 'Qāf', in *Encyclopaedia of Islam, Second Edition*, edited by P. Bearman, Th. Bianquis, C. E. Bosworth, E. van Donzel and W. P. Heinrichs, 12 vols. Leiden: Brill, vol. 4, pp. 400–2.

Ströker, Elisabeth (1987). *Investigations in Philosophy of Space*, translated by Algis Mickunas. Athens, OH: Ohio University Press.

Subtelny, Maria (2010). 'Templificatio hominis: Kaʿba, Cosmos, and Man in the Islamic Mystical Tradition', in *Weltkonstruktionen: Religiöse Weltdeutung zwischen Chaos und Kosmos vom Alten Orient bis zum Islam*, edited by Peter Gemeinhardt and Annette Zgoll. Tübingen: Mohr Siebeck, pp. 195–222.

Suleman, Fahmida (2013). 'Making Love not War: The Iconography of the Cockfight in Medieval Egypt', in *Eros and Sexuality in Islamic Art*, edited by Franscesca Leoni and Mika Natif. Farnham: Ashgate, pp. 19–42.

Suvorova, Anna (2004). *Muslim Saints of South Asia: The Eleventh to Fifteenth Centuries*, translated by M. Osama Faruqi. London: RoutledgeCurzon.

al-Ṭabarī, Abū Jaʿfar Muḥammad b. Jarīr (1960). *Taʾrīkh al-Ṭabarī: Taʾrīkh al-umam wa al-mulūk*, edited by Muḥammad Abū al-Faḍl Ibrāhīm, 11 vols. Cairo: Dār al-Maʿārif.

—— (1987a). *The History of al-Ṭabarī (Taʾrīkh al-rusul wa-al-mulūk), Vol. 6: Muḥammad at Mecca*, translated by William Montgomery Watt. Albany: SUNY Press.

—— (1987b). *The History of al-Ṭabarī (Taʾrīkh al-rusul wa-al-mulūk), Vol. 26: The Waning of the Umayyad Caliphate*, translated by Carole Hillenbrand. Albany: SUNY Press.

—— (1989a). *The History of al-Ṭabarī (Taʾrīkh al-rusul wa-al-mulūk), Vol. 1: General Introduction and From the Creation to the Flood*, translated by Franz Rosenthal. Albany: SUNY Press.

—— (1989b). *The History of al-Ṭabarī (Taʾrīkh al-rusul wa-al-mulūk), Vol. 13: The Conquest of Iraq, Southwestern Persia, and Egypt*, translated by G. H. A. Juynboll. Albany: SUNY Press.

—— (1989c). *The History of al-Ṭabarī (Taʾrīkh al-rusul wa-al-mulūk), Vol. 30: The ʿAbbāsid Caliphate in Equilibrium*, translated by C. E. Bosworth. Albany: SUNY Press.

—— (1991). *The History of al-Ṭabarī (Taʾrīkh al-rusul wa-al-mulūk), Vol. 19: The Caliphate of Yazīd b. Muʿāwiyah*, translated by I. K. A. Howard. Albany: SUNY Press.

—— (1997). *The History of al-Ṭabarī (Taʾrīkh al-rusul wa-al-mulūk), Vol. 8: The Victory of Islam*, translated by Michael Fishbein. Albany: SUNY Press.

—— (2001). *Jāmiʿ al-bayān ʿan taʾwīl āy al-Quʾrān al-maʿrūf bi-Tafsīr al-Ṭabarī*, edited by Maḥmūd Shākir, 30 vols. Beirut: Dār Iḥyāʾ al-Turāth al-ʿArabī.

al-Ṭabarī, Muḥibb al-Dīn (1970). *Al-Qirā li-qāṣid Umm al-Qurā*, edited by Muṣṭafā al-Saqqā. Cairo: Muṣṭafā al-Bābī al-Ḥalabī.

al-Ṭabarsī, Abū ʿAlī Faḍl b. Ḥasan (2005). *Majmaʿ al-bayān fī tafsīr al-Qurʾān*, 10 vols. Beirut: Dār al-ʿUlūm.

Tabbaa, Yasser (1985). 'The Muqarnas Dome: Its Origin and Meaning', *Muqarnas* 3: 61–74.

al-Tādilī b. al-Zayyāt, Abū Yaʿqūb Yūsuf b. Yaḥyā (1997). *Al-Tashawwuf ilā rijāl al-taṣawwuf wa akhbār Abī al-ʿAbbās al-Sabtī*, edited by Aḥmad al-Tawfīq. Rabat: Al-Mamlaka al-Maghribiyya, Kulliyyat al-Ādāb wa al-ʿUlūm al-Insāniyya bi-l-Ribāṭ.

al-Tahawy, Miral Mahgoub (2017). 'Reverence for the Beloved as a Religious Metaphor: A Study of Rajāʾa ʿĀlim's *Ḥubbā* (The Beloved)', in *The Beloved in Middle Eastern Literatures: The Culture of Love and Languishing*, edited by Alireza Korangy, Hanadi Al-Samman and Michael Beard. London: I. B. Tauris, pp. 102–30.

Tanındı, Zeren (1983). 'İslam Resminde Kutsal Kent ve Yöre Tasvirleri', *Journal of Turkish Studies* 7: 407–37.

Tezcan, Hülya (2007). 'Kaʿba Covers from the Topkapı Palace Collection and their Inscriptions', in *Word of God, Art of Man: The Qurʾan and its Creative Expressions: Selected Proceedings from the International Colloquium, London, 18–21 October 2003*, edited by Fahmida Suleman. Oxford: Oxford University Press, pp. 227–38.

—— (2017). *Sacred Covers of Islam's Holy Shrines: With samples from Topkapı Palace*. Istanbul: Masa.

Tezcan, Hülya and Selma Delibaş (1986). *The Topkapı Saray Museum: Costumes, Embroideries, and other Textiles*, translated by J. M. Rogers. London: Thames & Hudson.

Thackston, Wheeler (2001). *Album Prefaces and Other Documents on the History of Calligraphers and Painters*. Leiden: Brill.

al-Thaʿlabī, Abū Isḥāq Aḥmad b. Muḥammad b. Ibrāhīm (2002). *ʿArāʾis al-majālis fī qiṣaṣ al-anbiyāʾ, or Lives of the Prophets*, translated by William Brinner. Leiden: Brill.

Tibbets, Gerald (1992). 'The Balkhī School of Geographers', in *The History of Cartography, Vol. 2, Bk. 1: Cartography in the Traditional Islamic and South Asian Societies*, edited by J. B. Harley and David Woodward. Chicago: University of Chicago Press, pp. 108–36.

al-Tirmidhī, Muḥammad b. ʿAlī al-Ḥakīm (1958). *Bayān al-farq bayna al-ṣadr wa al-qalb wa al-fuʾād wa al-lubb*, edited by Nicholas Heer. [Cairo]: Dār Iḥyāʾ al-Kutub al-ʿArabiyya.

—— (1969). *Kitāb al-Ḥajj wa-asrārihi*, edited by Ḥusnī Naṣr Zaydān. [Cairo]: Maṭbaʿat al-Saʿda.

al-Tirmidhī, Muḥammad b. ʿAlī al-Ḥakīm and Abū ʿAbd al-Raḥmān al-Sulamī al-Naysabūrī (2003). *Three Early Sufi Texts: A Treatise on the Heart, the Stumblings of Those Aspiring, and Stations of the Righteous*, translated by Nicholas Heer and Kenneth Honerkamp. Louisville: Fons Vitae.

al-Tirmidhī, Muḥammad b. ʿĪsā (1937). *Al-Jāmiʿ al-ṣaḥīḥ wa huwa Sunan al-Tirmidhī*, edited by Aḥmad Muḥammad Shākir, 5 vols. Cairo: Maṭbaʿat Muṣṭafā al-Bābī al-Ḥalabī.

Toepel, Alexander (2013). 'The Cave of Treasures: A New Translation and Introduction', in *Old Testament Pseudepigrapha: More Noncanonical Scriptures, Volume 1*, edited by Richard Bauckham, James Davila and Alexander Panayotov. Grand Rapids: Eerdmans Publishing Company, pp. 531–84.

Toorawa, Shawkat (2016). 'Performing the Pilgrimage', in *The Hajj: Pilgrimage in Islam*, edited by Eric Tagliacozzo and Shawkat Toorawa. Cambridge: Cambridge University Press, pp. 215–30.

Toprakyaran, Erdal (2001). 'Osmanische Restaurationsmaßnahmen nach der Überschwemmung der Kaaba im Jahre 1630', unpublished MA thesis. Heidelberg: Ruprecht-Karls-Universität.

Tosun, Necdet (2012). 'Hajj from the Sufi Point of View', in *Central Asian Pilgrims: Hajj Routes and Pious Visits between Central Asia and the Hijaz*, edited by Alexandre Papas, Thomas Welsford and Thierry Zarcone. Berlin: Klaus Schwarz, pp. 136–47.

Toulan, Nohad (1993). 'Planning and Development in Makkah', in *Urban Development in the Muslim World*, edited by Hooshang Amirahmadi and Salah El-Shakhs. New Brunswick: Center for Urban Policy Research, pp. 37–71.

Trachtenberg, Marvin (1997). *Dominion of the Eye: Urbanism, Art, and Power in Early Modern Florence*. New York: Cambridge University Press.

—— (2002). 'A Question of Origins', *The Art Bulletin* 84 (4): 697–98.

Tuan, Yi-Fu (1977). *Space and Place: The Perspective of Experience*. Minneapolis: University of Minnesota Press.

al-Ṭūsī, Abū Jaʿfar Muḥammad b. al-Ḥasan (n.d). *Kitāb al-Ghayba*. Beirut: Manshūrāt al-Fajr.

—— (1992). *Tahdhīb al-aḥkām fī sharḥ al-Muqniʿa li-l-Shaykh al-Mufīd*, edited by Muḥammad Jaʿfar Shams al-Dīn, 10 vols in 5. Beirut: Dār al-Taʿāruf li-l-Maṭbūʿāt.

Tütüncü, Mehmet (2015). 'The Uppsala Mecca Painting: A New Source for the Cultural Topography and Historiography for Mecca', in *Hajj: Global Interactions through Pilgrimage*, edited by Luitgard Mols and Marjo Buitelaar. Leiden: Sidestone Press, pp. 137–62.

Umar, Ibrahim (1975). 'The Book on the Secrets of Pilgrimage (*Kitāb Asrār al-ḥajj*) by Abū Ḥāmid Muḥammad al-Ghazālī', unpublished MA thesis. Cairo: American University of Cairo, <http://www.ghazali.org/books/hajj.pdf> (last accessed 11 April 2019).

ʿUtbī, Muḥammad b. ʿAbd al-Jabbār (1858). *The Kitab-i-Yamini: Historical Memoirs of the Amír Sabaktagín, and the Sultán Mahmúd of Ghazna, Early Conquerors of Hindustan, and Founders of the Ghaznavide Dynasty*, translated by James Reynolds. London: Oriental Translation Fund of Great Britain and Ireland.

Vâlsan, Michel (1966). 'Le triangle de l'Androgyne et le monosyllable "Om"', *Études Traditionelles* 396–7: 218–25.

van Doorn-Harder, Nelly and Kees de Jong (2001). 'The Pilgrimage to Tembayat: Tradition and Revival in Indonesian Islam', *The Muslim World* 91 (3–4): 325–53.

van Gelder, Geert Jan (1991). 'Arabic Debates of Jest and Earnest', in *Dispute Poems and Dialogues in the Ancient and Mediaeval Near East: Forms and Types of Literary Debates in Semitic and Related Literatures*, edited by G. J. Reinink and H. L. J. Vanstiphout. Leuven: Peeters, pp. 199–211.

Velji, Jamel (2016). *An Apocalyptic History of the Early Fatimid Empire*. Edinburgh: Edinburgh University Press.

Vidler, Anton (1990). 'The Building in Pain: The Body and Architecture in Post-modern Culture', *AA Files* 19: 3–10.

Virani, Shafique (2007). *The Ismailis in the Middle Ages: A History of Survival, a Search for Salvation*. Oxford: Oxford University Press.

von Grunebaum, Gustave (1962). 'The Sacred Character of Islamic Cities', in *Mélanges Taha Hussein: offerts par ses amis et ses disciples à l'occasion de son 70ième anniversaire*, edited by Abdurrahman Badawi. Cairo: Dar Al-Maaref, pp. 25–37.

von Sivers, Peter (2003). 'The Islamic Origins Debate Goes Public', *History Compass* 1: 1–14.

al-Wāqidī, Muḥammad b. ʿUmar (1965). *The Kitāb al-Maghāzī of al-Wāqidī*, edited by Marsden Jones, 3 vols. London: Oxford University Press.

Warnier, Jean-Pierre (2006). 'Inside and Outside: Surfaces and Containers', in *Handbook of Material Culture*, edited by Chris Tilley, Webb Keane, Susan Kuechler, Mike Rowlands and Patricia Spyer. London: Sage Publications Ltd, pp. 186–95.

Watt, William Montgomery (1954). 'Ḥums', in *Encyclopaedia of Islam, Second Edition*, edited by P. Bearman, Th. Bianquis, C. E. Bosworth, E. van Donzel and W. P. Heinrichs, 12 vols. Leiden: Brill, vol. 3, pp. 577–8.

Webb, Peter (2013). 'The Hajj before Muhammad: Journeys to Mecca in Muslim Narratives of Pre-Islamic History', in *The Hajj: Collected Essays*, edited by Venetia Porter and Liana Saif. London: The British Museum Press, pp. 6–14.

Welch, Anthony, Hussein Keshani and Alexandra Bain (2002). 'Epigraphs, Scripture, and Architecture in the Early Delhi Sultanate', *Muqarnas* 19: 12–43.

Wellhausen, Julius (1887). *Reste arabischen Heidentums: Gesammelt und erläutert.* Berlin: G. Reimer.

Wendell, Charles (1971). 'Baghdad: *Imago Mundi*, and other Foundation-Lore', *International Journal of Middle East Studies* 2 (2): 99–128.

Wensinck, Arent Jan (1913). 'Kaʿba', in *E. J. Brill's First Encyclopaedia of Islam: 1913–1936*, edited by M. Th. Houtsma, T. W. Arnold, R. Basset and R. Hartmann, 9 vols. Leiden: E. J. Brill, vol. 2, pp. 584–92.

—— (1916). 'The Ideas of the western Semites concerning the Navel of the Earth', *Verhandelingen der Koninklijke Akademie van Wetenschappen te Amsterdam, Afdeeling Letterkunde, n.s.* 17 (1): iii–xii, 1–65.

—— (1917). 'Some Semitic Rites of Mourning and Religion: Studies on their Origin and Mutual Relation', *Verhandelingen der Koninklijke Akademie van Wetenschappen te Amsterdam, Afdeeling Letterkunde, n.s.* 18 (1): 1–101.

—— (1954a). 'Iḥrām', in *Encyclopaedia of Islam, Second Edition*, edited by P. Bearman, Th. Bianquis, C. E. Bosworth, E. van Donzel and W. P. Heinrichs, 12 vols. Leiden: Brill, vol. 3, pp. 1052–3.

—— (1954b). 'Al-Masjid al-Ḥarām', in *Encyclopaedia of Islam, Second Edition*, edited by P. Bearman, Th. Bianquis, C. E. Bosworth, E. van Donzel and W. P. Heinrichs, 12 vols. Leiden: Brill, vol. 6, pp. 708–9.

Wensinck, Arent Jan and Bernard Lewis (1954). 'Hajj', in *Encyclopaedia of Islam, Second Edition*, edited by P. Bearman, Th. Bianquis, C. E. Bosworth, E. van Donzel and W. P. Heinrichs, 12 vols. Leiden: Brill, vol. 3, pp. 31–8.

Wensinck, Arent Jan and David King (1954). 'Qibla', in *Encyclopaedia of Islam, Second Edition*, edited by P. Bearman, Th. Bianquis, C. E. Bosworth, E. van Donzel and W. P. Heinrichs, 12 vols. Leiden: Brill, vol. 5, pp. 82–8.

Wensinck, Arent Jan and Jacques Jomier (1954). 'Kaʿba', in *Encyclopaedia of Islam, Second Edition*, edited by P. Bearman, Th. Bianquis, C. E. Bosworth, E. van Donzel and W. P. Heinrichs, 12 vols. Leiden: Brill, vol. 4, pp. 317–22.

Westermarck, Edward (1899). 'The Nature of the Arab Ǧinn, Illustrated by the Present Beliefs of the People of Morocco', *The Journal of the Anthropological Institute of Great Britain and Ireland* 29 (3–4): 252–69.

Wheatley, Paul (1971). *The Pivot of the Four Quarters: A Preliminary Enquiry in the Origins and Character of the Ancient Chinese City.* Edinburgh: Edinburgh University Press.

—— (1983). *Nāgara and Commandery: Origins of the Southeast Asian Urban Traditions.* Chicago: Department of Geography, University of Chicago.

—— (2001). *The Places Where Men Pray Together: Cities in Islamic Lands, Seventh Through the Tenth Centuries.* Chicago: University of Chicago Press.

Wheeler, Brannon (2006). *Mecca and Eden: Rituals, Relics, and Territory in Islam.* Chicago: University of Chicago Press.

Whitcomb, Donald (1994). 'The *Miṣr* of Ayla: Settlement at al-ʿAqaba in the Early Islamic Period', in *The Byzantine and Early Islamic Near East, Vol. 2: Land Use and Settlement Patterns*, edited by Geoffrey King and Averil Cameron. Princeton: The Darwin Press, pp. 155–70.

—— (2001). 'Archaeological Evidence of the Early Mosque in Arabia', in *Religious Texts and Material Contexts*, edited by Jacob Neusner and James Strange. Lanham: University Press of America, pp. 185–97.

—— (2007). 'An Urban Structure for the Early Islamic City', in *Cities in the Pre-modern Islamic World: The Urban Impact of Religion, State and Society*, edited by Amira Bennison and Alison Gascoigne. Abingdon: Routledge, pp. 15–26.

—— (2010). 'An Umayyad Legacy for the Early Islamic City: Fusṭāṭ and the Experience of Egypt', in *Umayyad Legacies: Islamic History and Civilization*, edited by Antoine Borrut and Paul Cobb. Leiden: Brill, pp. 403–16.

—— (2012). 'The Miṣr of Ayla: New Evidence for the Early Islamic City', in *The Byzantine and Early Islamic Near East, Vol. 2: Land Use and Settlement Patterns*, edited by Fred Donner. Ashgate: Variorum, pp. 369–87.

Wilbaux, Quentin (2001). *La médina de Marrakech: formation des espaces urbains d'une ancienne capitale du Maroc*. Paris: L'Harmattan.

Wing, Patrick (2016). *The Jalayirids: Dynastic State Formation in the Mongol Middle East*. Edinburgh: Edinburgh University Press.

Winkel, Eric (2014). 'Translating, and Understanding, the *Futūḥāt al-Makkīya*: the First Chapter', *Journal of the Muhyiddin Ibn ʿArabi Society* 55: 1–32.

Winter, Tim (2004). 'The Chador of God on Earth: The Metaphysics of the Muslim Veil', *New Blackfriars* 85 (996): 144–57.

Witkam, Jan Just (2007). 'The Battle of the Images: Mekka vs. Medina in the Iconography of the Manuscripts of al-Jazūlī's *Dalāʾil al-Khayrāt*', in *Technical Approaches to the Transmission and Edition of Oriental Manuscripts: Proceedings of a Symposium Held in Istanbul, March 28–30 2001*, edited by Judith Pfeiffer and Manfred Kropp. Würzburg: Ergon Verlag, pp. 67–82, 295–300.

—— (2013). 'The Islamic Pilgrimage in the Manuscript Literatures of Southeast Asia', in *The Hajj: Collected Essays*, edited by Venetia Porter and Liana Saif. London: The British Museum Press, pp. 214–23.

Witztum, Joseph (2009). 'The Foundations of the House (Q 2:127)', *Bulletin of the School of Oriental and African Studies* 72 (1): 25–40.

Wolfe, Michael (1997). *One Thousand Roads to Mecca: Ten Centuries of Travelers Writing about the Muslim Pilgrimage*. New York: Grove Press.

Wolfson, Elliot (2009). 'Das Kleid der Kaʿba: Verhüllung und Entschleierung in den Bilderwelten des Sufismus', in *Taswir: Islamische Bildwelten und Moderne*, edited by Almut Bruckstein and Hendrik Budde. Berlin: Nicolai Publishing, pp. 153–7.

Woodward, Mark (2011). *Java, Indonesia and Islam*. Dordrecht: Springer.

Wootton, Brian (2015). *The Invention of Science: A New History of the Scientific Revolution*. New York: HarperCollins Publishers.

Wright, William (1967). *A Grammar of the Arabic Language: Translated from the German of Caspari and Edited with Numerous Additions and Corrections*, 3rd rev. ed., 2 vols in 1. Cambridge: Cambridge University Press.

Yaqin, Amina (2016). '*La convivencia, la mezquita* and al-Andalus: An Iqbalian Vision', *Journal of Postcolonial Writing* 52 (2): 136–52.

al-Yaʿqūbī, Aḥmad b. Abī Yaʿqūb (1892). *Kitab al-Buldān*, edited by Michael Jan de Goeje. Leiden: Brill.

—— (2010). *Taʾrīkh al-Yaʿqūbī*, edited by ʿAbd al-Amīr Mahnā, 2 vols. Beirut: Sharika al-Aʿlamī.

Yāqūt b. ʿAbd Allāh al-Ḥamawī (1977). *Muʿjam al-buldān*, 5 vols. Beirut: Dār al-Ṣadir.

Yazdani, Ghulam (1947). *Bidar: Its History and Monuments*. London: Oxford University Press.

Yılmaz, Hüseyin (2018). *Caliphate Redefined: The Mystical Turn in Ottoman Political Thought*. Princeton: Princeton University Press.

Young, William (1993). 'The Kaʿba, Gender, and the Rites of Pilgrimage', *International Journal of Middle East Studies* 25 (2): 285–300.

—— (1994). 'A Response to Annemarie Schimmel', *International Journal of Middle East Studies* 26 (2): 363–4.

Zadeh, Travis (2016). 'The Early Hajj: Seventh–Eighth Centuries CE', in *The Hajj: Pilgrimage in Islam*, edited by Eric Tagliacozzo and Shawkat Toorawa. Cambridge: Cambridge University Press, pp. 42–64.

Zarcone, Thierry (2012). 'Pilgrimage to the "Second Meccas" and "Kaʿbas" of Central Asia', in *Central Asian Pilgrims: Hajj Routes and Pious Visits between Central Asia and the Hijaz*, edited by Alexandre Papas, Thomas Welsford and Thierry Zarcone. Berlin: Klaus Schwarz Verlag, pp. 251–77.

Zargar, Cyrus Ali (2011). *Sufi Aesthetics: Beauty, Love, and the Human Form in the Writings of Ibn ʿArabi and ʿIraqi*. Columbia, SC: University of South Carolina Press.

Index

Illustrations are indicated by page numbers in **bold**